Second-Order Change in Psychotherapy

Second-Order Change in Psychotherapy

The Golden Thread That Unifies Effective Treatments

J. Scott Fraser

Andrew D. Solovey

American Psychological Association

Washington, DC

Published by
American Psychological Association
750 First Street, NE
Washington, DC 20002
www.apa.org

To order
APA Order Department
P.O. Box 92984
Washington, DC 20090-2984
Tel: (800) 374-2721; Direct: (202) 336-5510
Fax: (202) 336-5502; TDD/TTY: (202) 336-6123
Online: www.apa.org/books/
E-mail: order@apa.org

In the U.K., Europe, Africa, and the Middle East, copies may be ordered from
American Psychological Association
3 Henrietta Street
Covent Garden, London
WC2E 8LU England

Typeset in Goudy by Stephen McDougal, Mechanicsville, MD

Printer: Victor Graphics, Inc., Baltimore, MD
Cover Designer: Minker Design, Bethesda, MD
Technical/Production Editor: Tiffany L. Klaff

The opinions and statements published are the responsibility of the authors, and such opinions and statements do not necessarily represent the policies of the American Psychological Association.

Library of Congress Cataloging-in-Publication Data

Fraser, J. Scott.
    Second-order change in psychotherapy : the golden thread that unifies effective treatments / J. Scott Fraser and Andrew Solovey.
        p. cm.
    Includes bibliographical references and index.
    ISBN-13: 978-1-59147-436-4
    ISBN-10: 1-59147-436-1
    1. Psychotherapy—Methodology. 2. Change (Psychology) I. Solovey, Andrew D. II. American Psychological Association. III. Title.
    [DNLM: 1. Psychotherapeutic Processes. 2. Psychological Theory. 3. Treatment Outcome. 4. Models, Psychological. WM 420 F841s 2007]
    RC480.5.F7443 2007
    616.89'14—dc22
                                                            2006009553

British Library Cataloguing-in-Publication Data
A CIP record is available from the British Library.

Printed in the United States of America
First Edition

CONTENTS

PREFACE

We began the journey of writing this book some 30 years ago. It was then that we were introduced to a view on change that we came to believe was capable of describing the inner workings of all effective psychotherapy. In this work we offer this view as a process-of-change model.

The foundational concept that comprises our proposed process-of-change model, first- and second-order change, was developed in the late 1960s at the Mental Research Institute (MRI) in Palo Alto, California. Paul Watzlawick, John Weakland, and Richard Fisch (1974) were the innovators of first- and second-order change, which was translated from earlier work on cybernetics, logical types, and linguistics, among other rather complex theories. Yet, after a decade of early influence in the family therapy area, their seminal ideas on change were almost forgotten. We believe, however, that this says little about the importance of their thinking. Instead, it has more to do with what Everett Rogers (2003) described as the process of diffusion of innovations. In large part because of the complexity of the MRI group's perspective, the inherently paradoxical nature of change, and the way the MRI group's ideas contradicted the prevailing views of the time, their ideas were not embraced nor applied more widely.

In this book, we try to correct this error. First, we simplify the MRI group's concept of first- and second-order change through a wide range of examples and applications. We then apply this process-of-change perspective to unify the age-old psychotherapy research schism that separates the effects of technique from the therapist–client relationship. Finally, we apply the first- and second-order change model over and again in explaining how it integrates seemingly unrelated approaches to effective psychotherapy.

Along the way, we pay homage to Jerome Frank's (Frank & Frank, 1991) contextual model and to the stages-of-change model of James Prochaska and Carlo DiClemente (1982). Although we found these models to be excellent transtheoretical maps for understanding the change process, there was an important link missing. These theories did not get at the essence of the shift that occurs when change happens. We propose that our process-of-change model supplies this missing link and creates the possibility for binding these theories together in a unifying framework. In the end, methods and theories may differ, but the essence of change is always the same. In short, if sticking with a solution a little longer does not work, then the problem solver must engage in some type of action that is different or opposite from the current state of affairs.

We also have tried to honor the excellent work of a wide range of psychotherapy researchers who have endeavored to develop and affirm the effectiveness of the "best practices" covered in this book. However, if we have succeeded in our mission, it is mainly that we have "stood on the shoulders of giants," as have many before us. We personally owe great debts in particular to Paul Watzlawick, an Austrian gentleman and scholar, and to John Weakland, a sage and gentle friend.

All in all, we have written this volume in the spirit of celebrating the excellent work that has been done by a wide variety of therapists and researchers in the field of psychotherapy. Toward that end, we selected psychotherapy frameworks that are currently best known, are supported by research, and that represent diverse theoretical underpinnings. Unfortunately, in writing a book of this type it is impossible to include the entire range of fine work done by numerous outstanding therapists and researchers. For example, within our constraints, we were not able to review the excellent work of colleagues such as Jim Coyne and Sue Johnson, who have made significant contributions in the treatment of depression and couples. There was also a lengthy analysis of multisystemic therapy, functional family therapy, and brief strategic family therapy that we edited to make the text more readable. Despite this limitation, we believe that we have reviewed enough of the work in the field, on the problems we address, to maintain our assertion that first- and second-order change is at the core of all change in psychotherapy. Whether this assertion creates a first- or second-order shift for the reader remains for you to discover. Nonetheless, we hope these ideas are as exciting for you as they are for us!

This work would not have been possible without friends, colleagues, and family members who lent their support. More specifically, we would like to thank Mark Hubble for his assistance with writing the first three chapters of the text. Hubble also contributed his keen conceptual thinking and relentless pursuit of relevance. We would like to thank our wives, Beth Fraser and Donna Solovey, for their willingness to listen as we read to them passages of our writing and who read and edited numerous chapters of this work. Their suggestions were invaluable, and their emotional support helped us to stay centered during our journey. Words alone cannot express what we know you have offered us in addition to your love. We are also very fortunate to have children who not only understand our message but were willing to listen, read, and make critical comments. Our thanks and appreciation go to Heather Morrow Fraser, Chris Fraser, Nick Solovey, and Steven Solovey. We extend a special thank you to Heather Doyle Fraser for her support regarding the issues of publishing and writing style. We also give thanks to Anne Solovey, who proved the value of a degree in English.

There were also many professional colleagues who provided support for this book. We thank Andy's colleagues at Scioto Paint Valley Mental Health Center for their support, including Gary Kreuchauf (executive director), Mary Snyder, Sally Palmer, Landa Dorris, Vince Yaniga, Ed Sipe, Sue Peek, Kathleen Pallotta, and Anita Kefgen. We are grateful to the Scioto Paint Valley Mental Health Center Board of Trustees and their belief in the value of service to clients. A special note of thanks goes to Dwayne Smith and Rebecca Hall at Solutions Counseling, along with Michele Morris, MD; Scott Mackey, MD; Sarah Sams, MD; and Shelley Blackburn, MD for stimulating our thinking and collaborating on applications of the second-order change model in primary care medical practice. We are also grateful for Scott's former colleagues at the Crisis/Brief Therapy Center of Good Samaritan Hospital in Dayton, Ohio. Bill Hanlin, Gary Goetz, Tina Grismer, Phyllis Fisher, John Waterston, and John Davis, among many others, were all a part of the evolution of this work in practice. Scott also owes thanks to his doctoral students over the years in the School of Professional Psychology at Wright State University. His work with them has sharpened, simplified, and shaped these ideas into the form you find them in this volume today. We continue to be indebted to our wives, family, and colleagues who have supported and inspired us in our work. "Thank you" doesn't quite say enough, but thank you all, and then some.

Second-Order Change
in Psychotherapy

PROLOGUE: THE GOLDEN THREAD

The following figure is a labyrinth, the famous labyrinth of Crete. In Greek mythology, the warrior Theseus was given a golden thread to guide him to the center of this labyrinth, wherein a fierce Minotaur lived. Theseus had to defeat the Minotaur and then find his path back out. Over time, the phrase "the golden thread," has come to refer to a guide that helps us find the unifying pathway through disorienting and seemingly disconnected alternatives.

The Labyrinth of Crete

The next figure is the labyrinth at Chartres cathedral, near Paris, France. Religious pilgrims walk this labyrinth to discover that the seemingly separate quadrants and winding ways make up a unified whole that leads to a shared center. The golden thread traces this unifying pathway. It helps travelers realize the connections that make up the unified whole.

The Labyrinth of Chartres

In a similar way, today, we find that the apparent differences between effective psychotherapies create a labyrinth. There are disorienting twists and turns between effective treatments that emphasize techniques versus those that stress relationships and the therapeutic alliance that confuse therapists, theorists, researchers, students, and instructors alike. How can these apparently separate treatments be part of a unified whole? What pathways connect them? The premise of this book is that creating effective change, or *second-order change*, is what unifies all effective psychotherapy. It is the golden thread. We invite you, the reader, to join us in following this thread to discover the connections among effective psychotherapies and the unified core that they all share.

I

THE GOLDEN THREAD OF
SECOND-ORDER CHANGE

1

HOW DOES THERAPY WORK?

In decades past, researchers and policymakers focused on the question "Does psychotherapy work?" Researchers have now conclusively established the overall efficacy of psychologically informed treatments (Barlow, 2001; Hubble, Duncan, & Miller, 1999; Nathan & Gorman, 2002a; Norcross, 2002; Wampold, 2001), and the public, almost universally, has accepted psychotherapy as a viable remedy to many of life's problems (cf. Harris Interactive, 2004).

Now that that question has been answered (i.e., yes, psychotherapy does work), a new question has been posed: "How does psychotherapy work?" The answers to this question are not academic but have ramifications for everyone involved in the practice of psychotherapy. For example, policymakers at the governmental level and in the private sector (e.g., the insurance industry) increasingly determine whether therapy sessions will be reimbursed. For many patients, if not most, reimbursement is a key factor in deciding whether to seek or continue psychotherapy. Thus, policymakers in both the government and the insurance industry, and the providers they influence, need to better understand how seemingly disparate forms of psychotherapy work in equally effective ways. Researchers and theorists, rather than becoming polarized into warring camps, need to find a theoretical framework that cuts across all of the therapeutic approaches that have been empirically shown to be effective. An important purpose of this book is to provide such a framework.

HOW DOES THERAPY WORK?

So far, those claiming answers to this question have polarized into two camps. Members of the first, designated here as the *best-practices group* (often identified with *empirically supported treatments* [ESTs]), argue that sufficient evidence exists to prove that specific psychotherapy protocols are differentially therapeutic for specific therapy populations (e.g., people with major depression, people who abuse substances). The second camp, designated here as the *common-factors group* (often identified with the *therapeutic alliance*, or the *therapeutic relationship*), presents compelling data that all mainstream approaches to psychotherapy work equally well for most clinical populations, provided that a strong therapeutic alliance and other common curative factors are operating (e.g., a positive client–therapist relationship, a working alliance, perceived empathy, goal agreement, and collaboration, among other factors). Perhaps because of its close correspondence to current medical practice, the best-practices group has gradually gained the most credence with policymakers, and the result has been an increasing pressure toward conformity in the day-to-day conduct of psychotherapy. For example, across the United States, state mental health administrators and funding boards are requiring that providers adopt particular treatment models and protocols for specific clinical populations. Their most recent initiative comes as a demand that clinicians use the most effective therapies as they interpret them (Presidential Task Force, American Psychological Association, 2005; Task Force on Promotion and Dissemination of Psychological Procedures, 1995).

Professionals on the front line, treating patients, are confused and frustrated. Must we learn a different best practice for each clinical population? How do we practice with the majority of clients who have a mixture of problems and who fall into more than one specific clinical population (e.g., those who experience both depression and substance abuse?) Do we have no autonomy in practicing our profession?

As the debate continues between the best-practices and common-factors groups, with no end in sight, both have become increasingly polarized and increasingly bent on claiming the lion's share of positive outcomes for their approach. (Later in this chapter we review some of this research.) On one point, they both concur: The stakes are high and, no doubt, are getting higher, as the funds to pay for therapy become increasingly harder to find.

THE GOLDEN THREAD

In Greek mythology, the golden thread helped the warrior Theseus safely find his way to the center of a labyrinth and back out. It traced the pathway through seemingly endless, disorienting corridors in which one's movement was at times contrary to intuition. Today, there are a large and growing number of different, purportedly effective psychotherapies. However, their differences in approach and suggested mechanisms for change appear to contradict each other, creating a modern-day labyrinth for theorists, researchers, policymakers, professors, and graduate students. What makes these treatments effective? What do they have in common? What pathways do they share, and what thread, if any, connects them? Those encountering this dilemma cry out for a modern golden thread to find their way. We contend that second-order change is that golden thread.

WHO WILL MOST BENEFIT FROM READING THIS BOOK?

This book's audience includes those practical theorists, researchers, policymakers, professors, and graduate students who are struggling to find a pathway through the myriad effective psychotherapies and who are seeking a common thread that connects effective interventions. Each group runs into its own unique frustrations that are addressed by the second-order change model that we introduce.

Applied theorists have struggled for decades with the question of how psychotherapies are connected with one another. They have synthesized a number of useful schemes to integrate approaches, including technical eclecticism (i.e., using the most effective techniques without adapting the theories that underlie them); theoretical integration (synthesizing different theories underlying different approaches within a superordinate unifying theory); and a common-factors approach (identifying the core elements shared by all effective psychotherapies; cf. Norcross & Goldfried, 2005; for other perspectives, see psychological resources such as the *Journal of Psychotherapy Integration*). Each approach to integration has merit, and yet each is unable to explain the unifying pattern of change that underlies all effective psychotherapy models. By following the thread of second-order change, these practical theorists may gain a greater capacity for integration.

As researchers argue over the relative contributions to effective treatment of therapeutic techniques versus the therapeutic relationship, they have become caught in an unresolvable debate. This debate is reminiscent of Werner Heisenberg's (1958) famous *uncertainty principle* in physics (i.e., light being observed behaves as either particles or waves, depending on how it is measured). The kind of assumptions these psychotherapy researchers make, the subsequent questions they ask, and the way they approach answering them, determine what they find. The questions they ask and the kind of observations they make determine whether effective therapies are a product of either particular techniques or significant relationships. For these researchers, viewing techniques and relationships as inseparable aspects of second-order change should open new pathways of investigation.

Policymakers are now seeking the best treatments for clients within an economic climate of limited resources. They are increasingly insisting that so-called "best-practice protocols" be used by therapists in order for those services to be reimbursed. Although policymakers are trying to hold providers accountable for positive outcomes, providers are finding it nearly impossible to learn the broad array of seemingly very different best-practice approaches. Additionally, they complain that the mandates are much too restrictive. The second-order change model holds promise that policymakers will create more flexible guidelines that will allow practitioners a way of integrating effective approaches within a perspective that more flexibly fits themselves and their clients.

Professors and graduate students find themselves trapped in somewhat similar dilemmas. Should they not be teaching, and learning, the major theories of psychotherapy? And yet, once learned, how do they relate to one another? Is it a matter of picking one's favorite brand, or are there best practices to be learned for each disorder? Is it all about relationships or all about best practices? And what about diversity? How do these effective approaches handle differences between providers and clients, and how do they apply to most clients who do not have just one kind of problem? Most clinical trials have been conducted with clients with only one focused problem. For professors and graduate students, the second-order change model offers a hopeful framework for finding new pathways through these questions. We view this as the modern golden thread through the labyrinth of therapies that work. First, however, we will profit by taking another look at the current state of affairs in psychotherapy research.

THE GREAT SCHISM: RESEARCH PERSPECTIVES

At the risk of hyperbole, we maintain that the future of psychotherapy is uncertain. The prize is the undisputed claim to the lion's share of positive outcomes. For the common-factors contingent, the contest is already decided, regardless of how much influence the best-practices group may already wield.

For example, in an oft-repeated analysis of psychotherapy studies, Michael Lambert (1992; Asay & Lambert, 1999) surmised that a therapist's model or technique accounts for no more than 15% of the successful outcome variance. This effect was found to be no more potent than that explained by positive expectancy or placebo, also 15%. Next in importance for outcome, at 30%, were relationship-mediated variables, which accounted for as much as the previous elements combined. What is most impressive is that Lambert argued that, with 40% of the variance, extratherapeutic factors—those that are part of the client or client's environment that aid in recovery regardless of the client's formal participation in treatment—yielded the greatest impact on change. Lambert's findings markedly depart from the time-honored tradition of celebrating the contribution of the therapist's theoretical model and technique.

In a similar vein, Bruce Wampold conducted and published a series of meta-analyses[1] of the psychotherapy outcome research literature. As reported in his book, *The Great Psychotherapy Debate: Models, Methods, and Findings* (2001), he revised the percentagewise contribution of the factors discussed earlier. First, the total portion of the outcome variance attributable to treatment-mediated variables markedly diminished; that is, therapeutic modality (the therapist's model and technique) fell from 15% to only 8%. At least 70% of psychotherapeutic effects, he added, are general effects, representing the common factors underlying all psychotherapies. The remaining 22% of the variability is unexplained but is partly attributable to client differences.

With his startling (at least to some) results in hand, Wampold concluded that the medical model, implicit in the EST movement, which assumes that the outcomes of therapy originate in the specific ingredients built into a given treatment, is out of step with the facts. He endorses an alternative, a pantheoretical position, what he terms a *contextual model*. This model, closely associated with the now-famous work of Johns Hopkins University's Jerome Frank (see Frank & Frank, 1991), upholds the importance of common factors in promoting positive change. Wampold emphasized that there is no connection between the supposed underlying causes of psychological suffering and the treatments that effectively ameliorate it. Instead, he highlighted the critical role of the *healing context*: the therapist's and the client's belief in therapy, the relationship between the therapist and the client, the rationale for the treatment, the actions consistent with the rationale, and the meaning that the client attributes to therapy (Wampold, 2001).

Other works, such as *The Heart and Soul of Change: What Works in Therapy* (Hubble et al., 1999) and *Psychotherapy Relationships That Work: Therapist Contributions and Responsiveness to Patients* (Norcross, 2002), enlarge and underscore the body of literature upholding the common factors as important, if not the most essential, elements of effective psychotherapy. The evidence reviewed in these texts suggests again that the efficacy of mental health treatments will not be found in a specific therapy approach on its own. Instead, to understand the effectiveness of treatment, one has to look at the function and power of the therapeutic alliance and the resources clients bring to the work.

For all the forcefulness and authority derived from their research and writing, the common-factors contingent has yet to unseat the EST or best-practices group. The proponents of ESTs have amassed an imposing body of experimental evidence that, from their perspective, makes their case, hands

---

[1]*Meta-analysis* is a type of research in which sophisticated statistical techniques are used to review the range of studies that have been conducted on a similar research question. Significant effect sizes found in isolated studies may attenuate when meta-analytic techniques are applied. The effectiveness of ESTs is often based on effect sizes found in limited clusters of studies. In psychotherapy research, meta-analysis has not been able to verify the results found in the vast majority of ESTs that have been studied.

down. For instance, "exposure treatments" are frequently cited as the most effective interventions for anxiety (cf. Barlow, 2002). Certain texts, such as *A Guide to Treatments That Work* (2nd ed.; Nathan & Gorman, 2002a) and *Clinical Handbook of Psychological Disorders: A Step-By-Step Treatment Manual* (Barlow, 2001), are encyclopedic in their review of ESTs for a wide range of client problems. So impressive are these results that state and federal regulatory bodies are demanding that reimbursement from their resources become contingent on providers proving that they have used an EST appropriate to the problem treated.

The prospect of having a specific intervention for a given type of problem is especially appealing. The idea that therapists might possess the psychological equivalent of a pill or precision-guided weapon for emotional distress is also one that strongly resounds with the public and policymakers. Additionally, no one could argue with the success of the idea of problem-specific interventions in the field of medicine (e.g., surgery for acute appendicitis).

Setting aside the arguments for and against outside entities telling therapists how to do their jobs, encouraging practice of the most successful treatments is a very worthy and rational undertaking. If it is the case, as the best-practices group maintains, that we are on the verge of compiling a dependable psychological formulary, this is great news for clients, payers, and practitioners. In fact, it would mark the dawn of a new era, a revolution in clinical work. The usual doubt as to what to do in addressing a particular complaint would be gone. Sure and confident steps could be recommended to clients and, with their informed consent, the treatment immediately commenced. After the proper dosing and prescribed course, success would be evaluated and, if needed, modifications made to the treatment plan. A true standard of care could be established, with all that it would entail for training, supervision, continuing education, quality control, and funding. At the same time, the best of what is known about the therapy relationship (and other helpful treatment components; e.g., positive expectancy) from the common-factors literature could be applied to help ensure the client's compliance with the treatment regimen. Finally, the vexing problem of integration would be settled. Integration would be achieved at an empirical and practical level—hierarchies of therapies that best treat specific complaints.

In contrast, if, as the common-factors contingent contends, specialized treatments or ESTs are largely a chimera, then a major disservice is being perpetrated. In due time, those therapies currently touted as superior to the rest might be perceived as fads in a field already tarnished by so many misplaced enthusiasms. The stain on the profession sponsored by the inpatient-for-profit scandals, the recovered- or past-memories flap, and singular treatments still brings embarrassment. Those outside the field looking to pull the plug on psychologically based treatment would have yet another reason for giving physicians more control in the market. Psychotropic medication, the mainstay of the new biological psychiatry, is, after all, medicine, and everyone "knows" medicine works. Many psychologists, perhaps already having realized the prognosis, are clamoring to obtain prescription privileges.

From another perspective, should the common-factors position be correct, the structure of the profession could conceivably be challenged. For instance, if all treatments work equally well, and their effectiveness is found, as Wampold (2001) asserted, in the healing context and not in theories and specialized practices, then the current justification for separate training and even licensing of mental health practitioners is suspect. In a world won over by the common-factors contingent, programs of graduate study, with their many departments and different schools, philosophies, and doctrines would find recruitment especially trying. The appetite for specialized preparation in specific therapies with differing levels of certification (e.g., eye movement desensitization and reprocessing) would also be undermined. In time, such undertakings might come to be regarded as just moneymaking schemes for clever entrepreneurs. The implications for the field as a whole abound.

Regardless of what happens in the end, with a few exceptions (Norcross & Goldfried, 2005), neither side in the current debate is especially motivated to yield any ground. As a result, the field is left with two distinct bodies of research offering different visions for clinical practice. Because of this standoff, it is easy to empathize with those charged with administering mental health services. With limited time, shrinking budgets, and their own pressure groups nipping at their heels, planners must still try to identify and implement the best treatments money can buy. Expecting that the profession will provide them with clear and unbiased guidance any time soon may be a pipe dream.

A PATHWAY TO RESOLUTION

The definitive answer to the question "How does therapy work?" has yet to emerge. Furthermore, any answer that gains eventual acceptance is unlikely to evolve from an either–or proposition. On a moment's reflection, the schism in psychotherapy bears a distressing and strong resemblance to a vicious cycle (and vicious cycles are the hallmarks of problems from the perspective of what we call *first-order change*). The more researchers on the EST side attempt to prove that a particular treatment is the most effective, the more meta-analyses neutralize the findings. The word then goes forth, "All treatments work equally well. No critical technique exists, only relationships that work." Undeterred, the best-practices group pushes back, "Our work demonstrates the superiority of one method over another. We will research and validate the treatments. That will settle the score." More attempts to identify an ultimate therapy then trigger more reviews, more meta-analyses, and more impassioned claims for the common factors. Little imagination is needed to envision a continuance and escalation of this struggle.

This is an example in itself of what we describe as first-order change in the next chapter. Each view is based on reason and logic. The actions taken by each group not only are appropriate to their position but also affirm and reinforce their respective positions. To do anything otherwise would not make sense. The only way to take different or even opposite action is by moving to a different level of understanding. This kind of shift is what we presently define and extensively discuss as second-order change.

Despite the resilience of the vicious cycle to date, the divisions between the best-practices group and the common-factors contingent are much more apparent than real. Effective psychotherapy is not a member of any one category or owned by any particular advocacy group; on the contrary, all effective treatments are a member of the same class. Put another way, the proponents of technical approaches and of the relationship and common-factors approach are both correct.

Bearing this in mind, the common-factors people seem to be saying "You can't see the forest for the trees! Look at each given treatment, and you will fail to see what is common among all effective interventions." For their part, the best-practices group says "You can't see the trees for the forest! Blending all the effective approaches loses touch with those specific therapies that show differential efficacy." We are saying, "You are right; we agree! Looking is good." To paraphrase Carl Rogers (1957), we agree that the facts are always friendly. Yet it is now time to look in a different direction, to look at the common ground from which the trees grow. After all, whether it is one tree or a forest, they belong together. They spring from the same ground.

In all, the problem facing the profession is not about an ability to see the forest or the trees. In fact, we labor under an overabundance—trees of every size, shape, and description. Instead, the very ground from which a tree or a forest springs bears close examination. Because all effective psychotherapy initiates desired change, it is reasonable to conclude that change itself is the common ground.

By redirecting our attention to the nature of change, it may be possible to repair the rift in psychotherapy and achieve integration. The emphasis shifts from what is instrumental for change (techniques, common factors) to the underlying nature of change. In short, change is at the very core of problem resolution. Everything that a therapist does—or, for that matter, does not do—either supports or detracts from change. At this level of analysis, the many approaches reveal that they promote improvement in surprisingly similar ways. The lyrics, melody, and rhythm may differ, but the song remains the same. Looking at therapies that work from the perspective of how they promote change is a critical shift in viewpoint that allows new questions to be asked, new actions to be taken, and new integration to be understood. It is empowering. It is what we call a second-order change in itself.

In the midst of the claims and counterclaims that have created the schism in our field, we live in a time of accountability. Two pressing questions remain before us. First, what is the common denominator across effective therapies? Second, what do effective therapists do? Answering these questions is the purpose of this book.

OVERVIEW OF THE BOOK

We submit that a unifying perspective on change unites all effective psychotherapy. This shared perspective, termed here *the second-order change model*, weaves through all effective therapies. The foundation of this framework lies in an understanding of the nature of change. Although more types of change have been described (see Bateson, 1979), special attention will be directed to first- and second-order change. *First-order change* is defined as a class of solutions that do not change a problem or make a problem worse. In contrast, *second-order change* is a change of those first-order solutions, which results in a resolution of the problem. First-order change is related to stability; second-order change is related to transformation. First-order change is a change that occurs in a system that itself remains the same. These changes of intensity, frequency, duration, and so on, are solutions taken according to the existing assumptions and tacit rules of a system. Not only do they not change the system; they affirm the system by repeating its assumptions, rules, and patterns. When first-order change turns problematic, it invariably becomes a vicious cycle. First-order change may be seen in the frustrated folly of the client who attempts to force herself to sleep, or in the man who tries to will himself to become passionately aroused for lovemaking. In these and most other human dilemmas, the solutions become the problem. They create vicious cycles. Second-order change offers solutions that are most often viewed as counterintuitive or paradoxical from the original perspective. Sleep or sexual arousal occurs spontaneously as we allow ourselves to become immersed in the situation. As we may know, the answer to falling asleep or becoming aroused is to stop trying to will it to be so. Yet such a shift for the person caught in these dilemmas will typically not make sense, at least without some further frame or rationale. These kinds of shifts are examples of second-order change. We explain these central concepts on change in more detail in the next several chapters. In accordance with the thesis of this book, we show how second-order change is central to effective treatment.

Understanding the phenomenon of change in this way represents a second-order shift for theorists who are struggling with the integration of seemingly contradictory models of psychotherapy. The state of affairs that so much defines contemporary professional discourse reflects a competition of first-order solutions—who is on top, whose is best, mine is better. A new understanding of the nature of change redirects the debate from an either–or focus to a more productive both–and direction. We also show that as trainers, students, theorists, researchers, and policymakers understand the nature of change they will be able to integrate the best of what the principal warring camps have to offer. In effect, the blind alleys are only an illusion. Like a labyrinth, the passageway is clear when one follows the golden thread.

The book is divided in two major parts. In the first part, "The Golden Thread of Second-Order Change" (chaps. 1–5), we further elaborate the definitions of first-order and second-order change and apply them to the foundations of effective therapy. Chapter 2 addresses problem formation and the close relationship between stability, change, and vicious cycles. In chapter 3, we turn to second-order change. Examples showing the action of second-order change in a wide range of human dilemmas are presented, with a special focus on psychotherapy. Completing this section, in chapters 4 and 5 we assess what many refer to as the *fundamentals of effective treatment*. In particular, the contribution of the therapeutic alliance and other common factors are reexamined through the perspective of second-order change. These chapters create a framework to demonstrate how the golden thread of second-order change weaves its way through empirically supported therapies.

In the second part of the book, "Following the Thread: Empirically Supported Therapies" (chaps. 6–11), we review a variety of empirically supported approaches for common clinical problems. Specifically, in these chapters we address the two most common mood disorders; the two most frequent relationship complaints; and, finally, two special clinical challenges (e.g., substance abuse and dependency and high-risk emergencies, or *borderline* difficulties). The chapters comprising this major part, six in total, represent the core of the book in terms of applying the second-order change model to therapies that work.

Each clinical chapter follows the same format. To clarify the problem that is being addressed, we formally define the problem We then analyze the "best practice" or EST recommended for each clinical scenario, including a synopsis of the practical goals and steps and research supporting it. After delineating the approach, we examine the application, but with a difference. We show how second-order change operates as the underlying pathway to improvement in the therapy. Each clinical chapter concludes with a brief summary, titled "Following the Thread," of the principles of second-order change that underlie the approach.

The final chapter of the book, "Following the Golden Thread of Second-Order Change in Effective Psychotherapy," summarizes the implications of viewing and doing therapy from the standpoint of second-order. We present how this unifying perspective can structure and guide the integration of the various psychotherapies, mental health policy and planning, and clinical practice.

In the Greek myth, the warrior Theseus is seeking his way through the labyrinth to end the carnage of the beast, the Minotaur, by killing it once and for all. Divisiveness in psychotherapy is the Minotaur of our times. It creates an unproductive cycle of in-fighting when we should be proclaiming "What we do works and is worthy of funding." We can make this proclamation only after we realize what unites all therapies. This is the golden thread of second-order change.

2

PROBLEM FORMATION

Plus ça change, plus c'est la même chose [The more things change, the more they remain the same].

—Alphonse Karr, *Les Guêpes*, 1849

Change is at the heart of psychotherapy. Although many mental health professionals are eager to say they possess the royal road to change, little agreement in the field exists on precisely what is important to change. Behavioral therapies, for instance, emphasize extinguishing maladaptive behaviors and shaping new skills. The now-popular cognitive approaches stress challenging dysfunctional thought patterns and replacing them with more adaptive constructs. The psychodynamic tradition affirms the importance of a corrective emotional experience and replacement of neurotic relationship patterns with less defensive ones. The humanistic and existential school suggests that learning to become and experience one's authentic self in the moment is what change is all about. These are but a few broad statements on the nature of effective therapeutic change. Each is different and compelling in its own way.

If agreement cannot be reached about the nature of change at the theoretical level, then at the least it is reasonable to concede that stability is the opposite of change. Yet, on examination, even this turns out to be far from the case. Stability, in fact, is maintained by change. Stability and change are not found on opposite sides of the coin; they are closely related, entangled in surprising and sometimes complex ways.

A closer look at constancy or stability shows that continual change supports stability. For example, a tightrope walker makes constant adjustments, both large and small, to maintain balance or stability on the rope. Most people have had the experience of riding a bicycle, in which many changes in direction, weight distribution, and speed must be made to maintain equilibrium. Relationships, too, require continual adjustments and renegotiation to remain viable. Each example reveals a singular connection between change and stability.

Sometimes, efforts designed to maintain stability produce an unwanted effect, actually destabilizing the situation. This is observed with the tightrope walker who overcorrects while attempting to maintain balance. When handling a bike, if the rider holds the handlebars too rigidly and does not make needed corrections in direction (or undercorrects), the bicycle will inevitably tip over. Over- or undercorrection can induce a loss of balance and a tragic fall. The possibilities of over- and undercorrection further complicate the relationship between change and stability.

The connection between change and stability also diverges from everyday reasoning. Consider the following examples:

- In flying lessons, student pilots learn to stall an airplane and then bring the plane out of the stall. By climbing too steeply, the engine will stall out. Beginners exhibit a natural tendency to correct by pulling the controls farther back to go up. After all, they are trying to go up. When a plane goes into a stall, however, the pilot must counter this instinct and do the opposite. Breaking out of the stall requires one to push the controls forward to go down. The pilot literally tries to fly back toward the ground. This stops the engine from stalling and allows the pilot to guide the plane back on course.
- When mountain climbing on steep, sheer, and exposed rock faces, the novice's natural tendency is to cling tighter to the grips and freeze against the cliff. In such ascents, all climbers are *belayed*, or kept safe by being tied together and to the rock by ropes. One must trust the rope to let go of one grip and then move up to gain another. To learn this, however, the beginning climber must fall to avoid a calamitous fall in the future. The best way for beginners to understand that the rope will catch them and keep them safe is to test the rope. The idea of avoiding falls by learning to fall is sensible at one level but defies common sense at another. From his own experience, the first author found this task quite daunting. The mind insists that the reward for such folly is certain injury or death.
- In the decidedly safer and popular game of golf, examples abound of learning experiences similar to those of pilots and rock climb-

ers. In chipping the ball, for example, the objective is to direct the ball to fly up and over obstacles and then land on the green. Most beginners make the mistake of trying to lift their club and body up as they swing to make the ball go up as well. This fundamental error, called *scooping*, causes the club to hit the ground too far behind the ball, resulting in a poor shot. Good golfers learn to hit down on the ball to make it go up. Because it is so natural to scoop the ball, professional golfers spend countless hours practicing striking down on the ball. Even so, under the stress of a big tournament, the tendency still is to scoop.

Turning to the putting green, the final goal is to put the ball in the hole with as few strokes as possible. Golfers are taught to focus on the process of making a good putting stroke and not worrying about sinking the putt. Good putting reliably lands balls in the cup; focusing exclusively on the target lands golfers in a hole of frustration.

- Eastern philosophy and Zen in particular holds many comparable lessons. In his short essay *Zen and the Art of Archery*, Eugen Herrigel (1989) described how the Zen master instructs the student to focus foremost on the fundamentals: drawing the bow, breathing, and positioning the body. By directing attention to good technique, an archer is then much more likely to hit the target. Across all domains, the essence of Zen practice holds that using logical solutions to reach a goal inhibits rather than helps. Logic tells us to focus our efforts on results. This leads to anxiety. Anxiety then causes mistakes, making it even more difficult to achieve the desired outcome.

Returning to archery, the novice may begin an internal dialogue about hitting the bull's-eye. "Am I aiming too far right or left? The bulls-eye looks so small; how will I ever hit it?" These questions create tension and increase the likelihood of making a mistake. Zen practice breaks the student out of this mind-set. The student learns how to concentrate, notch the arrow, draw the string, and control one's breathing. In short, the student learns the process of shooting well. Hitting the bull's-eye is the final outcome of a good process. One hopes that the student will understand that in archery, as in all life endeavors, goals are more directly attained by not attempting to reach them directly.

Something akin can be seen in pain management. It is rational for most people with chronic pain to want an end to the torment. A common solution is for the patient to try to ignore her pain, or else to brace herself against it when she feels the pain. Through attempting to ignore the pain, she never learns to master it, and by bracing against it, she is likely to make the experience worse. In pain management programs the goal is for the person to pay attention to his or her pain and even intensify it to learn that he or she can alter the intensity either up or down. Paying attention and intensifying pain is the opposite of trying to stop it. It runs counter to the patient's goal. Yet pain becomes more manageable when the sufferer goes toward or embraces the pain that she is trying to avoid. In brief, the path to mastery includes the pain rather than ignoring it or acting in opposition to it. The psychologist Jon Kabat-Zinn (1990) showed potent effects by teaching pain patients to meditate and be mindful of their pain in just this way.

A moment's reflection on the preceding examples suggests that effective change often entails a paradoxical kind of effort. This kind of change, counterintuitive as it may first appear, is the golden thread running throughout effective therapy and the subject of this book. However, before proceeding to the examination of change that makes things better, we must first understand the sort of change that makes things worse. It is this class of change that creates and perpetuates problems and brings people to therapy in the first place.

PROBLEM FORMATION: STAGES AND CONSTITUENTS

There is always an easy solution to every human problem—neat, plausible, and wrong.

—H. L. Mencken, 1917

Clients' problems often resemble the predicaments of tightrope walkers and pilots-in-training. In particular, the natural steps clients take to maintain a pleasant, stable situation or to change a problematic one often make their situation worse. Their efforts to create stability or initiate change for the better often cause or aggravate problems and make them more persistent and impervious to change. Clients often indicate this when they say, "The more I try to get control of my anxiety, the more anxious I get." or "The more I try to move on from my grief, the more I find myself breaking down in tears."

An inescapable dilemma attends problems and problem formation. Most of the time, and for most people, the difficulties encountered in daily living are readily resolved with good old common sense. And yet, on occasion, the very same common-sense assumptions become the driving force in the development of serious problems. As we discuss later in this chapter, therapists can fall prey to these same traps.

Naturally wanting predictability, stability, and control, people first filter challenges through their beliefs and premises about how the world works. The goal is to make sense of the challenge: to define it; to establish its significance and parameters. The beliefs people use are derived from experience, precedent, tradition, culture, folk wisdom, or the conventions of the time. As well-conceived or ill-conceived as the premises may be, they are preconceived. They are what people bring to the table when a challenge is laid before them.

A premise is, at its core, a basic assumption about the way of the world. It is a proposition—or, better said, a set of presuppositions—from which conclusions are drawn and future actions are decided. In a person's psychological economy, these presuppositions perform an organizing function. As such, they are conservative, even protective, and surprisingly resilient.

The precursor to any problem is a stressor or adaptive challenge. Yet these occur all the time, for everyone, and not everyone develops problems. As the late John Weakland, celebrated therapist and coauthor of *Change: Principles of Problem Formulation and Problem Resolution* (Watzlawick, Weakland, & Fisch, 1974) put it, "Life is one damn thing after another, but it's the only game in town." (J. Weakland, personal communication, October 30, 1980.) Problems are caused not by stressors or challenges, but by how people experience these stressors or challenges. After the assessment of the stressor or challenge, people choose an action or solution for management. The solution is selected from the known universe of alternatives suggested by their beliefs and premises. They might decide to do nothing. They might decide to manage the challenge by changing it or themselves in some way. Perhaps they decide to contend with the difficulty by actively avoiding it. If the action or solution works, life goes on until the next inevitable "damn thing" presents itself.

Piaget (1947/1950) asserted that people often resolve life difficulties by assimilating or accommodating them into their familiar repertoire. Such frames and actions work much of the time. For example, parents often use rewards to help children directly achieve developmental goals (e.g., toilet training). Later, as they face other developmental stages, they return to the strategies that served them and the family well before.

This is fine and good so far, yet what happens if the solution does not work? For the stressor or adaptive challenge to devolve into a problem, and not remain one of life's many annoyances, two conditions need to be satisfied. First, the same solution or type of solution is selected. Second, the solution or type of solution is applied over and over again. Should this occur, a vicious cycle rapidly sets in motion. This is what is meant in a popular saying attributed to Albert Einstein, "Insanity: doing the same thing over and over again and expecting different results." Similarly, Weakland said that once a vicious or problem cycle takes hold, life changes from one damn thing after another to the same damn thing over and over again (J. Weakland, personal communication, October 30, 1980).

Failed solutions, it bears emphasizing, will be repeated until interrupted. It is as though they have a life of their own. In addition, repeating failed solutions almost always results in a downward spiral—this is the inevitable and terrible logic of the vicious cycle. Instead of creating improvement, the attempted and failed solution makes the problem worse. As the situation deteriorates, more of the same attempted solution is applied, exacerbating the problem and then provoking varying escalations of the solution. From this vantage point, the solution actually becomes a bigger problem than the original problem it was meant to solve.

The vicious cycle as just described might even be called a *solution-generated problem*. Over time, the problem will probably manifest little resemblance to the original difficulty. Such patterns are classic and, as we discuss further in chapter 3, occur in diverse contexts and at different levels of interpersonal commerce.

Once a person is familiar with vicious cycles, they are recognizable in many situations. An uncomplicated example, observed by one of us years ago, involves a bird trapped in a two-story vestibule of an apartment complex. At the front of the vestibule were double doors, with a large plate glass window directly above. It was spring, the weather pleasant, and so the double doors were left wide open. A bird, doing as birds often do with such an invitation, flew into the building. In short order, finding itself caught, the bird understandably decided to beat a hasty retreat. Resorting to what must have worked before to escape a comparable cul-de-sac, it turned around and flew up and at the plate glass window. At the risk of anthropomorphism, the poor bird's apparent premise was "If you can see forward, then that's the way out!"

Determined to free itself, the bird then engaged in a variety of solutions. It flew at the middle of the window, the side of the window, the top, and then the bottom. It flew soft. It flew hard. It flew into the glass with its head and with its side. As these attempts failed, the more intense and frantic the bird's efforts became. In short, the hapless animal was caught in a vicious cycle: a solution-generated problem.

One could surmise that in the bird's "mind," all its attempts were dissimilar. Flying at the top of the window is much different from flying at the middle or bottom. Striking the window with its side is much different from hitting it straight on with its head. If a soft impact did not release it to the outside, then surely a hard blow would force the way out.

To the onlooker, the resolution was not only logical but also simple— anyone could see it. Reverse the entire thrust of the solution. Hitting the top, middle, and bottom of the glass with its head or body, soft or hard, was patently not working for the bird. Thus, the bird should fly back and down, instead of forward and up.

Unfortunately, for the bird, such sound direction would have made little sense. All birds know that the way out is forward and up. If it can see forward, go there. To fly backward and down violated the bird's premise on what to do, regardless of whether it was instinctually derived or gained from experience.

As it turned out, the bird fortuitously achieved its goal. It hit its head so hard on the glass that it fell to the floor in front of the open door, stunned. On regaining its wits, away it flew.

People, of course, are not birds caught in apartment building vestibules. Nonetheless, they do become trapped in the same kind of solution-generated problems. To illustrate, almost within minutes of turning on the television, the viewer is bombarded with advertisements for medications such as Viagra. Apparently, the pharmaceutical industry would have the public believe that erectile problems in men (i.e., attaining and maintaining erections) are epidemic, sponsored by rampaging vascular difficulties. For all that, years ago, the renowned sex therapists Masters and Johnson (1966, 1970) demonstrated that most erectile problems are related to a vicious cycle; a solution-generated problem. The more a man feels anxious about whether he will have or keep an erection, the more his attention is riveted on the second-to-second performance of his sex organs. This is hardly stimulating, if readers will pardon the pun.

All men, for myriad reasons (e.g., fatigue, too much alcohol or tobacco, stress, prolonged bicycle riding, lack of rapport with a partner), will face erectile inefficiency. If accepted as inevitable and temporary, it remains what it is: an irritation or passing inconvenience. However, what if the inefficiency takes on a different meaning? What if the incident is regarded as a sign of something more serious or sinister?

Maybe the man interprets the lack of an erection as a demonstration of inadequacy or a lack of virility. He then might feel embarrassed or ashamed; humiliated before his partner. In this case, so the worse fears do not become true, the "failure" cannot be repeated. The erection, come hell or high water, must be achieved quickly, aggressively, and proudly. Fretting, the man's solution is somehow to make the erection happen using the right stimulation, the right position, the right mood or atmosphere. The result is predictable: Instead of enjoying the satisfactions of the moment, the man becomes mired in failed attempts to achieve deliberately a state that best comes spontaneously.

The resolution became obvious to Masters and Johnson (1966, 1970): Redirect the man's attention away from the erection to the sensuality of the total sexual encounter. By interrupting the man's solution (e.g., through sensate focus), calm returns, and pleasure is felt. Nature is then allowed to take its naturally arousing course. As with the beginner archer, the chance of hitting the bull's-eye increases when any anxious focus is diverted from the target.

Women who attempt to force themselves into an orgasm fall in a nearly identical trap. As with men, the joy of sex morphs into the job of sex. Again, the solution is not to work harder but to relinquish the solution.

In the following chapters, we describe many examples of problems. As they are presented, it helps to recall that a problem (either psychological or interpersonal) does not arise in the original stressor or challenge. Events that may precede problem formation are too numerous to categorize and, besides, people exhibit a wide variety of responses, many of which are adaptive and even growth promoting. In this sense, stressors are not and never will be the cause of a problem. The actual "kick point" for a problem is the solution that falls flat on its face. Should a person relinquish an ineffective solution and move on to one that actually manages the stressor, a problem still does not exist. Once the person repeats the ineffective solution, then the problem can be said to be forming.

With this in mind, recall the bird caught in the apartment vestibule: The events leading up to its being caught in the vestibule are far less important then the necessity that it does something different from repeatedly smashing itself against a plate glass window. How a man first experiences an episode of erectile inefficiency matters little against his anxious, repetitive, and protracted attempts to force an erection into being.

From this point on, we refer to the misguided and repetitive attempt to accomplish a change for the better by whatever means as a first-order change. It is a change derived from the first (preexisting) set of premises a person uses for managing a challenge. In considering first-order change, remember that it does not always give rise to failure. This is an important caveat. Often enough, first-order solutions are chosen because they worked in similar or past situations. They may very well resolve the current difficulty. If the solution works, then no problem ensues.

However, if the solution fails or falters, then a change of a different order is needed. This type of change, called a second-order change (discussed in depth in the next chapter), is derived from a second, or altogether different, set of premises that fit the situation as well as or better than the first. The alternatives that arise in second-order change represent a whole new set. Because they do not reflect the person's current worldview, they are commonly experienced by the individual or participants trapped in a vicious or first-order cycle as strange, weird, out of the blue, paradoxical—often contrary to common sense.

Although the language of solution-generated problems and first-order change presented in this chapter may be unfamiliar, the field of psychology has long been fascinated with vicious or problem cycles. We now turn our attention to the role vicious cycles have played in several therapeutic systems. As will be seen, over the years, the import and impact of vicious cycles have been recognized and documented. Knowing the foe from many different perspectives strengthens one's power to defeat it.

VICIOUS CYCLES REDUX

It's déjà vu all over again.

—Yogi Berra

An unfortunate trend has been observed in recent years among professional therapists: When someone conceives an idea or theory for treatment, it is publicized, especially in workshops and seminars, as though it were the next best invention since sliced bread. The pursuit of celebrity status peaked in the 1990s, yet the incentives to make unique or original claims for one's work remain. When it comes to vicious cycles, despite the temptation, no special claim can be justified or rationalized. This concept has been a touchstone across several therapeutic models and the subject of inquiry for more than 100 years. A brief sampling of what has been said and understood follows.

Psychoanalysis

With the *repetition compulsion*, the psychoanalytic tradition introduced the vicious cycle as a prominent, if not defining, feature of maladaptive behavior. For Freud, neurotic individuals displayed a compulsion to repeat traumatic events over and over, without regard to the damage rendered to their individual and interpersonal relationships. In his writings, particularly his metapsychology, the impression arises that he (and those who followed him) could never fully account for the phenomenon; above all, for the unconscious purpose it served.

In some places, the repetition compulsion is described as a vain quest to achieve mastery of an earlier trauma. The aim is to gain a new beginning (i.e., a resolution of the trauma denied under the original circumstances), but the outcome is invariably failure. For others, the repetition of the trauma and the subsequent pain it engenders gives punishment for sins committed. The pain provides contrition, and alleviation from guilt, although the relief is only transitory. Last, it is thought that the client repeats the past neurotic pattern because it is known or familiar; a far safer haven than a change toward an unknown, uncertain future.

The most recognizable, even extreme form of repetition compulsion is seen in the ritualized acts of an obsessive–compulsive person. Consciously, the acts are *ego dystonic*; that is, the person recognizes the absurdity of the behavior but cannot withstand the internal pressure to perform the act. Examples of compulsive rituals are legion.

One of the authors, during his internship in a locked unit of a state hospital, was called out by the female nursing staff. A male patient would not quit his morning shower. On entering the patient's bathroom, it was obvious that the young man had been standing under the shower for quite some time. His skin was puckered and bright red from the extended exposure to the hot water. When asked to finish, it was as though he had two minds. Nodding his head repeatedly, he agreed he needed to get out and said he would, all the while continuing to scrub himself vigorously. After several attempts at persuasion, he finally relented. Keenly embarrassed, he hurriedly dried himself, dressed, and then rushed out to the dayroom. The author found the moment poignant, almost surreal; the compulsive washing appeared to have an existence separate from the patient. Under the sway of the vicious cycle, the young man felt helpless and humiliated.

Although less dramatic than the last example, the repetition compulsion is invoked to account for people who repeatedly choose inherently destructive relationships. The prototypic case is of the man or woman who, almost unerringly, finds someone to punish, reject, or offend him or her. As soon as one relationship ends in disappointment, another is found, and the sad history is repeated. The cycle continues even though the person may be told by family, friends, and even therapists that the relationship is a mistake, doomed to bring more heartache, more injury.

Because repetition compulsion, as an explanatory concept, has never reached a final, conclusive form, its principal value comes as a description. At a minimum, psychoanalysts observed and recorded a consistency across problematic behavior. No matter how distressing the results, and no matter how many times failure was encountered, the person resorted to variations of the same solution over and over. If any consensus exists in the metatheory, it is that, through the repetition, the person is attempting to achieve some relief, if not resolution. This misguided and repetitive attempt to achieve a change for the better, by whatever means, is the hallmark of a first-order change.

Cognitive–Behavioral Therapy

Presumably combining the best of behavior therapy with cognitive therapy (viz., the work of George Kelly, Albert Ellis, and Aaron Beck), cognitive–behavioral therapy or modification elevates vicious cycles to a central place in the approach. They are posited as key offenders in depression, panic disorder, social phobia, hypochondria, bulimia, body dysmorphic disorder (BDD), obsessive–compulsive disorder, and other troublesome conditions. Detailing the presentation and operation of vicious cycles in all the disorders previously listed would exceed the scope of this historical review. For demonstration, however, the description of a vicious cycle as played out in BDD, the so-called "ugly disease," follows.

BBD refers to a preoccupation with one's appearance. To the afflicted, reportedly approaching as many as 5 million people in the United States, a real or imagined physical defect becomes a fixation. Although any feature may be the subject of intense focus, weight, complexion, face, hair, and legs are common imagined deficits.

Attending to the anxiety over the defect is a variety of action that people use to cope. To begin, some may attempt to groom the defect out of existence or minimize its impression (e.g., shaving, combing hair, removing or cutting hair, applying cosmetics). Using a form of camouflage or covering over apparel, or the closely timed and strategic placement of the hands over the imperfection is also pursued. Also seen are checking behaviors in which the person compares the appearance of the defective feature with others or frequently inspects the body part in mirrors and reflective surfaces. Mirrors may also become as loathsome as the defect, objects to be scrupulously avoided.

In social situations, the patient may repeatedly attempt to solicit reassurance about the flaw or even convince others of its ugliness. A commonplace remedy is to avoid any circumstance in which the perceived defect might be revealed. One woman, described by the psychiatrist Katherine Phillips in *The Broken Mirror: Understanding and Treating Body Dysmorphic Disorder* (1996), lived with her parents and rarely left her bedroom; when she did leave, she covered her face with a veil.

The solutions just described for managing the defect are at best partial and often more debilitating than the condition itself. Social avoidance exemplifies this point and provides an excellent example of a vicious cycle.

As noted, many people with BDD stay away from social activities. Fear of rejection drives the avoidance but the withdrawal, of course, provides fertile ground for the fear. For both men and women, the inevitable encounter triggers the idea that others are staring at them, noticing the defect, and forming a host of unfavorable opinions. Bound up by these ideas, the person shuts down, pulls back, and refuses or makes only a faint attempt at conversation and engagement. This is apt to be interpreted as aloofness or unfriendliness, leading others to pull themselves back or turn to easier, more congenial company. The client interprets this reaction as evidence of his or her worst fears: "I was right. They see it. I am ugly and undesirable." Hardly wanting a curtain call on such humiliation, the person resolves that withdrawal is the best course, adding more force to the cycle.

Perhaps the best example of vicious cycles from a cognitive–behavioral approach can be found in Aaron Beck's (Beck, Rush, Shaw, & Emery, 1979) approach to the operation of automatic thoughts and schemas. The proverbial cognitive–behavioral triangle of actions, thoughts, and body states sets up the first reverberating cycle of how the interpretation of environment affects our experience of emotions and shapes our subsequent actions. These actions, in turn, influence our environment, which further shapes our perceptions, interpretations, emotions, reactions, and so on. Once set in motion, these cycles can shape and reflect larger themes, called *schemas*. These schemas can drive further actions of people in a process that some find quite similar to the repetition compulsions described earlier in the discussion of dynamic perspectives. The point is that the core of this approach is the self-defeating, self-fulfilling prophecy of vicious cycles that are client problems, as we discuss in chapters 7 and 8, which focus on anxiety and depression. Barlow's (2001) approach to reversing the vicious cycle of panic attacks and anxiety disorders is just one example of how successful interventions from this perspective intervene in the vicious cycles of clients' problems.

Systems Theory Approaches

Another way of explaining vicious cycles of solution-generated problems is through the language of systems theory. These cycles have been called *positive feedback loops.* To be clear, the word *positive* has nothing to do with a value judgment that what is going on is "good." It may or may not be. A positive feedback loop refers to a circular process. Here, the more of A that occurs, the more of B occurs. The more of B that happens, the more this draws on A to happen. This is circular cause and effect, in which A causes B, which causes A, and so on. It is different from the linear cause-and-effect formula of A causes B, which leads to C. Positive feedback creates "runaways" in a system. Turning to human interaction, whether we label this resulting pattern a *vicious* cycle or a *virtuous* cycle depends on what value we assign to the process. The sexual problems discussed earlier involve positive feedback loops that we find undesirable. We might therefore label them *vicious cycles*. The results of interdicting a client's failed solutions to his or her sexual difficulties may lead to a new positive feedback loop that yields progressive passion, intimacy, excitement, and release. Valuing these as desirable therapeutic resolutions, we would then call these *virtuous cycles*. The positive feedback process is the same. The value judgment applied to it is what makes the difference between vicious and virtuous.

A common example from electronics is the positive feedback we have all heard from someone who holds a microphone too close to a speaker. Sound from the speaker is picked up by the microphone and is fed back through the receiver, which amplifies the sound and sends it to the speaker again, to be picked up as louder by the microphone and fed back, and so on. The result is the growing, deafening wail that we have all heard. The problem results from successive changes in a positive feedback cycle and ends only when the microphone is diverted away from the speaker. The cycle is broken; the pattern is interrupted.

As with each thumbnail sketch of the selected perspectives, there are many approaches within each perspective. There is not one system theory approach that will represent them all. There is, however, a foundation in general system theory that can be tapped. The works of Ludwig von Bertalanffy (1962) or Norbert Weiner (1961) are often brought forward as representatives of general systems theory. However, it was the sociologist Walter Buckley (1987) who did the best job of pointing out that there are qualitative differences among systems, from mechanical systems, to biological systems, to interpersonal systems of human interaction. Buckley's principles of process-level systems are most applicable to the kind of interpersonal system problems of human interaction that people bring to psychotherapy. The positive feedback cycle described earlier is at the core of human interpersonal systems from this view. In short, human interaction (including with ourselves) is described as a series of positive feedback cycles over time. The unit of interaction is communication that evolves over time. Reverberating cycles are described as vicious or virtuous depending on the value we attach to their process and outcome at any given point. Any one "kick-point" or original cause may generate a wide array of different cycle patterns. Similarly, the same kinds of problem cycles in different people may be generated from a wide array of initial starting points. They are functionally autonomous, to recall a term described earlier, from what initiated them. This perspective of process-level–human-interactional systems is the essence of the first-order and second-order change ideas that we are describing.

The Dialectical Perspective

The dialectical view is a systemic perspective that views all elements of human interaction as parts of a dynamic, ever-changing whole. It has ancient origins in both Eastern and Western philosophy. A basic premise of this view is that apparently polar opposite elements are viewed as poles of related dimensions and are therefore integrated at a higher order level of logic or organization. Furthermore, change, and not stability, is the essence of this view of human interaction. This assumption was shared from ancient origins by both the Greek philosopher Heraclites and the Chinese Taoist philosopher Lao Tzu. The German philosopher Hegel is a modern interpreter of the dialectical view. The dialectical view suggests that life problems come from vicious cycles as we get stuck at one level and are unable to move to the next to synthesize the poles of the dilemma. One way of viewing this is as movement from one pole to the opposite and, finally, to the integration of the two, or from thesis to antithesis to synthesis. Integration or synthesis is always moving to, accepting, and experiencing the world at a higher level of organization, or a higher logical level. Truth in this view is not fixed and is externally discovered and verifiable. Truth is relative to the system in which it evolves, and it is an emergent product of interaction within a social domain. This is similar to the social constructionist perspective, according to which the premises, assumptions, and concepts that evolve in each different system shape and direct what vicious cycles will uniquely develop. Although there are Eastern and Western philosophical traditions that embrace the dialectical perspective, this view is most often related to Eastern philosophies. The dialectical perspective is essentially the same as such non-Western perspectives as Zen Buddhism and Taoism. Because this perspective is so different from most Western assumptions, it is often experienced as illogical, counterintuitive, or paradoxical to most therapists in Western cultures. This non-Western perspective affirms a balance and affirmation of all actions and ideas. This is represented in the classic yin–yang symbol that has dark on one side, light on the other, and a dot of each shade in the middle of its polar opposite. The opposing elements combine into a circular whole, with the synthesis of opposites defining the essence of the whole at another level. The essence of human dilemmas is being out of balance, which initiates vicious cycles that take on lives of their own. These are but a few of the major bases of the dialectical perspective.

The view supporting first- and second-order change that we use throughout this book assumes that all human interaction is part of a dynamic, ever-changing whole, exactly as does the dialectic view. The way we negotiate interactions and change within a systemic whole is the focus for understanding and changing people within these systems. This is a perspective that focuses more on the process of change and less on the content and formal structure of the issues or systems at hand. Reality, truth, premises, and related assumptions on the way things are evolve and emerge from cocreated social interaction among group members. In this view, the only thing constant is change. As we discuss in the next chapter, ideas from group theory and the theory of logical types are used to describe the types of change.

As we discuss presently, first-order change is that which occurs yet does not change the system. Because changes are in accordance with the accepted premises, rules, and assumptions guiding the system, these changes are logical or make sense to those within the system. We will explain that first-order change operates according to the rules of group theory. Second-order change is a change that changes the system itself. This happens by moving to a higher order of organization in understanding and interacting within our world; to a synthesis or integration of the poles of the first-order level. Because second-order change alters the assumptions and related rules of interaction within systems, such change is often experienced as counterintuitive or paradoxical when viewed from within the assumptions of the system undergoing second-order change. We will explain that second-order change operates according to the theory of logical types. First-order change typically involves the acceptance of a set of assumptions on the nature of correct and incorrect, right and wrong parameters for action within a given system. Problems are often resolved by applying negation, or the opposite of what needs correcting. Frequently, this action works; often, it creates escalating vicious cycles, yet always it maintains the system. Second-order change resolves the polemic and escalating vicious cycles of first-order solution patterns by redefining the nature of the system and integrating the poles in a new synthesis, thus eliminating the solution patterns that are the essence of the problems at the first-order level. Said another way, second-order change alters the solutions of the first-order level and changes the assumptions on which they were based. The dialectical perspective and the process view of systems from which first- and second-order change emerge are one and the same.

THE MENTAL RESEARCH INSTITUTE

That vicious cycle
Ridden solely on perceptions.

—Unknown poet

The shoulders on which we stand to put forth our approach are those of the staff of the Brief Therapy Center at the Mental Research Institute (MRI) in Palo Alto, California. Paul Watzlawick, John Weakland, and Richard Fisch have been the core members of this group. They have jointly and individually authored a number of influential books on their work, but none is more influential than their book *Change: Principles of Problem Formation and Problem Resolution* (Watzlawick et al., 1974), and its more practical companion, *The Tactics of Change* (Fisch, Weakland, & Segal, 1982). They were powerfully influenced by their association with Gregory Bateson, Milton Erickson, Donald Jackson, Jay Haley, and various other creative thinkers and practitioners. They were the first, however, to apply the concepts of group theory and the theory of logical types to human problems and thus articulate and apply the ideas of first-order and second-order change to problems and their resolution. We owe an immeasurable debt to their work, from which we will continue to draw and to which we refer directly and indirectly throughout these first foundational chapters. This MRI group has made two major contributions: First, they have provided an understanding of how and why problems persist and change; second, they have provided a typology of problem formation and resolution.

First, we have built our discussion of how problems persist by using the MRI group's definition of first-order change and the nature of people's assumptions or premises. In observing people locked in a vicious cycle, it is tempting to be judgmental. "What is the matter with them? Can't they see what they're doing?" The more important question is why people persist in the face of failure.

When faced with an apparent difficulty, we tend to convert preconceived ideas into a convenient set of premises or rules for problem solving. We typically choose the set of assumptions that have worked well for us in the past. However, people have an affinity to choose a particular set and then follow the associated rules of solution. Therefore, even in novel situations people have a tendency to choose a frame that will lead to a simple set of related rules. These rules form a logical system that determines what solutions are reasonable. This becomes a problem only when the premises are flawed.

The nature of vicious cycles and how well-intentioned people get trapped can be further understood as a function of human pride, dignity, predictable safety, and dogged determination. Unlike computers, we have strong protective emotions attached to our premises. The fear of mistakes can turn first-order change into an emotionally compelling and very personal dilemma. We are confronted with potential embarrassment or shame if others become aware that some of our deeply held assumptions may be mistaken. Furthermore, our premises and related assumptions about the nature of the world have an existential dimension. Our premises regarding the way things are help us to create predictable safety in our world. We might disagree on many levels on whether our world is, in fact, predictable and safe; however, giving up a position that has served us well in the past for an untried new assumption is often experienced as a risky proposition. This is even truer when we feel that the stakes are high, time is pressing, and the risk of loss is great. Such is the case at most crisis points. Finally, many of us have been raised with admonitions such as "If at first you don't succeed, try and try again!"; "Don't give up the ship!"; "Damn the torpedoes, full steam ahead!"; and "When the going gets tough, the tough get going!" These are just a few examples. Such platitudes become deeply held and unexamined. We become doggedly determined to stay our course as we remember these directives. Each factor keeps us wedded to our premises. We continue to act with tireless persistence. As we hold tightly to our cherished beliefs, our solutions become the problem in a familiar vicious cycle. (On reflection, this same allegiance to a viewpoint applies equally to psychotherapists and their cherished theories and practices of psychotherapy.) We recall that it is said that Milton Erickson, who very much influenced the MRI group, suggested that the art of therapy was helping people to bow out of their symptoms gracefully.

Second, the MRI perspective on change provides a typology of problem formation that implies pathways to their resolution. The MRI group looked closely at the way problems evolve and provided a nice classification scheme. Because of the importance of this scheme, we discuss it in depth under the next major heading. To recount the purpose of this section, however, the concept of vicious cycles that lead to solution-generated problems is not new. It exists across theories and perspectives from psychodynamic to existential–humanistic, to cognitive–behavioral, to systems theory, to the ancient dialectical view and, finally, to the perspectives we now discuss that were developed by the MRI group. Again, we stand on their shoulders as they have stood on those of others before them. Their categorization of the types of change will serve us as a guide to the golden thread that we will follow through the empirically supported therapies reviewed in the next section of the book.

THE ROADS BETTER NOT TAKEN: THE EVOLUTION OF PROBLEM CYCLES

The Greek philosopher Heraclitus (ca. 500 BC) said, "Nothing is permanent but change." Change is at the heart of clients' problems, and change is the core element in all effective problem resolution. It is the nature of the change that determines whether it is problematic or a resolution. Referring again to the book *Change: Principles of Problem Formation and Problem Resolution*, its authors, Watzlawick and colleagues (1974), described three basic ways that problems may evolve.

1. *Action is necessary but is not taken.* This might be described as denying that something is a difficulty when it actually is. Some common clinical examples may be seen when family members deny that sexual abuse is occurring in their family, or when a battered woman does not acknowledge the seriousness of domestic violence in her relationship, or when parents overlook the need to correct a persistently unruly child. This is a set of *underreactions.*

   In child sexual abuse, it is all too common for family members to deny its existence and thus find no need to act. Children drawn into sexual abuse cycles with a perpetrator usually have multiple incentives—for example, shame or fear—to not disclose the abuse to others. Too often, however, a child's attempts at disclosing are met with the same responses as the fabled child who claimed that "The emperor has no clothes!" They are often shamed, blamed, and punished by those who might otherwise take needed action to break the cycle. This usually leads to more isolation and secrecy, and the cycles of abuse continue. Action is needed but not taken. The woman in a power-dominant, abusive relationship is in a similar dilemma. The classic cycle of tension building, abuse, and respite often draws women into a pattern of trying to understand and adjust their relationship with their partner. Traditional gender roles tend to put women in charge of relationships with their partners. The cycle itself evolves greater power dominance and further isolation from others. Often, embarrassment, shame, love, and commitment prevent women from disclosing to others. Others often do not find out about the relationship because they feel they want to honor the couple's privacy and do not want to intrude. However, when women do disclose, common reactions tend to shut the woman down further and isolate her more. Action is needed but not taken, and the cycle goes on.

2. *Action is taken when it should not be.* This is taking action when the perceived difficulty is in essence unchangeable, or it is not really a problem. Some examples are trying to close the "generation gap" when it will always exist; trying to "remember to forget" our grief when we simply need to allow it to be; trying to "will" an erection or climax, as we have already mentioned, when these are the natural by-products of the experience of passion; or suppressing a sad or anxious thought to master depression or anxiety rather than viewing them as a normal and passing occurrence. This is the set of *overreactions.*

For example, the parents of a teenager may try to convince her that her choice of her boyfriend, Spike, is a problem. They can act on this goal in numerous ways. They can tell her that Spike's family background, religion, or ethnicity, and so on, is too different from theirs. They can raise their voices in telling her this. They can tell her of bad things they have heard from the police or school that Spike has done. They can forbid her from seeing Spike, among many other options. As we know from this familiar interaction, these different processes of convincing their daughter that they know best about her boyfriend often reach the same outcome. She loves Spike and will do what she can to be with him. Within the group of parents and teenagers who are in conflict over dating, these actions most often maintain or escalate the conflict. The process varies, but the outcome is the same. The role of good parents of a teenager is not to impose their will upon their youth. It is to allow their teenager, within certain safe limits, to make his or her own choices and learn from natural consequences. Closing the generation gap with adolescents, or attempting to make an oppositional teenager conform to the will of his or her parents, is doomed to confirm that gap. It is only by looking across centuries of generations that we can see that the generation gap has always existed. It may even persist partly because of each generation's attempts to close it. The problem cycle begins when action is taken and it should not be.

3. *Action is taken at the wrong level.* This occurs when first-order change is attempted and only second-order change can resolve the difficulty. This is the case with insomnia, when one must stop trying to get to sleep in order to sleep. Directly pursuing sleep interrupts the spontaneity of falling asleep and creates the insomnia. This is also the case when a person demands spontaneous shows of affection from his or her partner, when these can happen only spontaneously. At the same time, vicious cycles are also triggered when second-order change is attempted and first-order change is all that is needed. An example of this is when parents demand attitude changes from their child when behavior changes are all that are needed. It may be fine that their child doesn't like doing his or her homework, as long as he or she does it. These examples illustrate how action at the wrong level can lead to overreacting or overpursuing the problem.

A further illustration of overpursuit is the dilemma faced by a person who is attempting to get his or her mate to show expressions of love, or of self-determination. The more I tell my partner how to show me love or how to be self-directed, the more his or her responses will fail to meet my goal. If my partner complies with my directives, then he or she may not be showing his or her own genuine wishes. If my partner refuses to comply, then I am somehow failing to get what I need. The problem, of course, is that in all cases I am initiating the action and not my partner. Free-will gestures of love or self-determination can only come from the other.

Vicious cycles can be initiated when a problem is conceptualized at the wrong level of simplicity or complexity. If the problem is viewed as more complicated than necessary, the problem solver will read too much into the problem. This in turn leads to either taking unnecessary actions or not taking actions that are needed. Viewing a problem too simplistically results in not reading enough into the situation, and again the problem solver may not act when it is needed, or may repeat actions that are unnecessary. As previously stated, failure to take necessary actions can be understood as an underreaction to the problem.

For example, consider a man who is distressed because he believes that his wife has lost interest in him. She has told him many times that if he would help out more with household tasks, then she would have more time for sex. The man decides that it can't be that simple, that the real reason for his wife's lack of interest is that she has lost interest in his physical body. Instead of helping out at home, he spends time at the gym trying to develop his muscles to look more attractive. His wife, however, loses more interest because he is gone more. As she loses more and more interest, he works out more often, and for longer periods. Finally, he has an affair. In his mind, he is hoping that his wife will see that other women are attracted to his body. This example, which occurs more frequently than one might expect, illustrates how making a problem more complex than is necessary creates a situation in which many unnecessary steps are taken. In this case, the unnecessary steps missed the point. The husband may feel that he did a great deal of work, especially in the beginning, to solve his marital problem. In the end, his response was an underreaction to the problem at hand, namely, failure to help his wife keep the house clean. His wrong-level solutions made the problem even worse.

Across all of these problem variations, a common theme is the vicious cycle. Invariably, the more a solution is ineffective or exacerbates a problem, the more it is applied. This is a *positive feedback loop*. Most problems take on this characteristic spiral of ineffective change. The more clients try to master their anxiety by avoiding it, the more anxious they find themselves. The more sleepless clients try to will themselves to sleep, the more it keeps them awake. The more I attempt to confront alcoholics with their drinking, the more adamant their denial grows. The more I try to prevent clients from repeatedly cutting themselves because they feel that no one understands and can help them, the more they feel misunderstood by me and want to cut themselves. Vicious cycles occur between clients and helpers, such as therapists, as easily as they do between clients and their own perceived dilemmas. These problem cycles may be initiated in several ways but, once initiated, the cycle is the same. The content may be different, but the process is the same. Problems involve stability and change. Problems are vicious cycles, positive feedback loops, and solution-generated problems.

FOLLOWING THE THREAD

Stability and change are closely related. In human affairs, to keep things stable, they must change. Furthermore, attempts to change may result in stability. As we describe in the next chapter, stability and change can relate to one another in a proverbial finger trap. From this viewpoint, problems are stable, and problems are similar. Problems are the same damn thing over and over again when viewed through this lens of change. There are several ways that the process may start, but once it has begun the process is the same for all problems. If this perspective on change leads to this view of problems, then what does it say about the effective resolution of problems? What unites effective therapies? Do effective therapists do the same things? We address these questions in the next chapter. Understanding second-order change will offer answers.

3

PROBLEM RESOLUTION

Never assume the obvious is true.

—William Safire

If you can't fix the problem, change the problem.

—J. R. Freeman

Consider the following list of interventions. Each describes an example of sound, evidence-based practice; yet each is relatively counterintuitive.

- A therapist, working with a client who has panic attacks, asks her client to bring on panic during the session.
- Another therapist, working with someone who has been recurrently depressed, teaches his client to allow depressing thoughts to pass through her mind without needing to respond to those thoughts.
- Still another therapist asks a quarreling couple to pick a fight with one another when they are not mad.
- A sex therapist prohibits a couple from having intercourse despite prescribing arousing exercises.
- Another client is told that there may be good reasons not to change.
- A parent, needing to regain control of her child's behavior, is taught to take charge by not directly taking charge.
- Another therapist tells his client that he can't blame her for wanting to harm herself when she becomes emotionally frustrated. He then asks her to experience more emotional frustration while considering other ways to react to it.

In the last chapter, we described how clients' problems are most often the result of attempts to create stability through first-order change. In fact, virtually all problems brought to psychotherapy can be understood as the result of vicious cycles that are initiated and maintained by well-intentioned first-order solutions; that is, these first-order change processes unintentionally stabilize, and typically worsen, the undesirable condition. Therefore, effective therapeutic interventions are targeted as changing solution patterns. Each intervention is an example of effective psychotherapy. Each approach is well supported by research. Each therapist understands his or her intervention within his or her chosen theoretical framework. Yet all of these interventions appear to be ironic and counterintuitive. The objective of this chapter is to show that this shared irony points to a powerful unifying framework that is at the heart of all effective psychotherapies. It is the ground of change from which all of them grow. It is the golden thread of second-order change that runs through the fabric of all of them.

Clients are changing, and yet not in the ways they desire. In the last chapter, we drove home the point that problems are most often a product of first-order folly—that is, virtually all problems brought to psychotherapy can be understood as vicious cycles that are initiated and driven by well-intentioned, failed solutions. In a strange way, the attempt to restore a desired state of stability escalates the problem pattern. We find ourselves in a contradictory situation in which the problem-producing process unintentionally stabilizes the undesirable condition. In other words, the more we attempt to resolve the problem, the more stable the problem becomes. Therefore, effective interventions are targeted as changing solution patterns. The essence of problem resolution is a shift in the pattern of failed solutions. Even the term *resolution* may be thought of in this sense as a "re-solution," or the introduction of alternate solutions to the problem at hand. At the most fundamental level this is second-order change, the focus of this chapter. We argue that second-order change is the catalyst for problem resolution that runs through all effective psychotherapies.

WHEN FIRST-ORDER SOLUTIONS SUFFICE

There are several key differences that distinguish the type of psychotherapy that occurs in clinical trials from psychotherapy in the field. A critical difference from the perspective of first- and second-order change pertains to client selection. Empirically supported treatments (ESTs) are designed for clinical conditions that have evolved to a degree of severity that second-order change will almost always be necessary. Clients are chosen to participate in a clinical trial because they have a problem that meets specific problem severity criteria. Psychotherapy in the "real world" of clinical practice has become highly popularized in Western culture. Clients may seek advice before a vicious cycle has actually begun to unfold. In such situations, direct advice or suggestions may be the most effective approach.

For a therapist to attempt a second-order intervention when a first-order one will suffice is for the therapist to fall into one of the three options for initiating or perpetuating problems noted in the last chapter—that is, making a simple problem more complex or intervening at the wrong level. Sometimes, simply reinforcing consistency in already-existing solutions, re-engaging clients in their own tried-and-true solutions, adding a new variation on a current set of solutions, or slightly redirecting a current set of solutions is all that is needed. A parent who has been inconsistent in offering rewards or consequences may experience success with his child by simply rewarding the child more frequently or applying consequences in a more consistent fashion. A woman who has always resolved life difficulties through sharing with her sister may be helped to reengage with her sister for some sisterly support. Noting clients' strengths and skills, refining those skills, or directing them in a slightly new path are other examples of what are, in essence, first-order level interventions by therapists. Experienced therapists will remember that many clients have been helped when they reassured them that they, in fact, aren't crazy or actually are headed in the right direction. (The bicycle rider or the tightrope walker we mentioned in the last chapter may need only to be reminded about over- or undercorrecting to maintain his balance and his course.) Effectively assisting clients with engaging in or refining first-order solutions requires that they are involved in the treatment and compliant with the therapist's suggestions. This is the essence of the working alliance and positive trusting relationship we discussed in chapter 1 of this volume. Such compliance is sometimes simple, direct, and forthcoming. If it is not, another type of vicious cycle may ensue. This involves a cycle within the therapeutic relationship in which the therapist gives advice and the client does not follow it. When this occurs, a second-order intervention is needed at the therapeutic alliance level. We discuss this further in the next chapter. In sum, second-order change should never be attempted when first-order change will suffice. This is a rule for both clients and therapists.

WHEN FIRST-ORDER CHANGE IS NEEDED

For the most part, clients enter therapy with strongly entrenched problems that are vicious cycles of first-order solutions. A key element in effective psychotherapy is the initiation of second-order change. It will help to revisit the definition of second-order change, pick it apart some more, and offer a few more simple examples and experiences with it before turning to how effective psychotherapists bring it about.

Recall how we defined *second-order change*: a change of a group or system's primary premises and related rules and interaction patterns. It is, in essence, a change of the change process itself. Changing the change process is a de-

ceptively simple proposition; however, because the logic involved in problem generation is compelling, it is easy to produce apparently new solutions
that turn out to be more of the same old solutions. The previously mentioned
parent struggling with an oppositional child may come up with a novel reward. If rewards have repeatedly failed, a more novel one will only perpetuate the cycle. Second-order change usually involves strikingly different or
opposite interactions. It is the difference between the new novel solution
and what has been tried before that transforms the group or system. Such
change also appears illogical or counterintuitive when viewed from within
the original premises and rules of the system in question. This is a function of
how logical systems operate. Logical systems establish parameters that define
what makes sense in problem solving. Solutions that are within the parameters of a given logical system "feel right." Solutions that are outside of the
system are experienced as strange, unusual, counterintuitive, ironic, or even
forbidden. For that parent who is trying to gain control of an oppositional
child, a second-order solution may entail a way of interacting that avoids
rewards or direct consequences. This will most likely make no sense within
the context of a system that is predicated on such reinforcements.

THEORETICAL ROOTS

The implications of this view on change are extraordinary for the practice of psychotherapy. This perspective suggests that change operates on principles other than what has been described in the major theoretical frameworks that comprise the behavioral health field. Yet what is the basis for the
operant principle that is at the heart of change? Without a psychological
theory to describe the relationship between stability and change, theoreti-
cians at the Mental Research Institute turned to theories of logic that are
found in mathematics. When the terms *first-order change* and *second-order
change* were first defined in the book *Change: Principles of Problem Formation
and Problem Resolution* (hereafter we refer to this work as *Change*; Watzlawick
et al., 1974), the authors used *set theory*, or *the theory of groups*, as the explanation for first-order change, and the *theory of logical types* as the rationale for
second-order change. Although these theories serve as a sound foundation
for understanding how change occurs, they are highly complex, rather ab-
stract, and often confusing to follow. Because of the conceptual challenge of
these theories, most people familiar with the work have overlooked or forgotten them. They are, nevertheless, firm foundations for understanding
change, and they deserve attention.

GROUP THEORY

There are aspects of group theory and the theory of logical types that
are important to the case that is being made for the golden thread. For the

purpose of our current discussion, we will describe these two theories very simply. Turning first to group theory, a group may comprise any kind of like members, from people to ideas. The theory of groups suggests that once a group is set, all interactions within the group, according to the assumptions and rules of the group, will maintain the group's identity. Thus, once set, all interactions preserve and perpetuate the stability of the group. There can be many changes in the interactions of the group and no change of the group will result. A group may not change itself from within. Groups are defined and bounded by their group definitions and related interaction rules. In applying this mathematical analogy to human dilemmas it does not mean that if the group contains people that people cannot change the group. It does mean that change cannot be initiated with the same assumptions and interactions that have initiated the problem. This is impossible from the perspective of formal logic. In other words, human folly is rooted in how a problem is understood. Understandings of problems are shaped by premises and assumptions on the way things are. Once problem-solving constructs have been set, escape is difficult, if not impossible. This simple definition may seem so obvious as to be confusing. Suffice it to say that the theory of groups underlies what has thus far been described and exemplified as first-order change, with all of its vicious cycles of solution-generated problems. As with most mathematical theory, the basic ideas are rather broad reaching and universal.

THE THEORY OF LOGICAL TYPES

Second-order change is based on the theory of logical types, which is closely related to group theory. As previously stated, group theory demonstrates the futility of attempting to initiate change with the same set of constructs that have initiated the problem. The theory of logical types shows how constructs from outside a group can be incorporated into a group, resulting in a change in the original group's identity. (The synonym for group in logical typing is the word *class*.) To make such a foundational change in any group, the very assumptions that define the group and its interactions must be changed. To accomplish this change, one must move to what is called a *higher level* or *class* of assumptions and definitions that subsume the original ones and describe and explain them as well or better. This kind of change is a basic shift in premise or mental set. From a dialectical perspective, this is the synthesis that integrates apparently opposing positions.

Consider, for example, a client who comes for therapy with anxiety about making mistakes in social situations. In this case, the client has a mental set that classifies all social mistakes as bad experiences without redeeming value. This understanding leads the client to place enormous pressure on himself to avoid social miscues. In social situations, he focuses exclusively on his own behavior in an effort to perfect his socialization skills. Close self-scrutiny distorts his perception of himself in social situations, raises his anxiety, and increases the likelihood that he will make social miscues. This obviously paves the road to human folly. In this instance, a higher class of constructs might be a class that defines social mistakes as both bad experiences and necessary opportunities for social learning (also explained as an integration and affirmation of previously opposite poles under a new idea of how one gains social competence). The inclusion of "necessary social learning opportunities" into the set of bad experiences creates a novel classification: "bad experiences that have redeeming value." The new concept is similar to the old one because it recognizes social mistakes as bad experiences. At the same time, the idea of learning from mistakes can hardly be denied. The word *necessary* pushes the notion of the good in mistakes a step farther. This new twist on an old concept actually better describes how social leaning works. Once made, the shift opens multiple and cascading new options for action. In response to this new set of constructs, the client may become more self-tolerant or even begin looking forward to making social mistakes so that he can learn more quickly how to socialize with others. If he is daring, he might take this idea further yet and make small social miscues on purpose in an effort to learn socializing skills at a more profound level. Also, once the shift is made, it is very difficult to shift back. The subsequent actions based on the logical shift will be perfectly logical from within the premises of the new set, but they may appear impossible or certainly illogical from the prior set.

In *Change* (Watzlawick et al., 1974), the authors wrote about "terrible simplifications." The idea of levels in problem solving can be understood as a function of simplicity and complexity. Higher classes of ideas, such as "bad experiences with redeeming value," are considered to be complex because they are inclusive and tolerant of concepts that appear to be contradictory. In this way, the inclusive notion that "good can come from bad" is more complex than an exclusive idea such as "mistakes are simply bad; nothing good comes from them." As we stated in the previous chapter, vicious cycles are triggered when the wrong level is selected for problem solving. Another way to say this is that problems are initiated when the problem solver judges a difficult situation in a way that misses hidden complexities (i.e., is overly simplistic) or in a way that is overly complicated. An example of overcomplication might be family violence or sex abuse when problem solvers justify unacceptable behavior by finding redeeming value in it. In these types of situations there is a need for problem solvers to shift to a more simplistic understanding, such as that violence or certain types of sexual behavior are unjustifiable.

Another implication of the level chosen is the relationship between problem classification and action. Actions follow how the problem is understood. Unnecessary steps that start a pattern of problem avoidance or overpursuit are initiated by the problem solver's understanding of the difficulty. As indicated previously, denial of the problem is similarly linked to the problem solver's understanding of the problem situation. This is the foundation of second-order change. By its very nature, second-order change is both simple and confusing. It may be defined only in context of what was there before it. It is a premise shift. It is a pattern shift. Therefore, it makes sense only in terms of the first-order premises and patterns of related solutions. A few more illustrations may help readers further understand the interesting nature of pattern shifts.

PUZZLES AND DILEMMAS

We are not retreating—we are advancing in another direction.
—Douglas MacArthur

The Finger Trap

One of the simplest examples of first- and second-order change is the "finger trap" toy that so many children have had fun with over the ages. The finger trap is a small cylinder made of woven hemp strips. The cylinder is not firm but flexible. One child asks another to put the index finger of each hand into each end and then try to escape these "handcuffs" by pulling her fingers out. As you might remember, simply pulling your fingers out only causes the fibers of the finger trap to bind more closely to your fingers. The more you pull, the tighter the finger trap becomes. It is only by giving up the logical solution of pulling out, and instead pushing in, that the trap finally releases and your fingers may be gently removed. Pushing in to get out is a second-order change.

A question can be raised about the logic that drives problem-solvers to try pulling out of the trap as a first-order solution. The instinct to pull out is universal; virtually all children initially try to solve the puzzle in this manner. Most children then get stuck in the cycle of trying this method over and over again. More careful consideration may shed some light on the hidden complexities of the finger trap and of second-order change.

In the process of development, children learn many fundamental lessons about life. An important lesson involves solving certain challenges in daily living by "pulling out" of them. If a child places her hand on an object that is too hot or too cold, she instinctively pulls her hand away. She learns to pull her feet out of her socks; the same procedure is used for taking off her shoes. If she steps in a mud puddle and her foot becomes stuck in the mud, she pulls her stuck foot out. When she grows older, she learns more complex variations on the same theme: To find your way after getting lost, you retrace your steps. In other words, you find your way out of a challenging situation by going in the direction opposite from the way that you entered it. A child's mind thoroughly understands this rule. Upon seeing the finger trap for the first time, the child's mind immediately reads the problem, determines the problem-solving level, and goes into action. This process occurs so fast that it is almost instantaneous. There is only one problem: The finger trap represents an exception to the rule of pulling out. It cannot be solved that way.

This is an elementary example of first- and second-order change. The logical solutions of pulling one's fingers directly out only further trap the fingers. The harder one pulls, the tighter the trap becomes. More of the same solution breeds more of the same results. This is the now familiar vicious cycle. The solution makes sense to the child, but it makes the problem worse. The resolution is a classic second-order change. The resolution is a reversal of the first-order solution. Pushing the fingers together releases the trap and allows the child to gently slide free. This resolution is based on viewing the dilemma differently. It is a product of using a different level of logic. The child solves the problem by doing less of the same instead of more of the same. The resolution is paradoxical and counterintuitive to most children. It usually results in cascades of laughter after discovering the "trick" of the trap. These elements are also typical of second-order change. First-order change appears logical to those trapped in the problem cycle and thus second-order change seems ironic, illogical, or even funny when viewed from the original position on the problem. The finger trap puzzle, although simple in form, has many profound ramifications. As mentioned earlier, avoidance or pulling away is a common mistake that sets up many complex human problems. Depression, anxiety disorders, chronic pain, and many other clinical conditions share this same fundamental error in logic.

The Old Nine-Dot Problem

At the risk of overkill, we ask you to engage in one more classic example of second-order change. These days the phrase "thinking outside of the box" is so often used that is has become almost trite. Yet we all continue to be trapped in our own logical boxes on a daily basis. The "nine-dot problem" has become almost as common. Solving it, however, even after having done so before, continues to trap us in our own assumptions and solutions. For those readers who are familiar with this problem, we ask you to stick with us for a moment. We will have some additional challenges for you. As a matter of fact, we have chosen to use this problem *because* so many readers will have encountered it before and will be sure that they will know the answers. This is the kind of confidence that leads to more problems.

In his popular book on creative problem solving titled *Conceptual Blockbusting: A Guide to Better Ideas*, James Adams (2001) follows the nine dot problem through several increasing challenges. Referring to the following dots, the basic directions to the problem are these:

Puzzle 1: Draw no more than <u>FOUR</u> straight lines (without lifting the pencil from the paper) that will cross through all nine dots.

.   .   .

.   .   .

.   .   .

This puzzle is extremely difficult to solve if you see the nine dots as a box that you cannot go outside of with your lines. For those attempting this puzzle for the first time, that is the key clue. Think outside the imaginary box![1] However, before turning to the solution, or going smugly on if you know the solution, first try several more challenges with these dots.

Puzzle 2: Now draw no more than <u>THREE</u> straight lines (without lifting the pencil from the paper) that will cross through all nine dots.[2]

Got that one? OK. Now try this one:

Puzzle 3: Do the same with <u>ONE</u> straight line. (There are several solutions.)[3]

Finally, try this last challenge:

Puzzle 4: Do the same thing using <u>ONE POINT</u>. (Again, there are several possible solutions.)[4]

In each variation of this puzzle, the solution involves breaking a self-imposed set of logical assumptions. These assumptions are not intrinsic to the problem set out; they are something we impose on ourselves. Of course, once we accept these assumptions, they set implicit limits on the range and kind of possible solutions we can use. Breaking out of these self-imposed mental sets moves us to a new logical level with whole new realms of solutions open to us. What is more, these are solutions that seemed unimaginable or illogical before. The power of second-order change lies therein.

The nine-dot problem and its solutions also demonstrate the relative aspect of first-order and second-order change. First-order change, or what has been tried before, defines second-order change, or a solution that is outside of our current problem-solving assumptions. Once we reach outside of our assumptions and find a novel solution, the novel solution becomes part

---

[1]The first puzzle is solved by drawing the first line across the top three dots and beyond them so the second line can be drawn through the third dot on the second row and through and beyond middle dot on the bottom row ending below the first column of dots. The third line is drawn straight up the first column. The fourth line is then drawn diagonally from top left to bottom right to connect the remaining dots. To solve the problem, our lines must go "outside the box."

[2]This challenge is solved by drawing three lines in a "W"-like formation, starting above and to the left of the top left dot. The first line goes diagonally through the left corner of the first column dot, the middle of the second dot in that column, and the right edge of the bottom dot in that column, to a point below the dots. The second line goes up the middle column in the same diagonal way to a point beyond that column to the right. The final line goes back down diagonally through the last column of dots.

[3]One solution is to use a line so fat it covers all the dots as it goes across them. Another is to bend the paper into a cylinder and draw an angled line that goes continuously around the cylinder and through each row of lines as it passes around. There are other options as well.

[4]Folding or cutting the paper to stack the dots on top of each other allows one to stab a sharp point through them all at one time. There are other options here, too.

of a new set of assumptions. The new assumptions may again blind us from seeing other possibilities that might work as well or better in other similar situations. For now, the important point is that difficulties in problem solving are usually a function of our mind set. Mind-set problems are a naturally occurring phenomenon. As human beings, we all share the same susceptibility.

SECOND-ORDER CHANGE AT THE MACRO LEVEL

Although these puzzles present clear challenges, and they offer nice examples of first- and second-order change, they pose no urgency or threat to others or us if we don't solve them. Problems and life dilemmas offer no such luxury. Failure to resolve these situations may cause discomfort at the least, and real personal threat or loss of life at the worst. Because the stakes are higher, ignoring these dilemmas is much less of an option. Creative flexibility holds even higher risks. What if our solution doesn't work? What do we risk? Tried and true, less risky, and more conservative approaches feel like the safer and better choices. Furthermore, as these situations escalate, it becomes even harder to reverse our course or to choose another. These problems are not humorous. These are deadly serious dilemmas. That is why the following examples are so fascinating. The first two examples occur at larger social levels, and the third is a clinical intervention.

Vietnam War Demonstrations

Most readers will be familiar with the tragic killing of student protestors at Kent State University by National Guard troops during the Vietnam war. In retrospect, it appears to have been the product of a predictable set of logical yet escalating responses by both the student protestors and the Guardsmen. That is why it was so stunning when one of us witnessed the following during a massive antiwar demonstration at about the same time at a major midwestern university.

In the early 1970s, a small group of students stopped traffic by sitting down in the middle of Grand River Avenue in East Lansing, Michigan. This was in protest of President Nixon's bombing in Cambodia during the Vietnam war. Grand River Avenue is a major thoroughfare that runs past the campus of Michigan State University. It was not long before traffic was blocked for miles. The students in the street held up signs and chanted anti-war slogans. Upon arriving on the scene, the police ordered the crowd to disperse. This directive was ignored, and the students chanted more loudly and made abusive gestures toward the police. In response, the police called for reinforcements and shot tear gas into the crowd. The students refused to move, and the smell of tear gas brought out students from dormitories that were in the vicinity. They joined in with their fellow students, and in a short time the conditions for a major riot were set. Police fired more tear gas, which brought out even more students. Soon hundreds of students were rushing toward the scene from every corner of the campus. Many were only curious, but others were willing to join in. They began throwing tear gas canisters back at the police. In response, the police called in a large contingent of state police dressed in full riot gear. As they stood in formation, their leader came out with a bullhorn. He loudly shouted to the crowd that a decision had been made to let the students peacefully demonstrate in the street. The police that were fighting with the crowd were directed to back down so that the students could demonstrate. The riot police retreated to an area that was outside of the view of the crowd.

In response, the crowd began to cheer. Once the cheering stopped, there was a pause, as it was unclear as to what should be done next. Some students went back to their dorms and brought back blankets, beer, guitars, and other things for a party. By 3 or 4 in the morning, most of the students had gone home. By 6:00 a.m., nearly all of the students were gone, and the police returned to kindly ask the remaining stragglers to clear the streets. This was done without further incident. The traffic pattern was reestablished, and police then lined the outside of the streets so that students could not return. Within another day, the situation was normal, without the need for police presence. It is clear that the response of the police was unexpected. The group of students who organized the protest was dependent on an overreaction from the police. Initially, the police did overreact, and this nearly helped to create a riot. The sudden reversal of the police position stopped the escalation and left the students with little else to do but have an all-night party on Grand River Avenue.

The Siege of Castle Hochosterwitz

Paul Watzlawick, John Weakland, and Richard Fisch (1974) offered the following historical account in the preface of their now-classic book, *Change*. Because these authors were some of the first to apply the ideas of first- and second-order change to clinical problems and their resolution, we have chosen to recount one of the wonderful examples they used to begin their book.

When in 1334 the Duchess of Tyrol, Margareta Maultasch, encircled the castle of Hochosterwitz in the province of Carinthia, she knew only too well that the fortress, situated on an incredibly steep rock rising high above the valley floor, was impregnable to direct attack and would yield only to a long siege. In due course, the situation of the defenders became critical: they were down to their last ox and had only two bags of barley corn left. Margareta's situation was becoming equally pressing, albeit for different reasons: her troops were beginning to be unruly, there seemed to be no end to the siege in sight, and she had similarly urgent military business elsewhere. At this point the commandant of the castle decided on a desperate course of action which to his men must have seemed sheer folly: he had the last ox slaughtered, had its abdominal cavity filled with the remaining barley, and ordered the carcass thrown down the steep cliff onto the meadow in front of the enemy camp. Upon receiving this scornful message from above, the discouraged duchess abandoned the siege and moved on. (p. xi)

The AWOL Patient

Another of us came upon the following situation in the hospital where he worked.

Just before I arrived on the scene, a patient had just burst through the doors of the locked psychiatric ward and was headed for the elevator or stairs to go AWOL, or absent without official leave from the unit. He was extremely agitated and pacing. He threatened to jump over the stair-well and injure or kill himself if the staff came any closer. The unit staff, hot on his heels, were pleading and demanding that he come back to the unit and stay back from the stairs. He met this with louder and angrier threats and demands that he leave. The situation was dangerous and escalating.

Stepping into the situation, I asked him what was going on. Startled, he said he was going and that nobody was going to stop him. Pacing with him now, I agreed that obviously no one understood his position. I said how I hated that kind of thing. Asking him to explain more to me so I could advocate for him, he told me what was happening. Agreeing with his position and frustration, I sat down with him on a bench in the vesti-bule. We agreed to go over the head of the staff on hand. We returned to the unit to have a direct discussion with the physician in charge of the unit. From there we negotiated a resolution to the patient's dilemma. After he thanked the psychiatrist and me, we filled in the staff on the resolution.

Each dilemma was an escalating or desperate situation. The attempted solutions only made things worse. On the university campus, the more the police tried to control or disperse the protestors, the larger and angrier the crowd grew. At the castle siege, both armies were getting desperate and frus-trated. There seemed no end to the stalemate. For the psychiatric staff, the more they attempted to restrain or control their patient, the more agitated and dangerous he became. The resolution to each dilemma embodied a sec-ond-order change. When the police said they would allow the students to peace-fully protest, there was nothing to fuel further escalation. The police reversed their solutions from preventing protest to acknowledging and allowing it. They achieved their goals of avoiding harm and dispersing the crowd by not pursu-ing them directly. The protest ended peacefully the next morning. The occu-pants of the castle under siege, faced with eventual starvation or sudden sal-vation, were freed by throwing their last food to their enemies. This solution was the opposite of what anyone would expect from a besieged and starving garrison. Discouraged, the enemy left. When the angry patient found an advocate and not an adversary, he not only calmed down but also reversed his path and returned to the unit. A therapeutic alliance was achieved through unexpected validation instead of direct opposition. Not all second-order change is this dramatic, but it does share similar qualities.

Although first-order change does often resolve perceived difficulties, true impasses and problems result from repeated ineffective first-order solutions. The impasse of the castle siege, the potential for the police to fire on the protestors, and the agitated and dangerous patient were all products of escalating first-order solutions. The second-order resolution in each situation was a reversal that changed the nature of the situation and opened a whole new set of possible paths toward resolution.

SECOND-ORDER CHANGE IN PSYCHOTHERAPY

We have shown how dilemmas in these puzzles relate to human dilemmas. Yet how do the solutions relate to the resolution of clinical problems? In other words, what is the relationship between the solutions found in our stories and puzzles with effective psychotherapy? Exactly how, one might ask, are these concepts applied to effective psychotherapy, and how do effective psychotherapists bring them about?

The first answer lies in one of the basic tenets of the theory of logical types and second-order change; that is, second-order change may be understood only in relationship to first-order change. Therefore, again paraphrasing the words of John Weakland, it is critical to define what is the "same damned thing over and over again" (personal communication, October 30, 1980) before we can understand and initiate something different. From this perspective, therapists must first know the pattern of the problem before they can initiate a pattern shift. Without such knowledge, a therapist or any other helper runs the risk of being drawn into the same logical yet self-defeating solutions as all others involved in the problem. One source of this knowledge is the psychotherapy and psychopathology literature about the problem in question. Although it may be broad-reaching and varied, this literature may converge on several typical patterns for the problem and dilemmas for therapists. The simplest and truest questions, however, are the following: How is the problem being *defined* by all parties involved in it? *Who* is involved with the problem? What language, concepts, and assumptions are being used to define it? *How* is it a problem for the involved parties? What has been done about the problem by all involved? What has been done in similar situations? How has that worked? What are some *examples* of how the problem occurs, and how it is being struggled with? What are the *strengths* of those involved? What is *working*? What is going on when the problem *isn't happening*? What are the clients' ethnic, sociocultural and religious traditions, economic situation, gender, sexual preference, and so on, and how do these interact with those of the therapist? What is the *goal* of the involved parties?

These are only a few simple questions, among others, that help an intervener get an idea of the pattern of the problem and how he or she might interact with it. These questions are not rocket science, but they do get to the heart of first-order patterns. As we shall see in future chapters, many effective therapies pose these questions in very different ways.

Turning to how effective therapists facilitate second-order change from this perspective, these are but a few options:

- The first point to remember is that second-order change may begin with a shift in the relationship of the therapist with the client(s) involved. This shift may itself represent a second-order change for the client, or it may be a precursor for it to follow.
- Therapists may facilitate changes in a client's assumptions, frames, or premises.
- They may also block, reverse, or redirect first-order solutions.
- They may prescribe the formerly problematic interactions for therapeutic purposes.
- Finally, they will look for and support new assumptions and solution patterns and reinforce and amplify them as they are found or initiated.

This is a short list that sounds too simple. Admittedly, it is not complete, but these actions form a core of what effective therapists do from this view when fostering second-order change from different perspectives. They will be described in more detail in a subsequent section.

Premises and Corollaries

Recall from the last chapter that this model is based on the three common errors that set vicious cycles in motion:

1. *Unnecessary actions are taken to solve a problem.* Unnecessary actions are actions that move the problem-solver in a direction that goes away from the problem or in a direction that overpursues the problem. Movement away from the problem includes avoidance or other means of escape that involve attempts to rationalize the problem away or disqualify the problem. Movements that go to close to the problem involve efforts that are designed to make the problem go away by force or make something happen that can only occur more naturally.

2. *Not taking actions that are necessary.* This involves lack of action or failure to attend to situations that are becoming increasingly problematic.

3. *Efforts to solve the problem occur at the wrong level.* This involves the way that the problem solver understands the problem. Vicious cycles occur when problem solvers read too much into the problem or not enough. Reading too much into a problem can result in problem solvers creating new problems that must be solved as a prerequisite for solving the problem at hand, missing solutions that have occurred, or turning normal ups and downs of daily living into psychological disturbances. For example, some understandings are so complex as to create additional problems than the problem at hand. Asking the question "why" when solving a behavioral concern creates an additional problem of trying to understand the complex nature of human motivation as a prerequisite for solving the problem. This takes a problem that is already difficult and makes it far more difficult, if not impossible, to solve. Overly complex understandings may also cause the problem-solver to miss solutions when they occur. The parent who wants his child to "want to study" may miss the progress involved when the child complies with studying, especially if the child does not study with a big smile on her face. Making a problem overly complex can result in efforts to fix problems that are best left alone. In marriage, arguments that are designed to change the personality of one's partner rarely work. Although reading too much into a problem is a kick-point for vicious cycles, so is not reading enough into the problem. Oversimplifying a problem tends to trivialize the problem and its solution. Trivializing the problem ultimately dishonors the problem-solver and the difficulties of change. In response, the problem bearer may become embroiled in attempts to demonstrate that the problem is much more difficult than how it has been characterized.

Operationalizing Second-Order Change

Second-order change can be operationalized in the following ways for therapists. The phrase "something to do with" is used out of respect for the many ways that exist for bringing about second-order change. Because change is so complex, many of these elements may be observed in any given case.

- If the first-order solution is *to go away from the problem*, then the second-order solution will have something to do with *going toward it*.

- If the first-order solution is *to overpursue the problem*, then the second-order solution will have something to do with *stopping and reversing the pursuit*.
- If the first-order solution is *to not attend to the problem*, then the second-order solution will involve *acknowledging the problem* and *taking necessary problem-solving action*.
- If the first-order solution involves *making the problem overly complex*, then the second-order solution will involve *simplifying the problem* and *narrowing problem-solving efforts* down to the problem at hand and clarifying the problem's parameters.
- If the first-order solution is *to overintervene* with normal ups and downs of daily living, then second-order solutions will involve *tolerating and accepting* the amount of unpleasantness that is a natural part of the human condition.
- If the first-order solution *reads too little into the difficulty*, or *simplifies the problem so much as to trivialize it*, then the second-order solution will *honor the complexity of the problem*. To honor complexity entails both respecting and assisting the problem solver with building an understanding that clarifies the problem and its parameters in a way that is understood by the problem solver.

Once more, these options may appear overly simple right now. However, they will apply to the wide complexity of problems and their effective psychotherapies that we review in the chapters ahead. All of these positions and interventions will occur within the broad context of what Frank and Frank (1991) termed a *contextual model*, which we mentioned in chapter 1 of this volume. We discuss this contextual model in the next two chapters. For now, it may be helpful to look in more detail at a clinical example to bring these ideas into better clinical focus.

Revisiting the Effective Interventions

More light may be shed on this perspective by revisiting one of the therapy interventions that began this chapter. Recall the first therapist, who was working with a client who has panic attacks. She asked her client to bring on panic during the session. Exploring the kind of thinking that supports this intervention will help the ideas of first- and second-order change come to life clinically. This discussion will also offer a head start, or a brief glimpse of how we discuss effective interventions in anxiety in the first chapter of the next part of this book, "Following the Thread: Empirically Supported Therapies."

The ideas of first- and second-order change can be seen in the classic problem of panic attacks and their solution. Panic attacks often begin by some chance occurrence that causes us to react with symptoms of anxiety. The initial kick-point for the first attack can be almost anything that causes us to feel widely out of control, unsure if we can handle the situation, and worried that the situation is dangerous. Innate fight-or-flight mechanisms set in. These include such things as increasing heart rate; the blood moving to the center of our body and making our hands and feet tingle and feel numb; rapid, shallow breathing; hypervigilance and increased scanning of our surroundings; and rapid thoughts. Shallow and rapid breathing may also cause us to feel dizzy and faint and to have chest pains. These responses have been adaptive for our species over the ages, enabling us to prepare to fight off danger or to flee from it. They can also be terrifying in themselves.

If we are aware of the cause of our panic, and the innate nature of these physiological responses, then we may be able to categorize our reaction as unpleasant but natural. In so doing, we can often move beyond the incident. We might act directly on the situation that made us anxious. We might learn new skills to master it. We might decide that we misinterpreted the situation, or find that our view was correct yet there was nothing to worry about. In these instances, we will move beyond the incident with few, if any, residual effects.

However, we may become very alarmed and worried about the panic attack itself. How did we get that out of control? What happened to us? Is there something physically wrong? Are we having heart problems? How can we avoid ever having that happen again? We get anxious about having gotten anxious. This can be the inception of a vicious cycle. Our resulting solutions *become* the very things that produce the syndrome of escalating anxiety and ongoing recurrent panic attacks. Our solutions exacerbate the anxiety we seek to quell. Our solutions become the problem. This is a prime example of first-order change.

This description is more than hypothetical; it represents a general theme that characterizes most cases of panic. Clients attempt to master their anxiety by avoiding it. They become anxious about becoming anxious. At a more specific level, the process includes many predictable elements. Clients try to avoid anxiety-provoking situations at any cost. They become hypervigilant for any body sign of anxiety, such as shallower or more rapid breathing, sweaty palms, rapid speech, racing thoughts, and so on. What is more, they try to control any sign of these things at the first sign of any of them. The irony of these solutions is that this intense focus only heightens their anxiety. Heightened anxiety can kick in the automatic physiological response cycle that they are trying to avoid. These anxiety reactions then make clients feel more out of control and panicked. They begin catastrophizing their situation. They experience tunnel vision in their focus and black-and-white, all-or-nothing thinking: "I either need to escape or I'm going to die!"; "I must calm down!"; "I'm having a heart attack!" A self-fulfilling prophecy sets in, and they are well on their way to their next panic attack. Their solutions have become the problem. This is first-order change. It is often a vicious cycle of self-defeating behavior.

It is interesting that all empirically supported solutions to such panic attack problems involve blocking or reversing client solutions. You do not master anxiety by avoiding it. You master it by going toward it. It's not the panic that is the problem. It's the way the client is going about resolving it.

SECOND-ORDER STRATEGIES

Strategies that block or reverse failed solutions to difficulties change the class of solutions that are being used in problem solving. Class shift is a catalyst in the change process. In our panic example, the client fell into a trap in which all attempts at symptom resolution fit into a predictable pattern. The pattern may be labeled as *the class of all overreactions*. In effect, the client is overreacting to unpleasant internal experiences. The client's overreactions have a theme that involves attempts to flee from the symptoms. The therapeutic objective becomes one of stopping the overreaction pattern. Either blocking or reversing flight attempts accomplishes this.

Blocking and Acceptance

Blocking strategies are defined as approaches designed to stop solutions that are failing to solve a problem. Blocking and acceptance strategies are found in a number of different ESTs. An example is psychoeducational approaches in which acceptance is embedded in the educational framework. Clients are educated about the psychobiology of panic and how it works. The process is natural. The client may have mistaken their reactions for something else, but there is nothing to resolve. This is an acceptance strategy. For some clients, this is enough to help them relax. They don't need to use their solutions. Their panic goes away. Blocking also can take the form of engaging in behaviors that are mutually exclusive from the solution pattern. Mutually exclusive behaviors stop attempts to solve the problem by getting the problem solver involved with doing something else. Clients may be asked to identify situations that bring on different levels of anxiety and scale them. They are to locate exactly where their body begins to respond, and how the response occurs, and scale this. They are to keep thought records and note the kinds of thoughts that they are having when they become anxious. They are then asked to examine how true these thoughts and fears might be. Paying attention and scaling symptoms are actions that are mutually exclusive from escape. In following the assignment, the problem solver must stay with the symptom to accomplish the task that has been assigned. Staying with the symptom is a subtle way of going toward it.

Reversals

Reversals are defined as approaches that are designed to help the client use solutions that are counter or opposite to the solutions that are being used to solve the problem. Because avoidance is the theme with our panic-stricken client, the opposite would be strategies that direct the client to go toward her symptom. A reversal for panic might entail asking a client to imagine successively more anxiety-provoking situations while maintaining relaxation. Clients may be offered a "be spontaneous" paradox. This entails asking the client to experience anxiety and the sensation of being out of control, in a controlled and deliberate way.

Panic symptoms are notorious for occurring spontaneously—they seem to come out of the blue. The problem solver has the experience that she is unable to control her mind. Asking the client to deliberately engage in the symptom is inviting her to perform a naturally occurring experience on purpose. Doing something willfully is the opposite of having it occur involuntarily. This reverses the cycle. Instead of having panic attacks involuntarily, the problem solver is now trying to have panic attacks on purpose. Whatever anxiety she can conjure up will be more manageable because she has made it happen by her own choosing. This shift reestablishes the problem solver's confidence in her ability to control herself.

Invariably, in each empirically supported approach to panic a context is created in which clients must go toward the symptom. Mastery is gained through the process. The therapist treating a client with panic symptoms, described at the start of the chapter, used a reversal. The reversal was embedded in the request for the client to bring on anxiety in the session, in service of the treatment goals that had been previously established. Each intervention example described at the start of this chapter represents an attempt to interdict or reverse problematic client solutions. The theoretical rationales that support these interventions vary widely. They implicitly share, however, the common target of intentionally or unintentionally producing second-order change. We intend to explore each separate kind of intervention in successive chapters.

Before moving on, it might be helpful to briefly describe a list of other interventions that come from the perspective of interdicting first-order vicious cycles and initiating second-order change. These interventions are associated with intentional efforts to produce second-order change. Understanding how these interventions work will be helpful for seeing the common thread that runs through all effective therapies.

Restraining Change

Restraining clients from moving too quickly, or prohibiting them from directly attempting to achieve their desired goal, often produces a second-order shift. This is accomplished through the use of *soft restraints*, such as giving the client a directive to go slowly toward his or her goal, and *hard restraints*, which involve either prohibiting a goal-oriented action or offering challenges to clients. A very subtle version of a soft restraint is simply the absence of a directive to change. An example of this might involve a thera-pist giving a client the homework assignment of thinking about what changes he might want to make in therapy. This assignment does not contain a mes-sage that directs the client to change the problem. A harder restraint might involve the therapist giving a prohibition against changing or directly work-ing on the problem. The client might be told that the problem is too compli-cated and must be understood more completely before he or she even thinks about taking actions. Restraining techniques are based on the rationale that problem solvers often engage in too much self-pressure around change. Pres-suring oneself to change builds up strong internal resistance that enhances the likelihood of making errors in the change process. Also, as stated earlier, clients seek therapy because they want to change. The expectation is that the therapist is an agent of change. Psychotherapy is, in essence, a powerful change context. Restraining the problem solver from change takes the pres-sure of changing the problem off and is a reversal at the psychotherapy con-text level.

Normalizing

The intervention of normalizing attempts to put clients at greater ease by contextualizing their difficulties as normal reactions, given the constraints of their situations. This is another variant of a position of acceptance. Be-cause it allows clients to relax their self-pressured efforts to solve a perceived difficulty, normalizing helps them depathologize themselves and whatever they are struggling with. With normalization, the therapist does not deny that the client is feeling or acting badly; instead, the client is told that acting or feeling badly is expected under the circumstances. To emphasize this point the therapist might indicate that it is surprising that the client isn't function-ing even worse given the set of circumstances that she is facing. The client might be given outside readings, psychoeducation, or direct explanations about her condition to further illustrate this point. Reversing the perception of being abnormal can result in a second-order shift.

Framing, Reframing, and Deframing

Framing involves placing a person, situation, action, or problem in a particular context. An important aspect of the psychotherapy process is fram-ing or describing the problem(s) that will be worked on. We discuss this further in the next chapter. From the perspective of second-order change, problem solvers often come for therapy in a state of demoralization. Their problem-solving efforts have gone awry. They may feel exhausted and thor-oughly befuddled. Hope for solving the problem is quickly being lost. When the therapist listens to the concerns a problem solver and feeds them back in a way that helps the client make sense of what is wrong, loss of hope is reversed. Taking a problem that is confusing or that defies description and defining it in such a way that opportunities for change are apparent is a reversal of the problem at the problem description level. In some cases, this is enough of a reversal to support second-order change.

Reframing is the formal name for a class of interventions that involve shifts in the classification of meanings. This type of intervention involves putting a person, situation, action, or problem in an alternate but equally sensible and more useful context. (This was discussed previously in this chapter in the section titled "The Theory of Logical Types.") Therapists, to create rationales for making second-order shifts in the problem-solving process, use reframing. Good reframes make such shifts seem reasonable. Reframes may be given along with a directive to do something that is contrary to current problem-solving efforts. A reframe may also be given without specifically directing the problem solver to take action. In these situations, action is implied. In a previous example, a therapist reframed social mistakes by stressing the necessity of making such mistakes to enhance social learning. The therapist could have used this new construct as a rationale for suggesting that the client deliberately make social mistakes as part of a homework assignment. However, the therapist could have given the reframe and asked the client to think about it. In the former example, action on the basis of the new construct is explicit. In the latter example, new action is implicit, because the logic of the reframe suggests that solutions are opposite of what they seem. Well-formed reframes reverse constructs that support problems and are used to create new or different problem-solving efforts.

Deframing may be understood as a class of interventions that is opposite of reframing. Whereas reframing creates new mental constructs by adding levels, deframing reduces levels or separates classes that have been mixed in ways that are unhelpful to the problem solver. The process of deframing involves deconstruction of the context of a particular frame of reference to eliminate it as the cause of a problem, challenge its absolute reality base, or simply point out that it is a point of view. For example, pharmaceutical companies have had a powerful effect on consumers of mental health services. It is common for persons with serious behavioral disorders such as bipolar disorder to refer to themselves as having brain chemical imbalances. On one hand, this has reduced stigma about taking medicine, but on the other hand, this view has also created new problems. Consider a problem solver with bipolar disorder who has adopted the brain imbalance theory and now relates all shifts in mood, no matter how insignificant, to brain chemistry. Because medicine is what balances the chemistry of the brain, it becomes reasonable to assume that any perturbation in mood requires chemical adjustment. This sort of approach may well trigger a cycle of visits to the doctor for increases and shifts in medication. This problem can be further complicated by the fact that the medicines used to treat bipolar disorder can have unpleasant effects and feed into the cycle. In the end, the problem solver may end up taking multiple medications at very high dosage levels. The objective of therapy in such situations is to deframe chemical imbalance theory. This might be done by having the problem solver begin to think about the possibility that some changes in mood may be normal fluctuations or expected responses that anyone might have to certain stresses. The intent of the process is to separate behavior that is "bipolar" and in need of medicine from behavior that might be best classified another way. Over time, the elements in the bipolar category are significantly reduced. Because reducing the category is opposite to growing, this represents a second-order change.

Positioning

Positioning involves taking positions relative to problem solvers that are designed to facilitate change. We discuss therapeutic positioning in more detail in the next chapter, because it is inextricably linked with the therapeutic alliance. Therapist positions may include "cautious optimism;" "a one-down position;" "strategic pessimism;" or another position that is counter to the expectation of the client. Here again, the psychotherapy change context comes with certain expectations for how the therapist should behave. Reversals at this level can be sufficient for the problem solver make significant changes in the problem that has stimulated the need for therapy.

Prescribing Symptoms

We discussed prescribing symptoms earlier in the chapter as relates to panic attacks. It has a much broader usage in psychotherapy practice, although the rationale is similar to those for other problems. Symptom prescription involves asking clients to engage purposefully in some variation of the described problem behaviors. There are generally two types of situations in which prescribing the symptom is used. The first is when a symptom or problem behavior is experienced as automatic or "just happening." Such prescriptions make the problem pattern less automatic and put it more in the client's control. The second type of situation in which symptom prescriptions are used involves problem solvers who have difficulty forming cooperative relationships with therapists or others. Some problem solvers are extremely threatened about submitting to the authority of others and behave defiantly in an effort to protect their right to self-determination. In such cases, carefully constructed symptom prescriptions can provide the client with a face-saving way of changing a problem pattern. The problem solver improves by defying the therapist. This use of symptom prescriptions occurs at the therapeutic alliance level of psychotherapy and reverses the clients efforts to be uncooperative.

Predicting or Prescribing Difficulties or Relapses

Predicting or prescribing difficulties or relapses is a class of interventions used to deflect problem solvers from being discouraged by perceived setbacks or to consolidate gains by reencountering old perceived dangers. For example, clients might be warned that first efforts to bring about change might not work as well as expected and that the problem may actually worsen a bit before improvement occurs. Once the problem begins to show improvement, the therapist might normalize the possibility of relapse, discuss relapse prevention strategies, or even prescribe a relapse so that relapse prevention can be practiced. The sense of relief about making significant changes in a problem can lead to self-pressure in an effort to keep the problem from occurring again. This can lead to a relapse. Relapse preventions strategies are designed to reverse this pressure and reduce the likelihood or severity of a relapse.

Adopting a Goal-Oriented Future Position

When clients come for therapy, they are under the influence of their problems. They are locked into a present–past orientation, meaning that they can see the problem from present to past and from past to present. In their demoralized state, they cannot see beyond the problem to the future, when their situation will be better. The state of "better" may not be conceivable to them. An important process in psychotherapy is that of establishing goals. We discuss this further in the next chapter. The process of establishing goals involves a reversal from present–past to the future and describes the hoped-for condition. This reversal represents another type of second-order change that is inextricably tied to the therapeutic alliance. It is sometimes a sufficient shift to support change.

THE SECRET IS OUT

A partial sampling of quotes from some of the researchers and founders of several ESTs suggests a growing appreciation for the concepts of first- and second-order change. As reflected in their own words, even these widely known authors are beginning to recognize the common thread that runs through their approaches.

The first approaches represent interventions for couple's problems. Neil Jacobson, Andy Christensen, and John Gottman recently developed ESTs for marital issues, to be discussed in chapter 10 of this volume. The first of these was Jacobson and Christensen (1996). Referring to couple problems, they said,

As Paul Watzlawick, John Weakland, Richard Fisch, and others have been telling us since 1967, there are times when efforts to change one's partner actually have the opposite effect. Direct attempts to change an intimate partner are often self-defeating, both because the particular efforts are misguided and because such attempts are likely to have the opposite effect. (1974, p. 13)

Another force in ESTs for couples therapy is John Gottman, who had this to say about couple's problems:

I contend that the current emphasis in marital therapy on problem-solving is greatly misplaced . . . 69% of the time [couples] were talking about a perpetual problem . . . instead of *solving* these perpetual problems, what seems to be important is whether or not a couple can establish a *dialogue* with their perpetual problems . . . if they cannot, the conflict becomes gridlocked. . . . Our findings suggest that people, including therapists, need to change their expectations about solving fundamental problems in an intimate relationship . . . I think that the goal of most therapy around problem-solving ought to be to help the couple move from gridlocked conflict with a perpetual problem to a dialogue with the perpetual problem. (Gottman, 1999, p. 56)

These evidence-supported approaches to couples treatment are based in large part on interdicting ongoing and fruitless solutions that are applied between couples. They seek to disengage couples from problematic change attempts and to reengage them at another level to more effectively change their problems.

In a more recent example of an empirically supported approach to relapse prevention in depression, to be discussed in chapter 8, Zindel Segal, Mark Williams, and John Teasdale (2002) struck upon a similar idea. Referring to their mindfulness-based stress reduction approach (MBSR), they noted,

Instructors in MBSR encouraged participants to let go of the idea that problems might, with enough effort, be "fixed." If fixing worked, then fine. But the mindfulness approach was explicit about the danger that such attempts at fixing might merely reinforce people's attitude that their problems were the "enemy," and that once they were eliminated, then everything would be fine. The problem is that this approach may encourage further attempts to solve problems by ruminating on them, and these attempts often keep people trapped in the state from which they are trying to escape. This is something that family therapists have emphasized for years. (Watzlawick et al., 1974, p. 60)

FOLLOWING THE THREAD

Second-order change is being recognized, if not by the term, then by the concept, across a wide range of effective psychotherapies. We follow this thread through the six chapters of the next part of this volume. First, however, we must return to the polemic debate introduced in the first chapter. These interventions are approaches of the best-practices camp described earlier. Recall that there is equally compelling evidence that all of these ESTs are essentially similar in their effects. The common-factors camp reminds us that the therapeutic relationship, working alliance, and other general commonly therapeutic factors account for much more influence on positive outcome in the literature than do specific techniques. How can this be accounted for from the perspective of first- and second-order change? In the next chapter, we offer some answers.

4

THE THERAPEUTIC RELATIONSHIP

Every truth has two sides. It is well to look at both before we commit
ourselves to either side.

—Aesop

In this chapter, we focus on the therapeutic relationship and demonstrate how second-order change is central to the process by which therapists
develop effective relationships with clients. In support of this, we introduce
the contextual model as offered by Jerome and Julia Frank (Frank & Frank,
1991). The contextual model is a framework that has strong empirical support for predicting psychotherapy outcomes. Context model components
suggest a synergistic connection between the therapeutic relationship and
techniques or treatment methods. We will show how the golden thread of
second-order change weaves its way through the contextual model. When
viewing this in the larger psychotherapy tapestry, it becomes clear that the
therapeutic relationship and methods are cut from the same cloth. Because
they contain the same material, the therapeutic relationship and intervention methods are inseparable. The contextual model also points to the ultimate purpose of psychotherapy: reversing demoralization and restoring hope.
We end the chapter with a discussion about the implications of this viewpoint for "The Great Psychotherapy Debate" (Wampold, 2001).

STUDYING THE THERAPEUTIC RELATIONSHIP

Researchers who are interested in understanding how change works in
psychotherapy have applied principles from medical research to determine

what kinds of psychotherapies are most effective. The objective of such research is to isolate variables in the treatment process to determine what variable or variables are responsible for change. Medical research is aimed at determining whether a specific substance has more power than an inert substance, which is thought to have therapeutic value (placebo), in treating a specific condition. In other words, the idea is to determine whether the therapeutic agent has more power than the placebo. If it does, then the therapeutic agent is considered a valid treatment, provided that it does not have side effects that outweigh its therapeutic value. The therapeutic agent is even better if research further shows that it outperforms other therapeutic agents that are used for the same condition.

Along this line, researchers have identified ingredients or variables that are associated with favorable psychotherapy outcomes. In the ingredient-isolation process, relationship variables have been separated from intervention techniques. Interventions have then been tested to determine their impact on specific emotional disorders. Relationship variables have also been tested and then compared with specific intervention techniques as relative to changing power. The objective has been to demonstrate that specific interventions are the active ingredients in the change process. As we noted in chapter 1 of this volume, there is overwhelming and convincing evidence from decades of research that client–therapist relationship factors, a positive working alliance, and other common therapeutic factors account for the vast majority of influence on positive therapy outcomes. The often-cited estimates of Lambert (1992) conclude that 30% of the influence of successful psychotherapy can be accounted for by so-called common factors that can be found in a wide variety of different therapies such as warmth, empathy, and acceptance; encouragement of risk taking; and other similar factors. Extratherapeutic change, or fortunate events and social support in the client's environment, and unique strengths of the clients apart from the influence of psychotherapy, are said to account for roughly 40% of the influence (or variance) in successful treatment. Lambert concluded that the client's faith and belief in the rationale and effectiveness of any treatment approach is as powerful as the approach itself. Belief in the intervention and the intervention approach itself each weigh in at 15%.

The more recent and scientifically derived analyses of Wampold (2001) support and extend these conclusions. As a result of extensive meta-analyses of the psychotherapy outcome literature, he concluded that at least 70% of the psychotherapeutic effects of effective treatment are general effects. Specific techniques account for no more than 8% of outcome variance.[1] Wampold

---

[1] Wampold (2001) used a statistical method to conduct his meta-analysis. The statistical method is based on probability. If intervention methods are 8% of outcome variance, this means that in 8 of 100 cases the intervention was the key to the outcome. As previously indicated, the alliance is the key factor in change in 21 to 26 of 100 cases. Through this method, Wampold also demonstrated that general effects are more powerful factors than the intervention method that the therapist uses.

goes as far as to conclude that "Decades of psychotherapy research have failed to find a scintilla of evidence that any specific ingredient is necessary for therapeutic change" (p. 204).

The Therapeutic Relationship Defined

Thus far, we have used the term *relationship* and particularly the phrase *positive therapeutic relationship* as if it were clear exactly what we were talking about. Yet the definition of a therapeutic relationship is anything but simple and clear. Historically, although it has traveled many paths, the importance of therapeutic relationships has been central to the psychodynamic work of Sigmund Freud (1912/1940) and the person-centered approach of Carl Rogers (1957). Both traditions view the relationship as the critical tool and focus of effective psychotherapy. Working from different assumptions, both traditions converge on the importance of the relationship as both a collaborative alliance and as a present focus to be used to resolve current and historical relational problems. Although definitions and practices have diverged, the curative influence of the therapeutic relationship has been sustained in both research and practice. The question remains as to exactly what it is, what makes it helpful, and how it exerts its influence on facilitating change.

Current Usage

The American Psychological Association (APA) Division of Psychotherapy (Division 29) convened a task force to review and comment on scientific evidence related to empirically supported relationships (Norcross, 2002). That group decided to adopt a general operational definition of the psychotherapy relationship advanced by Gelso and Carter (1985, 1994): "The relationship is the feelings and attitudes that therapist and client have toward one another, and the manner in which these are expressed" (Norcross, 2002, p. 7).

What was most helpful is that the task force went on to identify what they referred to as *elements* of the therapy relationship. These were defined more precisely. Most prominent among these elements determined to be core to the relationship were the alliance in individual therapy; cohesion in group therapy;[2] and the Rogerian facilitative conditions of empathy, positive regard, and genuineness–congruence. In addition, they included the dual elements of goal consensus and collaboration. They then proceeded to examine the research in support of these and other related elements.

As with the evolution of the definition of the therapy relationship, a difficulty inherent to research on the alliance is that researchers have not

---

[2]Cohesion is analogous to the therapeutic alliance but applies specifically to the group process whereby clients form bonds both with the therapist and group members. Group therapy is outside the scope of this work, although we expect that the same principles related to second-order change are applicable in the group therapy forum.

always agreed on precise definitions of the elements. For example, Tryon and Winograd (2002) conducted extensive research on goal consensus–collaboration. They found that collaboration on tasks and goals was too narrow of a construct for what was occurring in the treatment process. In response, they added engagement as a preliminary process, which precedes goal and task development. Engaging the client has empathic qualities and is necessary if the client is to stay in treatment long enough to establish goals and tasks. The term *engagement* was used to address the overlapping concept of empathy.

A difference in the way that key terms are defined has been a criticism of the research that has focused on relationship factors. Upon review of the scientific literature, the task force concluded that, despite definitional variances, the differential power of the treatment relationship is strong.

The Alliance

The alliance is a core element of the relationship and will be most useful later as it relates to second-order change. In many ways, the therapeutic or working alliance has come to be used almost interchangeably with the term *relationship*. The alliance, along with the previously noted Rogerian conditions, is one of the most heavily researched and supported elements in psychotherapy. In their research review of the alliance, for example, Horvath and Bedi (2002) concluded that "The therapeutic relationship in general, and the alliance in particular, is the quintessential common ground shared by most psychotherapies" (p. 37). How, then, is the alliance defined?

There have been varying definitions of the alliance throughout the history of psychotherapy, mainly grounded in the psychoanalytic tradition. Because the alliance is a foundational concept in all therapies, researchers have endeavored to develop a definition that is theoretically neutral.

Adam Horvath has been one of the most prominent recent researchers and interpreters of the literature on the alliance. As part of the APA Task Force on empirically supported treatments, he adopted a definition that embraced Bordin's (1975, 1989, 1994) work while incorporating emerging consensus in the field. His definition includes the following statements:

- The alliance refers to the quality and strength of the client–therapist relationship.
- This includes positive bonds such as mutual trust, liking, respect, and caring.
- It also includes cognitive components of the relationship, including consensus about and commitment to the goals of therapy and to the means or tasks of therapy by which these goals may be attained.
- It involves a partnership in which all parties are actively committed to their roles in the process of therapy and belief that all others are also enthusiastically engaged in the same process.

- The alliance is a conscious and purposeful aspect of the relationship whereby all parties can describe the quality of the alliance and in which there is a therapist or helper committed to providing assistance to the client or clients. (Horvath & Bedi, 2002)

As was said earlier, the therapeutic relationship, specifically, the alliance, has been found to account for a significant portion of the influence on outcome in therapy. With respect to the alliance alone, a meta-analysis of 24 studies linking the quality of alliance to outcome reported that it accounted for about 26% of the effect (Horvath & Symonds, 1991). A more recent analysis of 79 studies reported a somewhat smaller effect of 22% (Martin, Garske, & Davis, 2000). Horvath and Bedi (2002) found a similar average relation between alliance and outcome of 21%, with a median effect size of 25% across 89 studies. This effect is quite impressive compared with the much lesser power of intervention techniques. This research indicates that the alliance as a core element of the therapeutic relationship is obviously a crucial contributor to facilitating therapeutic change.

Goal Consensus–Collaboration

Another demonstrably effective element of the relationship from the APA Task Force analyses is goal consensus and collaboration. As noted, this element is also an explicit part of Horvath and Bedi's (2002) definition of the working alliance. Orlinsky, Grawe, and Parks (1994) defined *goal consensus* as patient–therapist agreement on the goals and expectations of therapy. As noted earlier, goal consensus is understandably well-correlated with outcome. This concept also correlates with empathy, because clients regard collaboration on goals and tasks as a sign of empathic understanding (Horvath & Greenberg, 1986). Research shows further that responding to clients' goals, intentions, and values is equally important to empathy as it is for the therapist to resonate with clients' feelings. In other words, an important aspect of empathy is goal consensus and collaboration with the client (Watson, 2002). Tryon and Winograd (2002) highlighted engagement, goal consensus, and collaborative involvement as pantheoretical concepts applying to all types of therapy and contexts. They defined *engagement* as the degree of involvement of the therapist and patient in the therapeutic process, often measured by patients returning to therapists after initial and successive sessions. They also cited research that suggests that client engagement in the first session is critical to the client's continuing treatment. *Collaborative involvement* refers to the degree of mutual engagement of the therapist and client in therapy and is usually measured by homework completion, measures of cooperation and resistance, and involvement in the patient role. Such understanding and agreement about the goals and conditions for therapy and the ways clients and therapists will mutually engage in it are what Orlinsky and his colleagues (1994) termed the *therapeutic contract*. It intuitively makes sense that such mutual collaborative involvement in the tasks of treatment should be broadly well-related to positive outcome. It is not surprising, from the literature reviews, that the more that clients and therapists agree on goals, actively engage in therapy, and are collaboratively involved in the process of treatment, the greater client satisfaction and the more positive outcomes are to be found (Tryon & Winograd, 2002).

Empathy

With respect to individual therapy, the APA Task Force's final element that has been shown to be demonstrably effective is empathy. Bohart, Elliot, Greenberg, and Watson (2002) concluded in the task force review that there is no consensus definition of *empathy*. Some developmental perspectives emphasize *emotional* elements of empathy, defined as feeling the feelings of the client and responding with appropriate care. Other definitions are more cognitive. It is interesting that both client-centered and psychoanalytic views have focused on a cognitive understanding of the client's frame of reference and way of experiencing the world. Both emotional and cognitive aspects of empathy do appear important. The most broadly used definition of *empathy* is, however, that of Carl Rogers (1980), "the therapist's sensitive ability and willingness to understand the client's thoughts, feelings and struggles from the client's point of view. [It is] this ability to see completely through the client's eyes, to adopt his frame of reference" (p. 85).

Barrett-Lennard (1981) set the standard for studying empathy by including three perspectives. The first is the *therapist's* appraisal of his or her ability to respond empathically with a client. The second is from the viewpoint of an *observer*, in terms of the quality of empathy he or she observes in a session or sessions. The third perspective is from the experience of the *client*, in their appraisal of the quality of empathy they feel they have received. It is not surprising that the results of general meta-analyses of 47 studies relating empathy to outcome across all sources of ratings reported an effect size between 25% and 32% (Bohart et al., 2002). What is important to know, however, is that (similar to previous findings of Barrett-Lennard [1981] and Parloff, Waskow, & Wolfe [1978]), client measures of their experienced empathy predicted outcome the best, at 25%; followed closely by observer measures, at 23%; and, finally, by therapist ratings of their own empathy, at 18%. Clients thus are the best judge of what is empathic, and when they experience empathy they are more likely to succeed in therapy. One can only speculate that such felt empathy in clients inspires faith and trust in the belief that the therapist is both able to relate to their distress and understand their perspective.

There are two last caveats from the research on empathy. The first is that different clients probably have a different need and capacity for receiving what therapists traditionally view as empathic communication (cf. Beutler, Johnson, Neville, & Workman, 1972, 1973; Ham, 1987; Henry, Schacht, & Strupp, 1986). Several sources suggest, for example, that clients who are highly sensitive, suspicious, poorly motivated, or reactive to authority tend to do worse with more empathic, involved, and accepting therapists (Beutler, Crago, & Arizmendi, 1986). Mohr and Woodhouse (2000) found that some clients prefer businesslike relationships over those judged as warm and empathic. These findings reinforce O'Hara's (1984) suggestion that in some cases it is most empathic for the therapist *not* to express the traditional qualities of empathy! Clients are the best judges not only of the quality of empathy but also of the type and amount of it they desire. The final caveat comes from a summary of potential contributions that empathy makes to successful therapy. Bohart and his colleagues (2002) cited Orlinsky et al. (1994) and suggested that client active involvement is the most important factor in making therapy work. They concluded by suggesting that "First, empathy promotes involvement. Second, empathy provides support for clients' active information-processing efforts. . . . Third, empathy helps the therapist choose interventions compatible with the clients' frame of reference" (Bohart et al., 2002, p. 101). We also need to be aware that this is true across approaches. Another interesting finding from Bohart et al.'s (2002) analyses was that, contrary to expectations, there was little evidence that empathy was more associated with outcome for experiential therapies than for cognitive–behavioral approaches. In fact, there was a hint that empathy might be more important for the cognitive–behavioral ones than for the others. Wampold (2001) cited similar results. Again, clients are engaged in therapy and focused on its tasks by the experience of their therapist relating to their emotional distress and understanding its sources. The amount and quality of empathy received enhances the working alliance and so fuels client and therapist bonds and agreement on goals and investment in the enterprise of therapy.

Intervention

Although the task force did not define the term *intervention*, we would like to offer a definition that we will use for this work. For our purposes, we use the term *technique* as synonymous with the term *intervention*. Therefore, techniques or interventions are purposeful strategies or methods designed to have influence in facilitating change in clients. Examples include cognitive restructuring, relaxation techniques, paradoxical intent, desensitization, and so on. As mentioned earlier, the objective of researchers has been to separate techniques from the alliance to ultimately determine what techniques work best for specific emotional disorders.

False Dichotomies

Researchers who support interventions as the most powerful element in the change process do not deny that that the relationship is an important factor. They suggest that the elements of the treatment relationship are process variables. They are both difficult to define and virtually impossible to replicate, as each therapeutic relationship is a bit different. Nathan and Gorman (2002b) pointed out that study of process variables has not shown consistent results. To empirical researchers, the previously noted difficulties with definitions of terms and fluctuations of effect sizes is not a trivial matter. It is also noteworthy that beliefs within the mental health culture currently favor interventionist arguments despite the strong evidence that relationship factors are the most potent force in change. Research on techniques has important advantages. Compared with process, it is far easier to define an intervention technique and develop a protocol for administering it. Specific techniques can also be assigned to particular conditions, such as depression or anxiety. By isolating interventions and applying them to particular conditions, researchers have been able to clearly demonstrate that psychotherapy is more effective than no therapy for virtually every condition that has been studied.

The problem occurs when the next step—comparing interventions to see which are the most effective—is attempted. Some effects can be shown in specific studies; however, when meta-analysis is done, the effects tend to wash out. All treatments seem to work just as well. This has been called the "Dodo bird verdict," from *Alice in Wonderland* (Luborsky, Singer, & Luborsky, 1975): "Everyone has won and all must have prizes." Researchers who are interested in proving the superiority of specific interventions are optimistic that improved research methods will eventually disprove the Dodo bird effect (Nathan & Gorman, 2002b).

We argue that research efforts designed to isolate specific variables either on the relationship or intervention side of the argument represent an oversimplification of the complexities that are involved in the psychotherapy process. Recall that in chapter 2 (this volume) we mentioned how oversimplification represents an attempt to resolve a problem at the wrong level and leads to a vicious cycle of failed solutions. The failed solutions will prevail until there is an interruption of the pattern and reversal of the underlying assumptions. In this case, we believe that attempts to isolate relationship and intervention variables create a false dichotomy.

In chapter 3 (this volume), we discussed logical typing and showed the relationship between incorrect classifications of experience with problem formation. Problems begin when relationship is denied. Denial of a relationship between members of a group creates an artificial duality. It simplifies through overexclusion. Good is simply good, and bad is simply bad; there can be nothing in the middle. For empirical research to be valid, clear distinctions must be made. Yet what if the relationship itself is an intervention? What happens to the ability of researchers to isolate variables if relationship factors also create the very effects that intervention strategies are designed to produce?

In psychotherapy research a false dichotomy is more than a philosophical issue. Here the current dichotomy presumes that treatment relationship and intervention variables are cut from different cloth. Variables can be isolated when they are made from different material. In such a world relationship building, assessment, and intervention are distinct entities. Because they are distinct they can be separated, measured, and compared for variable strength. However, there is compelling evidence to the contrary. This evidence supports the contention that relationship variables and intervention are cut from the same cloth. Evidence for this contention is based on interpretations of research findings and formal logic. The idea that relationship building and interventions are made of the same material does not imply that interventions are unnecessary for change or that power of the therapeutic relationship should be ignored. Instead, we are suggesting that if the current debate is to be resolved, then a unified understanding of psychotherapy outcome will need to be developed.

Influence

The argument for the inseparability of intervention from relationship building begins with the concept of influence. Recall that influence is integral to the definition of the term *intervention*. Interventions are defined as attempts by the therapist to influence change. Therefore, if interventions are to be separated from relationship building, we would need to prove that there is no influence involved in the relationship-building process; otherwise, it would mean that relationship building is an intervention. If this were the case, then there would be difficulty with attempts at disconnecting the two for research purposes.

Rogers's Unintended Influence

The impact of influence in the therapist–client relationship was made clear in Truax and Carkhuff's (1967) classic studies of Carl Rogers's therapy by way of analyzing Rogers's own therapy tapes. This analysis made it very easy to see how Rogers's own genuine responses to his clients, in keeping with his theory of humankind, selectively reinforced those elements of their interaction that were valued by his perspective. The work of Rogers was genuine, however. It was not some deliberate Machiavellian plot to shape his clients. It was just good therapy done be a master whose name is synonymous with the therapeutic relationship and a therapeutic alliance emphasizing accurate empathy, warmth, and genuineness.

As just stated, Carl Rogers was a master clinician considered by many as one of the great therapists of his day. His objective was to assist clients with finding their own way out of emotional problems by providing nondirective empathic feedback. The Rogerian method was designed in such a manner that therapist influence over clients was discouraged. It is ironic that despite efforts to deny influence his approach was found to be highly influential albeit in a very subtle way.

The Interpersonal Communication Perspective

Interpersonal communication thinkers were well aware of this reality when they offered axioms on influence in therapeutic relationships. The logic-based axioms on therapeutic communication stated by Paul Watzlawick, Janet Beavan, and Don Jackson (1967) make the relationship among communication, behavior, and influence very clear. They stated the following:

- Behavior has no opposite. In other words, there is no such thing as nonbehavior or, to put it even more simply: one cannot *not* behave.
- Now, if it is accepted that all behavior in an interactional situation has message value (i.e., is communication), it follows that no matter how one may try, one cannot *not* communicate.
- Activity or inactivity, words or silence all have message value: They influence others and these others, in turn, cannot *not* respond to these communications and are thus themselves communicating.
- All behavior, all communication has interpersonal influence. Therefore one cannot *not* influence. (Watzlawick et al., 1967, pp. 48–49)

In the therapeutic interchange, all actions of the therapist and client or clients have influence. What the therapist chooses to inquire about shapes the kind of information she receives from her client. Whether she chooses to confront or teach or simply remain silent all have profound influence on the moment by moment course of therapy, as do the way her clients choose to respond or not.

With this in mind, we turn to the contextual model of Jerome Frank. Here we will pick up with second-order change and propose a perhaps different understanding of how relationship building and techniques work. We will show more clearly how therapeutic relationship is a powerful intervention.

THE CONTEXTUAL MODEL

Jerome Frank first proposed a contextual model for understanding the nature of psychotherapy in his classic book *Persuasion and Healing*. Since the original work was published in 1961 there have been two subsequent editions (e.g., Frank, 1973). The most recent was published in 1991. Julia Frank, daughter of Jerome, coauthored this work (Frank & Frank, 1991).

Frank's contextual model represents a transtheoretical explanation of the process of psychotherapy, taking into account the role of relationship and technique factors. The term *transtheoretical* refers to a description of psychotherapy theory that operates at a general level of abstraction. From the general level it is possible to distill commonalities that run through psychotherapy frameworks despite significant differences that occur at more specific levels. For example, specific-level descriptions of psychoanalysis and behavioral therapy reveal distinct guiding theories and corresponding methods. Not only do these schools of thought have little in common but they also are directly at odds on many fundamental points. When observed from a transtheoretical perspective, common elements emerge. Frank's work shows not only common elements in seemingly disparate Western psychotherapy frameworks but also how Western psychotherapies are related to the treatments in other cultures, such as shamanism and religiomagical rituals.

Although there are several transtheoretical models that describe common elements in psychotherapy, Frank's contextual model is especially relevant to second-order change, for several specific reasons. First, Wampold's (2001) extensive meta-analysis of psychotherapy has brought significant credibility to the contextual model as an accurate predictor of psychotherapy outcomes. The contextual model clearly describes the inextricable connection between relationship factors and interventions. This model creates a contextual for understanding how relationship factors alone can create a second-order change in some client situations. Finally, the contextual model links change to the ultimate reversal—that is, from demoralization to hope. With this in mind, we will analyze Frank's contextual model as it applies to second-order change. From here on, we refer to the Frank's model as simply the *contextual model*.

The Assumptive World and Vicious Cycles

As previously stated, the contextual model is composed of common elements that can be observed in effective psychotherapy frameworks. These common elements are supported by underlying assumptions that we will review because of their implications for the power of the psychotherapy relationship. (Contextual model elements are described in the next chapter.) The underlying assumptions of the contextual model are remarkably similar to the assumptions that underlie second-order change.

They begin with an assumption about the general aim of psychotherapy—to help people feel and function better by encouraging appropriate modifications in their assumptive worlds, thereby transforming the meanings of experiences to more favorable ones (Frank & Frank, 1991, p. 30). The next assumptions in the model relate to the difficulties of making changes in the assumptive world.

The assumptive world is reflective of our need to make sense out of experience and is manifested by the automatic formation of certain assumptive systems, or schemas (Goleman, 1985), about ourselves, other persons, and the nonhuman environment. The totality of each person's assumptions may be conveniently termed his or her *assumptive world*. The perspective of second-order change is similar, except it is concerned with a more limited aspect of the assumptive world, the aspect that revolves around problem formation, maintenance, and resolution. In this sense, contextual *assumptions* and *premises* are interchangeable words.

Frank, referring to George Kelly's (1955) work, indicated that in the case of problem development assumptions made about causality are especially pertinent. False or incorrect attributions of cause and effect lead to assumptions about how to address a problem that may be disconnected from the reality that an individual is attempting to address. In other words, there is a disconnection between the assumptions that govern solution attempts and intended results.

An example is given of a paranoid person whose attributions about cause and effect lead to the assumption that people are motivated by malevolence. Such an assumption leads to acting in a very guarded way around people in social situations. In response, others act uncomfortably around our paranoid person, giving him more reason to be suspicious of people's motives. Here, Frank and Frank's (1991) assumptions about problem formation are almost identical with those of second-order change. Assumptions of the contextual model support the idea that vicious cycles are integral to symptom formation and that faulty assumptions are the basis for vicious cycles (first-order change).

The contextual model also provides an explanation for how such vicious cycles are maintained. It starts with the way the people process experience and the need for a stable, predictable sense of reality. To ensure predictable realities, biases are built into human information-processing systems. These biases shape information in such a way as to perpetuate an individual's picture of reality. Information that is too different must be addressed in some fashion. If novel information is accepted at face value, then we must reconcile the discrepancies between assumptions that define the current reality picture and assumptions that underlie the novel information. This is what cognitive theorists refer to as *cognitive dissonance*. Cognitive dissonance creates a dilemma for us. We can integrate novel information and in so doing change our reality picture or manipulate novel information in such a way that the current reality picture is maintained. In essence, cognitive theory indicates that people tend to take the latter route, especially when troubling social and emotional situations are involved.

Meichenbaum (1984) described two mechanisms that are designed to filter or shape experiences that are too inconsistent or dissonant with our assumptive world: (a) confirmatory bias and (b) avoidance. _Confirmatory bias_ is a kind of filter that emphasizes confirmatory experiences and deemphasizes contradictory experiences. Experiences that contradict our assumptions are either ignored or forgotten. _Avoidance_ refers to the tendency to avoid experiences that might provide new learning.

In chapter 2 of this volume, we suggested that vicious cycles are maintained by solution attempts that are based on false premises. We argued that false premises are perpetuated by logic, human dignity, and fear of what might occur if known solutions are abandoned or exchanged for a novel approach. Assumptions from the contextual model lend further support. Here, failed solution attempts are also maintained by biases that are embedded in human information processing. At yet another level, linguistic systems play a supporting role in the problem formation and maintenance process.

Demoralization

Beyond issues of information processing, logic, and language is yet another factor that comes to play in the formation and maintenance of problems from the contextual model: demoralization. According to Frank, demoralization plays a very interesting part in the process, because it has a dual role. On the one hand, demoralization worsens problems by creating a sense of desperation that further fuels the downward spiral of failed solution attempts. On the other hand, demoralization holds the key to second-order changes that lead a person out of vicious cycle processes. Frank described the demoralized individual as a person who is deprived of spirit and courage, disheartened, bewildered, or in a state disorder or confusion.

Persons who seek therapy have often spent considerable time and effort seeking their own solutions to social or emotional problems. As the cycle of failed solutions spirals on, demoralization begins to creep in. For many people, distress from this situation produces an assumption that they are somehow unique and that their problem is so complicated that they cannot put it into adequate words. Clients may assume that no one really understands them. They may think they cannot control their own feelings and that they are going crazy. These assumptions are characteristic of the demoralized state and go way beyond the original premises that started the first-order change process.

Frank supports the demoralization assumption on the basis of studies that reveal long time frames between the point when clients develop behavioral health problems and the point at which professional assistance is sought. The assumption is that prospective clients do not seek treatment until they have become demoralized from their failed problem-solving efforts. On this basis, Frank argued that it is demoralization that ultimately brings clients for treatment and not the emotional problem or its failed cycle of solutions per se. In other words, "_People seek help not in response to the symptoms themselves_

but because their efforts to cope with the symptoms have failed [italics added]"
(Frank & Frank, 1991, p. 38).

From the perspective of second-order change, we argue that demoralization folds itself into the vicious cycle and brings added premises that interconnect with the premises of the problem-maintaining system. As the client proceeds to engage in failed solutions, self-efficacy declines. The client is doing what seems right, but it is not working. Nothing else seems logical to try, and so the whole endeavor seems futile. This gives rise to new demoralizing premises as suggested earlier in this chapter, such as "This can't be done"; "I don't know what to do anymore"; "The solution that I am using works for everyone else, so because I am failing to make it work there must be something wrong with me"; and "This situation is so complicated that I can't even put it in words, so no one could ever understand me." When problem solvers lose confidence in this manner they become more fearful and even more reluctant to engage in new experiences. There is a need to pull within oneself and become avoidant. One is afraid that they cannot meet his or her own expectations for improving or match the expectations of others. In this state, persons may be ambivalent in their approach to therapy. There is a need for a novel experience if the client is to resolve his or her problem, yet in a demoralized state the client is fearful of trying anything new or different.

Through the process of interconnecting with the first-order change process, "Demoralization becomes a cause, a consequence, or both of presenting symptoms that clients bring to therapy" (Frank & Frank, 1991, p. 35). The importance of demoralization may also vary depending on how it has folded itself into the assumptive world of the client. Yet it is fair to speculate that much of what therapists ascribe to psychopathology may actually be clients' reactions to demoralization.

A driving force behind demoralization is the loss of *consensual validation*, a concept derived from the work of Hyman and Singer (1968), Festinger (1954), and Sullivan (1953). Accordingly, consensual validation emphasizes that a person's most significant experiences are social ones, and most attitudes and values can be validated by checking them against the behavior and attitudes of other individuals, especially members of groups to which a person belongs, or aspires to belong. This social comparison process exerts strong pressure on individuals to harmonize their assumptive worlds with those persons important to them. There are two remarkable aspects of this definition that require further explanation: (a) group and (b) or aspires to belong.

The term *group* refers to us in relationship to others. "Others" could be an individual or group of individuals. Others can also refer to opinions expressed through alterative media, such as newspaper articles, television, a computer program, or this book. Readers of this book will be hopeful that what we write reinforces premises they have formed around what makes their own therapy effective.

The phrase "or aspires to belong" refers to the idea that as individuals we have power to some extent in determining whom we will seek for validation of our assumptions. There may also be variances in the amount of validation power that a group has on the basis of the value that we ascribe to the group. For example, a person might seek validation for sports-related assumptions from one group and validation for opinions about art appreciation from another group. The person may not be negatively affected if a person from the sports group criticizes her taste in art. This will be especially true if our person does not think that the sports group friend is credible as an art critic. The main point is that loss of a consensual validation from a group of import can have a demoralizing effect that furthers the vicious cycle process. The following is an illustration that shows how the concepts of confirmatory bias and consensual validation work in the process of demoralization.

Consider a woman, Sally, who is caught in a relationship involving domestic violence. She has made several unsuccessful attempts to leave her husband and is stuck in a vicious cycle around the violence issue. Her husband is an individual who cycles between being a "very loving person" and an abusive person with a violent temper. The temper occurs periodically, versus every day, and usually is a response to some trivial mistake that Sally makes such as burning the toast for breakfast. The loving behavior that Sally's husband exhibits during respite periods has given rise to the premise that Sally can fix her husband by trying harder to be mistake-free. It is this premise that stops her from taking action that is necessary, placing responsibility for violent behavior on her husband, and leaving if he does not stop abusing her. Her premise is based on the need for consensual validation from her husband. To receive his validation she must accept his premise that Sally is the cause of his temper problem. Her refusal to accept this premise would risk further beatings or expulsion from her marital group.

A day after receiving a black eye from her husband, Sally went to visit her parents. She attempted to cover over her bruise with makeup, but her parents were able to detect the injury. They inquired into this situation, and after much hesitation Sally painfully revealed that her husband had hit her the night before. Her parents inquired further into the situation and learned that the reason for the abuse was that Sally had mistakenly matched one of her husband's blue socks with a black sock. He had discovered this after wearing the mismatched socks at work and had come home in an enraged state. Upon hearing this explanation, Sally's parents became extremely upset. Her mother and father both shared the opinion that Sally's husband was no good and that she needed to leave him and come live with them immediately. Sally's parents, although trying to help, were attempting to solve the problem at the wrong level. They were oversimplifying the problem. Without even thinking, confirmatory bias kicked in for Sally. She immediately picked up on her parents' oversimplification. Her husband could not be so easily described as a bad man. After all, he was usually very good to her. With this in mind, Sally found herself in an argument with her parents that involved her parents trying to convince her to leave her husband. Sally defended the situation on the basis that her husband was not as bad as he seemed and that he really does love her. As this argument unfolded, Sally's parents, who were attempting to be helpful, unknowingly sent a message to Sally that she interpreted to mean "If I don't leave my husband, I will not live up to my parents' expectations." In other words, Sally had a sense that she was losing consensual validation from her parents. As the larger pattern of Sally's marital relationship unfolded, the conflict between an unsolvable domestic violence pattern and loss of consensual validation escalated. Sally could not keep her secret from friends and coworkers. They expressed sentiments similar to those of her parents, and so Sally soon began to feel that she was being disqualified from all of her social groups. The only thing that made any sense was to keep trying to obtain validation from her husband by accepting his premise—"If I am a better wife, then my husband won't hit me." Through this process the reality of the problem did not change, and with each social group disqualification Sally felt more like a failure. She lost all sense of self-confidence and isolated herself, avoiding social experiences except for being with her husband. She grew depressed and totally shut down even at home. Sally finally made an appointment for therapy in an utter state of despair.

The Relationship, Second-Order Change, and Hope

So far, the contextual model portrays a rather dim view of the prospects that clients have for making changes in their assumptive worlds. In fact, Frank argued that because major assumptive systems, especially unhealthy ones, are resistant to change, the changes produced by psychotherapy are usually minor. On the bright side, most clients require or request not major changes in their assumptive worlds, only minor ones. Even better, the contextual model indicates that a change in a small part of the client's assumptive world can lead to changes in other aspects of the assumptive world and begin a virtuous spiral of change. In other words, because of the interconnectedness of premises that surround problem-generating systems, a reversal in any premise can lead to the reversal of other premises that are part of the system.

Frank gave the example of a person who, through therapy, gains a more favorable impression of his boss. This leads to him treating the boss differently, which in turn evokes changes in the boss's behavior, which heightens the client's self-confidence, initiating a wider circle of beneficial changes in the client's assumptions about himself and others. This assumption leads to another overall objective of psychotherapy as described by the contextual model, to "*break vicious cycles* [italics added] by confronting patients with discrepancies between their preconceptions and the world around them" (Frank & Frank, 1991, p. 33) This is in line with second-order change, which indicates that vicious cycles are shifted when clients take actions or make assumptions that reverse first-order premises, corresponding actions, or a combination of both. More specifically, we are referring to reversals of direction, such as going toward the problem as opposed to going away from it, creating space as opposed to overpursuit, taking necessary action versus avoiding action, or changing the assumptive level from complex to simple or from simple to complex.

The contextual model asserts that the real power of psychotherapy derives from the relationship between the client and therapist and is driven by the client's need for consensual validation. From this view, consensual validation is the key to the process that makes reversals or second-order change possible. When clients are in a state of demoralization they are hungry for consensual validation. Consensual validation is used in effective psychotherapy to introduce small changes in the client's assumptive world.

From this perspective, the therapist gains power to influence the client when the client determines that the therapist symbolically represents a group to which he or she aspires to belong. In other words, when the client comes for therapy she forms a new group with the therapist. If the client is to overcome confirmatory bias and other factors that are promoting a problem-generating system, the client must first empower the therapist to provide consensual validation that will support experiments with new solution approaches. Whether this occurs will depend on the degree to which the client believes that the therapist establishes a positive treatment alliance, conveys empathic understanding of her problem, and establishes collaborative goals. It is through these relationship-building processes that the therapist establishes herself as an agent of change who is not too much of a threat to the client's assumptive world. Interventions will not be effective unless a therapeutic relationship and its elements are first established. This position is supported by Horvath and Bedi (2002), who concluded that "the therapeutic alliance needs to be forged first, including a collaborative agreement on strategies to be deployed as part of the therapeutic work, before therapeutically sound interventions can be usefully implemented (p. 60)." We argue that the relationship-building process that sets the context for intervention ironically is not only an intervention itself but also that it has so much changing power that in many situations nothing more is needed. We presently provide more evidence to support this point.

The Relationship Is an Intervention

As stated earlier, clients often come to therapy in a state of demoralization. They may assume that no one can understand their situation or that they are crazy for having a problem. Through the relationship, the therapist may express empathy for the plight of the client and offer words that show that the therapist does understand. If the client has selected the therapist to be a member of his or her reference group, the therapist's understanding will reverse assumptions related to "no one can understand the nature of my problem." This reversal at the demoralization level of the client's assumptive world may be enough to start a cascading domino effect of changes as described earlier by Frank. This change may occur even though the therapist has not given the client any direct interventions. We can say that in this situation the therapeutic relationship is an intervention in and of itself. The relationship produces second-order change as it reverses demoralization and engenders the opposite perspective of hope.

Taking this further, the reversals of demoralization and reestablishment of hope within the context of the therapeutic relationship have more recently received scientific credibility. It would appear that the type of occurrence previously described might be much more than a logical theoretical construct. Reversals of demoralization and the establishment of hope may in fact be a major factor in the process of change.

Hope

Although the term *hope* may sound ethereal, cognitive theorists (C. R. Snyder, Michael, & Cheavens, 1999) have begun defining it in a more precise fashion for the purposes of investigation. Hope has been defined as a function of agency and pathways thinking. *Agency thinking* involves the client's belief that he or she is capable of achieving his or her goal. *Pathways thinking* is defined as the client's belief that he knows how to achieve a goal. From this perspective, difficulties in coping are considered a result of being unable to envision a pathway or make movement toward a desired goal (Klinger, 1975; C. R. Snyder, 1996, 1998).

When therapists explicitly or implicitly send the message that the client can expect successful change, increases occur in the client's opportunities for critical agency and pathways thinking (C. R. Snyder, McDermott, Cook, & Rapoff, 1997). We argue that in effective therapy therapists express hope for improvement through the process of establishing the therapeutic alliance and, more specifically, through empathic understanding, engagement, and goal-setting. Through the empathic processes of engagement, the therapist establishes credibility as a member of a group to which the client aspires to belong. The clinician gains credibility through the process of understanding the nature of the client's problem. In many instances, this may be an incredibly powerful and novel experience for the demoralized client. Through the experience of being understood, the client may form the assumption that "Because my therapist understands me, I know she can help me." This can have an immediate and powerful impact on agency and pathways thinking, resulting in a burst of creativity on the part of the client leading to a reversal of the entire first-order change process.

In goal setting, the client and therapist collaborate on a desired future state or time when the client will be doing better. Goal setting collaboration offers another opportunity for a second-order change. Demoralization often results in clients being preoccupied with past failures such that they lose a sense of future direction or how they would like to be when their situation is improved. The client has taken up residence in a "problem-saturated system." All he can think about is the pain and distress of his problem. In this state, the client may not know or remember what he is actually trying to achieve. Through understanding the problem and establishing mutually agreed-on goals, the client's vision of a more desirable future state is crystallized. If the client–therapist-generated goal seems reasonable to the client, then hope is born about the possibilities of achieving it. In many cases, the client will begin progress toward the goal before the clinician begins working with the client on intervention strategies. The reversal of the client's orientation to the problem from present–past to present–future represents a second-order change. This stimulates a reversal from demoralization to hope and another potential second-order shift.

There is compelling dose–response evidence that supports the contention that second-order change not only happens through reversals that occur within the therapeutic relationship but also that this is a more frequent occurrence than one might expect. C. R. Snyder et al. (1999) reported that 56% to 71% of outcome variance related to total client change can be accounted for by change that occurs in the early stages of treatment (Fennell & Teasdale, 1987; Howard, Lueger, Maling, & Martinovich, 1993). C. R. Snyder et al. (1999), quoting Ilardi and Craighead (1994), stated that,

> Such dramatic improvement occurring so early in treatment can hardly be a result of specific effects or interventions because clients have not usually learned the "active mechanism" for change by the time that improvement occurs in these early stages of treatment. (p. 184)

Other researchers have also documented these same early treatment effects and concluded that the reversal of demoralization to hope is the most parsimonious explanation (Goldstein, 1962; Peake & Archer, 1984; Peake & Ball, 1987; Wickramasekera, 1985; Wilkins, 1979, 1985).

To illustrate the points that we are making about the power of relationship as an intervention, recall Sally. She has now entered treatment and is at her first therapy session with her therapist, Lisa. Sally comes into the office and Lisa greets her with a warm smile. After introductions, Lisa asks Sally to tell her story. As Sally explains the history of her failed attempts to leave her husband, Lisa listens carefully and with only a few minor interruptions for clarification. Through the process, Sally reveals the losses of relationships with others and how she no longer feels that she can live up to the expectations of her family or friends. She knows that she should leave the relationship with her husband but still clings to hope that she might be able to do something that will change him. Upon hearing the story, Lisa takes a different approach than Sally has been used to. Rather than making negative statements about Sally's husband, Lisa says that it must be difficult to live in such a complex situation. This catches Sally's attention, and she leans forward in her chair to listen to more of what Lisa has to say. Lisa continues and affirms that if leaving her husband were easy, then Sally would have done it long ago. The problem is that the situation is so complex: "Although it is unacceptable that your husband becomes so intolerant and abusive, he does have many good points. Because there is so much good with the bad, it is difficult to determine exactly who your husband is." Lisa continued, saying that "It must be especially difficult because just when you begin to see your husband as being someone that you should leave, he does something wonderful like bring you flowers. This totally takes the steam out of your efforts to leave the marriage and perpetuates the belief that the relationship can be saved by trying a bit harder." As Lisa was providing this empathic understanding, Sally began sobbing. Lisa stopped and asked if she had said something to offend Sally. Sally said no, that she had finally found someone who understood her situation. Her tears were of sadness about her situation and gratitude that someone finally understood. At the end of the session, Lisa said that she was not going to tell Sally to leave her husband; "For now, it is most important that we understand the complexities of your situation and develop a safety plan to keep you from being physically hurt."

In this session there was no talk of action. Lisa and Sally developed a group, and because Lisa demonstrated such a keen understanding of Sally's situation, Sally granted Lisa the power of consensual validation. This was based on the sense of freedom that Lisa offered. Sally could be part of her group regardless of whether she could successfully leave her husband. This reduced any fears that Lisa might have about not living up to her therapist's expectations. Because Lisa exhibited empathic understanding of Sally's assumptions for staying in the marriage, Sally did not feel so guarded about her assumptive world. She left the session with hope that something different was about to occur in her life.

When Sally came back for a follow-up visit, she had important news. Her husband became mad at her during the time between sessions and hit Sally. In response, Sally said to herself, "this is unacceptable." She then packed her bag and left the house. She found an attorney and obtained a court injunction barring her husband from coming near her. Sally moved into a room at a motel and made an appointment for a job interview. Her plan was to get a job, establish a place to live, and then file for divorce. All of these developments were new, including her assumption that it is unacceptable for her husband to hit her even if she has made a mistake. Lisa expressed low-keyed pleasure about this development while emphasizing the difficulties around keeping this change going. Sally took the position of assuring Lisa that she could do it. Weeks and months passed with Sally growing stronger in her decision. She established herself independently and through good luck was able to secure a well-paying job with benefits. Eventually, Sally reconciled her relationship with her parents and former friends.

Further analysis indicates that Lisa never used a formal intervention in this case. Sally's lightning-quick move into action obviated the need to use the strategies that she had planned. Instead, she described her work as tracking with Sally and staying out of her way. In this case, the therapeutic relationship and an extremely important extratherapeutic variable—experiencing good luck in finding a job—created and sustained second-order change. Lisa closely matched Sally's presentation during the initial interview by respecting and understanding the complexity of her marital relationship. Her statement that abuse is unacceptable was in opposition to Sally's premise that she must fix the marriage; however, because she matched Sally's presentation so well and developed such strong credibility, Sally granted Lisa the power of consensual validation. This allowed the new premise suggested by Lisa to bypass Sally's filtering system. In the end, Sally moved out of the overly complex system that had developed within her marriage. She determined that her husband must take responsibility for his own behavior. When he failed to do this, she left and developed a new life for herself. Another important extratherapeutic factor was that Sally's family and friends welcomed her back into their groups without taking an "I told you so" type of stance.

In sum, we are arguing that the contextual model supports the conclusion that the therapeutic relationship is an intervention. In many cases, it is all that clients need to make second-order changes in problem situations. It exists as a vehicle for influencing clients to stop vicious cycles and experiment with new assumptions or premises in the problem-solving process. Consensual validation is a powerful social force that empowers the therapeutic relationship. It is an effective vehicle for change when the client ascribes credibility to the therapist as an important reference group member. Through consensual validation the therapist may stimulate a second-order change before ever constructing an intervention strategy with the client. The therapeutic relationship may also serve as a platform for developing intervention strategies when a positive alliance is not enough to produce desired changes. The ultimate treatment effect that psychotherapy seeks is the restoration of hope in the demoralized client. Hope restoration involves the stimulation of pathways and agency thinking.

FOLLOWING THE THREAD

The view that the psychotherapy relationship is an intervention may result in a need for us to reconsider our understanding about how effective psychotherapy works. Recall that first-order interactions are based on a set of premises or assumptions on the way things are in a given domain. These assumptions guide our actions, the results of which further perpetuate our assumptions. We as interveners and advocates of effective psychotherapy are subject to the same principles governing first- and second-order change as our clients. By developing a theory on the basis of a false premise, we may just as easily become trapped in similar vicious cycles. If our contention that the relationship is an intervention is correct, then it would follow that the current debate—about isolating elements of the therapeutic alliance from intervention for the purpose of measurement and comparison—is based on a false premise. When fabric is made of the same thread, comparison is confounded. This is tantamount to taking a medicine like aspirin, giving it different names, and then running a comparison study to see which drug is better. Although such studies have actually been done, the purpose has been to test the placebo effect and not the chemical properties of the drug. We suggest that the escalating debate over effective therapy is analogous to these studies. For now, we contend that shifting our assumptions to acknowledge the unity of technique and relationship is an important consideration in our understanding how change is effected in psychotherapy. For some, this may stimulate a second-order shift in assumptions about psychotherapy theories and their relatedness to change. We have more to say about this in the next chapter.

5

INTERVENTIONS AS
RELATIONAL ACTS

Getting rid of a delusion makes us wiser than getting hold of a truth.
— Ludwig Borne

In this chapter, we describe how the golden thread of second-order change weaves its way through psychotherapy interventions. In chapter 4, we argued that the therapeutic relationship is an intervention. In this chapter, we demonstrate the flip side, that interventions are relational acts. Frank and Frank's (1991) contextual model's components will be used to show that the therapeutic relationship empowers interventions and that, in turn, interventions empower the relationship. We demonstrate that second-order change is more than a simple reversal and that it often requires many reversals by clients and therapists if it is to be sustained. This makes for a complex process that we refer to as a *second-order relationship*. We argue that the second-order change model offers a unified framework that is at the heart of effective therapies. This framework is used in the next section of the book to demonstrate how second-order change is central to treatment methodologies that are gaining notoriety as empirically supported treatments. The chapter ends with a further comment about the debate over the role of common and specific factors in psychotherapy outcome.

CONTEXTUAL MODEL COMPONENTS

Before we more fully describe the contextual model components, it might be useful to define the term *context* as it applies to effective psychotherapy. The *American Heritage Dictionary of the English Language* (2000) defines context as the circumstances in which an event occurs. When we say that effective psychotherapy is *context bound* we mean that the variables that drive the change process are circumstantial and, to a large degree, subjective. This is the reason that seemingly simple terms such as *empathy* and *goal consensus* are so difficult to define; it is the client who determines what is empathic listening, and it is the client who ultimately determines when effective change has occurred. How clients make such judgments is determined by a host of factors that include personal values, life history, gender, age, ethnicity, race, culture, socioeconomic status, and so on. Consequently, the variables of psychotherapy that are measured by researchers are part of a stochastic process, a process that literally jumps around. Despite this movement, there are common features that can be found in effective psychological treatment. The contextual model defines the common features found in the relationship and in interventions. It also shows how the relationship and interventions interact to create change.

THE RELATIONSHIP REVISITED

An Emotionally Charged, Confiding Relationship With a Helping Person

Given the evidence that supports the power of the therapeutic relationship, it is not surprising that this is the first component of the contextual model. What is surprising is that Jerome Frank (1961) predicted the importance of the therapeutic relationship before the elements of the therapeutic relationship were fully tested. What is more, Frank also predicted that the relationship elements were contextual; that is, client driven.

The client's context for therapy is defined not only by the demographic factors listed earlier but also by the point at which the client is in the demoralization process. Yet no matter who the client is, or how demoralized he may be, it is predictable that he will be cautious about allowing a therapist to suggest changes in his assumptive world. As we reported in chapter 4, there is evidence to support the counterintuitive assumption that the more distressed the client is, the more cautious he will be about establishing a therapeutic relationship.

One may think of the psychotherapy process as operating within bilateral realities: the client's reality and the reality of the therapist. Within these two spheres there is a mutual assessment process. In one sphere we have the therapist. The effective therapist listens to problems, joins the assumptive world of the client, tracks with first-order change patterns, collaborates on goals, provides understanding and evaluates potential techniques that might produce second-order shifts. As clinicians are caught up in this process it is easy to forget that the client is also conducting an assessment. Within the client's reality sphere, he is determining whether he can trust the clinician with his assumptive world. He operates with a set of criteria that are based on his unique experiences with others and previous helpers. Before he will allow the therapist to be admitted into his inner sanctum, the part of him that is within his self-protective system, he needs to have a sense of the therapist's personhood. Is the therapist a person who is capable of understanding his problem? Does the therapist genuinely care about him and respect him despite his problems? Is the therapist genuine and congruent, or is there the hint of a hidden agenda? Does the clinician seem competent? Does the therapist know what do about the client's problem?

Clients base their decisions about whether to allow a therapist to intervene on the basis of how the therapist stands up to these questions. As we have explained, clients have different expectations about what makes the right answer. Whereas many clients prefer a clinician who takes a permissive approach, there are some who expect that the clinician will be more confrontational. They feel "handled" or "managed" when a clinician approaches them in a way that is too diplomatic. The research of Bachelor and Horvath (1999) indicates that clients and therapists often have different perceptions of the therapeutic relationship. They say that although the source of the divergence is not entirely clear, it may be true that therapists and clients use a different reference base when evaluating each other. Regardless of the source of this divergence, it is clear that to be effective, therapists must learn how to adjust their styles to fit the expectations of clients. Failure to meet the clients' expectations will result in a loss of credibility. Without credibility, therapeutic interventions are unlikely to be successful.

Another complexity is that there is no fixed point at which relationship building stops; it continues throughout the psychotherapy process. At any point in the process, the therapist can fall out of step with the client and lose the power that drives second-order change. For example, the therapist might pass the problem-understanding test and fail at goal consensus, or pass both the problem-understanding test and goal consensus and provide a task that makes no sense to the client. This may result in a loss of momentum that scuttles the change endeavor.

Herein lays yet another complicating factor, as was raised in the case of Sally in chapter 4 of this volume. Claiborn and Dowd (1985) argued the merits of a discrepancy model versus a content model of interpretations. Their position is that effective interpretations must be close to and yet somewhat discrepant from the client's point of view to be effective. We argue that this discrepancy viewpoint operates on many levels. At the relationship level, clients come for treatment in an ambivalent state. One of the key issues that emerges from this ambivalence is anxiety about how much of the assumptive world the client will need to open up for change. It might be said that clients enter treatment in a manner that is similar to us when we take our car in for repair. If the car is not operating properly, we know that some change is needed and will be upset if the mechanic tells us that the car's mechanical malfunction is a figment of our imagination. At the same time, we dread the possibility that the mechanic will tell us that we need to replace the car's engine. Therefore, another important factor in setting a context for intervention is that the clinician must find ways to simultaneously match the client's worldview and offer change. From a dialectical view, this represents confirming the status quo while equally affirming the need to change.

In sum, although the therapeutic relationship is at times powerful enough to facilitate change on its own, there are situations in which specific intervention approaches are necessary. The process of developing interventions emerges from relationship building. Readers should keep in mind the following points:

- Intervention techniques are an outgrowth of the therapeutic relationship and are effective only when the therapist has proven him- or herself to be worthy of the client's trust.
- Within the context of the relationship, the therapist must convey understanding of the client and his or her problem that are close enough to the client's worldview, so as not to appear threatening, but different enough to give the client hope that change will occur.
- Relationship-building elements are client determined and must be maintained throughout the treatment process. Effective therapists maintain the relationship by adjusting their approach to fit the client's understanding of how a therapist should be. As stated by the American Psychological Association Task Force (Norcross, 2002), "Monolithic theories of change and one size fits all therapy relationships are out; tailoring the therapy to the unique patient is in" (p. 12).

A Healing Setting

Another component of effective psychotherapy is the setting in which the clinician and client meet. The setting is directly tied to the relationship and has two important functions. The first is that it elevates the prestige of the clinician. The second is that the setting creates a place where the client is safe to share her failed problem-solving efforts. If the client is to transfer the power of changing her assumptive world to the clinician, she will need to have sufficient evidence that the clinician is both competent and safe.

The setting is another variable in the treatment process that is context bound, because clients have different ideas about what constitutes an impressive healing setting. In most states in the United States, law requires that the clinicians display diplomas, licenses, and professional disclosure statements so that problem solvers can immediately see that their clinician is qualified to provide psychological care. For many clients this is a sign that the clinician is competent and capable of addressing their problems. However, some clients may be put off by the amount of education that the clinician has and take this as a signal that the therapist is incapable of relating to their concerns. Many clients prefer to see their therapist at a professional office that is close to their home. This may be for the sake of convenience. Other clients are fearful that neighbors will see their car at the clinician's office and prefer to receive psychological treatment farther away from home, where they are less likely to be seen by someone they know.

Emerging empirically supported treatments for severe mental illness such as assertive community treatment (ACT; S. D. Phillips et al., 2001), emphasize the importance of natural settings. Clinicians who provide ACT, usually case managers, are required to provide care in client's homes and in other community settings. This is based on the nature of mental illness, which often involves vicious cycles around social withdrawal. Because social withdrawal is a symptom of certain mental illnesses, many severely mentally ill persons will not initiate actions that are necessary for social engagement. Consequently, they may not come to a clinician's office to receive care. This has been a contributing factor in treatment noncompliance and hospitalization recidivism rates. Clinicians who provide ACT are well aware of this phenomenon and are prepared to interrupt the client's social withdrawal pattern by bringing care to the client. This represents a second-order shift for the field. Previously, many clinicians read social withdrawal as a lack of motivation. It was thought that the client must come to the office as a sign that he is willing to participate in the treatment process. However, this only perpetuated the problem, as many clients simply never showed up for treatment. Instead, they would withdraw further and further into psychoses until hospitalization was necessary. With ACT, the clinician takes the first step by approaching the client in a setting in which the client feels safe. Many clients read this as a sign of positive regard: "My therapist cares so much about me that she is willing to come to my house." Once positive regard is established clients frequently become willing to open up and engage in the treatment process. The ACT clinician then begins the process of linking the client to other settings, such as the psychiatrist's office, church, drop-in centers, and even work. As the client builds on success, he becomes more active in care. The ACT clinician eventually transfers the client to a lesser level of care that might involve office-based services. The social withdrawal cycle is reversed as the client is now taking necessary steps in social engagement.

In sum, the healing setting plays a key role in the development of the treatment relationship and in some cases may stimulate second-order change. The setting has two functions: (a) It elevates the prestige of the therapist and (b) it provides a safe place for self-expression, thus increasing the likelihood that clients will allow interventions to be effective. As with all of the elements of the context model, the healing setting is context bound.

INTERVENTIONS

Once it is determined that relationship-building is insufficient for stimulating second-order change, the therapist must turn toward intervention methods. By understanding the client and sharing his aspirations, the clinician communicates in a powerful way that she is on his side and wants what he wants. It is the client's sense that the clinician is on his side that makes it possible for the therapist to effectively intervene. This solidifies the client–therapist group. The consensual validation that comes from this group makes the pain of correcting first-order errors worthwhile. We therefore argue that the first step in intervention involves the client transferring the power of consensual validation to the therapist so that the therapist may in turn validate changes that the client makes in the way he is addressing his problem.

The contextual model posits that a frequent source of social invalidation is when individuals have troubling emotional experiences that are so complex that they defy explanation, either within one's self or with others. Because we are social beings and meaning-makers, it is important that we can make sense of our experiences so that we can relate them to others. The loss of the ability to share meaning can result in a person feeling alienated from her significant social groups. She is carrying significant experiences that she cannot explain to herself or others, so she cannot be validated for what she is experiencing. This leads to assumptions that she is different from her group. In turn, she may think that she is "going crazy" and fall into a demoralized state. As we have written, the ultimate objective of psychotherapy is to restore hope in such individuals.

With this in mind, Frank and Frank (1991) described a two-step process that is crucial to intervention. First, the therapist provides a rationale, myth, or conceptual scheme for the client's symptoms, then the therapist offers a procedure or ritual that is designed to change the way that the client is trying to solve the problem. Evidence supports this two-step process as having healing potential regardless of whether the client carries out the therapeutic task. A logical description of the problem can reverse the client's alienation by restoring his ability to talk about his issues with others. The client's hope in getting better is elevated when he believes that the procedure will work. This then feeds back to the relationship and increases the therapist's credibility in a virtuous cycle.

The use of the terms *myths* and *rituals* in the same breath with *rationales*, *conceptual schemes*, and *procedures* may require some further explanation, as this may be a controversial confluence of concepts for some readers. Recall that the work of Frank and Frank (1991) was meant to be transtheoretical. In this case, the contextual model is not only transtheoretical but also transcultural. Because science is highly valued in Western cultures, we are naturally impressed with rationales and procedures that have a scientific basis. However, not all cultures place the same emphasis on science. Consequently, people from more indigenous cultures may reject scientific explanations for psychological problems and instead embrace mythical rationales and corresponding rituals. Because psychological healers from indigenous cultures have documented success rates that equal results in the West, Frank pays respect to the many different forms of psychological healing with their use of this terminology.

Given that varying types of psychological healing are effective throughout the world, and that there are many science-based healing rationales and procedures that work equally well, an important question is raised: To what extent must a rationale and given set of procedures be scientifically valid to be effective? In other words, what happens if, through advancements in science-based knowledge, we discover that there is little connection between energy release in catharsis and cure? What if it is demonstrated that there is no connection between eye movements in eye movement desensitization reprocessing and relief of symptoms of posttraumatic stress disorder? Does this rule these methods out as powerful treatment approaches? The contextual model says no.

From the perspective of the contextual model, powerful treatment methods do not have to be scientifically true to be effective. Instead, rationales must provide an explanation of the client's symptoms in way that makes sense to the client. In other words, the explanation must be plausible to the client and so therefore believable. Because the therapist must be congruent and sincere as part of the relationship-building process, the explanation or rationale for symptoms must also be plausible and believable to the therapist. Procedures that are designed to change the client's problem-solving approach must be linked to the explanation of symptoms in a way that likewise makes sense to the client and the therapist. In other words, the logical connection between the rationale and procedure must create a belief in the client that the procedure will be effective. Research shows (Wampold, 2001) that therapists must also believe in the efficacy of psychological procedures if they are to be effective. In fact, Wampold's (2001) meta-analysis shows that it is more important for the therapist to believe in her procedure than to perform it in a way that is in perfect conformance with a manual.

Here, once again, the term *contextual* comes out loud and clear. For rationales, conceptual schemes, and procedures to be effective, they must be aligned with the belief system, values, and culture of the client. Take, for example, two chemical engineers who enter treatment for depression. Both are to receive a similar treatment method; however, one of the engineers is an atheist, and the other has recently converted to Christianity. This difference in religious faith could have a significant effect on how they respond to a science-based rationale and treatment procedure. Even though the Christian engineer is a scientist, he may not appreciate a secular framework for understanding and treating his depression. However, the nonbelieving engineer would probably not appreciate a therapeutic rationale and treatment framework that emphasizes Christian metaphors. Plausibility and compatibility trump science when offering rationales and procedures.

This should not be taken in any way as a denigration of psychotherapy change frameworks. In fact, Frank and Frank (1991) listed six important functions of rationales, conceptual frameworks, and procedures in effective psychotherapy. The contextual model indicates that psychotherapy change frameworks combat alienation and demoralization, as described earlier in this chapter. The idea that the therapist has a method that is developed specifically for the client's problem, and that she conveys confidence in using the framework despite difficulties that may arise in the treatment process, links hope with the client's expectations that he will improve. Another aspect of the treatment process is emotional arousal. Here Frank indicates that, for many clients, learning that they can tolerate painful emotional experiences is critical to treatment success, and so *emotional arousal* is another important function. The clinician demonstrates that she can tolerate the client's emotional arousal and so, within the bonds of the therapeutic alliance, the client discovers that he can manage unpleasant emotions as well. This then leads to the idea of new *learning experiences,* which is the chief goal of psychotherapy. New learning experiences create opportunities for clients to experiment with alternative solutions in the problem-solving process. Because first-order change processes tend to become habitual, it is not expected that clients will make one reversal and be forever changed. On the contrary, there is usually a need to practice reversals in different situations to ingrain the change. An important function of psychotherapy change frameworks is that they provide a structure for practicing and maintaining change over time (Wampold, 2001). Once a change has been integrated, the client develops a sense of self-mastery over the problem, and hope is further enhanced. The client now has confidence that should the problem reoccur, he would know how to successfully manage it.

AN INTEGRATED VIEW OF INTERVENTION

Up to this point, we have described the concepts of first- and second-order change and their linkages to the therapeutic relationship and the contextual model. Because the second-order change perspective is so conceptually close to the contextual model, it may be unclear as to how it distinguishes itself. We argue that there is a reciprocal relationship between the perspectives of second-order change and the contextual model. They are both transtheoretical, support each other, and at times overlap. However, first- and second-order changes operate at slightly different levels of abstraction.

Although the contextual model identifies common aspects and functions of interventions, second-order change is more specific. Information yielded from the concepts of first- and second-order change makes it possible to describe the underlying change mechanism in the change process and predict at which point interventions will need to occur. In other words, the second-order change perspective describes the essence of change.

The Location of Change

The contextual model and the second-order change perspective agree that psychological ills are born from faulty assumptions that result in vicious cycles. Yet, as meaning-making machines, we develop assumptions about every aspect of our life experience. Our assumptive worlds are so complex as to be beyond adequate description. So, where should the therapist begin when determining what client assumptions need to be influenced or changed? Because second-order change can be understood only as it relates to first-order patterns, the location of change is defined by this relationship. In other words, therapists can ascertain faulty assumptions for intervention by understanding the commonality in the client's first-order solutions. Moreover, it is understood that these commonalities will fall into the error categories that we described in chapter 3.

As we have reported, there are several common errors that lead to vicious cycles, including taking unnecessary action, failing to take necessary action, or attempting to solve problems at an incorrect level of abstraction. We added to the description of common problem-solving errors by demonstrating that vicious cycles are directional. Problem solvers disqualify or move away from problems, overpursue them, or become frozen in a position in which they cannot take appropriate actions. This process is aided and abetted by assumptions that oversimplify problems or make them too complex. The second-order change view therefore predicts that psychotherapy in any given case will be related to correction of errors as are outlined earlier in this chapter.

The Essence of Change

Second-order change predicts further that solutions to psychological problems lie in opposites. This is another reflection of its dialectical underpinnings. Problems are formed when clients take a path that is opposite from the path that is needed to solve the problem. It is like a football player who, on receiving the ball, is hit and turned in the direction of the opponent's goal. Because problems form in opposites, solutions involve opposites as well. In effect, the therapist must help the problem solver move in the opposite direction of the direction that he is pursuing. More simply, the problem solver must stop his advance or retreat and go the other way.

Support System Configuration

Not only does the perspective of second-order change predict where problems and solutions lie, but it also predicts the configuration of problem solvers' support systems. In first-order patterns, support persons will line up on opposite sides of the continuum. Some may line up directly with the client's perspective and reinforce the idea that the first-order assumptions and solutions should work. Others may line up on the opposite side of the continuum and try to influence changes that are too dissonant with the client's assumptive world. Consider a fictitious person, George, who has come to therapy for depression. He has been trying to escape his depressed feelings by telling himself that there is no need to be depressed because he has a good family. Examination of his support system indicates that they have aligned on either side of the continuum. Some family members agree that George has many reasons that he should not be depressed. They are supporting George by telling him that not only does he have a good family but also that he is lucky to have a secure job. This support matches George's perspective too closely and so is unlikely to be helpful. George also has other family members that have expressed their opinions. They have argued that George needs to stop lying around and find something constructive to do with his time. Here again, the support is not working. The reason is that this part of George's support system is expressing assumptions that are too dissonant from George's perspective. He argues that depression makes him so tired that he doesn't have the energy to do anything but lie on the couch when he comes home from work.

The second-order change model further predicts that wrongheaded reinforcement of first-order solution patterns occurs with the best of intentions. In most situations, problem solvers want to do better and support persons want the same, it's just that the lure from the land of opposites is too powerful. For therapists, the ability to predict how support persons are responding to problem solvers provides invaluable information for facilitating second-order change. We know that our attempts to help must be closely matched with the client's perspective and yet different enough to make a change. In a sense, entrance to the client's inner sanctum is like threading a needle. This is a difficult but doable task.

With this in mind, we revisit common second-order change interventions, most of which were previously defined in chapter 3 (this volume). We argue that these interventions are supported by the second-order change and contextual models and are found across all effective psychotherapy frameworks.

Reversals and Blocking

By definition, all second-order interventions involve reversing or blocking the first-order change processes in which clients are engaging. The bird trapped against the plate glass window needs to go back and down, instead of forward and up, to free itself. The kid caught in the finger trap must push in to pull her fingers free. In short, reversals involve movement in the opposite direction of the first-order pattern. Blocking or stopping the pattern ultimately has the same effect: When the pattern is stopped, the client will usually reverse the direction of failed solution attempts. In the end, most effective change involves some sort of reversal.

The fundamental concept of reversals is easy to grasp—after all, we are simply dealing with opposites. Complexity comes with application and the multitude of levels that may be involved. The second-order change perspective helps us more clearly understand the main domains in which reversals are used in psychotherapy interventions.

These domains are *meaning* and *action*. Meaning and action form a reciprocal relationship. On the one hand, we act on our assumptions, and our assumptions drive our actions. Therefore, if we change our assumptions, new actions will follow; whereas, on the other hand, changing our actions affects our assumptions. For example, a paranoid person may sequester himself in his room to escape perceived harassment by his neighbors. He may then eventually seek treatment for stress from the harassment. An expert therapist might suggest that by sequestering himself, the person might be giving a message to any potential harassers that they are winning. To defeat them, it would be good for the client to go for walks and smile at people who pass him on the street. Once anyone who might be out to harass him sees that they cannot disturb him, they may stop their annoying behavior. In so doing, the client begins venturing out of the house to greet his neighbors. With this, he may begin to experience the pleasure of people smiling back at him, and so he comes out of his withdrawal even more to prove that he won't be bothered by harassment. In this case, the client's main assumption—being harassed by neighbors—remained the same. The therapist prescribed new actions for addressing the harassment. This led to new assumptions regarding how to stop it, and new actions led to new assumptions about how to solve the problem.

There is another point from this example that is critical from the perspective of second-order change. By observing the intervention just described, readers will notice that the expert therapist working with the paranoid person accepted the plausibility of the presenting problem at face value. In other words, because the client stated that harassment was the issue, the clinician directed her approach at reversing patterns that might be related to harassment. Therefore, the second-order change view predicts that reversals will be effective when they are specifically tied to the assumptions and actions that the client defines as problematic. This directly relates to the elements of empathic understanding, collaboration, and goal consensus, which are fundamental elements of the therapeutic relationship. The relationship empowers reversals and successful interventions further build the relationship. From success comes increased confidence that the therapist knows how to be helpful, now in the operation of a virtuous cycle.

Validation

Validation may be understood as a crossover intervention that lies at the intersection of relationship building and intervention. It is related to the concept of consensual validation and is one of the threads that connect the therapeutic relationship and interventions, making one common pathway. Validation is a therapist-initiated process in which the client's thoughts feelings and behaviors are accepted and considered completely understandable given the client's subjective experience of the world. The therapist genuinely accepts the client's presentation at face value and holds the belief that the client is doing the best he or she can. The therapist respects the client's experience of the problem by emphasizing its importance and empathically offers total justification of the client's experience (Duncan, Solovey, & Rusk, 1992).

Linehan (1993) broke down the process of validation into three steps:

1. Active observations of direct communication and public acts as well as intuiting the patient's unstated emotions, thoughts, values, behaviors, and beliefs.
2. Reflection of the patient's feelings, thoughts, assumptions, and behaviors.
3. Direct validation in which the "therapist looks for and reflects wisdom or validity of the patient's response, and communicates that the response is understandable . . . the patient's feelings, thoughts and actions make perfect sense in the context of the person's current experience and life to date" (p. 424).

The definition of *validation* and steps in the process suggests that validation is a directional, empathic process. In other words, validation involves understanding the client's perspective in the direction of justifying his or her incorrect assumptions and corresponding actions that drive first-order change. In some cases, validation is an intervention that produces second-order change by itself. It is not unusual for problems to develop in a manner by which the client is not validated by people in her support system. Simply hearing the therapist demonstrate how her symptoms reflect inner wisdom can reverse demoralization and produce a second-order change.

Some clinicians are troubled by the idea that the validation process involves justification of incorrect premises. They claim that, if the therapist truly believes that the client is operating from incorrect premises, such justification is insincere or manipulative. We argue that validation of incorrect premises is genuine, by definition, when the clinician is mindful of the context; that is, when the clinician is aware that incorrect premises are an artifact of the client's worldview. Understood this way, it is clear that the client is literally doing as well as possible under the circumstances. There is no insincerity or manipulation here.

Validation is also relevant to the two-step rationale-procedure process that was outlined earlier in the chapter. We argue that clients have a need to not only understand the nature of their problem but also to feel that they are justified for having the problem in the first place. Therefore, from the perspective of second-order change, effective rationales not only explain the client's dilemma but also validate the client for having the dilemma, by justifying it.

As we have stated, clients enter into treatment with ambivalence about change. The client knows that he must change to do better but does not know how much change is going to be needed to better manage his problem. The problem solver does not wish to make a dramatic shift. He is therefore caught in a change–don't change duality. The client is trying to change and prevent change at the same time. This is another dialectical dilemma. An analogy is a person who is running downhill. In so doing, the person must attempt to run and stop himself to slow the pace and not lose control. Validation juxtaposed with goal setting places the therapist in the position of justifying both sides of the change–don't change duality. This is a synthesis. Validation of the problem symbolically validates "don't change," and goal consensus symbolically validates "change." In other words, the therapist is saying, "I both justify your problem and your desire to do better." We discuss this in chapter 11 as the core intervention in dialectical behavior therapy for clients fitting the criteria for borderline personality disorder. As demonstrated in chapter 4 of this volume, this can be a powerful intervention. The second-order change model predicts that the positioning of the client's support system will play a role in determining the extent to which this dualistic stance promotes a significant second-order shift. It is unlikely that the client has persons in his social network who are taking such a complex position and so it is most likely that, at a minimum, this will represent a difference that will make a difference. It may become a part of a second-order relationship with the client that inspires hope that the therapist will be helpful.

Validation also sets the stage for other intervention approaches that may be needed and for this reason is usually a highly used intervention in effective therapy. Another way to understand this is that the client's self-protection system (as described by Frank & Frank, 1991) will permit changes if current premises are justified and linked to changed premises in a manner that appears plausible for solving the problem. This is what justifies the second-order shift. Recall from chapter 4 of this volume the case of Sally, who had been abused by her husband. Her first premise was that *she could stop the abuse by being a better wife.* The therapist used validation to justify the complexity that led Sally to this assumption while suggesting that there was no acceptable reason for abuse. The assumption that *there is no acceptable reason for abuse* ran directly counter to Sally's premise, and so an important question might be raised. Why would this apparent contradiction of her premise be taken as validation? In chapter 4, we explained that Sally's need for consensual validation played a role. We would argue that although this is true, there is also an additional reason that the therapist's alternative premise might be taken as validation. Other information provided by Sally indicated that at the time she came for therapy Sally was actually seeking help to leave her husband versus save the marriage. Her set of premises did not provide her with justification for following through on this action. Recall that she was struggling with a complex set of assumptions about the nature of her husband and what the abuse meant about him as a person. If he were really a good guy, then the abuse was her fault. However, Sally's support group had told her that he was a bad guy and that the abuse was his fault. If this were the case, then maybe he was a bad guy masquerading as a good guy. In essence, Sally's complex assumptive world was preventing her from taking necessary action. She was in a double bind and therefore was at a standstill. To continue with her premise was to continue the abuse. To accept the premise of her support group would mean that her assumptive world was entirely wrong. No matter which way Sally might turn there was a stinging loss that she would have to endure.

By stating that abuse was not acceptable, the therapist separated the abuse from the personhood of Sally's husband. This uncomplicated the web—Sally could easily accept the idea that abuse is wrong. She did not really need to judge her husband to make this determination, and so this assumption was not nearly as threatening to her assumptive world. She could now be right for seeing the situation as complex and right for not putting up with further abuse. This was the justifying link. Lisa, Sally's therapist, had effectively threaded the needle. Additional information from Sally's case indicated that there were points in the divorce process at which Sally's husband attempted to reconcile with her. At each point, her husband maintained his premise albeit in a disguised manner; that everything would be okay if they could only compromise. The compromise would be his trying harder to curb his temper and Sally trying harder to be a better wife. Sally saw her husband's offers as a prescription for more abuse, and so she followed through with her plan for a divorce. Another question that might be raised is what would have happened if Sally were not seeking justification or validation for leaving her husband? Our answer to this question is the therapist would have needed a different approach. The reason the approach worked here was that it fit with this specific situation.

Positioning

Positioning represents a class of relationship interventions that are variations on validation. Positioning is used to assist clients with making movement in the dialectical change–don't change duality. This duality is best thought of as a continuum versus a static position. Clients enter treatment at varying places along this continuum. Some may be anchored more on the change side of the continuum, whereas others are anchored on the don't-change side. According to the stages-of-change model (Prochaska & DiClemente, 1992), clients anchored on the change side fit the description of the action stage. (Prochaska and DiClemente's change model is more fully described in chap. 10 of this volume, on substance abuse.) It is not that these problem-solvers are totally lacking in ambivalence, it is that at this point they are highly motivated and so their ambivalence about changing may not be apparent. In some situations, clients in the action stage may begin a second-order shift during the time that transpires between calling for the initial appointment and the first session. It is not unusual that under these circumstances clients will progress far enough that they only need support to maintain the changes that they are already making. This support will come in the form of validating the change, validating difficulties that the client has overcome to make the change, and validating difficulties that may be yet be to come. Expert clinicians will not offer a change method to clients who are in the process of self-change. To offer a change methodology to a client who is already changing on her own could undermine her confidence in what she has accomplished and unwittingly facilitate a step back into demoralization.

Pro-Change Position

Many clients are highly motivated to change but don't know how to accomplish their goal. In response to this client position, the skilled therapist will validate difficulties in making a change and express optimism that the client will fulfill his therapeutic destiny. This type of response may be referred to as the *pro-change* therapist position. From this position, the clinician may give assignments that offer opportunities for making second-order shifts.

One of the therapeutic pitfalls with highly motivated clients is that therapists may become so caught up in the client's high motivational level that they miss the need to validate the client's don't-change ambivalent side. The clinician may adopt a cheerleading stance and lose credibility with the client if speedbumps develop in the change process. To protect the therapeutic relationship against such eventualities, the seasoned clinician will make statements about change along the lines of "I am very optimistic that therapy will be a worthwhile experience, because you are so motivated to change, yet I am aware that change can at times be very difficult even for persons who are as highly motivated as yourself." This statement emphasizes change while accepting whatever ambivalence the client may have. It creates a win–win proposition for the client. If he changes without difficulty, then he can surprise the therapist in a very pleasant way. If the client runs into difficulties, he won't need to be concerned about losing consensual validation within the client–therapist group. The client is now in a position in which he will receive consensual validation either way. This reduces pressure for the client and makes second-order change easier.

The Neutral Position

Some clients come for psychological treatment in a state that is close to the midpoint of the change–don't-change continuum. These clients are regarded as highly ambivalent about change. They may be somewhat suspicious of behavioral health providers on the basis of previous experiences or cultural considerations. Highly ambivalent clients may have issues such that a compelling case can be made for either changing or not changing. In these situations, expert clinicians are careful about being overly optimistic about the change process, because this might actually have the reverse effect of alienating the client. Here, the second-order change view predicts that a more neutral stance or position on change will be beneficial. A neutral stance frees the problem solver from expectations that she must change and creates space for the client to create her own decision. From the neutral position, the clinician validates the wisdom that is inherent to both sides of the change–don't-change continuum. Because both sides are equally valid, the clinician cannot rightfully know what is best. However, through mutual exploration of the up- and down sides of her problem situation, the client will be able to discover her inner wisdom and arrive at her own conclusions about whether change is needed.

Through this exploration the clinician refrains from advocating a pathway that the client should follow. The objective of this therapeutic stance is to convey to the client that he will receive consensual validation regardless of whether he makes a change. In some situations this therapist position is so powerful that the client will not only decide to change but will also realize that he knows how to create a self-induced second-order shift. In this case, the expert clinician will support the client from a pro-change position. However, after the shift the client may express a need for a change method. This is a green light for the clinician to work with the client on a change method that fits his concerns. In some cases, the client will decide that change is not needed. The expert clinician will validate the client's decision to not change at this time and invite the client to come back to therapy if the need arises in the future. It is not uncommon for problem solvers to follow through on this and seek the therapist out again when they are more ready to actively engage in the psychotherapy process.

Multicultural counseling practices (cf. Gonzalez, Biever, & Gardner, 1994; Sue & Lam, 2002) imply another situation in which a neutral therapeutic stance is often in order. Clients who are members of nondominant cultures may be accustomed to members of the dominant culture applying their norms and using their positions of power and privilege in relationships. The multiculturally sensitive therapist, who takes the one-down "not-knowing" position of a learner about the clients' perspectives, offers a powerful reversal or second-order shift in the traditional power-up relationship of therapists and clients. This may be a particularly powerful experience for ethnic minority clients or otherwise nondominant clients who are not accustomed to having their views and positions respected and privileged.

The Don't-Change Position

In very difficult cases, problem solvers may enter psychotherapy with a highly defensive posture. In such situations demoralization has set in and has gotten a foothold on the client. She is experiencing superambivalence; she is under great pressure to change, but the pressure to not change is greater. She knows she must change and feels that she can't do what is necessary to resolve her problem. In her own mind the forces that are preventing her from changing are too powerful to overcome. This client has reached a point of desperation, and that is why she is seeking psychological assistance. Yet, despite her desperation, she remains resistant to change.

In situations in which problem solvers are resistant to change the expert therapist takes a position that anchors the client's resistance. This position must be taken carefully, because clients in a state of resistance are also highly sensitive to invalidation. In practice, the expert clinician will make statements such as "I know that it is important that you change, but perhaps this is not the best time given all of the stress that you have been under." Here the therapist is validating both sides of the change continuum, but the emphasis is on not changing. For some therapists this type of therapeutic stance may seem counterintuitive or paradoxical. Beutler, Molerio, and Talebi (2002) made it clear that clients who may appear reactant or resistant to therapy have been demonstrably helped by such paradoxical-looking therapeutic relationships (see also meta-analyses by Hampton, 1988; Hill, 1987; and Shoham-Solomon & Rosenthal, 1997). Likewise, Horvath and Goheen (1990) found that patients with high levels of trait-like resistance improved with paradoxical interventions and maintained their gains beyond the period of active treatment. The important point is that when clinicians adopt a don't-change position in a manner that is respectful of the client's assumptive world, it is not unusual for the client to begin defending change. This creates a reversal of the usual client–therapist roles, and a second-order shift occurs on this level. The therapist, who is symbolically viewed as an agent of change, promotes reasons for the client to not change. The client, however, becomes the advocate for change. The clinician may introduce intervention approaches from the don't-change position, but she will do so by casting doubt on their utility. She might say, "If you were able to change, I would recommend that you become involved in some daily exercise activities so that there was not so much time to dwell on your problems. Yet this would be unrealistic given how depressed you are right now." In response, the client might come back to the next session and announce that he has just begun a new exercise regimen to help with his depression. Again, role reversals that emerge from the therapeutic don't-change stance are helpful only when the clinician fully understands the client's needs and aspirations. There must be a logical link in the mind of the clinician that connects the client's need for consensual validation with his goals. The don't-change position is merely a logical extension of the neutral stance. The client is placed in a win–win situation: He will be validated if he does not change and will ultimately earn the therapist's respect by changing beyond her expectations. In this sense the paradox is in the eyes of the describer rather than in the interventions (cf. Fraser, 1984).

The second-order change view predicts that expert clinicians will carefully evaluate client position before introducing a rationale and intervention approach. When clients are in the don't-change or neutral position, interventions will be targeted at shifting the client's position versus changing the presenting problem. Interventions that target client problems will be reserved for clients who are in the pro-change position.

Restraining

In chapter 3, we described restraining as a potential reversal at the psychotherapy context level. Restraining is similar to the position that therapists take with clients in the neutral and don't-change positions. Here we would like to emphasize that any steps a therapist takes to slow the speed of change is restraining. This often occurs naturally in the psychotherapy process outside of the awareness of the therapist. For example, when clinicians offer skills training, they often let clients know that they should not expect change until they have learned the skills that are designed to address their problem. This is an inadvertent restraint. The second-order change perspective predicts that if client and the therapist have a positive working relationship this may relieve enough pressure for the client to undergo a second-order change. This change may occur before the client is ever taught the skills that the clinician has in mind.

Normalizing and Acceptance

We have described normalizing as a way to place clients at ease by conceptualizing their difficulties as normal reactions, given the constraints of their situations. Normalizing is a very close relative of validation. It is different in that the implication is that no special actions are needed to make a change. If the client lets go of problem, it will resolve itself. The perspective of second-order change predicts that normalizing is more likely to be helpful when clients are unsure if they have a problem and are seeking reassurance. Normalizing may be understood as disqualification if the client is convinced that she has a problem that must be addressed. Some of the new cognitive-based psychoeducational frameworks are able to work around this concern by teaching clients to normalize their situations for very complex reasons.

Framing, Reframing, and Deframing

We have described framing, reframing, and deframing as a class of interventions that involves shifts in meaning. These interventions may directly reverse meanings that drive first-order change or serve as building blocks for prescribing alternative actions in the problem-solving process. The contextual model predicts that change in the assumptive world of clients and restoration of hope are the ultimate aims of psychotherapy. Toward this end, framing, reframing, and deframing are generally used to place a problem or problem solver in a more favorable light, to assist a problem solver with seeing the discrepancy between his solution attempts and goals, and to make new actions seem attractive. According to the discrepancy model (Claiborn & Dowd, 1985), plausibility and believability directly apply to the use of these skills. In other words, effective frames, reframes, and deframes must match the client's view of reality closely while offering a slightly different twist on the situation. At the same time, frames, reframes, and deframes must be plausible and believable to both the therapist and the client to be effective and ethical (Solovey & Duncan, 1992).

Prescribing

We have described prescribing as a subclass of reversal interventions that involve therapist-directed requests for clients to deliberately enact symptomatic behavior. The enactment is carried out for a different purpose than the one that is currently framed by the problem solver. Prescribing typically is done around involuntary symptoms. Clients are asked to enact the symptom on purpose in an effort to gain mastery over it. The contextual model predicts that this type of intervention is useful to clients as it helps them to master a symptom that seems to be out of control. The second-order change view also predicts that this intervention is effective because it requires the client to reverse direction and go toward the symptom versus having the symptom and trying to move away from it. Prescribing is consistent with consensual validation as it serves as an implicit permission from the therapist to engage in symptomatic behavior. This expands the client's sense that the clinician will continue to validate her despite having a problem. In this way, the client receives further encouragement to embrace the problem.

Predicting

Predicting is a class of interventions that are designed to sustain second-order change and the treatment alliance. Here, therapists predict that change will be difficult to sustain and that setbacks are opportunities to consolidate gains by reencountering old dangers. The second-order change perspective predicts that by reframing setbacks as opportunities the therapist symbolically extends consensual validation beyond termination of treatment. Pressure is lessened for maintaining change, which may prevent future reoccurrences of the problem. Furthermore, recurrence is not necessarily taken as another trigger for the same old solutions. The client may also return to treatment, if need be, for another learning opportunity.

Procedural Level

In chapter 3, we indicated that the second-order change framework makes predictions about what is effective at the procedural level of therapy. At the procedural level, clinicians develop strategies that are designed to interrupt first-order patterns that clients identify as problematic. From the perspective of second-order change, there are three main strategies that are found at the procedural level of effective psychotherapy. In any given case situation, clinicians may use one or more of these strategies, depending on how the case unfolds over time. The procedural strategies listed next may be used eclectically; they are also embedded in formal frameworks such as parent training, cognitive restructuring, or desensitization. Interventions from the previous section are used to carry out procedural strategies.

1. *Change the premise*: Therapists will use validation and other skills to help clients change premises that are driving first-order change.
2. *Accept the premise, change the action*: Therapists will accept faulty premises and restructure the logic in such a way as to offer the client a just reason to engage in more adaptive behavior—such as what occurred in the example of the paranoid client described earlier in this chapter.
3. *Prescribe the same action for a different purpose*: Therapists will ask clients to deliberately engage in symptomatic behavior, but for a different purpose—as described in the "Prescribing" section of this chapter.

Once a satisfactory second-order shift has occurred the expert clinician will structure the therapy in a manner that is designed to maintain the change after the client's treatment is concluded.

Second-Order Shift for Therapists

As we have demonstrated, psychotherapy is a highly context bound phenomenon. Expert therapists are flexible, very capable in building relationships, and gifted with language skills. Despite these extraordinary qualities, it is quite possible for therapists to become enjoined in vicious cycles with their clients. As therapists, we have the capacity for making first-order mistakes—there is no insurance policy that protects us from this aspect of the human condition. When therapists become caught in first-order processes they must make an internal second-order change, or the treatment is likely to fail. This is often best achieved in consultation with a colleague or in supervision with another therapist outside the therapeutic relationship. Such shifts may occur on different levels. Clinicians finding themselves in judgmental mode may need to reverse themselves to become more accepting of the client; sometimes it is necessary to shift from a pro-change stance to a don't-change stance. These are but two examples—the number of shifts that a clinician might need to make in a course of therapy are too numerous to describe. In the end, the purpose of the clinicians making second-order shifts is to increase the likelihood of helping clients. That is the clinician's higher calling.

Second-Order Relationships

We have described what works in effective therapy and that change occurs within the context of a relationship. At the micro level, it is the relationship among a bicycle rider, the bike, and the road. At a larger level, it is the relationship between parent and child. In psychotherapy, change occurs within the context of the relationship between therapist and client. The therapeutic relationship does not exist for its own sake; instead, clients and therapists endeavor to produce a certain kind of change, second-order change.

In the process of building a strong psychotherapy relationship, the client may undergo a second-order change. We argue that when this occurs the relationship itself is an intervention. At times, the relationship itself offers something so different from the client's current relational system that it is itself a second-order change. In other situations, the relationship serves as a platform for intervention techniques that also create second-order change. John Norcross (2002), commenting on the American Psychological Association's Task Force on empirically supported relationships, noted that "The relationship does not exist apart from what the therapist does in terms of technique, and we cannot imagine any techniques that would not have some relational impact" (p. 8). Put differently, techniques and interventions are relational acts.

Yet we know that change is not easy. There are many contextual variables that need to be in place for a second-order shift to occur. We also never quite know when we have threaded the needle. Sometimes we may have an excellent working alliance with the client but yet no change occurs. At other times, we may conceive a brilliant intervention and again, no change. We may help a client to make a shift and then lose track of our position and find ourselves in need of a second-order shift to salvage the treatment. When change does occur, it must be sustained, and this has its own set of challenges.

As we considered the way that the golden thread of second-order change weaves through the relationship and interventions, it became clearer that relationship and interventions are indeed inseparable. By combining all elements, we might better say that effective therapy is produced by a second-order relationship, which is defined as follows:

> A *second-order relationship* is a psychotherapy relationship where the client makes a second-order shift or series of shifts, such that the client achieves his or her goal(s) in therapy. Second-order changes may be an artifact of the psychotherapy relationship by itself or be a result of direct influence techniques. Direct influence techniques succeed only within the context of a positive working alliance. They have a reciprocal relationship with the alliance. It is the client who determines whether the changes that have been made in treatment are sufficient. Changes that the client has made must be maintained past termination of the psychotherapy relationship for the relationship to be considered a second-order relationship.

A UNIFIED FRAMEWORK

Now that we have described the unity of the second-order change perspective with the contextual model and therapeutic relationship, we are prepared to introduce a framework that will be used to evaluate effective therapy later in the book.

The purpose of the psychotherapy relationship is to produce change—second-order change. Second-order change is effected through the relationship. All actions that therapists take with clients involve the relationship. In many instances, the process of building the therapeutic relationship produces second-order change. In other instances, therapists and clients use the relationship as a vehicle for developing specific intervention approaches. Intervention approaches are effective when clients transfer the power of consensual validation to therapists. A prerequisite for transferring consensual validation is that the therapist establishes herself as understanding, trustworthy, caring, and competent. These therapist characteristics are contextual and therefore defined by the client.

To facilitate second-order change, the clinician's primary objective is to block or reverse the demoralizing vicious cycles that have brought him to therapy. This objective is attained through interventions that target meanings or actions that drive first-order change. We propose that what has been previously referred to as *techniques* are really highly specialized therapeutic relationship *skills*. There are a number of specialized relationship skills that go into the process of blocking or reversing demoralization. The most well known skills include the following:

- Validation: This is the cornerstone of effective therapy. It exists as a stand-alone set of skills and is the basis for all other skills that promote second-order change. It is a thread that must be woven through all other skills that are brought into a particular case.
- Framing.
- Reframing.
- Deframing.
- Normalizing.
- Prescribing (actions that reverse or block).
- Positioning (as relates to change).
- Restraining (a subcategory of positioning; there is always some restraint involved in second-order relationships).
- Predicting.
- Goal setting.
- Developing mutual tasks: These skills may be used in combination or in such a way as to overlap.

There are three basic therapeutic strategies at the procedural level of therapy, which are used to promote second-order change. The skills previously discussed are necessary for formulating and implementing these procedural level strategies.

1. Change the premises that support and direct the first-order solution pattern.
2. Prescribe new or different actions on the basis of first-order premises.
3. Prescribe first-order premises and actions for a different purpose.

Because clients empower the skills that therapists use in the treatment process, the selection of relationship skills and therapeutic actions is client dependent. Selection of strategies and skills is therefore arrived at through a collaborative process with the client. When skills and strategies facilitate sustained second-order change, the treatment relationship may be referred to as a second-order relationship.

The contextual model predicts that clients will be satisfied with the results of treatment when hope has been restored, that is, when agentic thinking (e.g., "I can do it") and pathways thinking ("e.g., I know how to do it") have been reactivated. The second-order change model predicts that hope has been restored when clients are approaching problems in a novel manner. In effect, clients are moving in a direction that is opposite from when they began treatment. These opposite pathways include the following:

- Clients who were oversimplifying a problem are now more appreciative of the complexities that are involved.
- Clients who were viewing the problem in a manner that was overly complex are now indicating that the problem was not as difficult as they had imagined.
- Clients who were attempting to trivialize the problem away or run from it are now embracing the problem, seeing its importance, or are no longer afraid of it.
- Clients who were trying to pretend that the problem does not exist are acknowledging it and taking appropriate actions to solve it.
- Clients who were overpursuing the problem are now creating space for its resolution.

FOLLOWING THE THREAD

In chapter 4, we indicated that it is difficult to predict that one therapeutic agent is superior to another if both are composed of the same active ingredients. We wondered what it means for research if therapeutic relationships are interventions, as the objective of researchers is to strip interventions from the relationship for the purposes of comparative measurement. Now we are arguing the flip side, that interventions are relational acts. If this is so, then the dodo bird may be wiser then we think. We will pick up with this story as the golden thread of second-order change weaves its way through some of the more widely researched, empirically supported treatments.

II

FOLLOWING THE THREAD: EMPIRICALLY SUPPORTED THERAPIES

6

ANXIETY

Fear has big eyes!

—Russian proverb

Anxiety is the paradigm case of vicious cycles, as we have noted several times in the previous chapters. We will draw on anxiety research and the perspectives of a variety of sources to detail the workings of the vicious cycles of anxiety. As we have already mentioned, anxiety comes down to mastery by avoidance, and resolution comes down to reversing people's solutions. We then describe the major empirically supported approaches to treating anxiety-related problems. Finally, we discuss these approaches in the light of first- and second-order change.

THE MANY FACES OF ANXIETY

[This is] the absolutely central problem in neurosis and therapy. Most simply formulated, it is a paradox—the paradox of behavior which is at one and the same time self-defeating! (Mowrer, 1950, p. 486)

Anxiety in one or another of its forms is one of the most frequently encountered emotional problems in both medical and mental health practice. From 18% to 20% of the world's population suffers from anxiety-related disorders, according to a convergence of epidemiological surveys (Barlow,

2002). Yet fear and anxiety alone are not necessarily problems. These two closely related emotions can offer great advantages. Whereas most sufferers would consider anxiety a burden they would gladly live without, most scientists and philosophers agree that "Paradoxically, [anxiety] may well have been responsible for the survival of the species" (Barlow, 2002, p. 2).

The Physiology of Fear

Most readers will recall that fear and anxiety are part of an overwhelming emotional response to potentially dangerous or even life-threatening emergencies. The built-in tendency to either escape or to stand and confront the danger (the so-called "fight or flight" reaction) has probably selectively preserved the lives and thus the species of most organisms. Fleeing to escape danger, freezing so as not to attract attention, or fiercely fighting for one's life have, in the past, served our species well. They have become ingrained. As such, there are well-known physiological reactions to such perceived emergencies that may be found across all organ systems. Cannon (1927) classically described the survival function of a range of these changes. At such times of perceived danger, the cardiovascular system plays a major part. Blood is redirected from the extremities to the torso to be available to vital organs and to the skeletal muscles to aid in potential combat. Decreased blood flow to the extremities and the skin may limit the potential for bleeding in a fight. These actions may also cause us to appear "white with fright," to feel tingling in our hands and feet, to shiver to produce body heat, and to have hot and cold spells as these adjustments occur. Oxygen to the brain to improve cognitive functions is facilitated by more rapid and deeper breathing, yet prolonged courses of this may cause dizziness or lightheadedness. The liver releases more sugar to energize the brain and needed muscles and organs. Pupils dilate, and hearing becomes more acute as signs of danger become the major focus of attention. The characteristically dry mouth that we experience at these points is a function of the digestive system being slowed down. Short-term urges to void our bladder and bowels to prepare for action may then be followed by vomiting and diarrhea to prevent absorption of noxious substances under prolonged emergency states. Fainting at the sight of blood has often been connected to a need to drop blood pressure and minimize blood loss and shock when severely injured. It is interesting that the experience of being "frozen with fright," or the phenomena of paralysis and waxy flexibility, is similarly related to the fight- or-flight mechanism. "Playing dead," freezing, and the like are related to the ancient and now-automatic survival mechanisms to prevent pending attack. Such conscious paralysis or waxy flexibility is not uncommon in the recounted experiences of survivors of sexual assault. All of these, among other physiological responses to perceived threatening situations, have been connected to reasonable and logical survival mechanisms that have evolved to become automatic for us all. These mechanisms probably have saved, and will save, our lives across generations. They also play a major part in the evolution and maintenance of anxiety.

Anxiety and Fear

Are anxiety and fear the same, however? Most philosophers and psychologists over time have distinguished between them on the basis of the presence or absence of cues. *Fear* is defined as a response to a specific, identifiable danger. *Anxiety*, however, is defined as a reaction to a potential danger that is more diffuse and less identifiable. It is said that Freud used the term *angst*, or anxiety, for general states of apprehension about the future without a clear object. He used the word *furcht*, or fear, when such apprehension had a clear object. Most dictionary definitions of these terms follow this convention today. So, anxiety is generally defined as an emotional state in reaction to an assumed potential, yet unclear, source of danger. In essence, anxiety becomes fear when the source of danger is identified. Again, anxiety is not always bad. Existential philosophers suggest that anxiety is a necessary part of the human condition that we must confront daily in terms of life's unpredictability. Without such struggle, we wouldn't evolve. It is said to be a core element of creativity, learning, entertainment, and artistic and athletic performance, to name but a few human endeavors in which anxiety often accompanies strong performance or achievement. The classic Yerkes–Dodson (1908) experiments found that animals performed better on simple tasks when they were made moderately anxious than when no anxiety was present. So, if anxiety can alert us to find the source of potential danger, and if it can facilitate so many human achievements, how does anxiety become a problem?

Clinical Variations and Definitions

Before looking further at how anxiety becomes a problem, it will be useful to discuss how anxiety difficulties are defined clinically. The *Diagnostic and Statistical Manual of Mental Disorders* (4th ed. [DSM–IV]; American Psychiatric Association, 1994) lists a range of anxiety-related disorders. In this chapter, we address three of the most common of these: (a) panic disorder and agoraphobia, (b) social anxiety, and (c) generalized anxiety disorder (GAD). As mentioned earlier, along with simple phobias, about one in four people will be affected by one of these anxiety-related disorders in their lifetime, and about 17% will experience some variant of these anxiety disorders in any 12-month period. There is also a greater prevalence in women than in men worldwide on a 2:1 ratio, most likely related to shared gender role prescriptions regarding the appropriateness of showing or acting upon fear or being allowed to avoid it (Kessler et al., 1994).

Definitions

Craske and Barlow (2001) stated that experimental, clinical, and longitudinal research support "The conceptualization of panic disorder as an acquired fear of certain bodily sensations, and agoraphobia as a behavioral response to the anticipation of such bodily sensations or their crescendo into a full-blown panic attack" (p. 1). They defined panic attacks as "discrete episodes of intense dread or fear, accompanied by physical and cognitive symptoms as listed in the panic attach checklist of the [DSM–IV]" (pp. 1–2). This list includes such physical and cognitive symptoms as palpitations; chest pain; sweating; trembling; shortness of breath; and numbness or tingling of extremities; along with such concerns as fear of dying, losing control, or going crazy. Such attacks often seem unexpected from the client's perspective in that clients often are not able to identify a clear trigger for them. They are results of activation of the fight-or-flight system. However, a significant number of people do experience isolated occurrences of panic without those instances growing into a pattern of panic disorder. What characterizes panic disorder is not the simple occurrence of panic on one or another occasion. Panic disorder is distinguished by recurring anxiety that panic will reoccur and will have catastrophic consequences. The DSM–IV requires recurrent unexpected attacks that peak within 10 minutes and that are followed by 1 month or more of consistent worry about the consequences of the attack (e.g., fear of dying or going crazy) or of changed behavior because of the attacks (avoiding situations or taking specific precautions). People struggling with this difficulty thus either are or become hypersensitive and aware of internal physical state changes. K. S. White and Barlow (2002) suggested that "the central problem of [panic disorder and agoraphobia] is anxiety focused on the symptoms of panic; hence the well known and commonly accepted characterization of agoraphobia as 'fear of fear'" (p. 329). The term *agoraphobia* refers to the tendency to avoid or endure with dread those situations in which escape might be difficult if panic might set in. This includes great concern over the potential embarrassment of losing control and fainting, vomiting, or losing bowel control, for example. Thus, having great difficulty traveling or needing to be accompanied outside the home, and always needing to have a quick escape, are common characteristics of agoraphobia. Although panic disorder may occur without such situational avoidance or dread, at least some mild agoraphobia is almost always present.

People with social anxiety disorder, according to the DSM–IV, are unusually concerned about a variety of social situations in which they fear being humiliated by being unable to perform adequately or by showing visible anxiety symptoms. Sometimes this is limited to only a few situations, such as speaking in public, performing, and so on, but more often there are more general social interactions involved, such as dating, engaging in meetings or parties, or going on job interviews. Because people struggling with social anxiety are acutely concerned about the reactions of others, they tend to be hypervigilant for early indications of disapproval from others and of anything in their own actions that might be evaluated negatively by others. As might be guessed, the clinical and research literature has shown that this hypervigilance may lead to actual performance problems, which may then result in the feared disapproval of others in the proverbial self-fulfilling prophecy. Turk, Heimberg, and Hope (2001) summarized this dilemma: "Negative predictions result in cognitive, behavioral, and physiological symptoms of anxiety, which eventually feed back into the negatively biased mental representation of the self and perpetuate the *cycle of anxiety* [italics added]" (p. 123). Once again, in social anxiety disorders it is the solutions that become the problem.

People who struggle with this form of anxiety characteristically experience severe restrictions on their lives, and they often underachieve in both job and social arenas. It is of no surprise that both epidemiological and clinical data suggest that a significant percentage of individuals with social anxiety abuse alcohol (Turk et al., 2001).

The *DSM–IV* defines GAD by noting the key feature of excessive, uncontrollable worry about a range of life events or activities accompanied by at least three of six symptoms of negative emotion and tension. These symptoms include restlessness or feeling keyed up or on edge, being easily fatigued, difficulty concentrating or having one's mind go blank, irritability, muscle tension, or sleep disturbance. Moreover, the individual perceives these worries as difficult to control; the worries are not focused on any specific area of concern, and this consistent worry results in increasing impairment in job or social functioning. The process of excessive worry, or "anxious apprehension," is the key feature of GAD. This seemingly uncontrollable repeated solution is defined as a future-oriented mood state in which one becomes ready or prepared to attempt to cope with upcoming negative events.

Borkovec (1994) provided one of the leading explanations of the function of such anxious apprehension or worry as a basic vicious cycle. He suggested that worry becomes negatively reinforcing because it is associated with escape from more distressing images or body sensations. Yet this distraction does not allow the individual to completely process the situation through effective problem solving and resolution before the person diverts to another area of worry. Heightened states of tension and alert are thus maintained and rarely resolved by the worry that distracts the person from resolving the tension-filled situation. Worry also becomes self-reinforcing, because it becomes associated with the nonoccurrence of negative outcomes (which usually are relatively unlikely to occur even without such worry or attention being paid to them). (If I continue to worry about the sky falling, and it hasn't done so yet, then maybe it is my worry that keeps the sky from falling.) Cognitively, people with generalized anxiety are said to overestimate the probability of negative events that are actually unlikely to occur. They are also found to make catastrophic judgments about situations that they view as intolerable, unmanageable, or beyond their ability to cope, without ever examining whether this is really the case. Thus the process of excessive rumination or worry becomes intensely self-reinforcing in another characteristic vicious cycle. It is the process of continual anxious apprehension or worry that makes it a solution-generated problem. In all of these cases, each client is trapped in a vicious cycle that becomes a spiral of anxiety that needs to be interrupted.

The Spiral of Anxiety

It is no mistake that we have used anxiety and panic so far as a case in point to explain the process of vicious cycles of solution-generated problems. Recall that the essence of first-order change is identifying a potential difficulty or threat and taking appropriate action to resolve it. We suggest that anxiety in the best of situations can alert us to a potential challenge or danger. Once we identify the source of danger, we may become afraid and yet take action to resolve the threat. However, if the source of potential danger remains vague and thus unresolvable, or if our solutions not only fail to resolve the perceived danger but actually maintain and perpetuate it, then we become part of a vicious cycle. Our perceptions of danger and attempts to resolve it maintain anxiety and make it worse. In chapter 3, we used the simple example of panic attacks to illustrate this process. As we said at that point, panic attacks often begin by some chance occurrence that causes us to react with symptoms of anxiety. The initial kick-point or trigger for the first attack can be almost anything that causes us to feel widely out of control, unsure if we can handle the situation, and worried that the situation is dangerous. Innate fight-or-flight mechanisms set in. If we are aware of the cause of our panic, and of the innate nature of these physiological responses, then we may be able to categorize our reaction as unpleasant but natural. In so doing, we can often move beyond the incident. We might act directly on the situation that made us anxious. We might learn new skills to master it. We might decide that we misinterpreted the situation or find that our view was correct yet there was nothing to worry about. In these instances, we will move beyond the incident with few, if any, residual effects.

However, we may become very alarmed and worried about the panic attack itself. How did we get that out of control? What happened to us? Is there something physically wrong? Are we having heart problems? How can we avoid ever having that happen again? We get anxious about having gotten anxious. This can be the inception of a vicious cycle. Once panic attacks have occurred, they tend to be maintained by selective internal attention to bodily events, safety behaviors to bolster the person against the traumatic situation, and avoidance or escape. Our resulting solutions *become* the very things that produce the syndrome of escalating anxiety and ongoing recurrent panic attacks. Our solutions exacerbate the anxiety we seek to quell.

Our solutions become the problem. This is a prime example of first-order change leading to a vicious cycle. Thus, in cases of social anxiety and generalized anxiety disorders, the same processes of first-order changes are involved with each vicious cycle. All are solution-generated problem patterns. It is merely the process of how the anxiety progresses that differs.

If the thesis of this book holds true, then effective psychotherapy should involve some variations of second-order change; that is, generally effective therapy should involve either a reversal of the first-order solution process or a shift in the assumptions or premises that underlie those first-order solutions, or some combination of both. A look at the literature on successful treatments for anxiety will confirm this prediction.

EFFECTIVE TREATMENT OF ANXIETY

Do the thing you fear and the death of fear is certain.
—Ralph Waldo Emerson

The main evidence-supported interventions for anxiety and panic with agoraphobia, in particular, are based on cognitive–behavioral theory. From this perspective, the vicious cycle contains three basic elements: (a) emotional reactions, (b) bodily sensations, and (c) negative thoughts about sensations (misinterpretations). K. S. White and Barlow (2002) suggested that the four "protective behaviors" that contribute to the vicious cycle of panic and agoraphobia are (a) agoraphobic avoidance, (b) interoceptive avoidance, (c) distraction, and (d) safety behaviors. The first of these involves avoiding public transportation, theaters, crowds, and so on, where one might feel trapped and unable to reach a safe person or place without embarrassment. Interoceptive avoidance includes an acute sensitivity to physical sensations associated with anxiety and panic and thus avoiding activities that produce similar sensations, such as exercising, having sex, or drinking caffeine. Distraction is another kind of avoidance whereby panic attacks are avoided by redirecting attention away from the anxiety-provoking situation by talking, reading, watching television, and so on. Safety behaviors are things a person does to help oneself feel safer or more protected should a panic attack occur. These may include carrying a cell phone, a pill bottle, or a water bottle, or being with a person who knows about the person's panic worries. As can be seen in each solution, they are all variations on a first-order solution of attempting to master the panic by avoiding it in some way or form. Thus, the core of effective treatment should involve a reversal or include mastery by exposure. This is the case in all effective approaches to the treatment of panic. This process of reversals begins with the rationale for treatment and continues through assessment, intervention, and maintenance phases of treatment.

Rationale or "Myth"

In the last two chapters, we have discussed the crucial role of the working alliance in effective psychotherapy. Along with a therapeutic bond between therapists and clients, two central elements of the alliance are (a) agreements on the rationale and goals of treatment and (b) investment in the procedures of intervention. The Franks' (Frank & Frank, 1991) contextual model emphasizes the critical role of therapists and clients mutually investing in a therapeutic rationale or myth that naturally leads to engaging in a set of related therapeutic procedures in which faith can be invested and from which hope springs. We have described hope as the by-product of finding a pathway toward problem resolution that generates the agency or energy to take action along that path. We have also said that relationship and intervention are inseparable and that there are actually second-order relationships that can become the central element of effective therapy. All of these elements are present in the basic approaches to effective psychotherapy for anxiety.

The rationale for a cognitive–behavioral intervention begins with explaining the natural physiological characteristics of the fight-or-flight response. Sometimes this explanation, even given by a sensitive and knowledgeable primary care physician, can be enough to redirect some patients out of their vicious cycle. Most often, this explanation, along with a discussion of the cycle of "becoming anxious about becoming anxious," provides a basis for understanding the reasons for the assessment and treatment and opens patients to commit to the procedures. What the client will be asked to do in many forms is to reverse herself and go toward something she has formerly avoided. This requires a significant amount of faith in the therapist, understanding of and investment in the rationale offered to explain the problem, and commitment to and hope for the assessment and intervention procedures that will follow. Above all, cognitive–behavioral interventions are compliance based, in that they specifically ask the client to engage in a collaboratively empirical relationship with the therapist and agree to do homework assignments or experiments both during treatment sessions and outside therapy between sessions. As we noted chapter 3 on the contextual model, investment and commitment to a structure for treatment and a rationale for it are critical to success. At the broadest level, an effective therapist using a cognitive–behavioral approach to anxiety may be viewed as establishing a second-order relationship with her client. Once both parties accept the rationale that anxiety is potentially the product of unexamined assumptions and misdirected attempts to master discomfort by avoiding it, a major part of the treatment has already been set in motion. The rationale itself first offers acceptance and validation for the client's current solution patterns and their related distress and, second, provides a rationale for the client to explore the plausibility of her assumptions and reverse her current solution patterns. This is the essence of second-order change.

Another reason for addressing therapy for anxiety first, in chapters 6 through 11 on empirically supported approaches, is that these collective cognitive–behavioral approaches to anxiety are clearly some of the most powerfully effective techniques among all approaches to psychotherapy. Clinicians and researchers using these approaches have been masterful in demonstrating support for this approach, and they have been some of the most vocal advocates supporting the ascendance of technique over relationship as the active ingredients of therapy. It is fascinating, therefore, to note how some of the leading advocates of these approaches have themselves noted the important contribution that both clients and therapists and their relationship make to support effective intervention. Craske and Barlow (2001), discussing approaches to panic and agoraphobia, noted that clients' understanding of the nature of their problem may be critically important to the success of cognitive–behavioral treatment. Clients who are most likely to drop out of these cognitive–behavioral approaches are those who have strong beliefs in the biochemical basis of their problems or who strongly believe that their problem has something to do with their past. Similarly, patients who attributed their problem to life stressors rather than their own beliefs and attitudes have been significantly more likely to drop out of treatment. Also, patients with lower educational levels and lower income, who are less similar to the therapist and have less agreement or understanding of the rationale and less discretionary time to engage in treatment, are less likely to engage in cognitive–behavioral approaches according to the standard protocols (Grilo et al., 1998). A patient's ability to understand and accept the cognitive–behavioral rationale for this approach is thus critical to moving forward with effective treatment.

Similarly, regarding the relationship, it has been found that patients who rated their cognitive–behavioral therapist as self-confident, caring, and involved performed better on tasks involving reversing their former patterns and going toward feared ideas or situations (Williams & Chambless, 1990). Reviews of behavioral treatment outcomes have clearly found that the Rogerian qualities of warmth, genuineness, empathy, and positive regard rated early in treatment predict positive results in cognitive–behavioral therapy, and therapists viewed as understanding and respectful have the most positive results (Keijsers, Schaap, Googduin, & Lammers, 1995). The development of faith, hope, and trust between clients and their therapists appears to be as important to a cognitive–behavioral approach to anxiety (and maybe even more so for this approach). In fact, a study of therapists using cognitive–behavioral therapy with panic disorder and agoraphobia found that empathic listening in the first session was related to better outcome, whereas directive statements and explanations in Session 1 predicted poorer outcome. The opposite result—empathic listening predicted poorer behavioral outcomes than did active and directive therapist statements and explanations—was discovered by Session 3 (Keijsers et al., 1995). When clients feel heard and understood, and when their pain and struggles are validated by therapists early on, they are more open to collaborating in the rationale for treatment and engaging in its procedures as therapy moves forward. Thus, mutual commitment and understanding of the rationale for explaining problems and supporting treatment (in this case, the cognitive–behavioral structure) is crucial to effective intervention. As we have said, the cognitive–behavioral rationale, if accepted by clients, may alone offer a second-order relationship that already begins the needed solution pattern reversals.

Assessment

Second-order change, by definition, involves counterintuitive solution pattern reversals. We have already pointed out that when clients accept a cognitive–behavioral framework for understanding their problems and pursuing treatment, the process of reversal has already begun. It is interesting to note that the assessment process in cognitive–behavioral therapy, and specifically in panic disorder, accelerates these reversals. Clients are asked, during treatment sessions, to create many of the bodily sensations of anxiety they most fear and to examine the plausibility of some of their most firmly held assumptions about their safety.

The major structure for such assessments of panic disorder with agoraphobia is a functional behavioral analysis involving several steps. These steps include varying combinations of interviews, medical evaluations, self-monitoring, standardized inventories, and behavioral tests. In essence, the interviews and inventories offer an excellent way of tracking the unique yet specific pattern of each client's particular view of his panic and his solutions to it. They track the exact situations in which the attacks occur, their intensity and frequency, the nature of the physical experiences the client feels, his greatest concerns, his solutions, and the consequences of his struggles. These assessments, combined with self-monitoring, lay the foundation for an exquisitely detailed description of the problem patterns. To further structure this collaborative process and set baseline markers of the patient's unique fears, a fear and avoidance hierarchy (Craske, Barlow, & Meadows, 2000)— that is, a rank-ordered list of the patient's feared situations—can be developed. Once the list has been compiled, the patient is then asked to rate each item on a 9-point scale that ranges from *none* to *extreme* in terms of the extent of his fear of and his avoidance of each. Conditions that would make the anxiety worse and those that would make the anxiety better, may also be added to each item. Other questionnaires measuring panic-related cognitions are available. In general, these questionnaires measure the beliefs associated with each patient's panic and the extent to which the patient believes them. These forms begin to address the clients' assumptions that guide their solutions. For example, the Agoraphobic Cognitions Questionnaire

(Chambless, Caputo, Bright, & Gallagher, 1984) and the Panic Appraisal Inventory (Feske & de Beurs, 1997) assess such things as clients' frequency of frightening thoughts about the consequences of panic or anxiety, or their anticipation of panic, assumed consequences of panic, and their perceived ability to cope with panic. Other questionnaires comprise measures of anxiety that focus on emotions or physical sensations. Scales like the Anxiety Control Questionnaire (Rapee, Craske, Broen, & Barlow, 1996), the Anxiety Sensitivity Index (Reiss, Peterson, Gursky, & McNally, 1986), the Body Sensations Questionnaire (Chambless et al., 1984), and the Body Vigilance Scale (Schmidt, Trakowski, & Staab, 1997) are often used. These scales assess things such as perceived control of reactions in emotional situations; the extent to which patients believe that anxiety symptoms may cause negative physical, psychological, or social consequences; the degree to which patients associate anxiety with specific body sensations; and how closely patients pay attention to bodily symptoms, how sensitive they are to these, and how much time they spend checking them. Measures of avoidance include such scales as the Albany Panic and Phobia Questionnaire (Rapee, Craske, & Barlow, 1995), the Mobility Inventory (Chambliss, Caputo, Gracely, Josin, & Williams, 1985), and the Fear Questionnaire (Marks & Mathews, 1979). These scales measure such things as clients' anxiety and avoidance of a range of situations based on internal body cues, ratings of the extent of avoidance of specific situations when alone or accompanied, and the extent to which they avoid a range of situations. As can be seen, this cadre of scales tends to triangulate on the specific nature, extent, and intensity of the unique panic disorder of each patient. Furthermore, the process of these assessments begins to offer clients an initial glimpse of the overall patterns of their problem and further reinforces many of the elements of the therapeutic rationale.

Self-monitoring offers an even more accurate appraisal of the patterns of anxiety than does retrospective recall. It also offers a baseline on the initial intensity of the problem and a method to use in measuring ongoing progress. In self-monitoring, clients are asked to use such forms as a Panic Attack Record (Barlow & Craske, 2000) to rate details such as exactly when each attack occurs; in what situations and with what triggers an attack occurs; whether it was expected or unexpected; the degree of fear they experienced, rated on a 9-point scale that ranges from *none* to *extreme*; and which of a range of physical symptoms they experienced. Daily levels of depression, anxiety, and worry about panic are also monitored with forms such as the Daily Mood Record (Barlow & Craske, 2000) at the end of each day using a similar 9-point scale. As might be imagined, keeping these records alone can be somewhat of an ordeal, and noncompliance is common, particularly for people who use the strategy of distraction and who are reluctant to do the opposite by focusing on that by which they are most discomforted. This again is a crucial point at which the therapist–client relationship and their mutual understanding of the rationale for treatment are crucial to success. However, when clients do comply, they are not only beginning to reverse their usual patterns through the assessment but are also gaining an external objective position on their attacks.

A particularly important point needs to be made here about the inseparability of assessment and intervention before going forward with the rest of the functional analysis. It is important to realize that assessing a problem by deliberately engaging in it toward some therapeutic end is a second-order change itself. The fact that I allow myself to look forward to the next attack, willingly go through the attack, and objectively attempt to rate and analyze it constitutes fundamental reversals. Because I am not deliberately avoiding the attacks any more, and because I am more deliberately engaging in them for the sake of resolution, I have already started interrupting the problem-maintaining solution pattern. Furthermore, because I am deliberately asking myself to step out of my immediate experience during the process of an attack to judge, rate, and rank the experience and its elements, I am disrupting the uncontrollable experience itself by attempting to place myself in such a position of neutral and objective control. These components of the assessment represent the heart of the paradox that is the hallmark of second-order change. Clients' problem patterns are changed by the process of assessing their problem.

Returning to the functional analysis, recall that a critical factor in panic disorder is acute sensitivity for and avoidance of bodily sensations similar to those of panic. Clients' first-order solutions are to both scan for any evidence of these sensations and shut them down whenever possible. It is interesting, therefore, to note that a central part of assessing for panic disorder is creating these very sensations in sessions. The behavioral assessment strategies of the functional analysis include both symptom-induction tests and behavioral avoidance tests. Symptom-induction tests involve having the patient purposefully engage in an exercise that produces bodily sensations similar to those they experience during panic attacks. These tests are best tailored to the client's uniquely reported sensations when experiencing panic. They can include such things shaking their head from side to side for 30 seconds, putting their head between their knees for 30 seconds, and then lifting it quickly, running in place for 1 minute, holding their breath for 30 seconds, holding complete body muscle tension for 1 minute, spinning in a chair or twirling in place for 1 minute, hyperventilating for 1 minute, or staring at a 40-watt light bulb for 1 minute and then reading a paragraph, and so on. Clients rate anxiety levels before, during, and after these exercises; the intensity of the sensations; and their similarity to natural panic sensations. These exercises help not only to confirm the presence of anxiety and panic but also to identify specific sensations that may elicit anxiety and panic. This is a prime example of what has in other discussions been called *symptom prescription and induction*. It is an exact reversal in that it asks patients to induce anxiety-provoking bodily sensations (which they commonly seek to avoid at any cost) and then deliberately reflect on them and rate them. Once more, the assessment becomes the intervention from the view of first- and second-order change.

Behavioral avoidance tests embody similar reversals in terms of avoidance behaviors. In a behavioral avoidance test, patients compile with their therapist a list of about five items from their list of feared situations, covering a range of difficulty levels from mildly challenging to a high ceiling of anxiety. They are then asked to engage in each situation over the course of about 2 hours and then return to the therapist. Clients are asked to rate their anxiety on the familiar 9-point scale ranging from *none* to *extreme* and then to attempt to actually engage in each situation. Therapists do not accompany clients to control for the safety factor that most patients feel in having a protective other along with them. Usually, another observer watches from a distance, or pedometers record distances walked or receipts are brought back, and so on, to verify compliance. Final ratings are made on 3-point scales with 1 representing complete refusal or avoidance, 2 representing partial completion, and 3 indicating completion or no avoidance. These assessment results and the task itself are then frequently used during treatment to measure success. Once more, it couldn't be clearer that clients are being asked to make second-order change or reversal of their solution-generated problem patterns as part of the assessment itself. There is nothing at all wrong with this. This is a powerful step in the direction of the desired goal of reversing clients' anxiety-inducing patterns even at the beginning of treatment as part of assessment. By the time treatment begins, clients are already well inducted into both the rationale for understanding their problem patterns and the pathway toward resolving them.

To complete our discussion of the functional analysis for panic disorder and agoraphobia, the analysis results in a profile for the client. This profile includes information on the topography of the panic attack (e.g., sensations, frequency, duration, apprehension, and types being expected or unexpected), antecedents (including situational and internal factors), misappraisals (in the physical, mental, and social spheres), behavioral reactions to panic attacks (including escape, help-seeking, and protection attempts), behavioral reactions to the anticipation of panic attacks (including avoidance, cognitive avoidance, and safety signals), consequences (including family, work, and leisure and social domains), and general mood (including concentration, sleep disruptions, muscle pains, sadness, hopelessness, etc.).

By way of example, consider the case of Ann, an elementary school teacher. For Ann, the sensations she experienced were feelings of unreality, shortness of breath, and stomach upset. These would occur on an average of three per week, lasting from a few seconds to 10 minutes. Most of these were expected, but occasionally they came out of the blue. They mainly occurred in public situations from which she felt there was no escape, such as in cars, if she were not the driver; movies or plays; or in her classroom. Her internal triggers tended to revolve around stomach distress accompanied by thoughts of vomiting and never being able to control this again. She was concerned that maybe this was all physical in that she had chronic gall bladder problems, but she also feared vomiting in public, loosing control mentally, and being humiliated. Her reactions to a panic attack invariably involved escaping from wherever she was, seeking help from therapists and a boyfriend, and being sure she had her medication bottle. She thus constantly avoided being out of control through speaking in public, driving with others, and being at restaurants. She cognitively would count to 10, tell herself things would be okay, and generally distract herself from her sensations, and she would always know where her boyfriend was. As a result, her boyfriend was supportive yet increasingly frustrated with her, her parents had become more distant, she was becoming concerned about losing her teaching position, she had stopped any performing as she did through college, and she was not going out with friends unless she was completely in control of the circumstances. Her mood had deteriorated to hopelessness, with frequent crying spells and greater isolation in her apartment. She was in a classic downward spiral when she reluctantly sought help from a therapist just one more time. We return to Ann's case to address intervention after considering the main empirically supported approaches.

Treatment Interventions

The majority of empirically supported approaches to panic and agoraphobia share the common components of education, cognitive therapy, and some form of exposure and coping skills training. One major well-supported integrated treatment protocol for panic and panic disorder with agoraphobia is referred to as *panic control treatment* (PCT; Barlow & Craske, 2000). This approach combines multiple procedures. First, clients are educated with accurate information on the nature of the fight-or-flight response, with clients being taught that they experience normal and harmless "sensations" and not "panics." This first intervention seeks to reframe one of the internal triggers for clients' escalating solutions as nothing that needs to be solved. The goal of this intervention is to interdict problematic responses to internal bodily sensations before they begin, by altering a basic assumption on their nature and their threat value. Next, therapists identify and challenge anxious thoughts and beliefs that focus on the overestimation of threat and danger associated with panic attacks. By collaboratively examining the plausibility of many of these assumptions, therapists and clients begin to reshape some of the assumptions that guide many of the client's problematic attempts to master their anxiety. Then information about the effects of hyperventilation and its role in panic attacks is offered, and extensive practice in breathing retraining is offered. This provides information on how the rapid, short breathing that sometimes accompanies panic attacks contributes to the sensations of the attack and thus normalizes those sensations. It also offers a self-control skill intended to counteract the tendency to hyperventilate. Finally, repeated *exposure* is initiated. One form of exposure is to the internal physical cues accompanying panic and is accompanied by practice in both cognitive and breathing strategies. Finally, the other exposure is *in vivo*, or real life, exposure to feared and avoided situations involved with the avoidance reactions of agoraphobia. This is not only a combined protocol but also, on the basis of evidence from earlier studies (cf. Craske & Barlow, 2001), is sequenced. Although there are elaborate and detailed protocols that guide therapists in these procedures, the detail of these procedures is less important to our discussion than the process of what is being done. Over and again, the key factors in these effective interventions involve exposure or reversals, which are the hallmarks of second-order change.

Recall from chapter 2 (this volume) that there are three basic ways that problems may evolve: (a) action is necessary but is not taken, (b) action is taken when it should not be, or (c) action is taken at the wrong level. Anxiety in general, and specifically panic and agoraphobia, are mainly the result of action being taken when it should not be. In essence, people who are caught in the cycle of panic and agoraphobia are constantly on guard against and attempting to avoid things that are not dangerous. Furthermore, they are trying to control things that do not need to be controlled. In a classic pattern, their solutions of hypervigilance and avoidance exacerbate the anxiety and panic that they seek to control and avoid. The goal of all effective intervention for such anxiety is thus to end the unnecessary solutions. In chapter 3 of this volume, we noted several ways that therapists across approaches facilitate second-order change. Two ways we mentioned were that (a) therapists may facilitate changes in clients' assumptions, frames, or premises, and (b) they may also block, reverse, or redirect first-order solutions. Similarly, two of the six points we made in chapter 3 to operationalize second order change for therapists across approaches were: (a) if the first-order solution is to go away from the problem, the second-order solution will have something to do with going toward it; and (b) if the first-order solution is to overintervene with normal ups and downs of daily living, then second-order solutions will involve tolerating and accepting the amount of unpleasantness that is a natural part of the human condition. Effective treatments for anxiety embody each point toward the ends of having clients stop unnecessary actions to resolve their anxiety and accept the formerly distressing sensations and situations as perhaps uncomfortable yet not dangerous or in need of being managed in some way.

We have already pointed out that educating clients about the fight-or-flight response is a first step in altering their premises or assumptions about the potentially dangerous nature and cause of the normal body sensations that accompany the response. The second set of interventions in the PCT protocol involves identifying and challenging clients' overestimations of threat and danger associated with panic attacks. This process of collaboratively examining the logic, reasonableness, and probability of clients' appraisals of danger directly attempts to change clients' assumptions, frames, or premises. If successful, these changed assumptions should lead to changes in behavior; in this case meaning that there is less need to brace against danger. Furthermore, the process of examining the utility of clients' assumptions usually includes experiments in which clients expose themselves to anxiety-provoking situations and collect observations on whether there was actually danger involved. These "cognitive" experiments are reversals in that they engage clients in going toward what they once feared and in tolerating what they once found intolerable. This second (cognitive–behavioral) component of the protocol does fit well with one of the several ways that therapists facilitate second-order change through altering assumptions or premises. However, there is some evidence that its major effect may be to engage clients through both discussion and action to expose themselves to formerly feared ideas and situations. In other words, clients are gaining mastery by reversing the solution process and going toward rather than away.

The component of the protocol that teaches clients about the effects of hyperventilation and teaches breathing retraining makes intuitive sense, yet it has been reconceptualized (Craske & Barlow, 2001). Not all clients experiencing panic disorder actually do hyperventilate. Furthermore, several controlled studies have found that breathing retraining does not add any clear benefits to the other components of the protocol. If it does have some effect, it may be through teaching a distraction technique or imparting a sense of control. These are both fine things for people who often feel wildly out of control and overly focused on supposedly dangerous things. However, the most potent elements of the protocol involve having clients expose themselves to anxiety-provoking sensations and situations with sustained attention to learn that they are safe. Distraction through focused breathing may run counter to that goal. Thus, the newest approach is to teach controlled breathing to show patients how their symptoms may be reduced by changing their breathing. Once clients are able to draw the conclusions that many of their symptoms are the results of overbreathing and are thus controllable and harmless, the focus on breathing is phased out to allow pure focus on exposure to the feared sensations and situations of the final phases of treatment.

The two most strongly empirically supported components on the PCT protocol involve exposure (cf. Craske & Barlow, 2001). *Exposure* is broadly defined as a client allowing herself to experience the sustained presence of feared sensations or situations without distracting herself or escaping from them. These techniques come under Point 5, in which therapists encourage second-order change by helping clients to tolerate and accept potentially distressing circumstances without needing to take action on them. There are two basic spheres to which clients with panic and agoraphobia respond. The first is internal sensations, and the second is external situations. *Interoceptive exposure* has the goal of reducing clients' fear of specific bodily cues through repeated and systematic exposure to those sensations. This technique is an extension of that done in the behavioral component of assessment. In this intervention, the unique bodily sensations that each client experiences during panic are repeatedly induced in the therapy session through the same methods noted earlier (i.e., jogging in place, spinning, hyperventilating). This is done in a graduated format, with therapists discussing the nature of these sensations with clients, noting their similarity to panic sensations, rating anxiety levels, and noting how harmless they have been. This is a clear reversal of the client's normal solution pattern to avoid these sensations at all costs and thus never getting information that they are controllable and harmless. *In vivo* exposure is repeated, systematic, real-life exposure to feared situations. These situations are typically those assessed earlier with clients to be variably anxiety provoking. The main objective is to keep the client in the situation, focused on her reactions and circumstances without escape or diversion for as long as she can tolerate it. These trials, if clients have been willing to comply with them, have been found to be highly effective in reducing or eliminating panic and agoraphobia across a wide range of studies. This has been true for both individual and group formats and for both massed intense exposure and the more common graduated exposure. The most important point is that successful clients have entirely reversed their first-order patterns through the very therapeutic procedures used to treat them. They learn that they do not need to be hypervigilant to either bodily sensations or formerly anxiety-provoking situations. They also do not need to either try to avoid or attempt to control either these sensations or situations to feel secure and comfortable. This is second-order change. Here we revisit the case of Ann to see how intervention progressed may help bring this more to life.

Ann's therapy followed most of these elements with some interesting caveats. Ann was bright and very motivated. She had been to several therapists before. She had also read extensively on anxiety and agoraphobia, and she could clearly define both. Despite all of this, her condition had steadily worsened. Her first therapist had wondered about her need to control others and had extensive discussions about codependence. Her next therapist discussed the potential that she had been sexually abused as a child. Despite much soul searching, talks with her mother about her past, and even praying about it, she failed to find any evidence that this was so. Her reading on panic and agoraphobia led her to another therapist who instructed her in deep breathing and had her placing marbles into a jar each time she mastered a challenging situation. This had been somewhat helpful to her, but she mainly found that she could now mask her anxiety from most others and at best tolerate and manage situations and distract herself enough to forestall the inevitable panic attacks. She was now less able to leave her home, and did so with only great effort and with antianxiety medication.

She reluctantly agreed to be seen by a psychologist in her doctor's office through her doctor's suggestion. Ann was recovering from a recent gall bladder operation. She shared with the therapist that she had always wondered if this had all been simply physical. Maybe she had always reacted to the sensations of chronic gastrointestinal problems. Most recently, she had noticed that she had drunk a lot of caffeine at breakfast while recovering from her operation, and she had all of the old familiar sensations in front of her class. She managed to stay with her class and noticed that her distress subsided.

The therapist in this case accepted Ann's hypothesis on the physical triggers and proposed some experiments to see how much of this was self-induced anxiety and how much was caused by simple stomach distress. Ann agreed to try an odd-and-even day experiment. On odd days, she was to go to her class and try to think of as many catastrophic things as she could to bring herself toward panic and then rate her anxiety while she stayed in class. On even days, she was to again drink coffee or Coke at breakfast (with her doctor's consent) and go to class, noting the sensations she experienced and rating her degree of anxiety while remaining in the class. As several weeks went on, Ann found herself able to both stay in class and she found that the familiar panic-inducing sensations seemed most associated with purposely irritating her stomach. She then expanded the same experiments to going out with friends, driving, and eventually going with a group out of town for a weekend. Ann experienced incredible changes for herself in that she found herself panic-free within 2 months and able to move freely both in her classroom and in her life. She decided that it all must have been caused by a lifetime of panicking over gall bladder symptoms. Ann had collaborated with the exposure experiments because her therapist had honored her own explanations of her problem.

Social and Generalized Anxiety Disorders

> What worries you, masters you.
>
> —Haddon W. Robinson

Barlow (1988) used the term *anxious apprehension* to refer to a future-oriented mood state in which one prepares to attempt to cope with anticipated negative events. T. A. Brown, O'Leary, and Barlow (2001) stated the following,

> Whereas the *process* of anxious apprehension is present in all anxiety disorders, the *content* (focus) of anxious apprehension varies from disorder to disorder. . . . Nevertheless, the process of anxious apprehension is viewed to be key in the progression of initial symptoms into full-blown disorder. (p. 159)

Thus, the general foundations of what we have discussed so far in addressing panic and agoraphobia applies as well to that of social anxiety disorder and generalized anxiety disorder. It is mainly the focus of the worrying that differs along with the focus of the treatment.

The literature on social anxiety disorder suggests that people struggling with this form of anxiety tend to have formed fundamental negative beliefs about themselves and others. They tend to expect to behave in inept and socially inappropriate ways in social settings and expect others to hold expectations that they are unlikely to be able to meet. Research has shown that these people tend to judge their own social behavior more harshly than others and to overestimate the visibility of their anxiety and any related social missteps or supposed stumbles compared with what others might actually notice. Devoting excessive attention to detecting social threats has been found to narrow their attention to threatening cues and social gaffes and interfere with their ability to process anything positive that might counteract their hypercritical appraisals (Turk et al., 2001). As noted earlier, this process often becomes a self-fulfilling prophecy resulting in actual social deficits from lack of practice and social and performance mistakes caused by the person becoming socially constrained and overly self-critical. As Turk et al. (2001) said, "Negative predictions result in cognitive, behavioral, and physiological symptoms of anxiety, which eventually feed back into the negatively biased mental representation of the self and perpetuate the cycle of anxiety (p. 123). Once more we find the vicious cycle of first-order change creating a solution-generated problem.

Cognitive–Behavioral Group Therapy

Cognitive–behavioral group therapy (CBGT) has been found to be a leading empirically supported treatment for social anxiety disorder (Hofmann & Barlow, 2002). Its proponents describe it thus: "CBGT works to break the vicious cycle of anxiety . . . through integration of cognitive restructuring and exposure techniques" (Turk et al., 2001, p. 123). As mentioned earlier in our discussion of panic, the addition of cognitive restructuring to pure exposure has not been consistently found to produce better results than pure exposure alone, yet discussing clients' overwhelming negative appraisals of themselves and beliefs about others and social situations remains so compelling a rationale for treatment that it continues to be used (cf. Turk et al., 2001, pp. 118–120, for further discussion). The exposure component interrupts the spiral by allowing clients to experience normal reductions in anxiety that come from repeatedly staying in social situations long enough and practicing social skills such as being assertive or asking someone for a date while in these situations; this allows them to check the correctness of their predictions that they will draw blanks or that everyone will notice their anxiety in these settings. The cognitive restructuring component addresses the usefulness of clients' beliefs and assumptions to see whether they actually make sense or are helpful and provides alternate ways of considering these situations. If successful, such reframes may lead to clients feeling less anxious as they enter social situations, thus experiencing fewer physical symptoms and being better able to devote their attention and resources to positive interaction and feedback. Furthermore, this cognitive restructuring serves as a key therapeutic rationale to encourage clients to reverse their avoidance of social situations and expose themselves to group interactions so they can conduct experiments and refine new skills. Such reversals are again the heart of second-order change. Once a client agrees to engage in the reversal, he is more than halfway home to his goal of becoming comfortable socially. As might be imagined, getting clients to agree to such group treatment has been a challenge, and dropping out can be a problem as well. One might say that the success of these groups may be based on the preselection of people willing to reverse their first-order solutions and enter social situations to begin with.

Once more, it is crucial that clients both trust their therapist and invest in the therapeutic rationale to become successful. Once engaged, however, there is no better controlled setting for social anxiety treatment than in a group. These groups usually have four to seven members and meet for 12 weekly 2½-hour sessions with cotherapists who guide the clients through a series of graded exercises tailored to each client's unique struggles, appraisals of self and others, and levels of anxiety. Group sessions include explaining the cognitive model; sharing goals; progressively identifying cognitive thoughts to examine in the group; group in-session exposure exercises; and continual homework exercises to be done outside the group, which are discussed in the following group sessions (cf. Turk et al., 2001). The more group members comply and engage with these processes, the more they gain both comfort with the situations they most feared and gradually shape new beliefs and assumptions about themselves and others as they build self-confidence and refine social skills.

A case example that illustrates this further involves John. John had struggled with all of the classic characteristics of social anxiety disorder and had also developed a severe alcohol problem. Numerous clinical and epidemiological studies indicate that a significant percentage of people with social anxiety abuse alcohol and, conversely, a significant rate of social anxiety has been found among alcoholics who note that they used alcohol to reduce their social anxiety. This presented a problem for John in that most alcoholic treatment programs rely on group formats, as does the group treatment of social anxiety discussed here. It appeared that John would need to reverse his usual avoidant solution to dealing with social situations to get treatment for either his social anxiety or his alcoholism. John, however, had lost so much through his social anxiety and drinking that he had become desperate. The key to his eventual success actually rested in the relationship he established with an extended family member and a therapist. His uncle continued to offer support and confidence messages from afar over the years. His therapist is the person who gradually helped John to consider taking steps toward the cognitive–behavioral group. Initially, John was helped by medication in attending the first few groups, but he soon discontinued it as he progressed in the group. He was eventually able to attend his first alcohol treatment group with the growing confidence gained through the CBGT treatment. He has now attended several large family functions, is in final interviews for a position in his field, and he has gotten his driver's license back. John would attribute his success to his therapist. We might suggest that it was this relationship that moved John to engaging in the kind of treatments which actively helped him reverse his solution-generated problems of social anxiety and alcohol use.

Worry, Exposure, and Acceptance

You cannot plow a field by turning it over in your mind.

—Anonymous

Generalized anxiety disorder eventually emerged as its own disorder in the diagnostic and statistical manuals only after a long history of being thought of as just excessive worry. However, as noted earlier, this pervasive worry pattern has taken over many people's lives to the extent that it has severely impaired their existence. The major interventions for GAD are typically a combination of cognitive therapy, worry exposure, relaxation training, worry behavior prevention, time management, and problem solving. T. A. Brown et al. (2001, p. 177) presented a useful summary table outline of a 13-session treatment protocol of this sort. Once again, we need to emphasize that the first 2 sessions are seen as crucial to the success of treatment in that they lay out the rationale for treatment, define the roles of therapist and client, and explain the nature of anxiety and the reasons for the vicious cycles of continual worry. Clients are also inoculated about the anxiety increases they will feel in treatment and the reasons for this. Investing in the rationale is crucial to going forward with therapy. Once it is set, then the rest of the elements can be engaged as allied procedures.

In the *cognitive therapy* component, clients are first instructed in the cognitive model and then proceed to learn about how people overestimate the probability of negative events and how they can get into the habit of catastrophic thinking about potentially negative outcomes. Much of this component includes in-session exercises and discussion of examples that further lay out the rationale for treatment and lead to homework exercises to check out the truth value and usefulness of their beliefs and predictions. The realistic likelihood of different feared events and the potential impact of the worst possible outcomes happening are collaboratively evaluated. Worry exposure is one of the key reversals in the approach. Again, the rationale is critical to having clients go toward what they most fear. In this case, the idea is that habituation has never happened because clients tend to shift rapidly from one worry to the next. Then clients are trained in session to imagine their two or three most common worries; trained in vivid imagery; then in imagining the worst possible feared outcome in a given sphere of worry; then holding that image clearly in mind during session for 25 to 30 minutes; and, finally, evaluating the degree of their anxiety. This is repeated for the next two spheres in session. The client is then instructed to practice this at home. *Relaxation training* focuses on training clients in the skills of progressive muscle relaxation until they can automatically induce this relaxation in other settings with a combination of centered deep breathing and oral repetition of the word *relax*. Clients then use this as a skill to counter anxiety sensations as they progress with daily life. *Worry behavior prevention* refers to first identifying the most common behaviors clients use to temporarily reduce their anxiety (e.g., calls to loved ones at work on at home, refusal to read negative stories in newspapers or listen to them on radio or television). Then the clients are asked to monitor how often these behaviors occur each week, and eventually they are helped with concrete ways to refrain from them and instead keep themselves exposed to the feared situations. The remaining two components, *time management* and *problem solving*, focus on moving clients out of the position of "spinning their wheels" in scattered worry work and feeling overwhelmed and instead teach the client efficient time management skills and proven problem-solving practices. In these ways, clients are enabled to actually address those things needing action and take care of them and allow or accept that others will take care of themselves.

Acceptance and Mindfulness

One of the most recent and interesting developments in the evolution of empirically supported treatments is the "discovery" and application of mindfulness and acceptance forms of interventions (Hayes, Follette, & Linehan, 2004; Kabat-Zinn, 1990; Segal et al., 2002). *Mindfulness* has been defined as "a process that involves moving toward a state in which one is fully observant of external and internal stimuli in the present moment, and open to accepting (rather than attempting to change or judge) the current situation" (Orsillo, Romer, Lerner, & Tull, 2004, p. 349). Acceptance is implied in this definition, in that current experience is validated and affirmed without judgment or need for change. Mindfulness parallels the meditative practices of such Eastern perspectives as Zen Buddhism. Acceptance is closely aligned with the dialectical perspective noted in chapter 3 (this volume) and is more explicitly discussed later, in chapter 11 (this volume), relating to dialectical behavior therapy. We return repeatedly to this concept of acceptance in many of the coming chapters, because the concept of acceptance and its related technique of mindfulness have contributed greatly to the success of many of the recent approaches to empirically supported treatments. A text titled *Mindfulness and Acceptance: Expanding the Cognitive–Behavioral Tradition* (Hayes et al., 2004) attests to the excitement this perspective has added. Not coincidentally, acceptance is closely related to the dialectical perspective, out of which comes the concept of first- and second-order change, the golden thread that connects effective treatments.

As applied to anxiety, and GAD in particular, mindfulness and acceptance have introduced some hope for even greater effectiveness (Borkovec & Sharpless, 2004; Orsillo et al., 2004). Much of this attention can be traced to the life's work of John Kabat-Zinn (1994), who applied mindfulness meditation to anxiety, pain management, and a wide range of other problems within a medical center setting. Ever since the success of an open trial of his mindfulness-based stress reduction for a mixed group of persons with anxiety disorders (Kabat-Zin et al., 1992), there has been increasing excitement and attention directed to the use of acceptance in commonly change-oriented approaches. Approaches such as acceptance and commitment therapy (Hayes, Strosahl, & Wilson, 1999), dialectical behavioral therapy (Linehan, 1993; see chap. 11, this volume), integrative couple therapy (Jacobson & Christensen, 1996; see chap. 8, this volume), and mindfulness-based cognitive therapy for depression (Segal et al., 2002; see chap. 7, this volume), have all heavily borrowed from this tradition. As it is applied to GAD in particular, it is used for purposes beyond being simply a variant of exposure.

The rationale and goal of mindfulness- and acceptance-based approaches to GAD are different from traditional exposure-based cognitive–behavioral interventions. In effect, mindfulness nips the vicious cycles of first-order worry in the bud by eliminating any need to control, fix, or act upon the worry, thought, situation, or experience associated with anxiety. Clients are taught to maintain a calmly present-centered focus on these thoughts, worries, experiences, and situations without the need to judge or change them. They are experienced as merely thoughts that may be passing by, just as clouds pass through the sky. In contrast to the basis of most cognitive–behavioral approaches, there is no attempt at control of these experiences, only acceptance of them. In fact, paradoxically, when clients attempt to use mindful acceptance as a way to control or eliminate their anxiety, they may actually increase their anxiety rather than decreasing it. Only when full acceptance is embraced will the client either experience less anxiety or be able to function effectively with the awareness of anxiety. This intervention is the essence of second-order change.

FOLLOWING THE THREAD

Anxiety is typically seen as the result of trying to master anxiety by avoiding it. The first-order vicious cycle is the result of hypervigilance and sensitivity to anxiety cues, which only provokes more anxiety and prevents mastery. Second-order interventions offer rationales explaining the cycle and the difference between fear and anxiety. They then prescribe reversals in the pattern by moving clients toward their anxiety to master it. Anxiety presents the paradigm case of first-order vicious cycles that are resolved by classic examples of second-order change interventions. It is an appropriate problem to start our journey through empirically supported psychotherapies, not only because of the classic vicious cycles but also because the golden thread of second-order change runs so richly through all of the fabric of these effective approaches. By staying grounded in this golden thread perspective of problems and their resolution, clinicians will be able to creatively, flexibly, and effectively apply the range of these effective approaches to their wide array of clients.

7

DEPRESSION

There is nothing either good or bad, but thinking makes it so.
—William Shakespeare, *Hamlet*, Act II, Scene 2

To be, or not to be: That is the question: Whether 'tis nobler in the mind to suffer the slings and arrows of outrageous fortune or to take arms against a sea of troubles, and by opposing end them.
—William Shakespeare, *Hamlet*, Act III, Scene 1

These two quotes regarding William Shakespeare's famous "Melancholy Dane," Hamlet, represent the major themes of two of today's prominent evidence-supported treatments for depression. The first theme is that our thoughts or cognitions have a major influence over our mood. Hamlet's thinking was pervaded by consistently dark thoughts about himself, his situation, and his future. The second theme is that interpersonal distress and relationship issues are the main cause of mood disorders like depression and thoughts of suicide. Hamlet considered his own suicide as a result of his overwhelming grief over his father's death and the subsequent loss of his mother's attention to her new husband, who may have murdered Hamlet's father. As we might guess, the two leading treatments for depression, cognitive–behavioral therapy (CBT) and interpersonal psychotherapy (IPT), focus their treatment on each of the two factors supposed to underlie depression: cognitions and relationships, respectively. Yet which is more effective? If they are both equally effective, how can this be so? These two assumptions or premises for treating depression seem to be so different. Furthermore, are there other, equally effective treatments? Both dark thoughts and interpersonal tragedy were equally present in Hamlet's life. Is treatment choice, then, more a product of what the therapist chooses to focus on, or what makes sense to the client, or is it a product of changing what is actually causing the client to be depressed? In this chapter we address the answers to these questions.

DEPRESSION DEFINED

Along with anxiety, depression is one of the most commonly seen problems by physicians and mental health providers alike. Major depressive disorder is the most frequently diagnosed disorder in adults. Over 19 million adults in America have some variation of depression each year, with lifetime rates among women ranging from 20% to 25% and from 9% to 12% for men (American Psychiatric Association, 1994; National Institute of Mental Health, 1999). These gender differences also hold up across populations. A leading cause of disability, depression has enormous interpersonal and financial costs in both the cost of treatment and in lost productivity.

Clinical Variations and Definitions

There are two main categories of depression that we address in this chapter. These are *major depressive disorder* and *dysthymic disorder*. The *Diagnostic and Statistical Manual of Mental Disorders* (4th ed. [DSM–IV]; American Psychiatric Association, 1994) offers the official criteria for each disorder. For major depressive disorder, the person must evidence marked distress or a decrease in her level of functioning. Furthermore, she must also experience a daily occurrence of dysphoric mood (tearful, sad, or empty) or lack of interest or pleasure in most activities. In addition, the person must also experience at least four of the following (three if both loss of interest in activities and depressed mood are present), with most occurring nearly daily: significant loss of weight or change in appetite; inability to get to sleep, or sleeping too much; psychomotor agitation or retardation; loss of energy or fatigue; feelings of worthlessness or excessive or inappropriate guilt; decreased concentration or indecisiveness; or recurring thoughts of death. Major depressive disorder has been the major focus of most treatment research and the source of greatest treatment success (Craighead, Hart, Craighead, & Ilardi, 2002). Dysthymic disorder was added to the DSM in 1980, and its diagnosis has continued to be refined to distinguish it as a chronic disorder rather than some form of personality disorder. It affects approximately 3% of adults in America and may account for as much as 36% of the population of mental health clinics, with women two to three times more likely to have the diagnosis than men (Markowitz, 1998). The DSM–IV sets out the criterion that the depressed mood is present for most of the day, for more days than not, for at least 2 years, with at least two or more of the list of six symptoms used for major depression present. The person must have never been without the symptoms for more than 2 months at a time over the previous 2 years, with no major depressive, manic, or psychotic episodes and no evidence of the depression having been the result of substance abuse, medication, or medical conditions. Overall, the symptoms must have caused clinically significant distress or impairment in social, occupational, or other important areas of functioning. Dysthymic disorder refers to a chronic depressed condition, and it has been much less successfully treated; even when treatment has appeared successful, there is a high incidence of relapse.

Two Competing Descriptions

There are a number of different perspectives that we might use to describe the process of depression. However, in keeping with our look at those treatments that have been designated as effective on the basis of available research, we will focus on two major evidence-supported treatments. The first of these is the cognitive therapy for depression (designated as CBT for cognitive–behavioral therapy), developed by Aaron T. Beck and his colleagues (Beck, Rush, Shaw, & Emery, 1979). The second is the interpersonal psychotherapy of depression approach (IPT), developed by Gerald L. Klerman and his colleagues (Klerman, Weissman, Rounsaville, & Chevron, 1984). To be clear, there is at least one other approach, behavioral therapy for depression, with at least the same demonstrated effectiveness as there first two. We address this third option later, along with another approach that is based in mindfulness and acceptance. However, our main focus will be on the CBT and IPT approaches to conceptualizing and intervening with depression. One reason for discussing these two alternative approaches is that they are based in very different psychological and philosophical traditions. The CBT traditions are based in cognitive, rational, empirical, and logical positivist assumptions. The IPT traditions are based on interpersonal, dynamic, and process assumptions. These separate assumptions generally lead therapists in very different directions in conceptualizing and treating depressed patients. The main reason for our choice, however, is the broad attention that these two approaches have gained by being selected for study in one of the largest and most carefully controlled studies to date on the effectiveness of different treatments for depression.

The National Institute of Mental Health Treatment of Depression Collaborative Research Program (NIMH TDCRP; Elkin et al., 1989) is the largest multicenter comparative clinical treatment trial in psychotherapy ever conducted to date. It compared medication and clinical management with the drug imipramine (IMI-CM) with CBT, IPT, and placebo with clinical management (PLA-CM). The study included 250 outpatient clients identified as experiencing major depressive disorder as measured by a number of widely accepted diagnostic scales. Each patient was randomly assigned to one of the four 16-week conditions noted earlier. All treatments were standardized, and manuals were used to train and supervise therapists. Treatment adherence measures were carefully monitored to be sure that the standard treatment was being applied. The treatment was provided at several separate centers, and a broad range of different measures were conducted throughout treatment. Although this massive study has been the subject of many subsequent analyses, many of which we discuss in this chapter, the major finding that has received so much notoriety is that, for those patients who completed the study, all three active treatments equally succeeded in reducing depression at posttreatment. For example, the percentages of patients who reduced their depression below the clinical level (Hamilton Rating Scale for Depression score of 6 or less) for each condition, respectively, was CBT = 36%, IPT = 43%, and IMP-CM = 42%. This and other, more refined results from the study became a strong statement that psychotherapy was at least as effective as medication in treating depression. This was reason for rejoicing among psychotherapists, yet it raised some equally compelling questions. The main question among these was how such apparently different approaches to depression as CBT and IPT have such similar effectiveness in helping depressed clients feel better. We address some answers to this question presently, but first we need to look at how each approach describes depression. Therapists practicing each approach are guided by these assumptions about the condition that they are treating.

Self-Fulfilling Prophecies

Aaron Beck's cognitive model (Beck et al., 1979) suggests three specific concepts to help explain depression. The combination of these three paints a picture of what becomes the self-fulfilling prophecy of depression for clients. The three areas are (a) the cognitive triad, (b) schemas, and (c) cognitive errors (faulty information processing). The cognitive triad is composed of three patterns that draw the person into viewing herself, her future, and her experiences in a unique way. First, the client develops a negative view of herself, assuming that because of her presumed deficits, she is undesirable and worthless. The second pattern is that the depressed person tends to interpret her ongoing experiences in a negative way, viewing situations as intolerable obstacles and confirmations of how bad things really are. The third component is that clients have negative views of the future, anticipating that their current difficulties or suffering will continue indefinitely. The resulting symptoms of depression noted earlier are thus viewed as following from the combination of these three client distortions of their reality. When clients are listless and withdraw to avoid their life demands, these actions are viewed as a result of clients' pessimism and hopelessness given that they expect negative events and a negative outcome of their efforts. Clients become increasingly dependant on others because they view themselves as inept and helpless and because they overestimate how difficult normal tasks will be and assume their efforts alone will only turn out badly.

Apathy and low energy are seen as logical results of the client's view that he is doomed to failure.

Beck agrees that most depressive episodes are triggered by the wide range of life difficulties that we all encounter. These may in particular include real or perceived losses but may also include the numerous economic, health, and interpersonal distresses that may arise. He adapts the concept of *schemas* from the work of Piaget (1947/1950, 1932/1960) and others to explain how a depressed person comes to act on these as triggers to evolve what we have called *solution-generated problem patterns*. He defined *schemas* as relatively stable cognitive patterns that serve as the basis for interpreting particular sets of situations. They help screen out, differentiate, and code stimuli into familiar, understandable, and predictable patterns that may then be responded to with an appropriate repertoire of reactions. Beck described people as evaluating experiences through a matrix of schemas that have generally been developed through early life events. These schemas are not particularly good or bad. As we discussed earlier, the concept of schemas is another way of describing the normal and natural process we all use to help make our world a little more safe and predictable. They tend to be the set of premises and assumptions regarding the way things are in a given domain that forms the basis of what we have described as first-order change. Beck suggested that many of these schemas lie dormant until they are energized by specific environmental inputs (e.g., stressful situations). A person's idiosyncratic schemas may or may not match those of most others for a given situation, but they will match that person's personal history and serve as a filter for her to arrange and react to it. In the case of depression, these schemas are described as particularly negative, distorted, and dysfunctional. However, the more those schemas are used, the more they drive the self-fulfilling negative prophecy, and the more widely they are evoked and applied. Eventually, these schema-driven patterns are said to take on a life of their own, becoming autonomous. The depressed person becomes less and less able to entertain the idea that her negative interpretations may be erroneous. She may eventually become preoccupied with pervasive negative thoughts about herself, her world, and her future, with all of the related symptoms of depression present.

Cognitive errors or faulty information processing is the final leg of this three-legged stool. These are a series of logical errors characteristic of depressive thinking that serve to maintain the person's belief in the validity of his negative concepts. Beck et al. (1979) described these errors as nondimensional and global ("I am fearful"), absolutistic and moralistic ("I am a despicable coward"), invariant ("I always have been and always will be a coward"), having assumptions about character diagnosis ("I have a defect in my character"), and irreversible ("Since I am basically weak, there's nothing that can be done about it"). These qualities are compared with more functional thinking, which is characterized as multidimensional, relativistic and nonjudgmental, variable, reversible, and leads to "behavioral diagnoses." Beck et al.'s list of thinking errors includes: *arbitrary inference, when a conclusion is drawn in the absence of evidence or in the face of evidence to the contrary; selective abstraction,* when a detail is taken out of context to characterize a whole experience, and other salient features of the situation are ignored; *overgeneralization, when one or more isolated incidents are used to draw a general rule or conclusion and apply it across broadly related and unrelated situations; magnification and minimization,* when perceived negative events or qualities are inflated and positive ones depreciated; *personalization,* whereby a person relates external events to herself when there is no basis for making such a connection; and *absolutistic, dichotomous thinking,* whereby all experiences are cast into one of two opposite categories. As might be imagined, each error and the combination of errors will tend to initiate and perpetuate their own vicious cycle of problems that characterize the depressed person's experience.

Beck et al. (1979) noted that a depressed person tends to have enough of an effect on her environment and those around him to actually create situations that match his expectations. He may isolate herself from others, and others may withdraw from him because he is not enjoyable to be with, and so on. This can create an interpersonal self-fulfilling prophecy whereby what the person expects from his world eventually shapes his interactions to match those beliefs. However, Beck et al. pay much more attention to what he described as "the primacy of cognitive factors in depression." They suggested that

> in taking a "cross section" of the symptomatology of depression, we have arrived at the position that we should look for the primary psychopathology in the peculiar way the individual views himself, his experiences, and his future (the "cognitive triad") and his idiosyncratic way of processing information (arbitrary inference, selective recall, overgeneralization, etc.). . . . If the diagnostician does not search for other pathology, he may miss the primary phenomenon in the chain of events, namely the thinking disorder. (Beck et al., 1979, p. 19)

Although the model does not address the ultimate etiology, or cause, of major depression, it does point to the way depressed people think of their selves, their experiences, and their future as the primary factor that drives the self-fulfilling prophecies of their depression.

Interpersonal Vicious Cycles

The IPT approach to depression follows a different tack to describe depression. This perspective locates the essence of depression in the interpersonal relationships of the depressed person. It is grounded firmly in the interpersonal dynamic views of Harry Stack Sullivan (1953) and on the attachment theory of Bowlby (1969). In their manual on the IPT approach, Klerman et al. (1984) stated that

> The theoretical foundation of the interpersonal approach has been best summarized by Sullivan, who taught that psychiatry involves the scientific study of people and the processes between people, rather than focusing exclusively on the mind, society, or the brain. Hence the unit of clinical study is the patient's interpersonal relations at any one particular time. (p. 47)

Thus, this perspective views disturbances in interpersonal relations as antecedents to emotional distress like that of depression. In their IPT manual, Klerman and his collaborators went on to state that

> While we believe that past and ongoing interpersonal relationships are related to depression, we cannot always establish the direction of causation . . . although disruptions of interpersonal relationships are not in themselves "necessary and sufficient" to produce clinical depressions, interpersonal difficulties are usually associated with clinical depression. (p. 51)

They cited Bowlby (1977) as suggesting that psychotherapy should help the patient examine current interpersonal relationships and understand how they have developed from experiences with attachment figures in childhood, adolescence, and adulthood. This is an area that should sound vaguely similar to that of Beck and his description of the development of schemas. However, the interpersonal approach makes much more of the reciprocal vicious cycles that evolve in the relationships of depressed people and those who interact with them than does the cognitive view. Markowitz (1998), in his IPT manual for treating dysthymic disorders, described this thus

> The fundamental concept of IPT is that depression does not occur in a vacuum, but rather in a social context. When bad things happen, you feel bad. Conversely, when you feel depressed, you tend to mishandle your social role, to interact ineffectively, and so bad things are likely to happen. This can result in a vicious cycle; bad events lead to worsening mood, which in turn leads to further bad events. (p. 44)

The interpersonal view emphasizes some very real reciprocal patterns that cocreate depressive patterns in the depressed person's partner relationships, family, work, and community activities. Klerman et al. (1984) cited the work of Coyne (1976), among others, who found that depressed people not only elicited unhelpful responses from others but also created mutual negativity and depressed reactions from the people with whom the depressed person interacted. Klerman et al. noted that depressed people are depressing to have around; they are evaluated negatively and often avoided. Thus a vicious cycle evolves whereby the depressed person not only feels negative about herself, her experiences, and the future but also those appraisals come to match her situation through coevolving interactions with others. As Markowitz (1998) suggested, "Depressed patients tend to withdraw socially and retreat inwardly, frequently spending much of their time alone or even laying [sic] in bed. . . . The patient who lies in bed thinking, 'I'm useless, I'm not doing anything' is in some measure correct" (p. 52). A depressing personal and interpersonal reality is thus created and is quite real. At one level, this view is at odds with the cognitive perspective that assumes that the depressed person's cognitions represent errors or distortions of her reality. The interpersonal position suggests that the depressed person's appraisals of her situation may in some ways be correct. Yet those depressing situations and relationships may be equally correctable as the depressed person examines her options and takes actions to change them.

The interpersonal viewpoint notes that sadness and an occasional depressed mood are a normal part of the human condition, with disruptions in interpersonal relationships resulting in nearly universal feelings of sadness. However, when a particular instance of interpersonal distress matches an important area of historical distress for a person, such as a critical loss of a loved one, or the threat of loss, and so on, this triggers responses similar to those discussed from the cognitive approach as schema-related. At times, our assumptions and related ways of interacting may easily assimilate our distress, help us adjust to it, or both. Problems develop, however, when our initial solutions fail and some variation is reapplied. This is an exact parallel to what we have discussed previously as first-order assumptions driving first-order solutions into the now-familiar solution-generated problems.

A major set of constructs that guide the interpersonal description of depression are that there tend to be four main areas on interpersonal distress around which depression evolves (Klerman et al., 1984). These interpersonal domains include (a) *grief,* which focuses on the person's reaction to the actual death of a person or people, either now or in the past; (b) *role disputes,* which involves analyzing interpersonal disputes with friends, family, partners, or coworkers; (c) *transitions,* which involve role change resulting from life events such as marrying, taking a new job, becoming a student, becoming a parent, and the like; and (d) *interpersonal deficits,* which relate mainly to interpersonal isolation and the related poor quality and quantity of the depressed person's interpersonal relationships. The key element here is that the depressed person responds to each area of interpersonal distress in a way that sets up a characteristic vicious cycle that eventually takes on a life of its own. The cycle eventually becomes an actual syndrome called *clinical depression.* One critical aspect of treatment, as we shall see, is educating the depressed client about depression and letting the client know that it is no more his or her fault than having diabetes or a broken leg would be. The interpersonal view suggests that the depressed symptoms are a natural result of failing to look at options to resolve critical areas of interpersonal distress and then take action to resolve them.

Solution-Generated Problems

Both approaches to depression view it as evolving from reactions to distressing yet common life events. In their chapter on cognitive therapy for depression, Young, Weinberger, and Beck (2001) emphasized the following quote:

> Research dealing with the onset of particular episodes of adult depression has concluded that the majority are provoked by life events or ongoing difficulties; the role of events has emerged as clearly the more important of the two. . . . Studies have suggested that about 66%–90% of depressed episodes have a severe event occurring within six months of onset. . . .The majority of these events involve some element of loss. (p. 265)

Similarly, in Beck et al.'s (1979) now-classic manual for conducting cognitive therapy in the treatment of depression, they state that "The precipitants of depression revolve around a perceived or actual loss" (p. 24). In his manual for doing interpersonal therapy for depression, Markowitz (1998) stated that "The fundamental concept of IPT is that depression does not occur in a vacuum but rather in a social context. When bad things happen you feel bad" (p. 43). In the original IPT manual for treating depression, Klerman et al. (1984) stated that "Clinical depression and related affective disorders involve an accentuation in the intensity or duration of otherwise normal emotions" (p. 29). But, just as with most problems, it is not the event that creates the problem but the way the event is handled or responded to that creates the pattern of the problem. People who develop the classic symptoms of depression have tended to take themselves and their emotions out of context. Thus, as they attempt to solve their distress, they focus on themselves and initiate a downward spiral that becomes a self-fulfilling prophecy. Furthermore, because feeling depressed is such a common emotion, Klerman and his colleagues also noted that "family and friends tend to minimize the severity of the patient's difficulties because the manifestations seem to be normal responses to life situations" (p. 30). This feeds the cycle of disconfirmation and alienation for the person feeling depressed, further locking in the downward spiral.

Describing this problem pattern of depression, Markowitz (1998) went on to say that

> when you feel depressed, you tend to mishandle your social role, to interact ineffectively, and so bad things are likely to happen. This can result in a vicious cycle; bad events lead to worsening mood, which in turn leads to further bad events. (p. 44)

Beck et al. (1979) echoed this analysis in suggesting that

> A person slipping into depression may withdraw from significant other people. Thus alienated, the "significant others" may respond with rejections or criticisms, which in turn, activate or aggravate the person's own self-rejection and self-criticism. . . . Thus the vicious cycle can continue until the patient is so depressed that he may be impervious to attempts by others to help him and show him love and affection. (p. 17)

Looking at a similar process, Young and his colleagues (2001) stated that "The severely depressed patient is caught in a vicious cycle in which a reduced activity level leads to a negative self-label, which in turn results in even further discouragement and consequent inactivity" (p. 281).

Both of these two major approaches thus describe depression in terms of what we have called solution-generated problems. Our past experiences shape our premises and assumptions, which in turn direct our actions or solutions, which in turn shape the pattern of our interactions. Once again, it is not the distressing event or change or perceived difficulty that is the problem. It is instead the pattern of how that perceived difficulty has come to be viewed and solved that becomes the problem. Change is constant and inevitable. It is the process of how we negotiate change that inevitably becomes the focus of our problem assessments and interventions. As therapists, our task is to help clients to change how they are negotiating change, that is, to help clients negotiate a second-order change, in this case, of the cycle of their depression. Both the CBT and the IPT approach take this goal as their task in their approach to psychotherapy for depression.

INTERVENTION

As we examine these two empirically supported approaches to treating depressed clients, an interesting paradox emerges. On one hand, the techniques of these two approaches (especially of the CBT approach) have often been broadly pointed to as evidence for the primacy of interventions over relationship in effective psychotherapy. On the other hand, the authors of these two approaches have jointly emphasized in their manuals for treatment the importance of relationship. Furthermore, Markowitz (1998), in his IPT manual for treatment of dysthymic disorder, explicitly parallels the IPT approach with the contextual model of Jerome Frank (Frank & Frank, 1991), which we discussed extensively in chapters 4 and 5 (this volume).

Beck et al. (1979) stated that

> The aspiring *cognitive therapist* must be, first, a good *psychotherapist*. He must possess necessary characteristics such as the capacity to respond to the patient in the atmosphere of a human relationship—with concern, acceptance, and sympathy. No matter how proficient he is in the techni-

cal application of cognitive strategies, he will be severely hampered if he is not adequately endowed with these essential interpersonal characteristics. (p. 25)

They devoted an entire section of their manual to describing desirable characteristics of the therapist, including, warmth, accurate empathy, genuineness, basic trust, and rapport gained through the therapeutic relationship. Turning to the interpersonal approach of IPT, it goes without saying that the client's relationships, including that with the therapist, are of paramount focus. However, Klerman et al. (1984) went further by supporting the contextual model of Frank: "Like Frank (1973), we believe that the procedures and techniques of many of the schools of psychotherapy have much in common (p. 14)." Markowitz (1998) elaborated on this in his manual: "IPT contains all the nonspecific factors conceded to be important to the efficacy of any psychotherapy (Frank, 1971): *providing a setting and a ritual for treatment, a sympathetic, understanding listener, an affectively charged therapeutic alliance, an explanation for the patient's woes, therapeutic optimism, and success experiences*" (p. 43, italics in the original). As we shall see, these elements hold true in the research regarding these two approaches. First, however, we need to examine exactly what each approach does in assessing and intervening with depressed clients. To integrate our discussion of the two separate approaches, we organize our description according to the elements of Frank's contextual model.

The Cognitive Approach

> Change your thoughts and you change your world.
> —Norman Vincent Peale

An Emotionally Charged Relationship

In introducing their cognitive protocol for treating depression, Beck et al. (1979) took extra care in emphasizing the need for therapists to foster all of the basic characteristics of warmth, genuineness, empathy, and other related characteristics that contribute to a trusting relationship and a firm therapeutic bond with clients. They urged flexibility in adapting their cognitive protocol to each client rather than fitting clients to the protocol. This has been found across numerous studies of a variety of approaches to be related to effective intervention. However, even before discussing the need to foster a strong therapeutic alliance, Beck et al. devoted an entire chapter to the role of emotions in cognitive therapy. Although most psychotherapy focuses on emotions as the key indicators of distress, the cognitive view treats them as a fulcrum to use in leveraging clients to change. Whereas cognitive therapy is often viewed as extremely rational and cerebral, the therapist's focus, in early sessions in particular, is on clients' emotional expression. As clients express emotion, their therapist uses these expressions as an opportunity to collaborate with the client in both learning the connection between thoughts and emotion and in examining what their emotions suggest about the way they are thinking about themselves and their circumstances. The emotional relationship in cognitive therapy is viewed as the door to both building the rationale for explaining and understanding the client's distress and for taking action to begin to help clients to relieve that distress. The classic question "What was going through your mind just before you began to cry?" along with other questions like it, is a hallmark of how therapists collaborate with clients to deconstruct the meaning of clients emotions.

The Rationale or "Myth"

One of the most important elements of successful cognitive therapy is presenting the general plan and rationale for cognitive treatment during the first and second sessions. Therapists explain the relationship between thoughts and feelings, using examples and taking advantage of clients' own emotions to show the connection with their thoughts. Therapists describe the natural course of depression and its symptoms and relate that course to common ways that clients have learned to think of themselves and their world. They note how these ways of thinking then become automatic habits, going unexamined and often becoming disconnected from what may actually be the case about themselves, their situations, and the future. Clients are offered hope as therapists explain that these common thinking patterns have been found to underlie depression and that a collaborative process of learning about these thinking patterns, examining their truth and usefulness, and taking action to alter their thinking and situations has been found to be very successful in relieving depression. The cognitive triad described earlier is set forward as the rationale for understanding depression and serves as the basis for the collaboratively empirical approach that therapists and clients will take to examining the evidence supporting or disconfirming clients' depressive assumptions.

A Set of Rituals or Procedures

Clients are then guided through the process of assessment and treatment that will help them discover how they are thinking about themselves and their circumstances, and what effect this has had on their lives, and then they will learn how to take action to change those patterns of related thought and action to make things better. The spirit of "collaborative empiricism," or the joint discovery of the truth and utility of clients' views and interaction patterns, is established early on. As a team, the client and therapist first seek out the nature of the client's automatic thoughts and schemas and then take them on as scientists address questions, treating each thought and schema as a hypothesis to be tested and gathering evidence that will either support or refute each hypothesis. To do this, clients will be asked to be very active in gathering data and examining evidence. In this way, clients are helped to discover the illogic or inconsistency with reality of their thinking on their own, rather than having therapists confronting them or persuading them of this. As clients learn the nature of automatic thoughts and thinking errors and their connection to ongoing events in their life, they also learn how important it will be to learn exactly how their thinking patterns operate in their own life. Assessment is begun at the first session and continued at every session. The most commonly used forms are the Beck Depression Inventory (BDI; Beck & Steer, 1987); the Beck Hopelessness Scale (Beck, Weissman, Lester, & Trexler, 1974); and the Beck Anxiety Scale (Beck, Epstein, Brown, & Steer, 1988). These scales are used to assess the client's depression at the beginning and throughout the course of treatment. Because the questions are so directly related to clients' thoughts, they are also used to help clients see the connections between their thoughts and perceptions and their emotions at the beginning and during treatment.

Rather than avoiding those circumstances that provoke anger, sadness, hopelessness, anxiety, guilt, and other emotions related to depression, clients are asked to attend to them in session and at home to learn more about them. Along with asking clients what thoughts precede their emotions in session, therapists may also ask clients to evoke these emotions in session by asking the patient to picture these emotion-evoking situations. Patients are often able to identify automatic thoughts connecting these situations with their emotions. Therapists also may role play interpersonal situations with clients to actively evoke emotions and reveal their related automatic thoughts. In essence, this and subsequent homework to be discussed are pattern reversals similar to the exposure we discussed extensively in the previous chapter on interventions with anxiety. They ask clients to move toward and deliberately experience formerly noxious, negative, and avoided situations and experiences in controlled, deliberate, thoughtful ways and for therapeutic ends. As in the case of anxiety, the rationale and early assessment and subsequent treatment are themselves second-order shifts for clients. These in-session exercises are then extended to clients' daily lives as they are asked to do homework. Clients are asked to make careful observations of their daily activities rather than simply moving automatically through their day. They are asked to keep a "daily record of dysfunctional thoughts" (see Figure 6.2 in Beck et al., 1979) to develop a record of the situations that trigger their emotions and automatic thoughts. The record has columns for the date and time, situation or stream of thoughts leading to the emotion, emotions and their degree of intensity, automatic thoughts and how strongly they are believed, rational response alternatives and how strongly they are believed, and the outcome or rerating of clients' beliefs in the automatic thoughts and the intensity of the related emotions. In this way, data are collected on the characteristic patterns of patients' thinking while the usually automatic flow of their daily lives is deliberately disrupted through observations that begin to deconstruct the patient's formerly firmly held beliefs.

Cognitive therapy's focus is on changing depressive thinking. Thus, as clients gradually bring in and share the patterns of their thoughts, emotions, and reactions to life situations, they then engage with their therapist in examining the evidence. The variety of procedures used include logical discourse and Socratic questioning, role playing, use of imagery and image restructuring, behavioral experiments and examining the evidence, and direct problem solving of dilemmas needing to be addressed. This is a very active treatment that requires clients to take consistent and deliberate action in their life; to solve problems they formerly felt were beyond hope of change through their own agency. As automatic thoughts and schemas are discovered, patients are then asked to list evidence from their own experiences for and against these hypotheses. Clients may also design experiments to further test these hypotheses. When the results of the experiment contradict patients' predictions, then their automatic thoughts need to be revised. Thus, clients are first asked to deliberately experience their depression and reflect on it. They are then asked to take designed action to engage in situations they would predict would be problematic and examine the results. Each exercise is a reversal, and each technique is designed to question the validity of the patients' premises and assumptions (schemas and automatic thoughts) that drive the pattern of the self-defeating vicious cycle that has become their depression. Direct reversals of patients' withdrawal and inactivity are designed to help them use their time more adaptively and become involved in more constructive activity. The most commonly used activities are scheduling activities that include mastery and pleasure exercises; role playing, and modeling and coaching to rehearse new and more assertive behaviors; self-reliance training that helps clients take increased control of routine activities, such as bathing, cleaning, cooking, or shopping; and diversion techniques whereby negative thinking is diverted through engaging in physical activity, play, work, social contacts, and so on. The "weekly activity schedule" (cf. Figures 1 and 2 in Beck et al., 1979) is used to help clients schedule hour-for-hour and day-by-day activities that are designed to offer clients more pleasure and a greater sense of control and accomplishment in their daily lives. As clients rate each completed activity for both mastery and pleasure, their ratings usually contradict their belief that they cannot accomplish or enjoy anything.

The course of treatment usually runs from 12 to 16 sessions over as many weeks. Each session is very structured, with the client and therapist setting the session's agenda, checking and evaluating homework, designing new experiments and tasks, evaluating progress, and getting feedback on the session to make it more helpful in the future. Young et al. (2001) described treatment as progressing in two phases. The first phase concentrates on induction into the rationale and process of treatment and on symptom reduction and includes all of the elements just described. This phase achieves direct reductions in depressive symptoms through keeping thought records, identifying and challenging dysfunctional thoughts through questioning and experiments, and constructing and following agendas and activity schedules until the client's depression is lifted. The second phase is designed as relapse prevention and focuses more on client's schemas. An assessment–education component and a change component are involved. The assessment–education component includes linking past experiences in the patient's history to current problems; using schema inventories to identify themes from these experiences, which have served the client as deeply held beliefs or premises; using imagery to activate or trigger these schemas in session; and educating the client on the nature of schemas as long-standing beliefs that may again be triggered in the future. Long-standing fears, such as fear of abandonment; fear of inadequacy; problems in entitlement or self-control; needing to subjugate to others or to self-sacrifice; or being overly self-punitive, inhibited, and negative toward oneself are but a few of the most common schemas rooted in patients' childhood, family, and social histories. Therapists then collaborate with clients in examining the evidence for these historical beliefs by examining the evidence and designing and carrying out experiments. Patients are encouraged to modify long-term interaction patterns that have reinforced their schemas throughout their life and ultimately act against the dictates of their beliefs. To prevent relapse, clients are encouraged to understand their own schemas and their origin and to learn how they will be triggered, reinforced, and maintained in the future unless they continue to be vigilant and use the tools they have learned in treatment to counteract these vicious cycles of self-fulfilling prophecies. Young et al. (2002) described the cognitive approach in the following way:

> Cognitive therapy helps patients understand the relationship among their thoughts, behaviors, and feelings. Cognitions are "put to the test" by examining evidence, setting up *in vivo* experiments, weighing advantages and disadvantages, trying graded tasks, and employing other intervention strategies. Through this process, patients begin to view themselves and their problems more realistically, feel better, change their maladaptive behavior patterns, and take steps to solve real-life difficulties. (p. 303)

The Interpersonal Approach

> Concern should drive us into action and not into depression.
> —Karen Horney

The Emotionally Charged Relationship

In the IPT approach, a major element of early sessions is to validate the depressed client's emotions as absolutely understandable, given the nature of his or her life situation. Clients' emotions are supported and made understandable to them as they are placed in the context of their current and past interpersonal relationships. At times, therapists marvel at how it is that their client has been able to go on, given the severity of their life situations. In contrast to the cognitive approach, clients are assumed to be having relatively reasonable emotional reactions to unreasonable circumstances rather than responding to dysfunctional thoughts about potentially reasonable situations. The two early tasks in IPT are (a) establishing a collaborative working alliance and (b) identifying the interpersonal focus that best represents the reasons for the patient's depression. The therapist is portrayed as the client's optimistic and realistic ally, supporter, and coach, who will help the client identify the current life situation troubling him, decide what he might like to change about it, and then find options available to make that change. Emotions in this therapeutic relationship are given the ultimate validation by the therapist, who confirms them as appropriate and then links them to relationships that are in need of action to be changed by the client. Therapeutic optimism is another relationship element that is explicitly emphasized. Clients are reassured that they are depressed and that depression is a highly treatable condition through several different alternative approaches. Depression is described as a common disorder that responds well to treatment. The outlook for recovery is excellent. Most people recover promptly with treatment, and the prognosis is quite good.

The Rationale or "Myth"

The straightforward rationale for IPT is that the depressed person's distress is not necessarily a function of her own flaws or inability to handle herself but instead is a reasonable emotional response to a distressing set of circumstances. The danger of such a normalizing position is that it may minimize the client's distress, or even cause her to get down of herself more because she has not been able to change things for the better. IPT addresses this by first validating the client's distress as very real and painful and then literally explaining the nature of vicious cycles and self-fulfilling interpersonal prophecies that are in fact very distressing and that can commonly take on a life of their own and develop into the syndrome of clinical depression.

Clients are discouraged from blaming themselves for the symptoms of depression through an important rationale of the IPT approach. IPT therapists give their patients the *sick role*, as both a rationale for their symptoms and a frame to discourage them from blaming themselves for their symptoms. This frame for depression follows from the work of Harvard medical sociologist Talcott Parsons's (1951) concept that being sick has both interpersonal privileges and responsibilities. In the case of depression, clients are excused for being depressed and excused interpersonally from a range of social obligations while they are working on getting better. Having an "illness" like depression, which takes on a life of its own, is no more their fault than would be having diabetes or high blood pressure. Markowitz (1998) noted that "The sick role shifts patients' blame from themselves to an illness, which the therapist blames for their suffering" (p. 51). This potent rationale tends to inter-dict clients typical vicious cycle of personalizing their problems and distress. This rationale becomes a form of an acceptance-based intervention. The client has no need to fix his symptoms as a personal flaw. The symptoms are actually commonly occurring results of chronically unresolved interpersonal difficulties that need to be addressed. The responsibility of the sick role is for the client to cooperate with treatment to get better. In the IPT approach, this entails identifying the current interpersonal challenges confronting the client, evaluating options to address them, and then taking action to change those relationship challenges in some way.

The Set of Rituals or Procedures

In their original treatment manual for IPT, Klerman et al. (1984) of-fered a concise outline of the phases, stances, and techniques of the approach to help clarify its structure. In the initial sessions, therapists help clients first by (a) learning about the general nature of depression and learning about the sick role; then (b) relating depression to the interpersonal context; (c) iden-tifying the major problem area; and finally (d) explaining the IPT concepts and contract. The phase of dealing with depression helps to set up a frame for clients to understand their problem and accept it through reviewing depres-sive symptoms, giving the syndrome a name, explaining depression and its treatment, giving the patient the sick role, and evaluating the need for medi-cation. The patient's current and past interpersonal relationships are reviewed as they relate to their depressive symptoms. The therapist then reviews the client's current and recent interactions with others, the client's expectations and unfulfilled needs, and what the client wants to change in these relation-ships. The client and therapist then jointly determine the most current and pressing problem area that relates to the client's depression and discuss what might change. Finally, the therapist outlines his or her understanding of the problem and looks for consensual validation of that explanation from the client. Thus, consensus is reached on both the focus and goals of treatment in the first or second session. The therapist explains that the procedures of IPT include a here-and-now focus, the need for the client to address current concerns and review current interpersonal relations in the area of focus, evalu-ate options and needs for action, and initiate action to change things. Treat-ment is usually explained as taking the form of 12 to 16 weekly sessions. All of these structures of the initial session, or first few sessions, are explicitly geared to directly increase the clients' level of hope by offering an under-standable explanation for their problem, a rationale for treating it, a pathway for change, and a clear contract and procedures for changing things.

Intermediate sessions are then devoted to resolving the interpersonal distress in the area of focus that was agreed to be the cause of the client's depression. As stated earlier, the four main problem areas are grief, interper-sonal disputes, role transitions, and interpersonal deficits. The essence of the work in each area is clearly pattern reversals in the vicious cycles triggered by each interpersonal life event. In grief, clients are directly encouraged to engage with the process of their painful and unresolved loss. Thus, clients are asked to master and integrate their grief by "remembering to remember," and experience the sadness and pain, rather than "remembering to forget." This is clearly a second-order change that is followed by reintegrating with others. For interpersonal disputes, the nature and pattern of the current vicious cycles of ineffective resolutions are analyzed and evaluated, and a new course of action is planned. Clients and therapists determine the stage of the dispute and decide whether a renegotiation is needed, whether there is an impasse, or whether the relationship needs to be dissolved. Clients' expectations and their assumptions that fuel their solution-generated problem patterns are evaluated, and other options are discussed and put to the test through role plays and actions in the clients' lives. Second-order change is clearly evident as clients change their assumptions and reverse their escalating solution patterns or accept the dispute and stop attempting to resolve it. The goals of working on role transitions (e.g., moving into the role of a parent, becoming divorced, becoming a student, etc.) are facilitating mourning of the loss of the old role, regarding the new role as more positive, and acknowledging anxiety and developing mastery in the new role. The therapist and client evaluate the escalating problematic patterns around the role transition, validate the emotions related to the change, and then plot a course of action to move out of the vicious cycles around the transition and integrate the change into the client's life. Finally, the area of interpersonal deficits is uniformly considered the most challenging and problematic for the IPT approach. This is mainly because these clients are depressed because they currently and historically have few social relationships and are socially isolated. Therapists often use their own relationship with these clients as a starting point for building closeness and new social skills and then move the client toward reducing isolation through encouraging new social relationships. The key to success in this area, as in all others, is to encourage clients to consider their depression as a reasonable reaction to recent life situations, examine their expectations and interactions that tend to fuel their impasses, and then take new and often very different (second-order) actions to resolve those difficulties. Depression is not the fault of the person experiencing it. It is a reasonable response to a set of unreasonable situations that will be resolved by acting on new options.

WHAT WORKS AND WHY?

As we look into what works in these two alternative yet equally effective approaches, it is important to state that these are actually not the only available approaches with strong evidence of being effective with depression. The cognitive and interpersonal views, by some quirks of sociopolitical scientific choice, just happened to be the two chosen for use in the massive NIMH TDCRP project. Equally available and well supported at the time were the behavioral and marital behavioral approaches that focus on behavioral activation and skills training (cf. Craighead et al., 2002). Another more recently supported approach for preventing relapse in successfully treated depressed clients is the *mindfulness approach*, which focuses on teaching acceptance. Each approach deserves a quick look to see what, if anything, they are doing that matches in some way what these cognitive and interpersonal approaches offer.

Behavioral Activation

Lewinsohn (see Lewinsohn & Gotlib, 1995, for an overview) was one of the first to develop a targeted program for depression, on the basis of the views of Skinner (1953) and Ferster (1973). This approach was closely complemented by the self-control therapy of Rehm (1977, 1990), among others. Behavioral approaches in their various forms all share the common assumption that major depression is related to a decrease of positive reinforcing behaviors. Consequently, they focus on increasing positive daily activities, improving communication and social skills, increasing assertiveness skills, decreasing negative life experiences, and increasing positive reinforcement contingencies for new adaptive behaviors. This behavioral approach has had results in treating depression that are as equally impressive as those of the cognitive and interpersonal approaches. For example, in a well-designed and well-controlled study that we discuss in some more detail subsequently (cf. Gotner, Gollan, Dobson, & Jacobson, 1998), a therapy including only behavioral activation elements was found to be equally effective (at the end of 20 sessions and at the 6-month follow-up) as one including behavioral activation and modification of automatic dysfunctional thoughts and a third treatment including the full CBT package. In another, more recent study, an approach focusing on the consequences of client's behavior and the teaching of social problem solving to resolve interpersonal difficulties (behavioral activation) was found to be equally as effective as an antidepressant medication (nefazodone), and the combination of the medication plus the behavioral activation therapy was more effective than either treatment alone (Keller et al., 2000; McCullough, 2000).

The behavioral marital therapy approaches of O'Leary and Beach (1990), and that of Jacobson and his colleagues (Jacobson, Dobson, Fruzetti, Schmaling, & Salusky, 1991; Jacobson & Margolin, 1979), have also been shown to be equally as effective as CBT for people with depression and marital problems. Furthermore, the behavioral marital therapy approach adds the advantage of decreasing marital discord and helping to reduce relapse. Behavioral marital therapy approaches focus on a similar set of interventions within the couple relationship. In essence, behavioral approaches function to help the client directly activate new and more positive behaviors that disrupt the old negative contingency cycles and substitute new, more positive interactions using a combination of behavior exchange and communication and problem-solving training. (We review these approaches in more detail in the next chapter.) After conducting a review of behavioral approaches, Craighead et al. (2002) concluded that both behavioral and marital behavioral approaches to depression had at least as great efficacy with depression as did the CBT and IPT approaches. The marital variation had significant advantages in reducing relapse among successful patients who had marital distress associated with their depression. Thus, activating a new path of action to redirect the former vicious cycle and enlisting significant others in supporting these changes has also received strong support.

It must be noted, however, that all of the approaches studied in the NIMH TDCRP had significant relapse rates. Craighead et al. (2002) noted that "Among patients who recovered during acute treatment, the percentages of patients who remained well during the 18 month follow-up were as follows: IPT (26%), CBT (30%), IMI-CM (19%), and PLA-CM (20%)" (p. 253). None of the active treatments was statistically significantly better than the placebo at an 18-month follow-up. Regarding behavioral marital therapy (which was found to be most effective in couples with a depressed partner), Jacobson's own research has found that at least one third of successful couples relapsed between the 1st and 2nd year of follow-up. So, what might be done to maintain gains in overcoming depression when they are achieved?

Mindfulness and Acceptance

Segal et al. (2002) addressed just this question in their new evidence-supported approach to preventing relapse, called *mindfulness-based cognitive therapy for depression*. They have developed an approach for people with three or more previous relapses or episodes of depression that nearly cut in half the relapse–reoccurrence rates over the follow-up period compared with treatment as usual. So, what did they do, and how did they develop this intervention? In studying clients who tended to have recurrences of depressed episodes, they noticed that these people were becoming more and more easily triggered into a characteristic vicious and ruminative depressive cycle in response to new situations that may have made them feel sad or distressed. Not only was there evidence that characteristic depressive thought patterns could produce depressed moods but also, conversely, that sad or depressed moods could also trigger familiar depressive thinking patterns. It is interesting that Segal and his colleagues described a person who relapses as being caught in the classic solution-generated problem cycle. A formerly depressed person might experience a sad or distressing mood from which she wants to escape.

Her solution is to try to think her way out of her distress, which in itself perpetuates the distress through rumination. Segal et al. suggested that

> He or she may remain upset, not so much because of the original situation, but because his or her mind goes round and round trying to work out why he or she got so upset in the first place . . . people dig themselves deeper into the very hole from which they are trying to escape . . . [thus] attempts to solve problems by endlessly thinking about them can serve merely to keep individuals locked into the state from which they are trying to escape. (p. 69)

This is the classic paradox that is the hallmark of a first-order vicious cycle in which the solutions have become the problem. It is interesting that the heart of Segal and colleagues intervention approach constitutes the kind of pattern reversal that is also the very hallmark of second-order change. What they teach these clients is techniques of waking meditation, or mindfulness, to practice and use as they move themselves purposely toward depressing moods or situations or as they encounter such distressing moods and situations in their daily lives. The idea is for clients to actively experience formerly distressing situations and, in essence, notice them pass without the need to act on them. This is the ultimate acceptance strategy. Clients learn to accept a perceived change or potentially distressing circumstance without triggering the actions or solutions that formerly created the vicious cycle of the solution-generated problem of their depression. This is the ultimate reversal of going toward the distressing situation and not doing the logical solution to resolve it. This is like pushing in rather than pulling out to escape from the child's finger trap illustrated in chapter 2 of this volume. It is, by definition, a second-order change.

What Are the Active Ingredients?

Given that there now at least several approaches to treating depression, each of which has impressive supporting evidence of its effectiveness, what, if anything, is the active ingredient or ingredients shared among them? We have focused on the cognitive and interpersonal approaches because not only are they different in their basic models and procedures but they also share extensive process and outcome data through the NIMH TDRC project. However, we have seen that there are at least several more equally effective approaches. As we note at the beginning of this chapter, what is most interesting in looking at the cognitive and interpersonal approaches is that they are very different but equally compelling in their premises and procedures, and yet they have been found to be equally effective. How can this be? Furthermore, if this is so, then how can the lessons learned from these two approaches as well as from other effective treatments guide treatment of depression?

Focusing again on the cognitive and interpersonal approaches for contrast, both approaches would agree that people who are depressed tend to be caught in vicious self-defeating cycles whereby they come to view themselves, their situations, and their future as overwhelmingly negative. Both view the origins of these depressive self-fulfilling prophecies as rooted in these people's early life experiences, learning, and interactions with significant others. Both view clients as needing to take new actions to bump themselves out of these vicious cycle patterns. However, the cognitive approach views the core problem fueling the cycle as the product of long-standing schemas and unrealistic thinking patterns that need to be examined and changed to resolve the depressed cycle, and the interpersonal approach views the core problem fueling the depressed cycle as based in current interpersonal dilemmas being mishandled as a result of early attachment and loss experiences. Depression will thus resolve as new options are taken to resolve the core interpersonal conflict driving the depressive cycle. Both descriptions and their related procedures are very compelling. Which is correct?

Evidence for Each Theory of Change

Imber et al. (1990) attempted to answer this question directly by administering instruments to the clients in the NIMH TDCRP multisite depression study to assess the hypothesized causal mechanisms for change in each of the three treatments used. The Dysfunctional Attitude Scale was used to measure the predicted change in cognitions of the cognitive approach. The Social Adjustment Scale was administered to detect interpersonal relationship changes predicted as the locus of change by the IPT approach. Surprisingly, however, few of the predicted relationships were found. At termination, there were no clear and consistent correlations found between changes in distorted cognitions for the CBT approach and success in treatment, or for changes in social adjustment scores for clients successful in the IPT approach. Although people got over being depressed in varying degrees, the predicted reasons for that success did not show up in either of the measures associated with each approach. This brings into question whether either cognitive change or interpersonal change is really necessary for resolving depression.

Is Cognitive Change Crucial?

Another often-cited study by the late Neil Jacobson and his colleagues (Jacobson et al., 1996) took a different approach to answering a similar question about the cognitive approach. The question concerned the necessary and sufficient components for change in the cognitive therapy approach. One would clearly assume that a critical component on cognitive treatment would be modifying dysfunctional schemas and automatic thoughts. To test this, Jacobson et al. (1996) broke down the key elements of CBT into a behavioral activation component, a component for dealing with depressing events and concurrent automatic thoughts, and a component for modifying depressive schemas. Then they dismantled treatment into three treatment approaches. The first treatment focused only on activating patient behavior. The second included that activation element and a treatment related to coping skills associated with automatic thoughts. The third was a complete package, including behavioral activation, coping skills, and identifying and modifying dysfunctional core schemas. Surprisingly, all groups were equally effective at both termination and follow-up. This casts doubt on the necessity of including the cognitive components of the cognitive approach. The IPT approach certainly did not include explicit procedures to challenge automatic thoughts or to draw direct connections among thinking, emotions, and depression, yet it was also equally or more effective than the CBT approach in the NIMH TDCRP study. Another related and surprising finding from the results of this massive TDCRP study was reported by Klein and Ross (1993). Recall that the BDI, which is heavily influenced by questions on cognitive distortions, was given as one of the outcome measures. One would expect that Beck's cognitive approach would produce superior results on this, his own cognitive scale. However, IPT was superior to CBT on the BDI among all clients completing treatment. This adds even more doubt and confusion regarding the mechanisms of change. How can an approach focusing on improving interpersonal relationships produce better results on a cognitively saturated measure of depression like the BDI than the cognitive approach of the scale's creator?

Adherence to Protocols

Another way of determining whether the particular approach to treatment (i.e., IPT or CBT or another view) was the active ingredient in change is to check to see whether the therapists who most closely followed the treatment manual or protocol had the best results. These results are also surprising with regard to depression. Shaw et al. (1999) examined the relationship between the degrees of protocol adherence of therapists in the TDCRP study as they related to outcome in treating depression and found that the degree of adherence was not related to outcome. This means that it did not matter exactly how perfectly the supposed active ingredient of each approach was delivered to the depressed clients. Similar results were obtained by Castonguay, Goldfried, Wiser, Raue, and Hayes (1996), who found that therapists who responded to alliance problems by increasing their adherence to a cognitive therapy protocol had worse outcomes than those who were more flexible. One might assume that applying more of the supposed active treatment would increase success when there were struggles, but in fact the opposite was found to be so. Similarly, in a series of studies that examined more interpersonal time-limited dynamic therapy, Henry and Strupp and their colleagues (Henry,

Schacht, Strupp, Butler, & Binder, 1993; Henry, Strupp, Butler, Schacht, & Binder, 1993) found the same phenomenon. Their studies found the surprising results that training therapists to adhere to a manual can result in *deteriorating* relationships between therapists and clients. There must be something other than the pure treatment rationale and procedures that is involved with change. Remember that each approach was more successful than a placebo and equally successful as antidepressant medication. Wampold (2001) noted that there have been other studies that have found some positive relationship between adhering to the structure of a therapy procedure and outcome. However, he concludes that this relationship appears to be more a product of maintaining a structure and a focus agreed upon between clients and therapists than a result of the core theoretical ingredients. Thus, it appears that the specific nature of the particular rationale and procedures of each treatment have much less to do with successful therapy for depression than does the way that the treatment is applied and the nature of the working alliance between clients and therapists.

Active Ingredients or Remoralization?

Another interesting study is that of Ilardi and Craighead (1994), who conducted an analysis of eight studies investigating the timing of changes in CBT for depression. They asked whether changes for depressed clients tended to happen after the key active procedures were implemented or before. Each perspective would assume that an early relationship is important to gaining compliance in engaging with the active procedures. It would be techniques, however, that would produce the major change in symptoms. They found that the majority of total symptom improvement (60%–80%) occurred within the first 3 weeks of treatment, well before the fourth session, when the cognitive manual recommended introducing cognitive restructuring techniques. Thus, the majority of change in these depressed clients across eight studies was achieved well before the supposed active techniques were applied. What was happening? These authors concluded that the timing of these changes are more a result of the early remoralization of the client: "Many patients improve very quickly in therapy, suggesting that their favorable response is due to the reassuring aspects of the therapeutic situation itself rather than to the specific procedure" (Ilardi & Craighead, 1994, p. 140). Such early remoralization may then help these clients to better comply with later homework and to take new action in their lives, which is implied not only by CBT but also by IPT and other treatments. Thus, early and strong elements of a working alliance appear to be active in effective treatments for depression such as the cognitive approach. Frank's (Frank & Frank, 1991) contextual model suggests that clients begin to change early in treatment and increase their gains throughout treatment through a process of reversing their demoralization about themselves, their situations, and their futures. This remoralization process would be expected to occur early in treatment, often before the supposed active ingredients of many manualized approaches are applied. If this is so, then what other elements of the working alliance might be involved with such success?

Empathy and the Working Alliance

The original manual for the cognitive approach emphasized that empathy and the treatment alliance were necessary, but not sufficient, conditions for change (Beck et al., 1979). Yet just how important is empathy to this relatively technical approach to treating depression? Burns and Nolen-Hoeksema (1992) used structural equation modeling to determine the role of empathy in the CBT treatment of 178 clients, using an empathy scale and the BDI, both completed by clients to measure the amounts of each quality present and change at 12 weeks. They found that clients with the warmest and most empathic therapists improved the most when all other factors were controlled. Thus empathy appeared to be as potent a change agent, or an even stronger change agent, than cognitive restructuring in this very carefully crafted modeling on the effectiveness of a CBT approach.

Studies of the effects of the treatment alliance on outcome in the NIMH TDCRP study have also had consistent results. Kropnick et al. (1996) found that positive measures of alliance were consistently positively related to outcome across all treatments. Furthermore, early alliance was so strongly related to success that a one-unit increase in alliance score predicted a three-fold increase in the probability of successful treatment of depression. Similar results relating the strength of therapist–client alliance across therapies to both successful treatment of depression and to decreasing dropout rates further support the strong influence of the therapeutic alliance, regardless of treatment approach on successful treatment of depression in the NIMH TDCRP study (Blatt, Sanislow, Zuroff, & Pilkonis, 1996; Horvath & Symonds, 1991). It is clear that the working alliance is a key component of effective therapy for depression, regardless of the approach and rationale used.

Allegiance

As Frank's (Frank & Frank, 1991) contextual model suggests, the effectiveness of any organized approach to treatment is also in part caused by the therapist's belief in the model and his or her enthusiasm about its effectiveness. This is also referred to as the therapist's *allegiance* to a model. This has also clearly been true with treatments for depression. Although early research on most models has shown effectiveness (especially when the research was conducted by advocates of the model), later studies by more neutral parties have inevitably found less strong effects. Robinson, Berman, and Neimeyer (1990) reviewed 58 studies of depression published before 1986. The treatments compared in these studies were classified as either behavioral, cognitive, cognitive–behavioral, or general verbal therapies. Initial meta-analyses of these studies found significant and relatively large differences in the effectiveness of these treatments; however, when the allegiance of the researchers conducting the studies was factored out, all of the treatment differences disappeared. Similarly, more recent meta-analyses comparing different approaches to treating depression and factoring out the effects of allegiance have had similar results (Gloaguen, Cottrauz, Cucherat, & Blackburn, 1998; Wampold, Minami, Baskin, & Tierney, 2002). The enthusiasm and allegiance of the therapists and researchers for their approach was considered to have made the greatest differences in the findings of superior effectiveness. Stated positively, these results confirm that therapists who are enthusiastic and invested in their approach tend to increase the effectiveness of that approach, regardless of their theoretical foundations.

Alliance, Allegiance, Structure, and Focus

It is abundantly clear that both the cognitive and interpersonal approaches we have discussed describe people who are depressed as caught in vicious cycles of first-order changes. Their respective approaches redirect this cycle to create second-order change through different rationales and procedures and yet through the use of the same core elements that we have emphasized in discussing Frank's (Frank & Frank, 1991) contextual model. Remember that the logic behind clients' first-order solutions is very compelling for them. Also, most clients are understandably reluctant to attempt anything new or different when they are in situations that already feel so distressing and seem so risky. Thus, for a client to consider doing something not only new but also often counterintuitive from his or her current perspective, there needs to be some compelling conditions present to help him or her do so. As we have suggested, these conditions are provided by the therapeutic alliance, offering a rationale and structure for treatment that is believed in and adhered to by both therapists and clients, and maintaining a flexible focus of treatment. The research evidence on treatments for depression supports this position.

Wampold (2001), in his review of studies and meta-analyses of treatments for depression, reached the same conclusions regarding the conditions important across effective treatments for depression as well as for other problems. These conditions not only are supported by the research evidence reviewed but they also match those projected as being important by Frank's contextual model. To support clients in making the kind of second-order change needed to step out of their solution-generated depressive patterns, a set of key elements needs to be offered in the relationship between clients and therapists. In brief, they include the following components representing an amalgamation of components from the working alliance and the contextual model:

- Empathic validation of clients' distress, including their emotions and the context for them.
- Provision of a rationale explaining the symptoms that makes sense to both the client and the therapist.
- Agreement between the client and therapist on the related goals and procedures of treatment and an enthusiastic and collaborative investment in the enterprise of it.
- Maintenance of the agreed-on structure and focus of this treatment contract throughout the treatment.
- Support for new learning and active engagement in new skills and actions both within and outside therapy.
- Consistent appraisals of progress and flexible adjustments to build success.
- Reinforcement of successes and predictions and inoculations of future challenges to build resilience and reduce the chance of a relapse.

These are the elements common to each of the effective treatments for depression that we have reviewed in this chapter, with the exception of one overriding common factor: All elements must be directed at altering the vicious cycles of the core solution-generated patterns that have come to characterize the patient's depression.

FOLLOWING THE THREAD

Depression is commonly seen as a vicious cycle of attempts to cope with overwhelming stress through self-disconfirmation, oversimplifying complex situations, and withdrawal. The first-order vicious cycle results in self-doubt, blame, and withdrawal from life situations that only make it worse. Negative cognitions become self-fulfilling. Second-order interventions offer various rationales to affirm clients' depression as appropriate to context and to their habitual solutions. Clients can then reverse the pattern through exercises in checking out their assumptions and addressing their challenges. Regardless of the approach, effective psychotherapies for depression direct second-order change by establishing validating relationships; investing faith in a rationale; and committing both clients and therapists to a set of active procedures to reverse the self-fulfilling, solution-generated problem of depression.

8

PARENT–CHILD
RELATIONSHIP PROBLEMS

Mom to kid: "If you would just clean up your room, I could stop nagging and then we'd be happy."

Kid to mom: "If you would just get off my back about the stupid room, I would behave better and then we'd be happy."

The disruptive behavior disorders described in the literature include attention-deficit/hyperactivity disorder (ADHD), oppositional defiant disorder (ODD), and conduct disorder (CD). These disorders have also been referred to as *externalizing* or *acting-out disorders*. In recent years, there has been a growing number of empirically supported treatments pertaining specifically to the treatment of CD and ODD. The proliferation of approaches offers an opportunity for a comparative analysis within the context of second-order change. Toward this end, discussion of the disruptive behavior disorders in this chapter is limited to CD and ODD.

Kazdin (2002), reporting on treatments for CD, indicated that a number of treatments have been shown through research to be either promising or probably efficacious. As with psychotherapy in general, these treatments have theoretical underpinnings that are often at odds. Kazdin further indicated that there is a paucity of studies that attempt to understand the basis of therapeutic change. We argue that what Kazdin said about CD also applies to ODD. In both cases there is not only a paucity of studies directed at understanding how therapeutic change occurs, but there also appears to be little interest in developing such theories. Kazdin further stated the following

Theory is needed to sort through an indefinite range of factors and to explain how these factors relate to the treatment process. In both research and clinical practice we wish to maximize therapeutic change. This requires knowing what the critical factors are in treatment and how change occurs. (p. 77)

In this chapter, we define the disruptive behavior disorders, look at the vicious cycle phenomenon as it is described from a variety of well-known perspectives, and propose a hypothesis that addresses Kazdin's (2002) request for a theory about change. We then show how change, in the most researched clinical treatments for disruptive behaviors, can be understood within the context of our hypothesis. Our objective is to show that although the main researched treatment methods are organized around a wide range of differing theoretical constructs, there is surprising commonality at the procedural level of therapy. Each researched method produces second-order change by reversing the sequence of how parents are attempting to get their children or adolescents to comply.

DEFIANCE DEFINED

Oppositional Defiant Disorder

According to the *Diagnostic and Statistical Manual of Mental Disorders* (4th ed. [*DSM–IV*]; American Psychiatric Association, 1994), ODD refers to a recurrent childhood pattern of negative, defiant, disobedient, and hostile behavior toward adult authority figures and that are developmentally inappropriate. There are specific behaviors that are associated with ODD. To qualify for the diagnosis, the child must exhibit four or more behaviors from the following list: often loses temper, often argues with adults, often actively defies or refuses to comply with adults' requests or rules, often deliberately annoys people, often blames others for his or her mistakes or misbehavior, is often touchy or easily annoyed by others, is often angry and resentful, and is often spiteful or vindictive. In addition, these behaviors need to cause clinically significant impairment in social, academic, or occupational functioning.

Barkley (1997) indicated that establishing a diagnosis of ODD for treatment purposes is more complex than what can be ascertained by the *DSM–IV* checklist, because noncompliant behavior is a normal aspect of development for most children. For this reason, he established criteria for his treatment program that include the *DSM–IV* but also are more specific:

1. The child's behavior is developmentally inappropriate or statistically deviant in that it occurs to a significantly greater degree than is common for children of this age group. The child meets *DSM–IV* criteria for ODD or CD.

2. The child's behavior results in an appreciable degree of impairment. The child's adaptive functioning is at or below the 10th percentile for age as detected through clinical interviews and child behavioral rating scales such as the Vineland Adaptive Rating Scale and the Normative Adaptive Behavior Scale.

3. The child's behavior results in a significant degree of emotional distress or harm, either for the child or, more likely for parents, siblings, or peers of the child. The child's distress may be established through self-report measures of emotional adjustment, such as ratings of anxiety or depression. Parents' distress may be measured through parent self-report instruments such as the Short Form of the Parenting Stress Index (Abidin, 1986). (Barkley, 1997, pp. 20–21)

Barkley (1997) summarized his treatment inclusion criteria by stating,

Regardless of the specific methods used to evaluate intervention criteria, the clinician's objective is to establish that the child's defiant behavior is outside the bounds of normally appropriate child conduct or that it is impairing the child's adjustment in some way or is creating distress for the child, the caregiver, or others such that there us a need for clinical intervention. (p. 21)

Conduct Disorder

Kazdin (2002) stated that the term *antisocial behaviors* refer to a variety of acts that reflect social rule violations and actions against others. Such behaviors as fighting, lying, and stealing are seen in varying degrees in most children. CD refers to antisocial behavior that is clinically significant and beyond the realm of "normal functioning." The extent to which antisocial behaviors are sufficiently severe to constitute CD depends on several characteristics of the behaviors, including their frequency and chronicity, whether they are isolated acts or part of a larger syndrome with other deviant behaviors, and whether they lead to significant impairment of the child. The overriding feature is a persistent pattern of behavior in which the rights of others and age-appropriate social norms are violated. Isolated acts, when severe enough, such as physical aggression, destruction of property, stealing, or firesetting, are sufficient to warrant concern and attention in their own right.

Risk Factors

Kazdin (2002) indicated that because CD often has its roots in ODD the two disorders share similar risk factors that include the child's temperament; neuropsychological deficits; poor bonding and attachment; and subclinical levels of CD that occur in elementary school, at home, or in the community. There are parental risk factors as well; these include psychopathology and criminal behavior in the family; harsh and inconsistent parent–

child punishment; less parental acceptance of the child; less warmth, affection, and emotional support; and less attachment. There are also low monitoring of the child, poor supervision, lack of monitoring of the child's whereabouts, and few rules about where the youth can go and when he or she can return. The family may engage in fewer community activities. Large family size, sibling antisocial behavior, and socioeconomic disadvantage are also risk factors. Other factors include prenatal complications, exposure to violence, antisocial peers, and school situations in which there is little emphasis on academic work. School settings often reflect a lack of teacher time on lessons, infrequent teacher use of praise and appreciation of schoolwork, little emphasis on individual responsibility of students, poor working conditions for pupils, unavailability of the teacher to deal with children's problems, and low teacher expectancies.

These risk factors are thought to combine in highly complex ways to produce defiant behaviors in children. We will have more to say about this later in the chapter. For now, we look more specifically at characteristics of children and parents that are associated with disruptive behavior disorders. We then describe contextual factors that also play a role.

Child Characteristics

There is a range of child characteristics that contribute to the development of disruptive behaviors. Research indicates that the child's temperament is significant factor. In fact, negative temperamental features of the child are among the strongest influences in the process (Olweus, 1980) and may be sufficient to generate parental risk factors that include psychopathology and poor marital or family functioning (Tschann, Kaiser, Chesney, Alkon, & Boyce, 1996).

Temperament

In describing the effects of temperament in the development of defiant behaviors in children, Greene (2001) turned to the work of Turecki (1989). *Temperament* is defined as the natural, inborn style of behavior of each individual. This style is innate and not produced by the environment. Turecki delineated a number of temperamental characteristics that are associated with difficult-to-rear children. They include high activity level, withdrawal from or poor reaction to new or unfamiliar situations, poor adaptability (to changes in routine), negative persistence (strong willed, whiny, rigid), low sensory threshold (child may complain about the tags on his shirt, or smells, or textures of food), and negative mood (cranky, irritable).

According to Greene (2001), children with ODD often exhibit a mixture of these traits during infancy, although some do not manifest temperamental issues until later (between ages 1 and 4). This understanding of temperamental features of children with defiant behaviors is well supported by other researchers. According to Barkley (1997),

> In particular, children who are prone to emotional responses (high emotionality) are irritable, have poor habit regulation, are highly active, and/or are more inattentive and impulsive, are more likely to display disruptive behavior disorders and, therefore, to demonstrate defiant and coercive behavior than are children not having such negative temperamental characteristics. (p. 39)

Attention-Deficit/Hyperactivity Disorder

As indicated earlier, many children who meet diagnostic criteria for disruptive behavior disorders usually have ADHD as a comorbid condition. Greene, Ablon, Goring, Fazio, and Morse (2004) indicated that ADHD is a diagnostic label used to describe children who exhibit developmentally extreme levels of inattention or hyperactivity–impulsivity or both. Children with ADHD often have deficits in neurological skills referred to as *executive functions* (Greene, 2001; Greene et al., 2004). Although there is some disagreement as to the precise cognitive skills that comprise executive functioning, there is agreement that this is an important factor in ADHD and the development of ODD. Greene further suggested that delays in the development of any or all of the executive functioning skills places a child at risk for developing ODD. Executive functions include the ability to shift efficiently from one mind-set to another; the ability to organize a coherent plan in problem solving; the ability to simultaneously perform multiple thinking tasks; and the ability to regulate emotional arousal in the service of a goal-directed action.

In general, children with deficits in executive functioning often come across as demanding, self-centered, and lacking in empathy and social tact. Self-awareness and empathy require a fairly continuous process of reflecting on and rethinking of past experience and perspective-taking, and this process is short-circuited by deficits in executive skills. From this perspective, Greene (2001) argued that children's defiant behaviors only appear to be willful disobedience. From this perspective, behind the mask of willful defiance is a child who is inflexible and frustrated with his inability to meet the demands of adults.

Motivational Factors

Although concurring that some children who exhibit defiant behaviors are inflexible, Levy, O'Hanlon, and Goode (2001), offered a contrasting view on child characteristics that emphasizes motivational factors in the development of defiant behaviors. They indicated that defiant children tend to be strong willed and need external motivation to cooperate. Although all children crave love and attention, there are differences in how they are motivated. Some children are achievement oriented; they are considered to be high achievers or perfectionists by parents and teachers. Other children are motivated by relationships; they seek friendships and relationships with others. Children in these categories usually do very well and are easy to rear. Defiant children, more than other kids, crave control in their lives. They will do just about anything, even things that seem to produce the opposite result, to try and get, maintain, or regain control. They are socially exploitative and are usually very quick to notice how others respond and to use those responses to their advantage in both social and family environments. They are blind to their role in a problem. Not only can they not see how they affect their own problems but they also convince themselves that people around them are the cause. Defiant children are also able to tolerate a great deal of negativity. They actually seem to thrive on large amounts of conflict, anger, and negativity from others. They will win most times in escalating battles of negativity.

Despite differences in how child factors are emphasized, there are important areas of convergence in the literature about the children who develop disruptive disorders. All the authorities that we have reviewed agree that disruptive children are very difficult to parent. They manifest problematic temperament characteristics early in life, which challenges parent–child bonding. Defiant children are usually impulsive and often have deficits in cognitive functioning. These children usually lack awareness of their own role in the development of transactional problems. Finally, children with disruptive behaviors may bring out pathological traits in parents, which can have a negative effect on parents as individuals and as a family unit. Parental problems may in turn further feed the development of defiant behaviors.

Parent Discipline

In addition to parent risk factors noted earlier in the chapter, Chamberlain and Patterson (1995) identified four subtypes of "parent inadequate discipline" that contribute to coercive parent–child interchanges: (a) inconsistent discipline; (b) irritable explosive discipline; (c) low supervision and involvement; and (d) inflexible rigid discipline.

Greene et al. (2004), however, were critical of research that separates child and parent risk factors. It is difficult to determine, on the basis of the characteristics of children who have disruptive disorders, whether the child's defiance provokes poor parenting or poor parenting provokes defiance. In other words, there is a circular or reciprocal relationship between parent and child behaviors that either prevents or encourages the development of disruptive behaviors. For this reason, Greene (Green, Ablon, & Goring, 2003; Greene et al., 2004) argues in favor of a transactional model that integrates parent and child characteristics. When viewed in this way, the concept of goodness of fit emerges. Goodness of fit is the degree to which the characteristics of the child are compatible with those of his or her parents. If an impulsive, poorly emotionally regulated child has a parent who is patient and slow to anger, then goodness of fit is considered compatible, and the child will be less likely to develop disruptive behaviors. However, if the same child has a parent who is also impulsive and quick to anger, then goodness of fit is incompatible, and the child will be more likely to develop disruptive behaviors.

Barkley (1997) indicated that larger contextual events, such as stress, marital discord, parental isolation, or events affecting the family from the outside, may increase the probability of defiant child behavior. This occurs by virtue of the toll these events take on the consistency of parental management of the child, the positive reinforcement of compliant child behavior, and the general monitoring of child activities by parents. Levy et al. (2001) reported that family crisis situations can contribute to defiant behavior and noted that this can be observed when children develop defiant behaviors fairly soon—a couple of days to a few months—after a stressful event.

THE VICIOUS CYCLE

Although described in different terms, a common theme among researchers and clinicians is that disruptive behavior disorders are triggered in multiple ways, and yet they are maintained by a vicious cycle. The child, parents, and others who become involved in the cycle share a strikingly similar characteristic: They are all unwitting participants. As unwitting participants, all parties develop premises and actions that direct their participation in a worsening situation. Participants are generally unaware that they are contributing to the problem. This is a now-familiar repetition of our core argument. Problems across domains of concern, and the effective psychotherapies for those problems, target vicious cycles of first-order change patterns and succeed by initiating second-order change. This is the golden thread connecting them as effective treatments. We presently share the main views on the cycle and then show how the golden thread weaves through these variant viewpoints.

Barkley's Vicious Cycles

Russell A. Barkley (1997) is a preeminent researcher and spokesperson for Parent Training (PT). He provides a comprehensive description of the parent–child vicious cycle that characterizes the development and maintenance of disruptive behaviors. His understanding is grounded in learning theory. However, Barkley goes beyond traditional learning theory by describing the development of disruptive behavior as a social process. Through the process, there is an acquisition of coercive behaviors in both children and parents. The following summarizes Barkley's (1997) perspective on how disruptive behaviors develop:

- The sequence is usually initiated by a command, given by the parent, for the child to engage in a task that is not considered enjoyable or reinforcing by the child.
- Most often, defiant children will not comply with the initial command; when the child does not comply, the parent will repeat the command.
- When the repeated command is not followed, it is repeated again, and so on. The sequence of repeated commands followed by noncompliance may be played over and over again, 5 to 15 times or more, in various forms.
- At some point, parental frustration increases, and the emotional intensity of the interaction escalates. The parent may warn or threaten the child that if the child does not follow instructions, some punishment will occur.
- Here, the child may continue to be noncompliant because threats are frequently part of the sequence and most often do not actually occur; hence the parent does not have credibility.
- Over time, both the child and parent escalate their emotional behavior toward each other, with voices rising in increasing volume and intensity as well as displays of anger, defiance, and perhaps destructiveness.
- This sequence may end in several ways; on rare occasions, the parent will perhaps send the child to his room and deny some privilege; more frequently, the parent will acquiesce to the child, allowing the command to be either partially or totally uncompleted. (pp. 28–29)

In some situations, the parent may obtain full compliance from the child, and herein lays the rub. In these situations the parent may believe that she has won the battle with the child because she has finally made the child comply. However, from the child's point of view, he has at a minimum delayed following through on the command. This is doubly reinforcing, because he is able to continue with the desired behavior for a little longer while delaying the unpleasant task. Therefore, to his parents' chagrin, he is highly unlikely to give up his defiant behavior, because the child does not understand that he has lost. To make matters worse, as the cycle of defiance unfolds over time, the parent may resort to coercive tactics in an effort to deescalate the child's emotional outbursts. Offers may be made to treat the child if he will settle down. In other situations, the child may injure himself while acting out, and the parent may soothe or comfort the child. This additional reinforcement accelerates the acquisition and maintenance of defiant behavior. Through this process, the child becomes locked in the cycle because of unwitting parental reinforcement. Parents become locked in the cycle because of partial success with the child.

Another outgrowth of the continuing cycle is that parents may tend to shy away from the child, perhaps to avoid confrontations. Consequently, the parents will miss opportunities to provide reinforcement for prosocial or appropriate behaviors of the child. Even when they know that the child is behaving well, the parents may withhold comment or fail to notice. Failure to notice may also allow the defiant child to engage in additional deviant behaviors. Lack of parental monitoring is associated with the later development of antisocial behaviors, such as lying, stealing, and destruction of property, and is a precursor to the development of CD (Frick et al., 1992; Hinshaw & Anderson, 1996; Loeber, 1990; Loeber et al., 1993; Patterson, 1982; Patterson, Dishion, & Chamberlain, 1993; Patterson, Reid, & Dishion, 1992).

As the process continues to unfold, parents of defiant children may become so angry with the child that they inadvertently punish prosocial behavior. This may occur by making sarcastic comments when the child exhibits prosocial behavior or insinuating that the child's prosocial behavior is instigated by malevolent ulterior motives.

Worse yet, J. Snyder and Patterson (1995) indicated that rapidly escalating episodes of mutual aggressive behavior of parents and children are self-reinforcing, because when the aggression peaks the episode typically terminates with either the child acquiescing to the parents' command or escaping the directive. Therefore, termination of the conflict followed by partial success reinforces more conflict. Both parents and children come to believe that perhaps one more episode will settle the growing war in their favor. This leads to a never-ending cycle of final showdowns.

Greene's Vicious Cycles

Ross Greene (2001) also described a vicious cycle but views it from a different angle. As previously stated, Greene argued that noncompliant behavior is fueled by the goodness of fit between parents and children as it pertains to a variety of temperamental, developmental, neurological, and social traits found in both children and parents. Furthermore, he views these traits as skills that, when delayed, result in uneven development for the child. Skill deficiencies cluster in such a way as to form an inflexible child. An inflexible child is easily frustrated when demands are made that require skills outside of his narrow repertoire. This feeds a vicious cycle as follows:

- When children are noncompliant, they behave as if they are attempting to escape from parental commands; however, this is illusory. In effect, the child wishes to be compliant but is unable to do so because he cannot shift gears quickly enough to satisfy parental expectations.

- This creates frustration, which then causes the child to shut down or go into what Greene (2001) referred to as a mental form of *vapor lock*. Vapor lock is a metaphor taken from automobiles when under certain conditions a car's engine stalls and will not run.
- In frustration, parents are prone to read vapor lock as defiance. When parents read the child's noncompliance as willful, they are compelled to impose their will on the child for fear of losing their authority.
- This then stimulates an emotional, symmetrical escalation that is similar to that described by Barkley (1997).

Such escalations are likely to be repeated because the child is unable to expand his flexibility skills in an environment where there is much pressure and either little teaching, or teaching that is mistimed, during the middle of an emotionally escalating situation. As long as the parents view the child as engaging in deliberately coercive behaviors, they are unlikely to change their style. Greene (2001) referred to the escalation sequence as a *meltdown*. His formula for a meltdown is inflexibility + inflexibility = meltdown.

DISRUPTIVE BEHAVIORS: THE CONNECTING THREAD

The Mental Research Institute group (Fisch, Weakland, & Segal, 1982) offered a transtheoretical view of vicious cycles that we believe contributes to a common understanding of disruptive behaviors. The foundations of this view were laid out earlier, in chapters 2 and 3. Here, the view is that there are two common strategic errors, made by parents, which contribute to disruptive behavior formation and maintenance. Both errors have a similar theme: They involve trying too hard to obtain compliance from the child, resulting in overpursuit. In essence, trying too hard to obtain compliance is synonymous with the term *coercion* (to force someone to act or think in a given manner).

The first of these strategic errors involves parental strategies that are designed to reach accord with the child through opposition. Here the parent who is preoccupied with authority issues becomes involved in haranguing the child in an effort to obtain compliance with specific behaviors. The harangue overshoots the mark because it is really directed at forcing the child to treat the parent with the respect, care, or the deference that the parent feels is due. In effect, to be in compliance the child must not only perform the required task but also acknowledge that the parent is "one-up." This requires compliance and places it at a higher level than simply obeying a request. Consider a child who has been directed to brush her teeth. If she obeys but makes a look on her face that appears disrespectful, then she will not be in compliance. This will trigger a harangue about showing the proper respect for her parent. The Mental Research Institute group (Fisch et al., 1982) wrote that "this form of problem solving provokes the very behavior the complainant wishes to eliminate, whether the demand for one-upness is phrased as being right or being in charge, and whether it is pursued by threats, force, or by logic" (p. 140).

The second type of strategic error is another form of overpursuit that takes on a more manipulative quality. This involves attempts to obtain compliance through volunteerism. Here the parent is afraid of being seen as dictatorial. Consequently, she engages in endless attempts to get the child to agree with or want to follow directives that are necessary but perhaps unpleasant. This type of error is summed up in the statement "I would like him to do it, but even more, I want him to want to do it." Again, directives that come out of this mode go far beyond a simple request for compliance. To follow such a directive the child must change his internal emotional state. Any sign, verbal or nonverbal, that he has not done so will bring on lectures and sermons that ultimately result in a meltdown or explosive episode.

In sum, this perspective offers an elegantly simple explanation for the vicious cycles in disruptive behaviors that have important implications. As parents become frustrated with their inability to obtain compliance from the child, they initiate a pattern of overpursuit. In this pattern, the parent goes beyond efforts to obtain compliance with specific requests. Instead, each request represents an effort by the parent to obtain categorical compliance from the child. The parent is in essence trying to transform the child's nature. Furthermore, as Greene, Ablon, Goring, Fazio, and Morse (2004) indicated, categorical compliance "is a developmental milestone on the trajectory of emerging self-regulation and affective modulation" (p. 372). Hence, from this perspective, the parent is unwittingly attempting to force the achievement of human developmental milestone. This is akin to trying to make a young child instantaneously acquire a full complement of language skills.

Sequentially, a two-step process is apparent. The first step involves the parent attempting to coerce change in the child. The second step is withholding validation until change occurs. In response, the child resists change and is deprived of validation. The child in turn invalidates the parent through noncompliant behavior. A vicious negative affect cycle then ensues that is characterized by mutual invalidation. This is a key first-order trap for parents and children.

THE SECOND-ORDER CHANGE SEQUENCE

After carefully reviewing empirically supported disruptive behavior treatment methods, we found that there are a number of common process outcomes that occur with effective treatment. The general order of this sequence is as follows:

1. Step 1: Parents and other caregivers adopt a more charitable view of what motivates the child's defiant behaviors. (New rationales for the child's behavior allow a more validating relationship.)
2. Step 2: Parents and other caregivers develop a proactive plan that narrows problem-solving efforts to a subset of specific target behaviors. (Parents reverse their demands to change everything and focus only on a small set.)
3. Step 3: Parents and other caregivers decrease or eliminate arguments with the child by refusing to engage in argumentation. (Parents reverse their willingness to fight.)
4. Step 4: There is a shift to rely on natural consequences as the primary mode of teaching the child. *Natural consequences* are defined as consequences that occur as a direct result of nature, such as becoming hungry if one doesn't eat (Levy et al., 2001).
5. Step 5: Parents dramatically reduce the use of punishment or significant consequences. If these techniques are used at all, they are reserved only for serious situations, are part of a larger proactive plan, and are enforceable.

These process outcomes occur within the context of a new pattern of parent–child interaction that is established through the treatment process. The new pattern reverses the "force change, then validate" sequence by having the parent validate the child before requesting change. The central challenge in treatment is obtaining compliance from parents and other caregivers with following the reversed pattern. More specifically, the steps are as follows:

- The parent shows interest in the child; this interest is shown by noticing the child when she is playing or engaging in independent activities. Interest may also be shown in problems that the child is attempting to resolve. (A new rationale initiates a new parent–child relationship.)
- The parent looks for ways to validate the child or take the child's perspective. (This starts building a newly validating relationship.)
- The parent establishes specific behavioral goals or expectations for the child. (Treatment rationales reduce the opportunities for defiance.)
- The parent reduces or restrains expectations for categorical change in the child. (The pattern of demands is reversed.)
- The parent looks for and validates incremental changes as they occur. (This includes the related procedures of each approach.)

We propose that the previously described five-step sequence explains how change occurs in effective therapy with disruptive behavior disorders. In effect, we are hypothesizing that the answer to Kazdin's (2002) question about the theory of change lies in the previously stated pattern reversal or second-order change. These also tend to match Frank and Frank's (1991) contextual model components as noted earlier. Recall that those components common to all effective treatments include an emotionally charged validating relationship; a set of rationales or "myths" to describe the problem and set a direction for treatment; and a set of related procedures to produce that change. Again, the pattern of "force change, then validate" is reversed to "validate, then work toward gradual change." This is a new change sequence.

FOLLOWING THE CHANGE SEQUENCE IN EFFECTIVE TREATMENTS

In this section, we review family-oriented methods of treating disruptive behaviors from the perspective of the second-order change sequence. The treatments that have been specifically chosen for review include Barkley's (1997) PT and Greene's (2001) collaborative problem-solving (CPS) approaches. These are two leading empirically supported approaches that focus on parent–child interaction. Limiting our comparison to these two should help make our point in a less complex way. With some minor exceptions, they will occupy our main discussion. However, there are a variety of other empirically supported approaches that also merit close attention by anyone interested in working with this more severely disruptive range of children and adolescents. These include multisystemic therapy (MST; Henggeler, Schoenwald, Rowland, & Cunningham, 2002), functional family therapy (Alexander & Sexton, 2002), and brief strategic family therapy (Szapocznik, Robbins, Mitrani, Santisteban, & Williams, 2002). There will be several points from each approach that we will draw forward. We have chosen to omit stand-alone cognitive therapies (i.e., problem-solving skills therapy; Kazdin, 2002) from the review because of the growing emphasis on family work in this area. A similar change sequence may be found, however, across all of these related approaches.

For now, we will mainly compare Barkley's (1997) and Greene's (2001) approaches to follow the thread of the change sequence. We begin by discussing assessment and its effects on change. Then we generally follow Frank and Frank's (1991) contextual model components to organize the rest of our comparisons. We first discuss how therapists enhance their relationship with parents and then the parents' relationship with their children through new rationales and validating interactions. Then we move to how narrowing the focus of behaviors needing change and the general procedures of both approaches enable multiple reversals or second-order shifts in the ways parents interact with their children. Last, we reemphasize how the change sequence of these two empirically supported treatments represents a second-order intervention that has produced impressive results with disturbed disruptive parent–child problems.

Assessment

The first step in the process of engaging families with disruptive children in treatment is assessment of the child and family. Although all of the reviewed treatment methods involve an elaborate assessment process, the precise focus of the assessment varies. For example, in addition to behavioral checklists, Greene (2001) stressed the importance of psychoeducational testing that is aimed at understanding difficulties that the child may be experiencing in a wide range of domains, including cognitive functioning, achievement skills, executive functioning, language processing, and developmental delays. Barkley (1997), although interested in similar domains, placed special emphasis on the parents filling out a variety of checklists that are specifically directed at assessing the child's disruptive behaviors at home and in school.

Although we will not track other family-oriented approaches beyond the assessment process, it may be helpful to address their similarities at this phase. MST engages the family in a more ecologically based assessment. The MST therapist shows interest in understanding the combination-of factors that sustain the identified problems. This interest is expressed by interviewing family members and relevant relatives, neighbors, friends in the family's social network, teachers, and school personnel. Other persons who are involved in community activities attended by the child and family also may be interviewed. In brief strategic family therapy, family functioning is stressed as part of the assessment and is measured with the Family Systems Ratings measure (Szapocznik et al., 1991).

Despite differences in focus, there are several objectives that family-oriented therapies have in common as pertains to assessment. The first is to ensure that the child demonstrates disruptive behaviors that rise to the threshold of a disorder. In programs such as MST (Henggeler et al., 2002) an additional requirement is that the child is at risk of out-of-home placement. The second is to understand the repeating familial or community patterns that are maintaining the problem. In other words, the vicious cycle as understood through the lens of the treatment method is evaluated. Third and foremost, through assessment the therapist shows interest in the family. Henggeler et al. (2002) pointed out that parents or caregivers of disruptive youth often feel poorly served, if not blamed, by mental health professionals. Consequently, interest is shown toward parents in a way that confirms their status as the executive officers of the family. This is consistent with each family-oriented framework we have reviewed. Placing the parents in a leadership role is accomplished by taking the parents' concerns about their child seriously. From the perspective of the second-order change, the parents' premise that the child is the problem bearer is accepted. Despite agreeing with the parent that the child has the problem, great care is taken to also show a nonjudgmental interest in the child, affirming a dialectical balance in accepting both positions equally.

Enhancing the Parent–Child Relationship

Each family framework has within its method a procedure or set of procedures that are designed to assist the parent in developing a renewed interest in the child. As previously stated, the authors concur that at the heart of disruptive behaviors is a "toxic negativity cycle" between parent and child (Alexander & Sexton, 2002). This cycle involves reciprocal attribution of negative motivation ascribed by parents toward the child, and vice versa. The assessment process and interest that the therapist shows in the child is a first step with assisting the parent with viewing the child in a more favorable light. In Barkley's (1997) PT, the parent is taught a technique for engaging the child in nondirective play early in the therapy process and long before addressing the child's noncompliant behaviors. With this technique, the parent is directed to spend 5 to 10 minutes daily joining the child while he or she plays. The parent is to show interest but not attempt to direct or correct the child. If the child engages the parent in competitive play, the parent is instructed to let the child establish the rules and allow the child to win. The parent is also instructed to go along with the child if he breaks the rules. This begins reestablishing a parent–child bond while allowing for increased positive interactions and validation.

In Greene's (2001) method, the therapist creates a new interest in the child by using information gleaned from the child's psychological tests to show that the child's noncompliant behavior is a function of difficulty with thinking clearly through frustration. In effect, Greene reframes willful noncompliance as a set of skills that the child is unable to perform. This is a central therapeutic rationale. He then indicates that the skill set can be learned. He reported that when parents have a better sense of why their children behave as they do, later strategies for helping the child improve become clearer.

The important common thread is that treatment begins with a demonstration of interest that goes from therapist to parents to child. Sequentially, therapists of each studied method refrain from the use of change techniques while building a therapeutic relationship with the family. The authors of functional family therapy (Alexander & Sexton, 2002) have conducted noteworthy research on the early phase of treatment, which they refer to as *engagement*. They reported that relational skills are the therapist's most important tool during engagement. Barkley (1997) concurred, citing specific evidence that supports the importance of relationship-building with parents and children as a critical factor in outcome variance (Crits-Christoph & Mintz, 1991).

Validation

As we have stated, clients often come for therapy when they are in a state of demoralization. However, with the disruptive disorders comes a twist: The parents of the child are usually in a demoralized state, whereas the child has little or no insight into his or her problem. For this reason, family-oriented approaches have evolved in such a way that the therapist develops a partnership with parents around changing the child's behavior. This is a relatively new development in the field and runs counter to the tradition of attempting to treat the child in individual therapy. Henggeler and associates (2002) wrote that

> Mental health services for children have traditionally placed parents on the periphery of treatment or viewed caregivers as the problem, not the solution. MST involves a shift from child-centered services to the family as the client. This shift is extremely difficult for many clinicians. (p. 8)

The shift to family-centered therapy is not isolated to MST but is readily observed in all of the family-oriented approaches that we have reviewed. In effect, the shift of reference from child to family represents a second-order change in the child therapy field.

Validating Parents

In family-centered approaches, the parents or caregivers are treated as the primary client. Given this, family-oriented therapists use validation as a tool for building a relationship with parents first. To validate parents, the therapist makes a distinction between parental *intent* and *actions*. The child or adolescent is viewed as posing special challenges for parenting. Parents, unaware of the hidden complexities, engage in parenting practices that may seem reasonable but that do not work. From this perspective, parents have good intentions; they are unfortunately operating on false premises that guide their parenting practices. In other words, the parents' failure to properly raise their child is validated or justified on the basis that the parents are doing as well as can be expected given their current understanding of the child's behavior. Although the reviewed approaches all use this same approach, they do so in a variety of ways.

In Barkley's PT (1997), providing a frame or rationale that validates parents is the primary focus of the first treatment session. Blame is taken off of the parents by demonstrating how complex the causes of misbehavior are. This starts with temperament contributions; physical characteristics of the child and developmental abilities, which can complicate problem solving; and the child's ability to comprehend and follow commands. The objective is to demonstrate that the child's misbehavior is not entirely the parents' or child's fault. From here, a shift is made to show how children misbehave to gain positive consequences or rewards or to escape from currently ongoing unpleasant, boring, or effortful activities. The concept of intermittent reinforcement is used to demonstrate how children do not have to be successful all the time with escaping or avoiding unpleasant activities to show noncompliant behavior in response to most commands. The therapist then explains the role of stress events and how family stress may cause parents to fluctuate with their commands, supervision, and use of consequences with the child. The therapist summarizes by saying that many times characteristics of the parent or child are such that they will naturally prove irritating to the other. The objective of the treatment is to change the fit between parent and child where possible and to lessen the behavioral problems of the child.

Greene and his colleagues (Greene, 2001; Greene et al., 2004) have indicated that in CPS emphasis is primarily placed on the child's characteristics. This major rationale places special emphasis on emotion regulation, frustration tolerance, adaptation, and problem-solving skills. He stated that a major objective is to help adults who interact with the child to develop a clear understanding of his or her unique difficulties, including specific factors that fuel his inflexibility–explosiveness (Greene, 2001). Furthermore, he argued the importance of achieving this understanding before initiating interventions with the child's problem behaviors. Here again is a rationale providing validation for the parents. Greene (2001) takes blame away by focusing on the child's problems, which are described as being neurologically based. Furthermore, improving the child will require a special kind of care. The child will need a "user friendly" environment. The rationale implying that special care is needed for a neurologically based problem also justifies or validates why the parents may not have known the proper way to raise the child in the first place.

Establishing Validating Parent–Child Relationships

After the process of validating parents, family-oriented clinicians then seek to initiate a process in which the parents validate the child. Barkley (1997) stated that the value of parental attention is quite low at the beginning of therapy. This makes efforts to motivate the child toward improved behavior useless in many cases. Therefore, early PT sessions are designed to assist the parent with increasing forms of attending to and appreciating the child's behavior. Barkley stated that consequences, positive or negative, will not have much effect on the child until the parent–child relationship has been restored. Levy and colleagues (2001) echoed this position and warned readers, in their manual for parents, not to read ahead to the intervention chapters unless the parent–child bond is solid.

The work of Greene (2001) has a similar pattern. Treatment starts with the previously described no-fault framing or rationale that is used to validate the parents. Embedded in this frame is a no-fault frame for the child as well. The child is not responsible for his temperamental difficulties, as these are inborn. He is not responsible for physical characteristics that make him prone to defiant behavior; neither is he responsible for developmental disabilities that may also contribute to the problem. Therefore, if the child's behavior is to ultimately improve, he will need a user-friendly environment, in which problem behaviors are seen as incoherent as opposed to a sign of a badly behaved child. In other words, the child's misbehavior is validated or understandable given his impairments. This rationale is geared to blocking the parents' formerly demanding-and-withholding patterns and initiates collaborative and affirming interactions in their place. The similarity in methods across treatments is that they each attempt to undermine the belief that the child's misbehavior is motivated by ill intent.

Establishing Goals (Narrowing the Field of Change)

As we have previously indicated, the core issue around the treatment of children with disruptive behaviors is that parents try too hard to obtain compliance from the child. There is a loss of perspective as parents attempt to coerce compliance on a wide range of issues that range from trivial to major. Because the parent is in essence attempting to bend the will of the child, all issues may be treated with the same amount of intensity. For example, the same level of importance may be assigned to picking up toys as playing with knives. In other situations, priorities may be hierarchical but highly faulty in terms of their relative importance. Here more attention may be paid to picking up toys than playing with knives.

Effective parent–child treatments counter these problems through the process of goal setting. Each framework has a method for placing parents in charge of developing a plan that establishes specific parenting priorities. Each method also assists parents with ignoring issues that are of lesser importance. Here we see two subtle second-order changes. First, there is a shift from reactive to proactive parenting, because parents are now preplanning what behaviors they will seek to change and what behaviors they will let go. Second, changing specific behaviors is the opposite of seeking categorical compliance and so represents another second-order shift in the parents approach to the child. Notice that these shifts occur before any direct efforts are made to change the child's noncompliant behavior.

Coaching Parents to Revise Their Goals

Greene and his colleagues (Greene, 2001; Greene et al., 2004) have developed a method for assisting parents with establishing priorities that they refer to as a *basket framework*. He asks parents to imagine three baskets in a row: Basket A, Basket B, and Basket C. The baskets are then used to assist the parent in establishing priorities and goals for the child.

Basket A represents situations in which the parent needs to maintain authority. These are situations that involve safety, such as harm to self, others, animals, and property. Greene (2001) offered parents a 3-point litmus test to help determine whether a behavior should go into Basket A: First, the issue must be important enough to endure a meltdown. Second, the child must be capable of successfully exhibiting the behavior on a fairly consistent basis. Third, the parent must be able to enforce his or her wishes.

The first point in the litmus test is very interesting from the perspective of second-order change. Greene (2001) pointed out that in limited situations the exercise of parental authority is necessary. He instructed that in such situations parents should be prepared, because they will most likely induce a meltdown. This line of logic is consistent with *symptom prescription*, because now the parents are deliberately enacting their contribution to the child's meltdown. Parents are typically unaware of the role that they play in meltdowns and view these episodes as occurring spontaneously.

Basket B involves a list of behaviors that are important but that are not worthy of a meltdown. Basket B is considered to be most important basket because it is here that the parent is going to do the work of teaching the child flexibility and frustration tolerance skills. This is the field of change.

Basket C contains goals and behaviors that were once a high priority but will now be downgraded. This basket is considered the largest basket or the basket that overflows. When children engage in Basket C behaviors, the parents are instructed to not even mention the behavior. A wide range of behaviors fall into this category, including decisions the child might make to go out in the cold without gloves or poor selections on what food to eat. Not responding to these behaviors and instead allowing natural consequences to take their course is a key second-order change for parents.

Barkley (1997) has a different approach for assisting parents with establishing parenting priorities for the child. His method is implemented sequentially. As indicated earlier in the chapter, at the beginning of treatment Barkley asks the parents to describe problems they are having with the child and general goals. This aspect of the treatment is then to some extent placed on hold until Step 4. Here parents are given assistance with establishing a token economy, which requires that parents list specific desired social behaviors and then place a value on each behavior. Colored tokens are used to symbolize the relative values of the desired behaviors. Here again we see a similar pattern. Specific goals for the child are expressed as desirable behaviors that have different values. This results in a hierarchical arrangement of parenting priorities. Also, in establishing the desired behavior list it is virtually impossible for the parents to define all possible desirable behaviors. Hence, through the process elimination parents deselect behaviors that will not be the focus of treatment.

Reversing the Parent–Child Relationship

Establishing specific goals or behavioral targets has an important effect on parent–child interactions. As previously indicated, Greene (2001) pointed to the importance of a user-friendly environment for the disruptive child. In such an environment, overall demands on the child for flexibility and frustration tolerance are reduced by judiciously establishing priorities among parenting goals.

The need to reduce stress on the child in order to speed the process of change seems counterintuitive and so represents another reversal or second-order change for parents. In essence, the therapeutic task is to help parents gain compliance with the child by decreasing stress and increasing positive interactions. This concept is in line with Frank and Frank's (1991) point that clients become more conservative when confronted with demands to change. We are suggesting that this same principle is observable with children who exhibit disruptive behaviors. Pressure to change increases resistance, whereas reducing pressure in a planned or strategic manner reduces the child's resistance, thus increasing the likelihood that the child will develop skills necessary for complying with adult directives.

Coaching Parents in Restraint and Validation

Once parenting priorities have been established, parents share their expectations or incremental goals with the child. This leads to another common thread: All models reviewed have built-in restraints to change. Restraints are used throughout the treatment process and during the period that transpires between the parents' establishment of goals and the child showing evidence of incremental change. Restraining is generally a blocking strategy that relieves the parent from pressuring the child to change. All methods also have a system for validating incremental change when it occurs. This represents Steps 4 and 5 in the change sequence: Wait for change or restrain from change, and then validate incremental change.

Barkley's Approach to Coaching Parents

Reviews of Barkley's (1997) PT usually emphasize the reward and consequence systems that have become the hallmark of this type of treatment. As we have already begun to show, however, the change pattern that underlies PT is far more complex than how it is usually represented. *Parent Training* demonstrates many second-order change strategies that are built into the treatment system. As was previously noted, the reward or reinforcement system is not introduced until the fourth step in the treatment process. During the fourth step, instruction is limited to the reward aspect of the system. Consequences are not discussed until the fifth step.

As was also previously described, early session interventions are aimed at rebuilding the parent–child bond. Parents are taught to change the environment so that there are fewer objects that the disruptive child can damage, engage the child in nondirective play, catch the child doing something good so that this can be validated, give simple commands once, redirect the child or ignore him when he does not follow commands, and engage the child in complementary activities. However, all of this is presented within a frame in which the parents are told that they should not expect the child to change yet. Reducing expectations for change is a classic use of restraint, because it reverses the forced change approach that is typical of parents of children with disruptive disorders.

At the session in which the reinforcement system is introduced, the therapist shifts gears and tells the parents to not be disheartened if they have not seen much change in the child, because today they will receive a powerful system for increasing compliance. Parents are then instructed on how to implement the first half of the token economy. This involves giving a directive that is part of the child's behavioral plan and waiting for the child to comply. The child is then paid with a token that represents the value of the task that has been performed. Here again we observe the use of restraint, or waiting. Parents are taught that it is normal for a child to take up to 15 seconds before complying with a directive (this is a longer interval than it seems). Also, recall that parents are given only the first half of the reinforcement system. Parents will implement only this half before the next session. They are warned against jumping ahead by taking tokens away or punishing the child; that will come later. From the perspective of second-order change, holding back the second half of the system is a way of suggesting to the parents that although awarding tokens is powerful, there is another intervention yet to come. Hence, the hope of change is increased, while pressure to change the child is simultaneously relieved.

There is another facet of the reinforcement system that is of interest. Rewarding the child with a token is framed as payment for work done. The token is translated into a flat exchange of privileges for accomplishment of a task. Tokens are not awarded until the task is completed. There is no urging, pleading, or begging by the parent to obtain compliance from the child. There are no sermons or harangues. The directive is issued only once. When behavioral compliance occurs, the child is given a symbolic validation or token in exchange. This completes the change sequence of wait or restrain and then validate incremental change. The previous coercive interactions are blocked by the process.

Greene's Approach to Coaching Parents

Greene's CPS method (Greene, 2001; Greene et al., 2004) is presented to parents within an overarching rationale that suggests that, through treatment, parents will develop a more realistic vision of who the child is and what the parent can hope to create with the child. This realistic appraisal involves reversing parental expectations for changing their child's nature and is there-fore by definition a restraint to change or second-order treatment strategy.

There is also a series of restraints that are built into Greene's (2001; Greene et al., 2004) basket framework. Let us first quickly turn to Baskets A and C. Recall that Basket A contains behaviors that involve serious risks to self, others, animals, or property. Parents are instructed to do what is neces-sary to stop behavior that occurs in this basket. The operant word is *stop* the behavior. In other words, parents are not attempting to directly change Bas-ket A behaviors. They are simply using their parental authority to stop the behavior so that the child or someone or something is not damaged. From the perspective of second-order change, stopping is synonymous with the term *restraint*, and so in Basket A parents are using a restraint approach. Parents are also trained to refrain from using instructional methods (e.g., sermons, lectures, etc.) when stopping a behavior in this category, because the child is incoherent and incapable of learning during a meltdown. This further blocks parental expectations of changing the child in this mode. This reversal takes pressure off both the parents and the child for changing during times when emotional intensity is at a peak. From the perspective of the second-order change, the combined symptom prescription and restraint makes Basket A a powerful intervention strategy. In effect, the meltdown is pre-scribed within a context of lowered expectations for change.

Recall that Basket C is the overflow basket. This basket contains a va-riety of behaviors with which the parent chooses not to intervene. All pres-sure is relieved from efforts to bring about change, and so here we identify another reversal or second-order shift. The shift occurs because, as mentioned earlier, behaviors in this category are behaviors that had a high priority be-fore treatment. Now parents will do an about-face and not comment on Bas-ket C behaviors at all. This reverses parental expectations for change in this category as well.

Basket B defines the arena in which parents will focus their efforts on changing the child. Here we again see subtle yet powerful reversals. The change method used in Basket B involves a win–win type of problem-solving method. The win–win approach is based on a general formula that has many variations depending on the situation. The general formula is as follows, "If you get to do what you want, you will be happy, and I will be unhappy; if you do what I want, I will be happy, and you will be unhappy." The child is then asked to think of a solution that will make both the child and parent happy.

In this process, the parent first shows that he or she understands the child's perspective and then gently represents the parent's own perspective. This is done crisply and with simple ownership: "Your choice will make you happy and me unhappy." The parent then does the same with his or her own preferred method of problem resolution, acknowledging that if his or her solution is adopted, then the parent will be happy and the child unhappy.

Acknowledging the child's plight in a respectful way represents a demonstration of parental empathy for the child and is therefore validating. Finally, the parents invite the child to do some mutual problem solving. Greene (2001) suggested that the parent may need to assist the child by giving examples of solutions that meet the dual requirement of satisfying the child and parent. By helping the child arrive at a win–win solution, the child begins to view the parent as an ally as opposed to an adversary. The win–win validates both the child's and parents' perspectives. The parents also remain in control because they ultimately determines whether the child's solution is acceptable. Greene went on to point out that negotiating in this way is very difficult for the inflexible child and can be almost as frustrating and arousing as when the parent takes a more authoritative stance as represented by Basket A. He further said that learning how to execute Basket B is an art that takes time to become skillful in. This is an embedded prediction that change will go slowly and is a reversal of parental expectations for immediate change in the child.

There are two additional points on the Basket B strategy that are particularly relevant to the second-order change sequence. There are two parts to learning the approach: (a) learning the win–win strategy, as may be applied to a variety of situations, and (b) determining in real time into what basket a particular behavior falls. For any behavior that the parent thinks falls into a basket she must first identify the behavior and then determine into which basket it falls. This decision-making process may not always be easy and forces the parent to stop and think before intervening. This blocks emotional engagement with the child.

Embedded in the process is the "validate, then ask for incremental change" sequence as the parent first validates the child's perspective before asking the child to develop a win–win solution to the problem. Each successful negotiation represents an incremental step in the direction of a more flexible child.

Greene, Ablon, Goring, Raezer-Blakely, et al. (2004) conducted a study that compared the CPS approach with Barkley's (1997) PT approach. The study revealed that CPS worked as well or better than PT in many domains. A limitation of the study was that the principal author supervised therapists in both conditions. Results were favorable enough that the authors recommended that the study be replicated independently. The second-order change model predicts that both methods are likely to be found to be equally powerful because they share a common feature, second-order change.

Significant Consequences

We have now fully described the five-step change sequence. In sum, the steps include (a) show interest in the family and child; (b) validate the family and child; (c) establish or point to specific behavioral goals; (d) restrain or wait for change; and (e) validate change when it occurs. This is a *reversal* of the common problem sequence between parents and their children of "demand, then validate."

Within this sequence we have not discussed the role of significant consequences or punishment (Levy et al., 2001). A review of the treatment methods suggests that this is somewhat of a controversial subject, as there is not agreement on the role of significant consequences in developmental change. Because significant consequences have a role in PT, and because PT is the most studied method for the treatment of disruptive disorders (Barkley, 1997, Kazdin, 2002), we now look briefly at how consequences are used in PT. Careful review of the PT method suggests that significant consequences are not part of the change process but are part of the structure for maintaining change once it occurs.

Barkley (1997) reported that by the time parents have learned how to validate the child through the token economy system many parents are reporting dramatic changes in their child. In fact, by this time, many parents are not seeing problems in their child's behavior. This suggests that the child at this juncture in the treatment program has learned compliance skills in a manner that is satisfactory to his or her parents. The use of time-out and penalties is taught to parents because it is assumed that there will be a honeymoon period with the token system and that the child will experience occasional noncompliance, despite the acquisition of compliance skills. This leads to several key points that are of importance to this discussion. First, as previously stated, significant consequences are used, but only after the child has begun demonstrating the compliance skills. Second, significant consequences are limited to the most serious situations that are part of a plan. They are not used in a haphazard fashion. Finally, significant consequences are meant to be mild and enforceable. Parents are taught not to threaten the child with a consequence that cannot be enforced. Consequences are also tailored to the age of the child.

Instead of supporting parentally applied consequences, all methods of treatment primarily rely on natural consequences as the instructor for the child. This further disengages escalating vicious cycles between parents and children or adolescents. Natural consequences occur intentionally or unintentionally through the process of narrowing the field of change. Narrowing the field creates room for the child to make interactional mistakes and learn on her own. For example, Basket C in Greene's (2001; Greene et al., 2004) framework would be viewed as from this perspective as the world of natural consequences. The elimination of the toxic negative interactive cycle also eliminates parental interactions that can transform natural consequences as learning tools into more of the same parent–child conflict. For example, Levy and colleagues (2001) recommended that parents react sympathetically when a child receives a natural consequence so as to not restart the cycle of negativity. It is harder for children or adolescents to escalate with their parent when they hear them say "I'm sorry that happened to you." The genuine soft emotions of this one-down parental position counteract the typical first-order vicious cycles of arguments and further defiance. Natural consequences replace parentally imposed consequences to reinforce ongoing change. Life becomes the best teacher.

FOLLOWING THE THREAD

Parent–child relationship problems are widely viewed as the result of vicious cycles whereby parents try to force compliance to their demands, and children and adolescents resist. Second-order interventions reverse the change sequence for parents by offering rationales for why the escalating battles happen and then having parents de-escalate their demands by validating their children first before gradually shaping collaboration. Second-order change finds its path through all of the approaches reviewed. Frank and Frank's (1991) contextual model holds true as it tracks the path of intervention through a sequence of steps that reverse what parents have typically done. Establishing a validating relationship for whatever rationale, and refusing to fight except in the most extreme instances, deescalates the vicious cycles and allows a new, more positive relationship to begin. Again, the inseparable foundation of first- and second-order change is at the center of another set of impressively effective treatments.

9

COUPLES THERAPY

It seems to me that most couple problems amount to two people trying
to reach accord through opposition.

—John H. Weakland

There is, perhaps, no other set of empirically supported treatments
(ESTs) that more explicitly target first- and second-order change than those
for couple problems. Couple problems are clearly described as escalating vicious cycles of solution-generated problems. With couples, and in couples
therapy, it's all about changing these cycles. Couples learn how to negotiate
change with their partner, how to avoid escalating demands for change, how
to deescalate a spiraling dance of change gone awry, how to repair failed
attempts at change, how to accept that there is no need for change, how to
change their view of their partner and of their life together, and how to
evolve through changes in their relationship over time. Therapists learn how
to balance negotiating the need for change in their clients against the prospect that what is needed is for clients to accept things the way they are.
Interventions are designed to either block or redirect partners' solutions to
challenges in their relationship. In all cases, second-order change is at the
heart of all of this.

That people experience problems in their relationships is supported by
divorce rate statistics in the United States; an estimated 50% to 67% of first
marriages and 60% to 67% of second marriages end in divorce (Gottman,
1999). It is no surprise, then, that beyond seeking help for anxiety and depression, people more often seek therapy for marital and partner difficulties

191

than for any other type of problem (Gottman, 1999; Veroff, Kulka, & Douvan, 1981). Gottman (1999) listed a range of consequences of such couple distress and dissolution, including increased physical illness and mortality from illness; decreased life span; and increased physical violence, suicide, and homicide, among other kinds of emotional and psychological distress. Therapists have been treating couples in distress using a myriad array of approaches for a long time. However, researchers have only recently looked into the validity of our assumptions about what makes for strong vital relationships and into the effectiveness of most common couple therapies.

We begin with a brief overview of what couple researchers John Gottman and his colleagues and Neil Jacobson and his colleagues have identified as myths and mistakes of marital therapy, along with their reviews of the effectiveness of most traditional couple treatments. After this, we turn to the recommended empirically based treatment approaches designed by these two related research groups as prime examples of the kind of ESTs that we are examining and integrating in this book. Finally, we will once more analyze these two related evidence-based couples therapy approaches from the perspective of first- and second-order change. As we have done at the end of each chapter, we conclude with a section that guides practitioners on how to flexibly put these ideas and approaches into practice.

MYTHS AND EFFECTIVENESS

John Gottman has been one of the premier researchers on couple relationships and couples therapy over the last several decades (cf. Gottman, 1999, 2000; Gottman & Silver, 1999). In one of the early chapters of his book, *The Marriage Clinic* (Gottman, 1999), he does a fine job of reviewing and refuting a range of widely held assumptions about couples and couples treatment. Many of these refutations help us redirect our thinking about not only what is important to positive relationships but also what should be the major areas of focus for effective therapy.

With all of these myths and hypotheses laid aside, what, then, do we have to say about successful couple relationships, and what should be done in successful couples therapy? Reviewing the literature on couples leads to the conclusion that it is mostly the process of how couples interact that determines their satisfaction and success. Consequently, it is the process of how couples negotiate their differences and less the content of the individuals' or couple's relationship that should become the focus of treatment. However, this seems all too close to what most typical couples therapy has done over the years. Thus, it would seem wise to look at how well the most tightly designed versions of couples therapy have done.

The late Neil Jacobson and his colleagues have been some of the most prominent researchers on the effectiveness of couples therapy. Jacobson was part of an early movement to design and test the effectiveness of behavioral approaches to couple treatment. Jacobson built on the first applications of behavioral principles to working with couples by Richard Stuart (1969, 1980) and by Gerald Patterson and Robert Weiss (Weiss, Hops, & Patterson, 1973), and some of the later findings of Harold Kelley's group, which studied close relationships (Kelley et al., 1983). Teaming up with Gala Margolin, and with the consultation of Andrew Christensen, Jacobson wrote one of the first manuals of traditional behavioral couples therapy: *Marital Therapy: Strategies Based on Social Learning and Behavior Exchange Principles* (Jacobson & Margolin, 1979). The two foundations of this approach, and most other related traditional behavioral couple therapies, are (a) *behavior exchange* (BE) and (b) *communication and problem-solving training* (CPT). In brief, BE techniques are designed to increase the ratio of positive to negative behaviors exchanged between couples at home. The more I have interactions with my partner that make me feel better, the better I feel about my relationship. Because there has been found to be an ideal ratio of five positives to every one negative exchange in satisfying marriages (Gottman, 1993), these interventions seek to decrease negative behaviors and increase positives at home for the couple. They are designed to create rapid change, yet not necessarily long-lasting change, in presenting problems, given that there are few new skills taught to handle future problems. CPT, however, de-emphasizes the presenting problem and focuses on training couples to be their own therapists through learning communication and conflict resolution skills. The better I learn to communicate and negotiate with my partner on issues that divide us, the better we will do as a couple at evolving positive agreements on how our relationship will go. After the short-term relief gained from the BE interventions, the skills taught in the CPT interventions are designed to extend the positive change and prevent relapse. The problem was that, although these combined interventions were effective, as predicted, and in just the ways predicted, the effects in the long run were not as impressive as initially thought.

Some classic studies found that an approach that combined BE and CPT outperformed either element applied separately (Jacobson, 1984; Jacobson & Follette, 1985; Jacobson, Follette, & Pagel, 1986; Jacobson, Schmaling, & Holtzworth-Munroe, 1987). Couples receiving BE experienced more short-term gain than in any other condition, changing the ratio of positive to negative behavior better than all other conditions. As predicted, CPT was most successful at teaching conflict resolution skills and exceeded all treatments in measures of enhancing communication. However, whereas the BE couples had a high relapse rate within 6 months, and whereas CPT couples were slower to relapse, there was more divorce in the CPT group after 2 years than there was in the BE couples. The researchers speculated that getting better at communicating while the couple experienced continued distress and little change may have helped the CPT couples to conclude more quickly that divorce was the best resolution. Not only did the combination of BE and CPT outperform the elements alone in regard to marital satisfaction but also, by the end of a 2-year follow-up, not a single couple had divorced. Although these were impressive results, there were some significant cautions brought up that cooled initial enthusiasm for this approach (as we have found in previous chapters on other problems).

To Jacobson's great credit, he led the charge at critiquing his own work and his own approach. The first point on which to be clear is that quite often a couple's problematic relationship tends to deteriorate over time without therapy. Thus, all organized approaches to couple treatment tend to outperform no-treatment control groups, if for no other reason than because control couples' relationships tend to deteriorate. Thus, even small changes are likely to be statistically significant compared with deteriorating control couples. However, Jacobson looked beyond statistical significance to devise a method of measuring *clinical significance*. Simply speaking, a clinically significant change would be rated as such if it returned the clients into a measured range similar to the normal, satisfied population (Jacobson & Truax, 1991). When these studies were re-evaluated from this perspective, it was found that for even the combined treatment, about one third of the couples didn't improve, and one third of those who did improve relapsed mostly within the first year of a 2-year follow-up. Thus, this empirically supported behavioral couples therapy was helping only about half the couples treated in therapy. However, this 50% success rate was not unique to the behavioral approaches; it was found on reanalysis of clinical trials of other approaches to be characteristic of all approaches to couples therapy (Jacobson & Addis, 1993). Thus, even with the most tightly designed and effective approaches, couples had about a 50–50 chance of getting better. This isn't the best of track records. It raises questions about who is more likely to benefit from these traditional couple therapies and who won't.

In line with these questions, these same researchers followed up on these findings to try to find out what sort of couples succeeded and who tended to fail at combined behavioral couple treatment (Jacobson et al., 1986; Jacobson et al., 1987). They found five factors that discriminated between couples who succeeded and those who failed. These five factors, labeled (a) *commitment*; (b) *age*; (c) *emotional engagement*; (d) *traditionality*; and (e) having *convergent goals* for the marriage, were found to contribute to partners' ability to accommodate, compromise, and collaborate with each other. Couples more willing to collaborate with treatment and to accommodate each other tended to be more committed to each other, younger, emotionally engaged with each other, and egalitarian, and had similar goals for their relationship. Conversely, couples who were on the verge of divorce were older; disengaged from each other; more traditional; disagreed on the vision of an ideal marriage; and were much less likely to collaborate, compromise, and accommodate one another and therapists. What became clear was that traditional behavioral couples therapy was built on the assumption that couples would be able to accommodate, compromise, and collaborate. Couples unable to do those things gained little from behavioral approaches that were based on joint definitions of the problem, good motivation to change, willingness to collaborate, and enthusiastic willingness to comply with treatment. The problem is that the most challenging and distressed couples, if not the majority of couples seeking therapy, don't fit this profile.

In response to these and other findings, proponents of the current leading ESTs in couples therapy have, in short, changed their views on change. One might say that the newest EST couple therapies represent a second-order change for both researchers and treatment teams. Instead of consistently advocating for change in couples and assuming their willing and enthusiastic compliance, these newer approaches are both teaching couples how and when to not demand or expect change and are teaching couples therapists how to do the same in their relationship with these couples. This is a reversal of former well-meaning solution-generated patterns for both couples and couples therapists. As one might expect of such second-order changes, they have realized impressive gains in helping couples become more effective and satisfied with their relationships and for couples therapy in its effectiveness, especially with the 50% of those couples who formerly were not getting help from more traditional approaches. Before we go on to describe how these empirically based couples therapies have implemented these changes in themselves, we need to look at their views on the first-order vicious cycle patterns in couples whom they are trying to change.

VICIOUS CYCLES

Bad solutions don't merely fail; they create an even bigger problem.
　　　　　　　　　—Christensen and Jacobson (2000, p. 98)

Both of the leading empirically supported approaches to couples treatment define couples problems as a series of first-order change escalations. These repeated escalations then become linked in an evolving vicious cycle of solution-generated problems. This larger problem pattern eventually defines the unique character of troubled relationships. These two complementary approaches to couples therapy do have something to say about what common elements contribute to these vicious cycles across most couples. We now turn to Jacobson and Christianson's (1996) work for professionals, *Integrative Couple Therapy*, and its companion for couples, *Reconcilable Differences* (Christensen & Jacobson, 2000); and to Gottman's work for professionals, *The Marriage Clinic* (Gottman, 1999); and the *Clinical Manual for Marital Therapy* (Gottman, 2000); and his companion for couples, *The Seven Principles for Making Marriage Work* (Gottman & Silver, 1999). After we review their descriptions of the vicious cycles couples get into, we discuss the essence of their approaches that embody second-order change for both couples and therapists.

Integrative Couples Therapy

Jacobson and Christensen's (1996) integrative couples therapy (ICT) is based on interdicting vicious cycles. Referring to the work of the Mental Research Institute's group on first- and second-order change (discussed earlier in this volume, in chaps. 2 and 3), they wrote the following about couple relationships: "There are times when efforts to change one's partner actually have the opposite effect. Direct attempts to change an intimate partner are often self-defeating, both because the particular efforts are misguided and because such attempts are likely to have the opposite effect" (Jacobson & Christensen, 1996, p. 13). These authors described couple problems in classic vicious cycle terms from an initial trigger, to a set of solutions that only exacerbate the problem, to a full-fledged solution-generated problem that takes on a self-fulfilling life of its own.

Incompatibilities and Vulnerabilities

Speaking about the transitions that lead to couple problems, Christensen and Jacobson (2000) wrote that "It is our belief that this painful transition begins with common, garden-variety incompatibilities between partners. The ways partners try to handle these incompatibilities often lead them along this painful path" (p. 23). The two general challenges they identify for all couples tend to be either (a) incompatibilities or (b) vulnerabilities. Marrying someone similar to oneself has a better prognosis for happiness than does marrying someone different, but both options can succeed. Conflicts are more likely to be caused by differences than similarities, but incompatibility on some dimension is practically guaranteed in all couples, no matter how similar they are. Earlier research on close relationships (Kelley et al., 1983) has identified two major areas of potential incompatibility: (a) level of desired closeness and (b) the extent of asymmetry in the couple. *Closeness* is defined as the extent, diversity, and intensity of interaction between partners. It describes the desired and actual amount of interaction, affection, and time partners spent doing things with each other. *Asymmetry* relates to the extent and nature of the differences between the partners. It refers to the roles the partners play in the relationship and the extent of each partner's power, control, and responsibility. *Vulnerabilities* are defined as personal sensitivities around universal themes of security ("Don't ever leave me"), freedom ("Help, I'm trapped!"), admiration and affirmation ("I'm somebody, too"), approval ("Tell me I'm OK"), and control ("Who's in charge here?"). Problems evolving from these areas spring from interpersonal sensitivities, disappointments, resentments, and the like. Incompatibilities generally evolve into differences that make a difference. Some things that were initially appealing in a partner may eventually become infuriating. Partners may find they differ on the degree of closeness they desire, with one craving gestures of frequent affection and the other greater distance. Differences in partners' expectations about rules, roles, power, dominance, and control may be influenced by cultural differences or gender role expectation differences and the like. Issues around the control and use of money, sexual intimacy, housework and child care, and individual career and related life choices are all fertile ground for differences between partners.

However, these and other closely related incompatibilities and vulnerabilities are merely potential triggers for difficulties. They occur in all relationships. They represent the content of the interaction. However, as we have discussed in some detail in the first several chapters, they don't necessarily have to evolve into problems. Each area of difference may be either assimilated by the partners or accommodated by one or both partners in the relationship as the relationship evolves and redefines itself. It is the process of how the couple solves these differences that determines whether the initial difference or perceived difficulty evolves into a true solution-generated problem. Both assimilating and accommodating solutions are, in fact, first-order solutions that work for the couple. It is those first-order changes that don't work, but are then reapplied in some form or variation, which become the vicious cycle of the couple's problem.

Solution-Generated Problems

Christensen and Jacobson (2000) agree that it is the couple's solutions that become the problem between them. They suggested that "As we cope ineffectively with the initial problem, created when our incompatibilities and vulnerabilities are triggered, we often generate a worse problem" (p. 104). Once these patterned ineffective solutions are reapplied, they increase in intensity and frequency as separate vicious cycles that evolve into a larger cycle over time to take on a life of its own. The cycle itself eventually becomes content for the ongoing frustration, hurt, and alienation between the parties. Christensen and Jacobson wrote of this when describing couples' ongoing arguments:

> They are criticizing each other for being critical. Now the process of their interaction, the way they cope with their problem, has become the content of their discussion. Their solution to the problem has become the problem. The "cure" has become the disease. (p. 104)

Once more, our familiar description of problems constituting vicious cycles of first-order solutions is vividly repeated. In their diagram of the "anatomy of an argument," Christensen and Jacobson picture the evolution of this cycle from an *initial problem* (the content of the argument, consisting of either provocations, incompatibilities, or vulnerabilities, or anger or hurts); to the process of *unsuccessful coping* with the initial problem (through accusation, blame, or coercion; avoidance, denial, or minimization; overreaction; or firming alliances or coalitions); and, finally, to the *reactive problem* (or the vicious cycle of the solution-generated problem in the relationship).

Each successive vicious cycle is described as proceeding through the characteristic phases, from escalation, to polarization, to alienation. *Escalation* between partners is not only the increase in tension, volume, or viciousness of the argument but also in the expansion of its focus to include other related or unrelated issues brought in to justify points or simply to retaliate. *Polarization* refers to the process of becoming rigidly fixed and extreme in our views through listening to our own reiterated arguments and using our partner's behaviors as proof for the truth of our position. *Alienation* is generally the result of escalated polarized arguments. It may be a product of frustration, or hurt, or refusal to address a problem, but it is always a negative development, with partners turning away from each other.

The other classic ABCs of heated arguments are referred to as a *toxic triad* or *toxic cures*. According to Christensen and Jacobson (2000), "Toxic cures are solutions that make the problem worse. They are treatments that aggravate the disease. Their intent is often to create change for the better: their result is to create change for the worse" (p. 107). The ABCs are accusation, blame, and coercion (and a "D" can be added for defensiveness). *Accusation* is simply pointing out that your partner has either done or not done something implicitly or explicitly expected in the relationship. This may take the form of accusing our partner of insensitivity, neglect, lack of collaboration, or a range of other perceived violations embodied in the triggering event. This accusation itself may be met with defensiveness or a counteraccusation that it was our reaction, and not their action, that was the problem. This can kick in the cycle right away. However, the addition of *blame* turns the cycle distinctly more negative. Here we start claiming that the cause of our partner's offense is his or her broadly defined negative personality characteristics. These may include the partner's moral character, mental or emotional instabilities, and personal failings or inadequacies, to name but a few. The point is that such statements become a personal indictment of our partner. Something deeply wrong with his or her character is at the root of the problem. All of this breeds defensive counterarguments from our partner. Finally, *coercion* goes beyond mere accusations and attacks. Coercion is intended to force our partner to do what we want through a barrage of demanding, nagging, criticizing, complaining, and making our partner feel guilty until he or she finally gives in. The inherent trap in this sort of coercion is that it most assuredly will escalate on the basis of how it works. One partner's coercion is reinforced because the other finally complied. The other's compliance is reinforced because the coercion stopped. However, future rounds of the same badgering are doomed by an intermittent ratio schedule of the partner's compliance and his or her habituation to the other's demands. In other words, we never know when our partner will finally relent and comply, and our partner may simply get used to the coercion. Thus, coercion is described as an addictive drug whereby early immediate effects require increasing doses to achieve the same effect. Partners may eventually deliberately ignore or actively resist these barrages and the positive feelings and loving atmosphere of the relationship eventually erode.

Polarization and the Mutual Trap

Jacobson and Christensen (1996) reflected on the process of partners trying to change each other's differences around some contentious theme by saying, "When two people engage in such change efforts simultaneously, the almost inevitable outcome is polarization or an exacerbation of the differences. When polarization occurs, the conflict increases rather than decreases" (p. 48). They referred to the *mutual trap* as the outcome of polarization. Although polarization doesn't necessarily stop, there comes a point when each partner feels trapped, stuck, helpless, and desperate. This is a separate, private, and rather implicit experience for each partner of a sense of entrapment in the very problem he or she is trying to resolve. The polarization process leading to the mutual trap is exactly what we have discussed as an escalating cycle of first-order changes leading to a self-perpetuating solution-generated problem. Each partner's solutions feed into the other and make the differences more extreme and more entrenched. Differences in a couple in their wish for closeness or distance, for example, can take on a focus around lovemaking. She pressures for him to have more interest in lovemaking (or his apparent distance cues her approach), which leads him to resent her intrusions and pull away; his pulling away makes her feel rejected and unloved; he responds to her hurt by forcing interest passion, or both, resulting in lack of arousal on his part, or, when he is successfully aroused, she reacts to his attention as being somehow not genuine or spontaneous. The cycle continues and reinforces itself. Similar mutual traps can develop around a wide array of general themes. Control and responsibility differences can evolve into mutual traps around such things as how to use resources and money, or who does what in the household or in regard to child care. Differences in partners' views of conventionality verses unconventionality, or in spontaneity versus conservatism, can create polarizing vicious cycles whereby each partner becomes more extreme in how they think they should spend their time, raise their children, or relate to their families or friends. One partner's position on these themes actually seems to be reinforced by the other's responses—as each tries to negate and change the other; their very attempts to change things further entrenches them and makes them more extreme. As we discussed in chapter 2, this is a defining feature of first-order change. Attempts to change something by negating it only affirm and strengthen what one is trying negate. The process of polarization that evolves mutual traps is the paradigm case of first-order change.

As with all first-order changes; the same dance is repeated, but with different steps. This is when alienation sets in, and the partners begin to disengage from one another, blaming their partner and turning away from them. Discussing the effect of these vicious cycles over time, Christensen and Jacobson (2000) wrote,

> Escalation, polarization, and alienation can occur gradually over time rather than in a single argument. As we repeat the same unsuccessful solution to our problems, persisting in wanting our partners to change, our tensions may escalate, our positions may become polarized, and we may become alienated from each other. (p. 116)

These are the solution-generated problems that the ICT approach targets for change, but as we shall see, change in a new and different way.

Gottman's Vicious Cycles

John Gottman is another outstanding research clinician. His work and that of his colleagues on what makes for happy marriages and what factors lead to divorce has had more to say on what makes for success in couples and what key factors must exist in couples therapy to build more satisfaction in distressed couples than nearly any other current research group. Almost all of their work describes the workings of solution-generated problems in distressed couples as they progress through repeated vicious cycles of trying to solve mostly unsolvable problems.

The myths and hypotheses presented at the start of this chapter are mainly the result of Gottman's reviews of the literature and of his careful study of happy and successful couples. One of his findings was that, contrary to what most couples therapists have assumed, there are many ways for couples to be successful. Gottman (1999) has said that

> There are three types of stable, happy couples, not just one. These three types—volatile, validating, and conflict-avoiding—have very different attributes, yet are similar in that they all have a 5 to 1 ratio of positive-to-negative exchanges. This ratio suggests that there is something like an "emotional bank account" that is operating to make these marriages very rich climates of positivity, yet very *different* rich climates. (p. 88)

It wasn't so much that these different types of couples didn't argue. In fact, they all frequently did argue, each in their own way; and this emotional engagement was vital to their success. They even exhibited many of the toxic elements of arguments that couples headed for divorce used. The difference tended to be how they argued, what they argued about, and how successful they allowed themselves to be in repairing the damage caused by these quarrels. The main element missing from how they argued was the use of contempt, which was most often present in couples headed for divorce. The couples seemed to accept a wide range of differences between themselves as tolerable, and they focused their disagreements on more solvable problems. Finally, they had enough of a reserve of positive regard for their partner to accept their partner's attempts to repair any potential damage done in their arguments. Gottman used these key factors, among a few others, to define the desired target for successful couples therapy.

Dow-Jones Ratios

Returning to various cycles, Gottman's research group has learned a great deal by studying couples arguing in their laboratory and then finding out what factors in their way of arguing predicted eventual divorce. One prominent factor alluded to in the quote stated earlier on the 5-to-1 ratio of positives to negatives in happy stable couples is what Gottman termed the *Dow-Jones ratios*. He calculated the sum of all positive things during one person's turn at speech minus all the negative things and found not only that the 5-positives-to-1-negative ratio predicted stability and satisfaction but also that couples whose ratios got closer and closer to 1 negative for each positive had greatly increased probability of divorce in the next 4 years. So, the more baseline negativity in couples' interactions, the more likely they were to split. The greater the positive ratio, the more positive was the couple's prospect of satisfaction. It wasn't the fact that couples argued that predicted further distress and eventual divorce; it was how they argued that mattered more. There was much more that this research group learned from the way these arguments took place.

Harsh Start-Ups

The first factor, after the ratio of positives to negatives, that predicted divorce turned out to be what Gottman termed *harsh start-ups*. It turned out that the way a topic of disagreement is introduced is critically important to predicting marital outcomes. Harsh start-ups (quick escalations from neutral to negative affect), particularly by the wife, was found to be highly associated with marital distress and divorce. As a matter of fact, in the graphs of the Dow-Jones ratios of couple positives to negatives in arguments, only the first minute of the argument was needed to predict divorce or stability for 96% of the couples. Harsh starts predicted harsh endings.

The Four Horsemen

However, the group gained even more richness from studying how these couples argued. They found in counting negatives that not all negatives were equal. Four behaviors, which Gottman eventually termed "The Four Horsemen of the Apocalypse," emerged. These four, found to be the most corrosive, were (a) criticism, (b) contempt, (c) defensiveness, and (d) stonewalling. *Criticism*, similar to the descriptions of the integrative approach described earlier, implies that there is something globally wrong with one's partner ("You always," "You never," "What is wrong with you?" "Why are you so

... ?", etc.). As can be seen, a healthy dose of toxic blame is imbedded within criticism, which can also include sarcasm. The second horseman is *defensiveness*, a common response to criticism. It usually includes denying responsibility for the problem, implying that the other partner is at fault, and fueling further escalation. The third horseman, contempt, turns out to be one of the deadliest in that it appeared in most couples who eventually divorced. *Contempt* is defined as any statement or nonverbal behavior that puts oneself on a higher plane than one's partner. It includes a universal facial expression combining pulling the corner of the lip to the side, rolling the eyes, and looking up. Mockery, especially in public, is a particularly harmful example, as is correcting one's partner's grammar during a fight. Contempt is the single best predictor of divorce to the extent that the amount of contempt found in happy marriages has been observed to be essentially zero.

The final horseman is stonewalling. *Stonewalling* is defined as any way in which one partner withdraws from interaction with the other. It occurs most often in men (85% in several of the group's studies). In fact, when stonewalling was found in women, it became highly predictive of divorce. Stonewalling is intimately related to what Christensen and others have described variously as characteristic *demand–withdraw*, or approach–avoidance patterns in married couples. It has been found that women are significantly more likely to initiate topics of disagreement than are men. Thus, men find themselves on the receiving end of complaints much more than women, resulting in the eventually greater stonewalling by men than by women. These demand–withdraw patterns occur in all marriages, however, and they are only exacerbated in distressed couples.

Gender Differences

Furthermore, lest women be blamed in this demand–withdraw pattern, Gottman (1999) has found that the pattern is triggered by early cues of agitation and withdrawal in male partners, drawing approaches or demands from the woman. Causality is circular, not linear. Gottman's group also found distinct differences in physiological reactivity between men and women. Based likely on evolutionary differences, men's cardiovascular systems remain more reactive than women's and are slower to recover from stress. Adrenalin will cause quicker responses to perceived danger, and blood pressure will be higher and stay elevated longer for men than women during and after a quarrel. In the face of danger, men are more likely to stay vigilant than women. Such heightened diffuse physiological arousal in men can lead to the phenomenon of flooding and related stonewalling and withdrawal in men. *Flooding* refers to the experience of being so overwhelmed with a sudden barrage of negativity from one's spouse that one shuts down and withdraws as a form of defense, leading to the phenomenon of stonewalling. In true vicious cycle form, however, such withdrawal may be met with frustration by one's partner and a new round of demands for the other to engage. The Gottman group also found that men were much less open to allowing themselves to be influenced by their wives than were women open to influence by their husbands. A man's willingness to accept influence from his wife was associated with greater marital satisfaction. Conversely, his unwillingness to accept such influence was correlated with greater marital distress. Thus women are often drawn into a demand–withdraw pattern by the multiple characteristics of their male partners. The downward spiral continues.

Downward Spirals Toward Divorce

Emotional disengagement, similar to that described by the ICT model described earlier, tends to be the eventual result of these cascading cycles on negative interactions. This is characterized as the absence of positive affect, partners leading parallel lives, little friendship, and unacknowledged tension with little soothing by either partner for the other.

Combining these and other related factors, Gottman and his colleagues have been able to predict divorce with 96% accuracy. These successive factors include harsh start-ups to disagreements, presence of the Four Horsemen, flooding (becoming emotionally overwhelmed); body language and cues of physiological discomfort, failed repair attempts, and pervasive negativity (bad attributions and memories). The four final stages of failed relationships are described as seeing the marital problems as severe; attempting to solve things on one's own; beginning to lead parallel lives; and finally, loneliness, which sets in as the members of the couple turn away from each other more and more. This is a clear downward spiral.

Repair Attempts

Gottman (1999) has suggested that the one greatest savior of all marriages is the ability to successfully repair potential damage during and after arguments. A *repair attempt* is defined as anything done by one or another partner that attempts to prevent negativity from escalating out of control in their disagreements. Repairs may consist of a comment on the communication itself, or a deferral to the other's position, or an expression of appreciation for the partner, or a softening of the complaint, or it can even include laughing about the argument as an example of how silly they can get, and so on. As noted earlier, in the three different yet successful types of marriages, their greatest strength was not that the couple didn't argue; it was that the partners were readily willing and able to accept each other's attempts at repairing their relationship during and after these quarrels. We should be clear that it is not simply that attempts to repair occur in distressed couples and that this is the problem. Attempts to repair occur in even the most distressed relationships. What makes a difference is whether the attempt to repair is successfully *allowed* and *received*. In fact, in highly distressed marriages there are frequent repair attempts during arguments, yet research has found that the higher the rate of repair attempts, the higher the rate of their failures in these highly distressed couples. The ability to receive a repair attempt appears to be related to the store of positives in a couple's "emotional bank account" and, subsequently, to their positive views of the partner and the relationship. This is a key element of being able to override negatives in successful, stable marriages. The remaining critical factor in distinguishing successful from distressed relationships is a couple's ability to distinguish between solvable and unsolvable problems. Perpetual arguments about unsolvable problems are, above all, one of the greatest core problems to be resolved in helping distressed marriages.

Perpetual Problems

As we have described, perpetual problems are long-standing, solution-generated problems. After studying the stability of marital interactions over periods of 4 or more years, and turning to the content of the arguments, Gottman (1999) concluded that "I contend that the current emphasis in marital therapy on problem-solving is greatly misplaced . . . we found that 69% of the time they were talking about a 'perpetual problem' that they had had in their marriage for many, many years" (p. 56). He went on to say

> We discovered that, instead of *solving* these perpetual problems, what seems to be important is whether or not a couple can establish a *dialogue* with their perpetual problems. If they cannot establish such a dialogue, the conflict becomes *gridlocked,* and gridlocked conflict eventually leads to emotional disengagement. Hence, I think that *the goal of most of the therapy around problem-solving ought to be to help the couple move from gridlocked conflict with a perpetual problem to a dialogue with the perpetual problem.* (p. 56)

Perpetual problems are those that tend to be based on the incompatibilities and vulnerabilities discussed by Jacobson and Christensen (1996) and when both parties have become polarized and entrenched in their position. Couples show little give-and-take in their discussions around these issues, and there is considerable hurt and wish for vilification. The ICT approach discussed earlier would describe this as the reactive problem in that the pattern of the problem becomes self-perpetuating and cause for hurt, mistrust, and alienation in itself. It becomes an example of what is wrong with the marriage. Gottman (1999) offered example lists of such perpetual problems. On the basis of his research, what he has found to be important is solving not the perpetual problem but the emotions that surround discussing the problem. If the Four Horsemen have taken over, there is little positive affect, and demoralization is setting in; then the couple is headed for further distress and potential divorce. Perception of the other becomes crucial in differentiating successful from unsuccessful relationships as the couple moves through these negative interchanges. In happy marriages, partners tend to evaluate negative actions of the other as transient and situational and to evaluate positives as a result of enduring internal qualities of their partner.

Conversely, in distressed couples, negative actions of the partner are ascribed to personal character flaws, whereas positive actions are seen as unstable, fleeting, situational, or even cause for suspicion. With these respective positive or negative overrides in place, arguments over perpetual problems become easier to categorize as either something harmless that just needs to be accepted or else another example of the malevolence of their partner and the hopelessness of their relationship. Gottman has noted that this pervasive negative perception has, in fact, caused distressed couples to underestimate the occurrence of actual positives in their relationship by a factor of about 50%. The relevance of this to ongoing arguments about perpetual unsolvable problems is that the growing negativity makes it more and more difficult for each partner to accept the repair attempts of the other partner either during or after disagreements. Happy, stable couples tended to be able to accept the inevitability of the unsolvable problems between them, work on the solvable ones, and accept repair attempts from their partner regardless of the problem with which they were engaged. The pervasive negativity of the distressed couples prevented them from accepting influence or repairs from their partner, and they continued them in the destructive cycles of perpetual problems. Thus, Gottman's targets are helping couples disengage from perpetual arguments over unsolvable problems, developing a dialogue around them, identifying solvable problems, building more positive perceptions of each other to allow for more positive interchanges, and ultimately to help the partners accept repair attempts from each other as they move forward in their relationship. In other words, like Jacobson and Christensen (1996), he seeks to reduce the triggers for solution-generated problems while having the couples go toward their inevitable arguments in new ways. This comes down to interrupting first-order change and pursuing second-order solutions. Turning to how these two ESTs for couples therapy assess and intervene in these solution-generated couple problems will complete the picture.

ASSESSMENT

As might be expected, both approaches assess couples for the dimensions of the problem they view as most salient as discussed earlier in their descriptions of the solution-generated problems characteristic of most distressed couples. It is interesting that both views tend to converge in both the theme of their assessments and of their feedback and contracts with couples.

Gottman's Assessment

At minimum, Gottman's assessment takes three sessions: one conjoint session of 1.5 hours, and one half-hour session with each partner separately.

His basic question areas look for both strengths as well as areas needing improvement in the couple. Gottman's *sound marital house theory* (1999) is used as a guide for the assessment. In brief, this view looks for an overall level of positive affect and an ability to reduce negative affect during conflict resolution. The four levels of the sound marital house to assess are as follows:

1. The foundation, which is composed of marital friendship in nonconflict contexts, and its ability to create room for the partner; fondness and admiration; and a turning toward, and not away, from the partner.
2. The extent to which either positive or negative sentiment overrides or affects the success of repair attempts during conflict.
3. How the couple regulates (not resolves) conflict, including establishing dialogue with perpetual problems, solving solvable problems, and self-soothing abilities.
4. How the couple creates shared meanings by meshing their individual life dreams and meshing rituals of connection, goals, roles, myths, narratives, and metaphors.

Assessment in these domains is guided by the detailed "Clinician's Checklist for Marital Assessment" (see Table 4.1, Gottman, 1999, pp. 115–116). Several formal paper-and-pencil assessments are sent to the couple ahead of time. General marital adjustment is assessed through the "Locke–Wallace Marital Adjustment Test," and divorce potential is assessed with the "Weiss–Cerreto Marital Status Inventory" (see Appendixes A and B, Gottman, 1999). The first part of the conjoint session is guided by the structure of the combined "Oral History and Meta-Emotion Interview" (see Appendix C, Gottman, 1999) to obtain a joint overview of their relationship. The couple is then asked to identify one perpetual problem, one solvable problem, and one topic they enjoy discussing. Then the couple is asked to talk about each topic uninterrupted for about 6 minutes while the therapist observes their interaction patterns, noting signs of key positive and negative elements of how they manage conflict. The perpetual problems are invariably the location of the escalating vicious cycles for distressed couples. These vicious cycles of first-order solutions are the target for either acceptance, meaning stopping the couple's first-order solutions, or for redirection of their efforts to problems they can do something about. Finally, the therapist discusses with the couple what matters most to them in their relationship, their disappointments, how they view the relationship now, and their hopes for marital therapy. In individual sessions, the therapist assesses for the presence of violence or extramarital affairs (no secrets are allowed), differences in personal goals, commitment to the marriage, each partner's hopes and expectations for the marriage, the cost–benefit analysis of staying or leaving the relationship, and the partner's own individual expectations for therapy. There is of course considerable detail to all of these steps, but this is the general format of the assessment. After the individual sessions, the therapist meets conjointly again with the couple to offer feedback on a formulation for the couple's problem and to make a contract for treatment. A key element is finding perpetual first-order vicious cycles or perpetual problems and offering a rationale to redirect the couple from trying to solve them.

Assessment in Integrative Couples Therapy

It is interesting to note that Jacobson and Christensen's (1996) assessment parallels Gottman's (1999) assessment format rather closely. They also require three sessions for assessment—one conjoint, and one with each partner separately, before doing a conjoint feedback session. The main purpose of the assessment is to come up with a formulation that will guide the treatment plan. A second overriding goal is to assess where the couple is on the dimensions that will lead the therapist toward interventions targeting change strategies or acceptance strategies. *Change strategies* encompass the behavior exchange and communication problem strategies of traditional behavioral therapies discussed earlier. *Acceptance strategies*, however, are designed to help the couple to disengage from their escalating struggles around key differences and begin to accept aspects of their relationship as not amenable to or needing change. This, of course, is exactly what Gottman is addressing when he helps couples identify unsolvable issues and perpetual problems around which to begin to accept and develop dialogue. The final implicit goal of the first, conjoint session is for it to be in some way both conducive toward building an alliance with the therapist and to provide some therapeutic relief and hope for the clients. To this end, if possible, specific problems are saved for discussion in the individual interviews and are assessed from formal evaluation surveys filled out by the couple separately before the sessions begin. The conjoint session builds on positive elements of the relationship.

As with Gottman's approach, a number of formal paper-and-pencil assessment scales are sent to the couple to fill out jointly and separately before the sessions. These scales include the Dyadic Adjustment Scale, to assess commitment and willingness to work on the relationship; the Marital Satisfaction Inventory (MSI), to assess the level of marital distress; the Conflict Tactics Scale, to assess for domestic violence; and scales authored by several of the authors and their colleagues, such as the Marital Status Inventory, to assess commitment to the relationship; the Areas of Change Questionnaire and the Areas of Change and Acceptance Questionnaire, to assess the amount and direction of desired change and acceptability of current behaviors; and, finally, the "Spouse Observation Checklist," to assess daily accounts of positive and negative spouse behaviors (see Gottman, 2000, Appendix A, for sample forms). In sum, the results of these inventories are combined with interview data to come up with the formulation at the end of the assessment.

The initial conjoint session focuses on getting information on the following questions: (a) "How did the couple get together?" (b) "What was their courtship like, and what was the relationship like before the problems began?" (c) "How is the relationship different now, on days when the partners are getting along?" (d) "How would the relationship be different if the problems that currently exist were no longer present?" Part of the goal of these questions is to create more positive affect between the couple while gathering information on the nature of their relationship and their hopes and expectations for its future.

During the assessment, the therapist tries to answer six questions, the answer to which will shape both the formulation of the couple's problem and the treatment plan. The resulting formulation is also framed using these six areas:

1. How distressed is this couple?
2. How committed is this couple to this relationship?
3. What are the issues that divide them?
4. Why are these issues such a problem for them?
5. What are the strengths holding them together?
6. What can treatment do to help them?

How distressed the couple is determines how therapy actually proceeds. Although all interventions in this approach begin with some acceptance, the more distressed a couple is, the more acceptance interventions are used. The less distressed the couple is, the more change strategies may be applied. Aside from observing how the couple interacts in the interviews and what they are complaining of and asking for, the Dyadic Adjustment Scale and Marital Satisfaction Inventory can also add quantitative and normative data to this judgment. The Conflict Tactics Scale can also provide private information on the level of potential domestic violence present. Marital work is explicitly rejected when there is domestic violence present.

The couple's *level of commitment to each other and the relationship* provides a good indicator of how much effort the partners are willing to invest in couples therapy. The more committed the partners are, the more change work can be initiated. Less commitment or unequal commitment calls for more acceptance work. The Marital Status Inventory measures directly the steps partners have taken to disengage from one another. Statements that they are on the brink of divorce, that this is their final resort before splitting, the setting up of private bank accounts, and extramarital affairs are just some markers of lower commitment.

Learning *what issues divide the couple* is an important step in identifying a theme for the couple's difficulties, and this is used as one of the core elements of the final case formulation. To identify a theme, it is necessary to find out what issues divide the partners. The therapist asks the couple what they argue about and discusses their points of view and positions on particular areas that differ between them. As already mentioned, these themes may include such things as differences in the areas of closeness versus distance, commitment versus independence, conventionality versus unconventionality, or control versus responsibility, among other general areas. Couples are usually able to identify these areas directly in the interview jointly and individually. However, the "Areas of Change Questionnaire" (see Gottman, 2000) can help with identifying lists of changes that couples may want. Also, the "Areas of Change and Acceptance Questionnaire" is particularly helpful in not only identifying what changes are desired but also how frequent many undesired behaviors may be and how acceptable they may be at their current levels. This helps in identifying some areas in which acceptance may be present already and others where it may be easier to begin.

Finding out *why these issues are such a problem* gets directly at information on polarization and the mutual trap. The therapist attends here to how the partners react to conflict and how they get stuck. As with Gottman's assessment, the process of how the partners engage in conflict is a critical focus, and couples may be invited to spend a short time engaging in discussion of one of these areas of difference, short of creating too much distress. The therapist looks for polarization in noticing how each partner's well-intentioned attempts to solve the problem initiates problematic behavior from the partner, in turn initiating problematic behavior from the first partner.

Learning of *the strengths that keep the couple together* builds on positives in the relationship and forms a continuing basis for acceptance work. Learning what qualities attracted the members of the couple to each other, and which of these keeps them attached to each other, can be used in framing the mutual-trap description in the case formulation to the couple in the feedback session. Differences that attract can also create stress. Noting both the positive and negative sides of these differences can form the foundation of acceptance work whereby the qualities that cannot be changed can be accepted. Learning how the couple has overcome some past differences and been resilient in the face of stress also provides a good basis for noting how this can again be done in treatment.

The final question on *what treatment can do to help* is cast as possibly the most important. Setting mutually agreed on, achievable goals is the cornerstone of a positive working alliance and treatment contract. Jacobson and Christensen (1996) stated that

> The goals of [integrative couples therapy] are almost always some combination of acceptance of differences and changes in conflict areas. Change typically involves increases in positive behavior, shaped and reinforced by natural contingencies, and more open, less blaming, and nondefensive communication. The therapist needs to pay attention during the assessment phase to areas where accommodation, compromise, and collabora-

tion are possible, as well as areas where acceptance may be possible. (pp. 76–77)

The balance of these elements becomes the goal of treatment.

INTERVENTION

It should now be abundantly evident that both of these ESTs for couple problems view these problems as vicious cycles of escalating first-order change resulting in solution-generated problems. It should also come as little surprise that they both seek multiple second-order changes in both couples and therapists to effectively achieve their goals. We will not go extensively here into the details of both approaches. Both approaches have excellent and detailed manuals with companion guides for couples. What we do want to highlight is the kind of second-order changes that are at the core of both approaches.

It should be clear by now that both the Gottman approach and the ICT of Jacobson and Christensen base their interventions on encouraging acceptance as well as supporting change in distressed couples. Both approaches view the way couples manage the perceived need for change as the core problem needing to be changed in these couples. Both couples and therapists need to change their views on change. This is the essence of the definition of second-order change.

Second-Order Change

The core second-order changes inherent in both of these approaches might be best highlighted by listing them here:

- Accepting that change is not always possible or desirable is a fundamental change. This is a paradox. It also allows other change in key related areas.
- When partners stop demanding change in each other, it opens the way for change to occur. When partners accept each other's position and agree not to invest in changing it, but develop a dialogue around the difference, they not only feel more empathy but also become more open to change in the absence of pressure to do so.
- When couples accept the premise that difference and conflict will always occur, they reduce their efforts to eliminate conflict, and they then experience decreases in the number, frequency, and intensity of the very arguments they assume will be inevitable.

- Once couples come to acknowledge and accept the nature of the trap their struggles have created, they have already made a step to change it.
- Couples are asked to enhance their intimate connection with each other by engaging with each other around inevitable differences rather than avoiding them or needing to eliminate them.
- When therapists give up their focus on helping couples solve their problems, they become more effective in helping couples solve their problems.

Recall that the general success rate for all couple treatment has been shown to be roughly 50%. By contrast, both the Gottman and the ICT approaches have increased that success rate significantly with the addition of acceptance-based interventions to the traditional approaches built on direct change. Jacobson and Christensen (1996), reporting on preliminary findings piloting work using their ICT treatment manual, stated that

> Virtually every couple thus far completing ICT showed significant improvement, and the vast majority (75%) recovered to the point that they were no longer distinguishable from happily married couples on measures of marital satisfaction. These differences appear to be holding up through a one-year follow-up: at that time, three of the eight [traditional behavioral couples therapy] couples had separated or divorced, compared to none of the ICT couples. (p. 20)

With similar positive results from the Gottman approach, what, in general, are they doing differently? To address this, we turn again to Jerome Frank's contextual model for describing all therapies, including the emotionally charged *relationship*, the therapeutic *rationale* or *myth*, and the related *procedures* to integrate these two approaches.

The Therapeutic Relationship

The fundamental difference in the relationship offered by the Gottman and ICT approaches compared with most approaches focusing on problem-solving and change is that therapists accept couple's distress and conflict as inevitable, and they urge couples to do so as well. Both approaches build their relationship on the basis of acknowledging the partners' dilemmas given the context of their disputes and validating the pain of their distress given the relationship traps in which they find themselves. The key difference in the relationship is that the therapist focuses on the process of how the couple managed their disagreements as the source of their problem rather than some inherent flaws in either partner individually or their relationship. Therapists in both approaches build working alliances around helping couples engage with each other through their perceived differences. This promises to enhance their closeness, fondness, and intimacy while better resolving those issues that can be solved; accepting and developing a dialogue around those that will always be there; increasing the positive experiences in their relationship; and using that positive reserve to better allow their partners to repair what damage might be done along the way. According to Gottman (1999),

> The two necessary "staples" of marriages that work (whatever their typology) are (1) an overall level of positive affect, and (2) an ability to reduce negative affect during conflict resolution. These two empirical facts give us the basics of marital therapy: To create lasting change in troubled marriages, interventions need to enhance the overall level of positive affect in both nonconflict and conflict contexts, and teach couples how to reduce negative affect during conflict by accepting one another's influence. (p. 105)

Although the ICT approach is in close agreement with these goals, they differ somewhat in the kind of relationship they advocate for therapists with couples. Whereas both approaches stress accepting many differences as inevitable and not needing change, Gottman's approach does this mainly in a supportive and validating yet mainly didactic teaching format, using lots of exercises and homework assignments to be completed. ICT therapists differ in their relationship in that they are much more process oriented, with an emphasis on accepting the couple and the individual partners in the same way that the therapist is encouraging these partners to do with each other. Jacobson and Christensen (1996) wrote of this statement

> We attempt to create an environment that fosters acceptance and change in part by accepting both partners to the degree that they might accept one another under ideal conditions. Our emphasis on validation and nonconfrontation created the paradox that we have to accept even their unwillingness or inability to be accepting of one another . . . the stance of the therapist is what most differentiates the integrative model from [traditional behavioral couples therapy]. This stance permeates the therapy and makes it recognizably integrative regardless of the particular focus of a therapy session. (pp. 18–19)

Relationship is one of Frank and Frank's (1991) three foundations for successful intervention (the other two being the rationale, or "myth," and the related procedures). Acceptance is not only a goal for couples to achieve but also an imperative quality for the therapist to have and to model for the couple. This is not always easy when a couple's process tends to draw therapists into their polarization, or when the polarized position of one partner tempts the therapist to confront, accuse, and blame that partner as does his or her mate. The acceptance stance grows out of the dialectical perspective mentioned earlier, in chapter 3, and we discuss it later in more detail in chapter 11. The basis of this perspective is that polarized opposites are sought to be synthesized and integrated in some form of higher level integration. This is the goal of the formulation in ICT. It represents the sort of second-order change that keeps couples from being drawn back into first-order vicious cycles, and it equally keeps therapists from being drawn into the same first-order processes with the couple. The essential therapist skills that contribute to this therapeutic relationship exactly parallel those discussed by Marsha Linehan (1993) in her dialectical behavior therapy for clients fitting the criteria for borderline personality disorder (see chap. 11, this volume). Not surprisingly, acceptance is at the heart of the dialectical behavior therapy approach also. These therapist skills include intuitive attention to the interaction process of a couple, to track the cycles of their problem; moment-by-moment flexibility in balancing interaction with the couple and for each partner with the other; the ability not to force an agenda on the clients but to balance acceptance of their pain, perspectives, and struggles, with the intention to help these change; the ability to maintain the focus on the formulation of the problem and on the position of acceptance; to skillfully use metaphor, humor, and the client's language to engage clients in the process of change; and overall to maintain a balanced, accepting therapeutic atmosphere in the relationship, despite severe conflict, without becoming blaming or confrontational. All interventions are embedded in, flow from, and are indistinguishable from this relationship.

This statement on the therapeutic influence of the position of the therapist in relationship to their clients in couples therapy echoes what we said about the relationship in chapters 4 and 5. The relationship *is* the intervention. Although techniques abound in these two approaches, the relationship is the vehicle of change. As we noted, and is implied in the description, this shift toward acceptance in couple therapists is often a second-order change for the therapist herself.

The Therapeutic Rationale or "Myth"

Both approaches strongly emphasize the importance of the therapeutic rationale or formulation to the success of treatment. There are two elements of the rationale. The first element is to have the couple accept the premise that their distress is caused by the way they handle their differences and disagreements and that it can be resolved by adjusting how and when they argue and how they maintain positives between them. The second element is to have the couple accept a formulation of their problem. This formulation describes the solution-generated patterns in terms and language that they will acknowledge and accept and that fits the therapist's theory of the problem and change. This later formulation implies that it is a combination of the therapist's concepts and the clients' language and worldview. The question is based less on some ultimate "truth" and more on "fit" and investment with both the therapist and the couple as they agree to working within that formulation. As noted earlier, the first element of the rationale is a second-order change for most couples. The cure does not lie in resolving their distress by doing something to help their partner or their self, or helping them resolve and eliminate their conflicts. Instead, conflicts are accepted as inevitable, and the way they manage their differences and disagreements in these conflicts is the pathway to greater love, intimacy, and happiness. The formulation is an extension of this second-order shift in that it describes the pattern of their solution-generated problem and implies that they can solve it by giving up their attempts to solve it. Furthermore, once the couple accepts the rationale and formulation, they have already begun to change. By accepting the self-defeating current patterns as the problem and opening themselves to changing how they engage in those cycles, they have already begun to disengage from the problem.

The ICT approach is clearest in their description of the formulation of the problem for couples. Jacobson and Christensen (1996) said that

> The *formulation* is the single most important organizing principle in ICT. In fact, if one were to generate a one-line description of the overarching goal in ICT, it is to get the couples to adopt our formulation . . . If they leave therapy with this formulation as a prominent part of their relationship history, they will in all likelihood have benefited greatly from therapy. (p. 41)

In the ICT format, the formulation always includes the three components of (a) a *theme*, (b) a *polarization process*, and (c) a *mutual trap*. The theme is shorthand for the couple's main conflict. the polarization process describes the elements of the vicious cycle once the conflict starts. and the mutual trap describes the "stuckness" couples feel that keeps them trapped in their dilemma and unable to resolve it despite (or because) of their best efforts once the polarization process has been set in motion.

Gottman spends less time on a structured formulation, yet he refers to the ICT format in discussing his view. Gottman referred to his case formulation as the therapist's healing image of the couple. It emerges from his oral history interview during assessment, and it is one of the few concepts that he leaves more to the therapist's intuition and explicitly relates it to the healing myths of shamans used to create faith, hope, and trust in the healer and patient. Of course, his more explicit formulations include descriptions similar to those in ICT. He details the vicious cycles of the couple's perpetual problems, the way they engage in conflict, the ways in which they self-soothe and soothe each other and repair their relationship during and after conflicts. He further discusses the nature of their "emotional bank account" and their positive or negative emotional override tendencies. He also uses his "Sound Marital House Structure" (see Gottman, 1999, p. 105) and the "Clinician's Checklist for Marital Assessment" (see Gottman, 1999, Table 4.1, pp. 115–116) to both structure his feedback to the clients and begin to teach them the most important components of sound and happy marriages, where they fall on these dimensions, and how they can enhance their picture to help resolve their distress and ensure future success. As in the ICT approach, once couples have understood and accepted this formulation, they are more than halfway toward the change they desire.

Therapeutic Procedures

Some of the major goals for both ICT and Gottman's procedures represent basic reversals or second-order changes. Both approaches ask couples to go toward and engage in their problems, often with no intent to solve them, rather than trying to avoid or resolve them. A major goal of ICT is to "convert problems into vehicles for intimacy" (Jacobson & Christensen, 1996, p. 12). One of Gottman's main goals for couples is to develop a dialogue around unchangeable problems instead of trying to solve them. Whereas both approaches include change strategies that have second-order shifts implicit within them, the ICT approach uses a number of explicitly acceptance-oriented procedures that highlight second-order changes in their couple interventions. Our intent is not to be exhaustive and detailed in our account of the procedures of these two approaches. We address instead an overview that will note their common change strategies and then focus on the more specific acceptance strategies of the ICT approach. Because Gottman's approach relies most heavily on change strategies, we start with his procedures.

Gottman's Procedures

One must remember that Gottman's basic approach implements a basic second-order shift in its premise that the couple doesn't need to solve all of their problems, needs to learn to disagree better, and needs to learn better skills by going toward their conflicts rather than by avoiding them. In the process of this, the couple needs to learn to increase overall levels of positive affect and reduce negative emotions during conflict. Gottman's concept of the sound marital house serves as the foundation for this. First, the marital friendship is enhanced to create positive feelings in nonconflict situations by creating "cognitive room" or creating "love maps," enhancing fondness and admiration, and turning toward versus away from the partner and building an emotional bank account. If successful, this leads to "positive sentiment override," which helps couples have success in repair attempts during conflicts. Next, the couple is taught to regulate conflict through establishing dialogue around perpetual problems, solving solvable problems, and learning mainly to soothe themselves physiologically during conflicts. Finally, couples are helped to create a shared meaning system that includes meshing individual life dreams and meshing connection rituals, including goals, roles, myths, narrative, and metaphors. As this final level evolves, it further strengthens the foundation of the couple's friendship and helps them become even more resilient through their next inevitable conflicts.

Gottman's intervention assumptions are as follows:

- Therapy is primarily dyadic, between the couple with therapist as coach.
- Couples need to be in distressing emotional states to learn how to cope with and change them. Couples are encouraged to become emotional in conflicts to learn best how to self-soothe, soothe their partner, or take a break.
- The therapist should not do the soothing; the couple needs to learn to soothe themselves and each other.
- Interventions should seem easy to do. They should make sense and feel safe.
- Couples therapy should be mainly a positive experience. Couples should not be criticized for what they have done wrong but instead coached and supported for doing things that will help them.
- Rather than having lofty ideals for the couple, a "good enough" partnership that works for them is good enough for the therapist.

Gottman parallels these assumptions in eight principles shared in his couples self-help manual (Gottman & Silver, 1999). They include the following principles:

1. First, the couple learns how to *enhance love maps*. A *love map* refers to each partner's knowledge of the other's psychological worlds. Couples are encouraged to learn more about each other by playing games in session to see how much they know about each other, creating maps of their partner's everyday life, identifying things they admire and appreciate in their partner, appreciating how their partner has been hurt, what their triumphs and goals are, and so on. These are collaborative, change-based interventions.
2. Next, the couple is helped to *nurture fondness and admiration*. This is massively based in collaboration and change. It guides the couple through further exercises, in session and at home, to assess their fondness and admiration for each other, noting the things they appreciate about one another, collaborating on the history and philosophy of their relationship, and participating in a 7-week course of daily exercises designed to get the couple used to thinking positively about each other.
3. The couple is also taught to *turn toward each other rather than away*. The idea of an emotional bank account is put forward

to help the couple find ways of putting a vast balance of positives in their relationship from which to draw when conflicts arise. Couples are taught to have stress-reducing conversations by learning to show genuine interest, communicating their understanding, taking their partner's side, learning to take a "we against others" attitude, expressing affection, and validating emotions. They also engage in other exercises to learn what to do when their partner doesn't turn toward them.

4. Another skill the couple, and especially men, learn, is to *let your partner influence you*. Here couples engage in exercises to practice yielding to their partner in conversations and conflicts. Other exercises involve such things as having the couple come to some resolution on what to take or leave in an imaginary predicament and then analyzing who gave in and how it felt to negotiate give and take.

5. A critical task is *separating the two kinds of conflict into solvable problems and perpetual problems*. Here couples are given examples of solvable and perpetual problems and learn the differences in discussion with the therapist. They then list, assess, and categorize their own conflicts and track and analyze several recent conflicts to identify feelings, triggers, causes, and each partner's contributions.

6. The couple is then set on the task of *learning to solve their solvable problems*. Here they learn and practice how to soften their start-up, by complaining and not blaming; using "I" statements; describing and not judging; and being clear, polite, and appreciative. Next, they learn what a repair is through examples and then practicing this in session and at home. The couple also learns to soothe themselves and each other, recognizing times when emotional flooding occurs, and practicing soothing techniques. The final exercises include tasks to teach compromise and learn tolerance of each other's faults.

7. Overcoming gridlock is the next-to-last set of tasks to be learned. Recall that gridlock occurs around perpetual problems, resulting in polarization and isolation. Here couples learn first about each other's dreams and engage in exercises in detecting and respecting them. Then the couple is engaged in a gridlocked problem in structured exercises, learning to soothe each other and come to ending compromises and realizations of the issue that will remain. Couples thus learn to identify gridlocked problems, identify the dream within the conflict, find negotiable areas and areas of flexibility, build temporary compromises, predict future conflicts, and thank their partner for the effort.

8. Creating shared meaning comprises the final set of exercises. Couples assess their relationship by identifying rituals of connection and their respective roles, goals, and symbols. They then go on to design family rituals to which they can truly look forward, design roles through which they feel comfortable and fulfilled, identify their goals and mission in life and design ways of fulfilling them in the relationship, and identify the symbols that lend meaning and significance to their relationship.

These are rather extensive categories of exercises that are only a sampling of tasks and questionnaires and exercises that help couples build the qualities found to support positive marriages and partnerships. They are all, however, heavily reliant on the couple being engaged in the process of change. If learned, they are very effective in building resilience and even happiness in couples. They are, in the main, change strategies.

Integrative Couples Therapy and Acceptance Strategies

Accepting that change is not always possible, or even desirable, is a fundamental tenet of how couples approach the need for change and how they negotiate change. This is what first- and second-order change is all about. Recall from the first few chapters that people often get drawn into vicious cycles of solution-generated problems when they try to change something that is essentially unchangeable, perpetual, or not really a problem. A prime example given is attempting to close the generation gap between parents and teens. This generation gap has been lamented in writings from early history. It has always been there, maybe necessarily so, and it is generally widened, and not closed, by attempts to close it. Similar examples occur in abundance. In fact, it is not the *content* of the issue that is deemed as a problem that needs fixing but the *process* of deciding there is a problem, and setting out to fix it, that becomes the problem. In such cases, the solution is some combination of reframing the nature of the difficulty into something not needing to be solved, and interrupting or redirecting the present pattern of solutions. These are some core operations leading to the process of second-order change.

If the partners in a couple agree that their conflicts or polarized distance is a problem that needs to be changed, and if they are open to the information and influence a therapist has to offer, then they may greatly benefit by change strategies such as those Gottman developed. These change strategies directly reframe the need to solve some problems, thus stopping those perpetually gridlocked vicious cycles at their source. Furthermore, as couples redirect themselves to generating positive interactions and learn new skills to solve problems and derail potential vicious cycle arguments from moving again to gridlock, the process of their problem is changed. However, over half the couples seen in therapy are not like this. They are highly distressed, relatively less committed to each other, and invested in polarized issues that divide them and draw them back into the gridlocked, repeating, vicious cycles of their problematic relationship. Given this state, they are unlikely to agree on many things, much less that their problem doesn't need solving, and they are often equally reluctant to comply with therapists on how to change things. This is when the acceptance strategies of ICT find their greatest value. The intent of these acceptance strategies is the same as that of the change strategies. The action, given the couple's level of distress, lack of agreement, and reluctance to comply, is less direct and more subtle in its application.

The following is a set of explicitly acceptance-based strategies used in the ICT approach. They are not mutually exclusive and, in fact, they generally overlap in that they flow from the basic premises of the acceptance-based perspective. Acceptance strategies are generally described as both tools for turning problems into vehicles for intimacy and as processes for increasing tolerance for that which may not change. In most cases, acceptance strategies are used first with couples, and then change strategies are added. Acceptance strategies are the major focus with highly distressed couples:

- *Empathic joining around the problem* is one of the first acceptance steps. Therapists emphasize the pain and honest efforts of each partner without accusation. The formulation itself becomes a central vehicle for this joining by casting the couple's dilemma as flowing from an honest difference that naturally led to polarization and eventually alienation. Therapists emphasize using "soft" rather than "hard" emotion descriptions in their reflections, and they encourage the partners to do the same. Hard emotions, such as anger and resentment, which imply assertion, power, and control, are most often expressed in couples who are in defensive positions. Soft emotions, such as hurt, fear, and disappointment, convey doubt, uncertainty, and vulnerability and are more easily accepted by partners. The use of these may be taught, prompted, coached, or modeled by the therapist.
- *Encouraging unified detachment, or making the problem an "it,"* follows from empathic joining. Here the couple is encouraged to continually engage in more detached intellectual analyses of the problem using the formulation as a guide. Rather than blaming each other, the problem is externalized and often given a metaphorical name as an "it." "Two porcupines trying to dance" is an example. Couples are then asked to analyze their conflicts at home, putting the imaginary therapist or the problem in a chair to address as they track the common sequence of their conflict according to the formulization and polarizing process rather than directly and spontaneously engaging in it.

- *Highlighting the positive features of negative behavior* relates directly to the dialectical or polarized nature of the couple's dilemma. As partners begin to acknowledge the positive qualities of negative actions (creative vs. flighty, decisive vs. bossy, deferring vs. uncommitted, etc.) they begin to merge these actions into a more unified whole. This continues the basic acceptance in the relationship by both affirming distress and confirming positives. It reduces polarization. Complementary differences usually create balance in relationships. These differences can even become a positive aspect of the couple's relationship and something for them to be proud of and feel close about.

- *Role playing negative behavior during the therapy session* is a core reversal of usual patterns common to both Gottman's approach and the ICT approach. It is basically a symptom prescription that puts the couple into a be-spontaneous paradox of engaging in the problem deliberately for therapeutic purposes. The couple may no longer spontaneously act out their pattern but must instead deliberately engage and disengage in it to track and analyze its process. Problem cycles are harder to enact deliberately, and this may undercut the pattern itself. However, information the couple gains by analyzing the pattern may be invaluable to recognizing and changing it in the future. This is parallel to the goal of couples developing a dialogue around their solvable and perpetual problems, as emphasized by Gottman. It changes the context for future arguments and is designed to promote tolerance when such arguments inevitably occur in the future. Arguments at home may also change as a result of the same factors. Finally, this is also in essence an exposure technique that, if repeated, may produce effects analogous to extinction. All of these elements are part of this basic second-order shift intervention.

- *Faked incidents of negative behavior at home, or "faking bad"* is a prime counterintuitive example of the second-order sort of intervention that undercuts the process of the vicious cycle patterns by its very application. It is explained as a way to promote tolerance by desensitizing partners to negative behavior. Partners are asked to deliberately pick fights or to deliberately do or not do something that creates conflict when they would not ordinarily do this. The faker is then asked to observe the process of the vicious cycle, the polarization, and the pain, to better track and learn from it. Directions are given with both partners present, and they are told not to divulge when they are doing it. This is another symptom prescription that basically undercuts the couple's problem patterns. Neither partner is able to know whether this is a real conflict or one staged for therapeutic purposes. It has powerful effects in deescalating fights and reinforcing the formulation of how the conflicts occur.

- *Preparation for backsliding* is an inoculation used as progress is made. It is basically relapse prevention that inoculates the partners against both assuming that the problem has started again and trying again to fix it using the same old vicious cycle first-order solutions.
- *Emotional acceptance through greater self-care* has two elements. The first is to have each partner begin doing things for him- or herself to feel better and to learn self-soothing. The second is to learn to do self-case during arguments, polarization processes, and other instances of negative behavior. This is, of course, similar to Gottman's teaching of self-soothing and having couples practice it during in-session and at home conflicts.

These are again only a sampling of the acceptance strategies used by both the ICT and the Gottman approaches. They blend together in that they flow from the same perspective on change. In the final analysis, both Gottman's approach and Jacobson and Christensen's ICT approach gain their increased effectiveness as ESTs for couple problems through adding acceptance to the traditional change strategies of couple therapies. The concept of acceptance is closely aligned with second-order change in that it ultimately allows couples to resolve their differences by not trying to change them.

FOLLOWING THE THREAD

Couple difficulties are typically described as vicious cycles wherein partners try to force change on each other. These conflicts become polarized and erode positive feelings within the couple, making it harder to tolerate common couple conflicts. The more the members of the couple try to fix the relationship, the worse it gets for the fixing. Second-order interventions first offer rationales to affirm the universal and more unique reasons for conflict. Reversals include asking partners to go toward conflicts, develop dialogue around and accept those irresolvable differences, and evolve positive experiences and futures with each other. The concept of acceptance is closely aligned with second-order change in that it ultimately helps couples resolve their differences by not trying to change them. Irony is the mark of second-order change.

10

SUBSTANCE ABUSE
AND DEPENDENCY

We learned that we had to fully concede to our innermost selves that we were alcoholics. The delusion that we are like other people, or presently may be, has to be smashed.
—Alcoholics Anonymous (1976, p. 30)

In this chapter, we show how second-order change is woven through empirically supported treatments for substance abuse (addiction). From there, we review the historical underpinnings of treatment and contrast these with a current understanding of what works in alcohol and other drug problems (AOD). A case will be made that the addictions field is in the process of undergoing a second-order change and that clinicians need to go through a second-order change to keep up with the changing field. We then look more specifically at the stages-of-change model, motivational interviewing, and 12-step approaches that are modeled after Alcoholics Anonymous (AA). We will show how these approaches produce second-order change for clients.

For readability, the terms *addiction*, *dependence*, *alcoholism*, and *substance abuse* are used interchangeably in this chapter. Although we believe that there are differences between AOD abuse and dependency (i.e., the main difference being that the AOD abuser may have more latitude for controlled use than a person who is chemically dependent), effective treatments for both contain similar elements, particularly elements that lead to second-order change.

SUBSTANCE DEPENDENCE (ADDICTION)

The *Diagnostic and Statistical Manual of Mental Disorders* (4th ed. [*DSM–IV*]; American Psychiatric Association, 1994) defines *substance dependence* as a cluster of cognitive, behavioral, and physiological symptoms associated with substance use such that the individual continues use of the substance despite significant substance-related problems. There is also a pattern of repeat self-administration that usually results in tolerance, withdrawal, and compulsive drug-taking behavior. Substance dependence can be applied to every class of substances except caffeine. The symptoms are similar across classes, but for certain substances some symptoms are less salient. In a few instances, not all symptoms apply. For example, withdrawal symptoms do not usually occur with hallucinogen dependence. Although not listed as a criterion, most persons with substance dependence experience craving, or a strong subjective drive to use the substance on which they are dependent. Dependence is defined as a cluster of three or more of the following symptoms occurring in a 12 month time period: increased tolerance; withdrawal; a pattern of using more drug than is intended, persistent failed efforts to quit or cut back on use; spending considerable time to obtain, use, and recover from use; giving up important social, occupational, or recreational activities to use; and continuing use despite knowledge of negative physical or psychological consequences. (Readers are referred to the *DSM–IV* for a more detailed description of these symptoms.)

DiClemente (2003), reporting on Orford (1985), indicated that in recent years the scope of the term *substance dependence* has expanded to include substance use or reinforcing behavior that has an appetitive quality, is self-destructive, and is experienced as difficult to modify or stop. Through this expansion, a wide variety of relationships and behaviors, such as excessive work, problematic interpersonal relationships, and excessive exercise, have been redefined as addictive.

USE VERSUS ABUSE VERSUS DEPENDENCY

Many drugs or substances can be used in a manner that is not problematic. Illegal drugs by definition are subject to abuse because any use, if discovered by law enforcement authorities, can lead to untoward consequences. However, even when legal, drug use can lead to difficulties that do not rise to the threshold of dependence. For example, a person drinking more than five or six drinks several times per week may not develop substance dependence. However, overuse of alcohol can lead to high blood pressure or other physical consequences. With this in mind, the *DSM–IV* defines substance abuse as a maladaptive pattern of use manifested by recurrent and significant adverse consequences related to substance use. Tolerance, withdrawal, or patterns of compulsive use are not necessarily involved.

ADDICTION RATIONALES

William Miller (2003) wrote that the development of the modern treatment system for substance abuse stems from the 1960s. Rationales that explain the acquisition of addictive behaviors emerged in reaction to the view that addicted persons are morally deficient. Alcoholics Anonymous (1976), the first to challenge the moral deficit model, argued that the cause of addiction is both constitutional and spiritual. In effect, there is something different about the physiological makeup of an alcoholic that causes excessive AOD consumption. The syndrome is best understood as a progressive disease, similar to diabetes or hypertension. Over time, the disease damages the human spirit, resulting in loss of meaning for any activities other than consuming the addictive substance. Recovery is based on a spiritual transformation versus punishment.

Following on the heels of AA, other models of alcoholism have developed. The medical model has achieved great credibility, as have learning theory, the interactional approach, and the sociocultural perspective. Two points are important from the perspective of second-order change. The first is that, despite theoretical differences, a commonality among current ways of understanding addiction is validation of the problem. Addiction is viewed as perfectly understandable given the person's genetic makeup, the reinforcements of AOD use, and the individual's sociocultural milieu. Second, current rationales describe the process of becoming addicted as a vicious cycle. Patterns of the vicious cycle of addiction are exemplified in the following models.

VICIOUS CYCLES AND FIRST-ORDER CHANGE

The Alcoholics Anonymous Model

According to AA (1976), addiction is characterized by countless vain attempts to prove that one can drink like other people. The same would hold for other drugs; for example, some persons can moderately use substances such as tobacco or marijuana and not become addicted. Furthermore, the idea that one will someday be able to control and enjoy one's drug use is considered the great obsession of the abnormal drinker (AA, 1976). It is the blind belief that control is possible that drives the addict in a continuous cycle of use despite untold negative consequences. The more he uses, the more he fails to control use, the more he drinks to prove he can control his use, and so forth. In effect, use to control use becomes the failed solution and characterizes the first-order solution pattern.

Moreover, AA clearly defines this as a classification error. From the perspective of second-order change, the addict overcomplicates a simple problem. The use of complex defenses such as rationalization, denial, and splitting obscures the simple fact that he cannot drink or use drugs like many others. From the perspective of AA (1976), the addict will not be able to take necessary steps for resolving his drug problem until he classifies himself as a person who cannot control his use. The necessary steps involve, of course, abstinence.

As stated earlier, the field of substance abuse is wider than addiction per se and encompasses a broad range of problematic patterns that do not rise to the threshold of dependency. Despite this, we believe that there is validity to the fundamental AA principle; that is, AOD problems are fueled by a vicious cycle that involves a classification problem. A person who receives a citation for driving under the influence of alcohol may not fit the category of alcohol dependence. However, because of strict laws regarding repeat offenses, she is compelled to realize that she no longer fits the category of a nonoffender. To avoid future arrests and consequences, she must change her self-classification and take necessary steps to avoid another citation.

Conflict Theory

According to Miller and Rollnick (2002), conflict is an important concept in many psychological theories and comes in three varieties. The most vexing conflict and type related to AOD problems is approach–avoidance. Included in this category is a more toxic derivative known as the *double approach–avoidance conflict*.

In approach–avoidance conflicts, the person is both attracted and repelled by the same object, relationship, or person. As an individual proceeds down the path of addiction, a relationship develops between the person and the substance or substances that he enjoys using. On the one hand, he is drawn toward use by enjoyment and pleasurable effects that the substance provides. On the other hand, he is repelled by the negative consequences that begin to accumulate, such as hangovers, arrests, and loss of significant others. This creates a vicious cycle wherein the person indulges in the behavior and then resists it. When he is experiencing a hangover, he makes promises to himself that he will stop using, but he is then drawn to the substance when he is feeling better. As the approach–avoidance cycle unfolds, a double approach–avoidance cycle emerges. Here the person may move in the direction of abstinence or modification. When the downside of abstinence or controlled use is experienced, he may then be drawn back to use, perhaps more than before. Now, going toward the substance moves him away, and moving away drives him toward the substance.

This type of cycle creates what Miller and Rollnick (2002) referred to as a *state of ambivalence*. From this perspective, the addicted individual becomes stuck or locked into a pattern of continued use. Ambivalence can be construed as a solution attempt. In fact, Miller and Rollnick described ambivalence as a step in the direction of ultimately solving the problem, because before becoming ambivalent the individual was engaging in problem behavior while oblivious to the consequences. However, it is also clear that ambivalence is a first-order solution, because it produces more and more problematic AOD use. While a person is in a state of ambivalence, he or she is unable to take necessary problem-solving steps.

To solve the ambivalence, two steps must be taken: (a) The person must determine that the disadvantages of AOD use outweigh the advantages, and then (b) she must make a decision to stop or modify AOD use. This closely resembles the AA process, although it is nuanced differently. In general, the addicted person must reclassify use as falling into a problem category. This is necessary for taking action. However, in this model there is a de-emphasis on the need for labeling. In other words, the person may determine that her use is problematic without labeling herself as an alcoholic or a drug addict.

Systemic Family Consultation

The systemic family consultation model proposed by Rohrbaugh and Shoham (2002) is discussed here because familial involvement in the development and treatment of AOD problems is well established. In fact, Rohrbaugh and Shoham (2002) argue with substantial empirical support (Baucom, Shoham, Mueser, Daiuto, & Stickle, 1998; McCrady et al., 1986; O'Farrell, Choquette, & Cutter, 1998), that, to date, the most effective outpatient psychosocial treatment approaches involve spouses or significant others. Rohrbaugh and Shoham (2002) identified two types of cycles that characterize the familial context that plays a role in the development of addictive behaviors: (a) demand–withdraw interaction and (b) the negative affect cycle. An understanding of these cycles also leads to a hypothesis that we have formed about how change occurs in the modern AOD treatment frameworks.

Demand–Withdraw

The demand–withdraw interaction is a common pattern in couples with AOD issues. This type of interaction involves first-order solutions that involve overpursuit. Here, one partner attempts to influence the AOD behavior of the other by criticizing, nagging, or making demands for modification of substance use. In response, the partner who is being criticized distances, defends, avoids, or withdraws. In effect, he does not take necessary steps to solve the problem. This pattern was documented by Christensen and Heavey

(1993). Within the pattern, each partner inadvertently stimulates more of the same behavior in the other. In response to nagging and criticism, the using partner may hide AOD use or defend it. This then brings on more nagging and criticism. However, the partner who hides and defends use provokes anxiety in his partner, which stimulates more nagging and criticism. Partners in the nagging-and-criticizing role were previously referred to as *codependent* because their behavior was thought to enable the addictive pattern. From this perspective, both parties are seen as engaging in failed first-order solution patterns. The addictive aspect of the pattern represents an unfortunate and unwanted outcome.

HISTORICAL UNDERSTANDING OF TREATMENT

Engaging in denial, rationalization, evasion, defensiveness, manipulation, and resistance are characteristics often associated with substance abusers (Miller, 2003). Vernon Johnson (1973), a leading proponent of this view, argued that as addictive disease progresses the chemically dependent person develops stronger defenses, which in turn become real mismanagement. This serves to erect a secure wall around the alcoholic's negative feelings about himself. The end result is that the alcoholic becomes walled away from those feelings and becomes largely out of touch with himself:

> Not only is he unaware of his highly developed defense system; he is also unaware of the powerful feelings of self-hate buried behind it, sealed off from conscious knowledge, but explosively active. Because of this, his judgment is progressively impaired—and impaired judgment, by definition, does not know that it is impaired. (Johnson, 1973, p. 25)

According to Miller (2003), this line of thinking led to aggressive, argumentative, denial-busting methods for confronting people with alcohol and drug problems. The idea was to break through the previously mentioned walls and impress reality on clients because they were unable to see it on their own. Such confrontation was integrated into the Minnesota model and became the staple of many chemical dependency treatment programs in the 1960s and 1970s. Along with confrontation came an importance for the client to accept the label of alcoholic or drug addict. Again, it was thought that acceptance of the label meant that the client was finally facing reality.

With the confrontational style came a type of intervention that was applied by family members and significant others to the chemically dependent person (Johnson, 1973). The objective of the intervention was to impress reality on the chemically dependent person in an effort to force him or her to accept some form of treatment. With this method, family members, employers, and significant others would meet with a therapist to develop a confrontation plan. The plan generally involved the following components:

- Meaningful persons would invite the chemically dependent person to a meeting. At the meeting, they would be prepared to present facts or data about physical complications or behavior patterns indicating presence of the disease.
- The data would be specific and describe events that have happened or conditions that exist.
- The tone would be nonjudgmental.
- The chief evidence would be tied directly to alcohol or drug use: "After the company picnic, I saw you leave, a bit under the weather. I assumed your wife drove home, but I learned you drove 100 miles per hour on the freeway with your family in the car."
- The evidence of the behavior would be presented in some detail.

During the 1980s and 1990s, research was conducted on the effectiveness of confrontational approaches to persons with chemical dependency. Confrontational approaches were found to be associated with high dropout rates and relatively poor outcomes. In a New Mexico study, the researchers were able to predict clients' alcohol consumption 1 year after treatment from a single counselor behavior: The more the counselor confronted during treatment, the more the person drank (Miller, Benefield, & Tonigan, 1993). As a result of research and poor results, some of the major substance abuse treatment institutions moved away from such methods. In 1985, the Hazelden Foundation officially renounced the "tear them down to build them up" approach, expressing regret that such confrontational approaches had become associated with the Minnesota model (Miller, 2003). Despite admissions by such well-known institutions as Hazelden, movement away from confrontational approaches has been slow. To this day, many substance abuse counselors continue to use aggressive confrontational approaches.

SECOND-ORDER THEORY SHIFTS
IN THE SUBSTANCE ABUSE FIELD

According to Miller (2003), research has failed to show that substance-dependent persons, as a group, have abnormal defense mechanisms. Instead, addicted persons react in a fashion similar to the way most other persons do when they are confronted with information that threatens the loss of consensual validation. Denial, rationalization, resistance, and arguing are common defense mechanisms many people use instinctively to protect themselves emotionally (Brehm & Brehm, 1981). The idea that defensiveness is a normal response to confrontation is the opposite of psychopathology and represents a second-order conceptual shift in the field. Once this is accepted as a foundational principle, other second-order shifts follow.

Counselor Effects

Leading researchers in the addictions field, such as Miller and Rollnick (2002), have linked counselor effects in substance abuse treatment to similar research in the general field of psychotherapy. They emphasize that counselors working in the same setting, and offering the same treatment, show dramatic differences in rates of client dropouts and successful outcomes. These differences exceed the magnitude of differences between treatment approaches. Miller and Rollnick further stated that the Rogerian conditions of accurate empathy, nonpossessive warmth, and genuineness are not only applicable to substance abuse counseling but also help to explain differential outcomes. They argued that the therapeutic relationship stabilizes quickly in early sessions and that the nature of the client–counselor relationship in early sessions predicts retention and outcome. Here we see another second-order shift. Previously, the focus of the clinician has been on the defensive posture of the addicted client. Now, the emphasis is placed on the therapeutic relationship, or how the therapist and client are relating. To make this shift, clinicians must move from an authoritarian stance to an empathic one, in which the client is viewed as an active partner versus passive recipient of treatment (Miller, 2003). The shift from passive to active represents a reversal in the way that clinicians conceptualize client roles and therefore meets the definition of a second-order change for clinicians.

Denial Revisited

As stated previously, a major shift has occurred in how denial and resistance to change are conceptualized in substance abuse treatment. The next conceptual step from normalizing resistance has been to accept responsibility that certain treatment procedures set clients up to react defensively. Miller (2003) argued that when clients are labeled pejoratively as alcoholic or manipulative or resistant, and are given no voice in selecting treatment goals, they are likely to respond with defiance. Treatment strategies that involve aggressive confrontational tactics are also likely to produce the same negative effects. Miller (2003), reporting on Jones (1977), argued further that one reason that high levels of denial and resistance are seen as attributes of substance-dependent individuals is that their normal defense mechanisms are so frequently challenged and aroused by clinical strategies of confrontation. This becomes a self-fulfilling prophecy. Iatrogenic resistance represents still another major conceptual reversal in the field of chemical dependency. Whereas previously defensiveness was viewed as coming from the client, resistance is now understood as a function of treatment procedures that are being used by the therapist.

Ready, Willing, and Able

Another major shift in the addictions field is the manner in which the concept of motivation is understood. Motivation was previously conceptualized as a static client characteristic. If a client was perceived to lack motivation for changing an addictive behavior, then coercive methods were used. These included confrontation, punishment, restrictions, losses, nagging, and bugging. In effect, imposing or coercing motivation has appeared to be the method of choice for many family members, treatment personnel, and policymakers who see substance-dependent persons as actively fighting consideration of change (Donovan & Rosengren, 1999; Liepman, 1993).

Currently, a more interactional view of motivation in the substance-dependent person has been offered. Miller and Rollnick (2002) offered a conceptualization based on discrepancy, which comes from self-regulation theory (J. M. Brown, 1998; Kanfer, 1986; Miller & Brown, 1991). From this perspective, motivation to change is linked to the degree of discrepancy that exists between a person's actual behavior and desired state. When the present reality is within desired limits, no change will be deemed necessary. Once a person begins to see a discrepancy between how she is and how she wants to be, motivation for change will grow. Motivation itself may be construed as comprising three dimensions: (a) willing; (b) able; and (c) ready.

Willing relates directly to discrepancy. As the discrepancy between the current state of affairs and what is desired grows, the substance-dependent individual becomes willing to consider change. However, being willing is not enough. As the discrepancy gap widens, the substance-dependent person must see an avenue that will make change possible. Similar to hope restoration, as described in earlier chapters, the substance-dependent person must develop a sense of general efficacy and self-efficacy. *General efficacy* is the belief that one has found a method of change that will work; *self-efficacy* is a belief that the person can follow through on the method. The concept of self-efficacy comes from the work of Bandura (1986, 1988, 1997). Realizing that one needs to change, having a method, and being willing to follow through, however, are still not enough; the substance-dependent person must also be ready to change. Readiness to change is a function of priorities and of where in a larger scheme of priorities the individual places the need to change an addictive behavior. Here again lies another significant shift for the field. It was previously considered pathological for a person to rank changing an addictive behavior as a low priority. Miller and Rollnick (2002) offered a reversal of this stance. They suggested that ranking priorities is a normal function of human behavior. A person with an addiction may have legitimate reasons for not being ready to change at a given time. The addicted person may also have multiple substances on which he is dependent. He may be ready to make changes in the use of one or some but not all substances. As we will see, respecting the client's priorities has the counterintuitive effect of enhancing her motivation to change.

STAGES OF CHANGE

James Prochaska and Carlos DiClemente (1982, 1983, 1986) began developing a transtheoretical model of change in the early 1980s. The initial elements of the model came from an analysis of theories of therapy and highlighted processes that could be identified across various perspectives (Prochaska, 1979; Prochaska & DiClemente, 1986). Through studying the broader perspective of psychotherapy models, they became especially interested in how people change addictive behaviors. Their initial forays into the area of addictive behaviors involved investigations into how nicotine-addicted smokers were able to quit smoking. It is most interesting that much of Prochaska and DiClemente's early work involved naturalistic studies, in which they followed individuals who were at different points in the process of quitting smoking on their own, to see how they did it. Later, when comparing self-changers with persons who quit as part of a treatment program, a framework emerged. It was evident that the process of change was generic and that it could be best understood from a temporal perspective—that is, quitting smoking was a process that unfolded over time. It was also determined that the change process could be conceptualized as occurring within the context of predictable steps or stages. Further research indicated that the same stages and process of change could be assessed across various addictive and health behaviors (DiClemente, 2003). Over the years, the stages-of-change model has become regarded by scholars in the addiction field as the gold standard for conceptualizing how addictive behavior changes over time (Flores & Georgi, 2005; Miller, 2003). Yet for many clinicians the idea that clients change in stages is still a radical concept. In this section, we briefly review the stages of change and the concept of stage-based interventions. We then describe motivational interviewing and how it fits with the stages-of-change model. We briefly review the 12-step model of treatment and conclude the chapter with a discussion about the second-order implications that underlie these frameworks.

Precontemplation

Carlos DiClemente (2003) wrote elegantly about the process of acquiring and changing addictive behaviors:

> By definition, the end-state of addiction is a well-established way of behaving that is consistent, stable, and resistant to change. Change requires dissolution of this established pattern and involves a shake-up or

perturbation of the status quo for some period of time until a new pattern can be established that replaces the old. Then, once again, there is a period of stability until change is again needed or wanted. (p. 25)

From this perspective, *precontemplation* is both the end-state of addiction and the place at which change begins.

Persons in precontemplation are not considering change in the foreseeable future, defined as a period of 6 months to 1 year. They are either satisfied with the addictive behavior or are unwilling to go through the disruption that is necessary for change. As long as the current pattern seems functional, the addicted individual will see no reason to change it. It is very difficult, however, to maintain an addictive pattern without incurring negative consequences over time. Through the human developmental process, many influences shape a person's perspective on what is important in life. Consequently, the previously described discrepancies are prone to surface, creating a classification problem as was previously described. This creates a growing gap between whom the addicted person is becoming and whom he wants to be. For example, a woman who has just received her third DUI may realize that she is now viewed as a criminal versus a traffic offender. As a traffic offender, she used oversimplification to place drinking and driving in the same category as speeding. "Drinking and driving, speeding, running a stop sign, they're all the same thing. No big deal." Now with laws that make a third DUI offense a felony, she realizes that drinking and driving falls into a much more serious category. It's not the same as other driving offenses. The situation is more complex then she had considered. As discrepancies such as this become apparent, there is a shift in concern about the addictive behavior and awareness of reasons for change. Although there is no definite time frame for any of the stages, it is the growing discrepancy gap that triggers the beginning of the change cycle. Change starts as the addicted person begins to question whether she can continue to categorize her AOD use as "no problem."

Contemplation

Once the discrepancy gap is wide enough, the addicted man enters a period of instability. He is no longer satisfied with the addictive behavior, while at the same time he is not yet ready to change. The addicted person has made a significant categorical shift. He now recognizes that substance use falls into the problem category, yet he is not ready to change his behavior to be consistent with his new category of problem drinker or drug user. Consideration of change entails struggling with ambivalence about leaving one behavior pattern and moving to another (Miller & Rollnick, 2002). This involves a process whereby the individual evaluates the risks and benefits of changing the addictive pattern. Because change is difficult and will involve disruption in a person's life, the case for change must be compelling. It must also meet the perceived needs of the individual.

Going back to the woman who just received a third DUI; on the surface, the case for change appears to be clear. The criminal penalties should by themselves create a sufficient case for change. Yet in this situation the person works as a bartender at a restaurant where alcohol is served. The culture at the restaurant is based on drinking. Her drinking pattern involves abstinence while working and staying after work to have a few drinks with her coworkers. She is able to use public transportation to get to and from work, and so she is not concerned about the loss of her driver's license. From this perspective, although the person feels distressed about being labeled a criminal, her entrenchment in a drinking culture outweighs the need for change at this time. She may be willing to live with the discrepancy between her criminal status and behavior indefinitely. She justifies this on the basis that she is willing to give up driving to maintain her addictive behavior; this reduces the risk of another DUI. She may say, "Maybe I do have a problem, but how is that different from anyone else? I can deal with it."

The need for change, however, may strengthen with new circumstances or situations. A person in a similar situation might learn from his or her doctor that alcohol use has damaged his or her liver and that stopping alcohol consumption can prolong his or her life. This might be enough to tip what Miller (2003) referred to as the *decisional balance* in favor of change. Once the scale is tipped in favor of change, the client begins preparing to revise meanings, categories, and behavior to achieve congruence. To change, he or she has two alternatives. The first is to revise categories, meanings, and behavior in a manner that is consistent with a responsible drinker. The other is to revise categories, meanings, and behavior in a manner that is consistent with a nondrinker. He or she must decide which way he or she will go before he or she can establish a goal.

Preparation

According to DiClemente (2003), *preparation* is a stage of change that entails development of an action plan and the commitment needed to implement the plan. Changing a behavior pattern requires attention and energy devoted to breaking the old pattern and starting a new one. Planning is the activity that organizes the environment and develops strategies for change. With a shift in the decisional balance, the previously described woman will need to develop a plan for her recovery. This will involve establishing goals and methods for achieving those goals. As suggested earlier, this process is fraught with thorny questions. Will she develop a plan for controlled drinking or abstinence? If she opts for control and fails, will she then seek abstinence? If she opts for abstinence, what will she do about her entrenchment in a drinking culture? Can she still work in a bar? Should she stop socializing with friends who drink? What will she do instead of drinking? Will she go for a simple solution and just stop? These are but a few questions that a person must resolve before taking action toward behavioral change. Preparation is the stage in which individuals formulate such questions and devise their change plan. This is also a time for summoning the energy that will be required to successfully implement the change process.

Action

The implementation of the change plan represents the *action* stage of change. This involves stopping the old pattern and engaging in a new one. Most people equate this stage with change (DiClemente, 2003). Action represents a clear shift from the first half of the change process. In the early stages of change the focus was on intentions, considerations, and plans; now, the emphasis is on behavior change. As was stated in earlier chapters, it is not good enough for a shift to occur once. The new behavior must be structured in a manner as to be repeated over time. DiClemente (2003) indicated that the old pattern retains its attractiveness and that returning to it may be easier than establishing a new pattern. For frequent behaviors such as daily drug use, the action stage may last for 3 to 6 months. For less frequent behaviors, such as weekend binge drinking, the action stage may last longer, for up to 1 year.

Maintenance

DiClemente (2003) stated that for a new behavior to become a habit it must become integrated into the lifestyle of the individual. In other words, the addicted person must develop a lifestyle that is congruent with his new view on drug use. During the maintenance stage, the new behavior pattern becomes automatic and no longer requires conscious effort. "The new behavior becomes fully maintained only when there is little or no effort or energy needed to continue it and the individual can terminate the cycle of change" (Prochaska, Norcross, & DiClemente, 1994, p. 29). As the person heads in the direction of terminating the change cycle, however, there is still a danger of returning to the old pattern. There is a tendency to relapse when changing an addictive behavior and so movement through the cycle of change is viewed as a circular rather than linear process.

DiClemente (2003) argued that the stages of change seem most like stages of development as described by Erik Erikson (1963). Erikson viewed psychological development as a series of tasks that build on one another, that become important in different points of development, and that can be more or less successfully resolved as the person proceeds through life. In a similar fashion, persons proceed through the cycle of change at different rates of speed. Tasks involving motivation, decision making, efficacy, and coping activities have an ongoing role throughout the change process. How one resolves issues regarding these tasks will determine the degree of success that the individual has as he or she progresses through the change stages. Relapse followed by recycling through the change process is considered to be typical for most addicted persons. Through relapse and recycling, the addicted person gains knowledge about flaws in his change plan and has an opportunity to develop better strategies. Research shows that the spiral movement over time and the process of recycling through the stages until the individual achieves successful recovery provide an optimistic framework for addictive behavior change in the long run (DiClemente, Carbonari, & Velasquez, 1992; Prochaska, DiClemente, & Norcross, 1992).

STAGE-BASED INTERVENTIONS

Segmenting the process of changing addictive behaviors, over time, has created important implications for the addictions field. As was suggested before, clinicians and program developers have historically ignored the first half of the change process. Consequently, addictions treatment has centered on coercing addicted persons into action. "It has been a time honored assumption that to move the addicted alcoholic only one of two options is available, hitting bottom or confrontation" (DiClemente, 2003, p. 122). Unfortunately, this view has consistently led to poor results for clients. DiClemente (2003) further cited many examples of the ineffectiveness of external pressure as a means of coercing change.

Breaking change into stages has assisted clinicians and program developers with conceptualizing the first steps of change in a new way. The place at which the addicted person begins reclassifying use as problematic has been reevaluated and is now considered a critical intervention point. It has also become apparent that there are many intervention points along the pathway of change and that the needs of addicted persons are different at each point. With this has come awareness that there are specific tasks at each stage of change and that in turn intervention points are related to stage-specific tasks. For example, the major task of precontemplation is increasing awareness of the need for change. Contemplators need to focus on weighing pros and cons, persons in preparation need to increase commitment and make strategic plans, persons in action need to implement strategies for change, and maintainers need to sustain change and establish new behavior patterns (DiClemente, 2003). From this perspective, the change of addictive behaviors bears a striking resemblance to the change of disruptive behaviors that we discussed in chapter 8. Because change is developmental, coercing change is similar to forcing language development or toilet training. Coercion fosters defiance and further feeds first-order vicious cycles.

DiClemente (2003) argued that it is important to intervene with strategies that are designed to address the developmental stage of the addicted person. Helping the client resolve stage-based issues allows the client to move forward in the change cycle while feeling supported. For example, stimulus control—the avoidance or removal of triggers for addictive behaviors—and counterconditioning—changing one's response to the stimulus through activities such as relaxation training, distraction, constructive self-talk, or desensitization—are cognitive strategies that are frequently used to assist addicted persons with controlling craving and urges to use. A clinician who is informed in regard to the stages-of-change model does not assign these techniques to a client who is in precontemplation. Doing so could rush the client, resulting in a pattern wherein the therapist overpursues change while the client withdraws further into a pattern of not taking necessary steps to address his addiction. This places the client and therapist at risk for development of a vicious cycle regarding the client's resistance or "yes, but" interactions.

Instead, a clinician informed about the stages-of-change model works with the client in precontemplation on increasing awareness of substance use as a problem. Discussion about change techniques is placed on hold until the decisional balance is tipped in the favor of change and the client is ready to develop a plan for abstinence. The argument against rushing change with addicted persons has become an empirically supported standard of care in the addictions field (Miller, 2003). It is also a second-order reversal for therapists from their previous standard of demanding that clients admit their problem and take action on it.

MOTIVATIONAL INTERVIEWING

Motivational interviewing is a clinical strategy designed to enhance client motivation for change. It can include counseling, client assessment, multiple sessions, or a 30-minute brief intervention (Miller, 2003). Motivational interventions have been correlated with the stages-of-change model. Such interventions may be used to enhance motivation for engaging in treatment, or they may be used as a stand-alone approach. A recent review of 11 clinical trials of motivational interviewing concluded that this is a useful, efficient, and adaptive therapy style worthy of further development and research (Noonan & Moyers, 1997). Three trials confirmed the usefulness of motivational interviewing as an enhancement to traditional treatment, and five supported the effectiveness of motivational interviewing in reducing substance-use patterns in medical settings for other health-related issues (Miller, 2003). In Project MATCH (Project MATCH Research Group, 1997), the largest ever clinical trial to compare different alcohol treatments, motivational interviewing was found to yield identical outcomes to longer outpatient methods and was more effective with angry clients.

Motivational interviewing is predicated on the notion that confrontation decreases the likelihood of change in substance-abusing or substance-dependent persons. "Getting in the client's face may work for some, but for most it is exactly the opposite of what is needed—to come face to face with a painful reality and change" (Miller, 2003, p. 10). Instead, addicted individuals respond much more favorably to a therapist who is empathic and respectful of the client's freedom to change or not change.

The Righting Reflex

Miller and Rollnick (2002) reported that professional helpers become therapists because of a broad desire to help people set things aright. They referred to this desire as the *righting reflex*. Consequently, when we encounter an individual who is struggling with a substance abuse problem, our natural instinct is to attempt to "right" the individual's behavior. This immediately sets up a dichotomy wherein the client defends her substance use while the therapist argues the case for change. Earlier in the book, we described this in the context of change–don't change ambivalence. Also as previously described, many substance abuse clients enter treatment after being subjected to confrontations by their spouse, court personnel, their boss, significant others, and perhaps previous therapists. For this reason, they may be highly sensitive to further confrontations and quite prepared to defend the "don't change" side of their ambivalence.

For this reason, Miller and Rollnick (2002) recommended that clinicians inhibit their righting reflex. They indicated that this may feel wrong, similar to the car driver who must learn to steer into a skid, but that it is necessary if the clinician is to form a successful treatment alliance with the client. Within the context of the alliance the clinician will attempt to interact with the client in such a way that the client argues for change. This is accomplished when the therapist, in the initial phase of treatment, validates the good that comes from the client's substance use. By validating the good, the client is free to begin discussing the not-so-good aspects of his addictive behaviors.

The One-Down Position

Miller and Rollnick (2002) described their positioning form of treatment as an evolution of Carl Rogers's work (1957, 1980). It is similar in the sense that they are working to help the client discover his own motivation for change by creating a condition of acceptance of the client as a valid person. The approach is client directed; the client is free to continue using alcohol and drugs without condemnation from the therapist. To create the condition of acceptance, the therapist takes a *one-down stance*, which is described as analogous to the TV character Columbo, played by Peter Falk. This stance is also remarkably similar to therapist maneuverability as recommended by the Mental Research Institute (Fisch, Weakland, & Segal, 1982). From the one-down position, similar to the Columbo method, the therapist recognizes that she does not have the power to change the client. The client's situation is somewhat of a mystery that she is helping the client sort out. As the mystery unravels, the therapist can help the client build on discrepancies with the idea that the bigger the discrepancy, the more likely the client is to undergo change.

Miller and Rollnick (2002) also acknowledged that although the motivational approach is client directed there is also a consciously deliberate aspect. It is directly aimed at assisting the client with resolving her ambivalence in the service of changing addictive behaviors. With this in mind, there are four basic principles that underscore motivational interviewing.

Express Empathy

Reflective listening and accurate empathy, as described, are the fundamental skills that form the foundation of the motivational approach. Through skillful listening, the clinician hopes to understand the client's feelings and perspectives. This is done without judging, criticizing, or blaming. The attitude is one of listening with a desire to understand the client's entire viewpoint. Miller and Rollnick (2002) reported that, as has also been previously stated throughout the book, this kind of acceptance paradoxically frees clients to change. However, nonacceptance immobilizes the change process.

Within this perspective, the clinician seeks to validate the client's experience. Ambivalence about modifying or abstaining from addictive behaviors is not only considered normal but also represents a necessary step in the change process. This logic is based on the precontemplation stage. Because clients start out believing that addictive behaviors are under control and not a problem, the recognition that there is a discrepancy means that progress has been made. At the same time, addicted individuals can become stuck in their ambivalence to change, and this is also considered quite normal.

Develop Discrepancy

As stated, motivational interviewing is intentionally directed at resolving ambivalence in the service of change. A major feature of motivational interviewing is to create and amplify discrepancies between the current state of affairs and the state to which the addicted person aspires. There are two caveats to this point that are important to note. The first is that discrepancy is used to describe the importance of change versus the wideness of the gap. The key here is the value that is ascribed to the discrepancy by the client. In some situations, the discrepancy may not need to be large for a client to desire change. However, a very wide gap might be demoralizing and inhibit change for the client. Therefore, the terms big and *wide* refer to the importance of the discrepancy as defined by the client. Second, the discrepancy must be the client's. A sense of coercion occurs when a person feels that the therapist is imposing her values or goals on the treatment.

Roll With Resistance

In regard to *rolling with resistance*, Miller and Rollnick (2002) referred directly to the work that comes out of strategic family therapy and second-order change. From the motivational perspective, the clinician seeks to stay out of arguments with the client. He or she does this by not directly arguing for change. New perspectives are invited, not imposed. When a client begins to show resistance, the therapist interprets it as a signal to respond differently. The therapist views the client as the primary source of answers and solutions to problems. This position is taken out of respect for the person as a competent autonomous individual. Advice may be given, but it is given in a permissive way. Clients are invited to "take what they want and leave the rest" (Miller & Rollnick, 2002, p. 40).

Support Self-Efficacy and Optimism

As stated previously, *self-efficacy* is defined as a person's belief in his or her ability to carry out and succeed with a specific task. It is linked to hope as a key element in motivation for change and a predictor of treatment outcome (Frank & Frank, 1991; Miller, 1985; Shapiro, 1971). Self-efficacy is fostered first by the clinician's belief that the client can change (Jones, 1977; Leake & King, 1977; Parker, Winstead, & Willi, 1979). It is also fostered by the clinician's attitude of "If you wish[,] I can help you change" (Miller, & Rollnick, 2002, p. 41.).

In sum, motivational interviewing is guided by four principles: (a) express empathy; (b) develop discrepancy; (c) roll with resistance; and (d) support self-efficacy. Other techniques associated with this method, such as asking open questions, measuring self-efficacy, eliciting change talk, and agreeing with a twist, are designed to actualize these principles in the treatment process. Motivational interviewing is often used to facilitate progress through the early stages of the addictive change cycle. It is also used to assist clients with developing change plans and to set up intervention strategies, such as stimulus control and counterconditioning, in the latter stages of the change process. Motivational techniques are used in the maintenance stage of change to normalize relapses and speed recycling toward long-term change.

12-STEP PROGRAMS

Addiction programs fashioned after AA are based on a 12-step approach found in the *Blue Book* (AA, 1976). As previously described, the 12 steps are designed to interrupt a cycle of futile attempts to drink or use drugs normally. This cycle is interrupted through an anonymous fellowship wherein persons with a similar condition give up the idea that they can control substance use and that they can stop through their own willpower. This giving up or surrendering of control is accomplished through a series of specified steps that involve proclamations, confession, making amends, and providing service to other persons with addictive behaviors.

In this approach, the addicted person is required to label himself as an alcoholic or an addict. Working progressively through the steps becomes central to the person's life and is done over time. The expectation is that addicted persons assist each other as they become more comfortable with sobriety. Persons who have more experience with sobriety mentor those with less sober experience. Special coins or medals are given to mark sobriety anniversaries. Fellowship meetings involve members telling personal stories of their fall into addiction and the steps on which they are now working as part of their recovery. The AA mantras are "One day at a time" and "Easy does it." This refers to the need to be ever vigilant about relapses and work daily on sobriety. It is believed that the best source of help for the addicted person is another person who is also recovering. Confrontation is used and is considered more palatable because the confronting person is a fellow addict.

ADDICTION AND SECOND-ORDER CHANGE

Although written about in different words, it has been known for many years that changing addictive behaviors involves second-order change. Dr. Silkworth (AA, 1976) wrote that

> Strange as this may seem to those who do not understand—once a psychic change has occurred, the very same person who seemed doomed, who had so many problems he despaired of ever solving them, suddenly finds himself easily able to control his desire for alcohol, the only effort necessary being that required to follow a few simple rules. (p. xxvii)

It is clear that Silkworth is describing an individual who has undergone a second-order change, as has been defined in this book. The question, then, for researchers and clinicians has not been about the need for addicted persons to undergo a transforming experience but how it should be arranged. As we have been demonstrating throughout this chapter, research has been identifying methods that produce change. Yet what Miller and Rollnick (2002) stated about motivational interviewing may be said about the field in general: "There is reasonable evidence that motivational interviewing works in certain applications, but the data thus far are less clear in documenting how and why it works" (p. 26). We argue that the golden thread is at the heart of the questions "how" and "why."

Second-Order Change for Therapists

We have shown that since the 1980s theories used in the addictions field have gone through a radical second-order shift. The same is true for therapists. Much of the change has been related to the stages-of-change model and motivational interviewing. Before these frameworks were developed, change in addictive behaviors could be construed as having three components (confront, change, and prevent relapse). As suggested earlier, confrontation was used to facilitate each step.

From the perspective of second-order change, the most common first-order pattern for addictive behaviors involves a bidirectional vicious cycle in which significant others overpursue change, while in response the addicted person refuses through oversimplification ("There is no problem.") or by using highly complex defenses to deny a problem. Consequently, necessary actions are not taken to quit or modify the addictive behavior. In the end, demands for change reinforce refusal to change, and refusal to change reinforces more demands. With this in mind, it is fairly easy to see how and why treatments that are based on confrontation are generally ineffective. A confronting clinician in a cycle wherein change is being demanded is, in essence, adding more of the same solution to the problem. Because second-order change is about difference, it makes sense that helpful clinicians provide input that is opposite of the input that comprises the vicious cycle interactions. In this case, the opposite would be empathy and feedback provided in a manner that supports the client's freedom to choose. Despite this general rule, it is also true that confrontation in the old style does have a track record of working sometimes.

Rohrbaugh and Shoham (2002) identified unusual situations in which significant others fail to take necessary steps, meaning that significant others take the approach that is opposite from the usual one. The addictive behavior is ignored or not addressed. In response, the addicted person escalates his or her patterns of substance abuse. Here, confrontation is the opposite of a permissive approach and perhaps sheds light on why it has been effective in some cases.

This has important implications for therapists. Whereas therapists have traditionally been formally trained to rely heavily on confrontation while using an empathic approach sparingly, the reverse now seems more appropriate. As Miller and Rollnick (2002 described, this will seem incorrect or counterintuitive for clinicians who have been trained in confrontational approaches. Hence, for many clinicians adopting an approach such as motivational interviewing will create a need to undergo a second-order change.

The stages-of-change model may have a similar effect for clinicians. Past models that promoted coerced change were based on the error of oversimplification. The stages-of-change model takes a temporal view of the change process, and second-order change is implicit in its application. Breaking change into segments, and applying different strategies on the basis of the client's stage of change, requires a more complex understanding of change and places a restraint on the therapist's "righting reflex." For example, it is recommended that when working with precontemplators and contemplators therapists provide specific information about AOD use from the perspective of "how it is good and not so good" (DiClemente, 2003, p. 145). For some therapists, the idea that there is anything to embrace about substance abuse is a radical shift. Also, the client is left to consider the ramifications of use for himself. This is also a major shift for therapists who have been trained to believe that they have the power to change clients' belief systems through aggressive means.

Second-Order Change for Clients

When clients enter into treatment, whether they come alone or with significant others, they bring experiences of how others have responded to their addictive behaviors. This creates expectations for how the therapist will behave. Consequently, in many cases the client expects that the therapist will move quickly to condemn AOD abuse and try to rush the client into change.

If the clinician has been trained in the stages-of-change model and motivational interviewing, then many reversals of the client's expectations will occur. The therapist will convey a desire to partner with the client as opposed to taking an authoritarian stance. She will acknowledge an upside to AOD abuse and do so before exploring the problems involved for the client. As we described in chapter 4, this creates a change-empowering form of validation. The client has good reason for having a substance abuse problem and is right for wanting to change it.

The therapist will seek to understand where the client is in the change process and accept the client's position even if it is different from where others expect him to be. The therapist will make it clear that change is up to the client and that she will help but not tell the client what he must do. If the client is ambivalent about changing, she will explore the pros and cons of change while not imposing change on him. She will go over the choices of abstinence or controlled use and possibly prescribe a controlled-drinking experiment to help the client determine whether he can control his use. Once the client has decided to change, she will work with him on establishing his own goals and developing a plan for goal achievement. This will include decisions that he will make about establishing a supportive social network. She will offer a menu of change alternatives from which he can choose. As he progresses through the change cycle, she will work with him on identifying triggers for relapse. She will normalize relapse so as to preserve the therapeutic alliance should he fall back into use. The work will occur at a pace that is comfortable for the client.

As stated previously, this type of open stance tends to create a paradoxical effect in that it promotes change. We argue that it does so for an important reason. The open position of the therapist is opposite from the vicious cycle pattern that is maintaining the client's addictive behavior pattern. In the pattern, others are attempting to restrict the addicted person's freedom. Here, the clinician is reversing the pattern by creating space for the client to make her own choices on necessary steps that she will take to address her addictive behaviors.

The 12-step model, from AA, also has embedded reversals. This was originally pointed out by Gregory Bateson (1971) in his cybernetic theory of alcoholism. Bateson postulated that the main reversal is around the notion of control. As stated, from this perspective addicts are understood as engaging in a symmetrical escalation with the addicting substance. The objective is to prove that one can use like others. Each failed attempt to prove this point is followed by another failed attempt to prove the point. The reversal is to give in and admit that the substance is in control. Surrender is reframed as victory and is celebrated with a legion of others who have also surrendered. Once the war with the substance is over, the recovering addicted person begins engaging in a new life that involves confession of past sins, making amends, serving others, and humbly admitting that this type of change could come only from a power that is greater than he. From the perspective of second-order change, the steps following surrender serve as a blocking strategy such that the recovering person engages in activities that are mutually exclusive from using alcohol or other drugs.

FOLLOWING THE THREAD

Addictive behaviors are generally formed and maintained by a series of problem-solving errors, as described in chapter 3 (this volume). The addicted person attempts to solve the problem at an incorrect level of abstraction. This results in a refusal to classify addictive behavior as problematic, which is followed by failure to take other necessary actions for change. In response, significant others overpursue methods of interaction that are designed to convince the addicted person that he must change. Research shows that when overpursuit is reversed, and the addict's reasons for use are validated, a therapeutic space is created. From this space, the addict is freed to take necessary steps for ending or modifying his addiction. Necessary steps include problem identification, establishment of a change plan with specific goals, willingness to make the plan a priority and confidence that the plan will work. Once these steps have been achieved, the long-term outlook for permanent change is good even though there may be relapses along the way.

11

SELF-HARMING AND SUICIDAL CLIENTS

A serene acceptance of what <u>is</u> promotes health, but by keeping the mind clear it also puts a person in a better position to change things that need changing.

—Bernie Siegel

Hold on to the center and make up your mind to rejoice in this paradise called life.

—Lao Tzu

Most therapists agree that responding to patients who injure and mutilate themselves, who threaten suicide and make numerous attempts at it, and who may become demanding and angry at us, as therapists, for the way we are trying to help, is one of the most stressful parts of our work. There is nothing more frustrating for a skilled and compassionate therapist than to work with such clients. Engaging in therapy with them may become a sort of "devil's pact," wherein the more we try to offer help, the more it is apparently not enough. Clients become more distressed, needy, and self-harming, and we become more alarmed and intent on intervening to keep them safe. As this cycle continues, both therapists and their clients become equally stressed, frustrated, and blame each other for not making things better. Our efforts are then redoubled, and the vicious cycle is locked in.

Recall that first-order change is defined as change that occurs in a system that itself remains the same. These changes of intensity, frequency, duration, and so on, are solutions taken according to the existing assumptions and tacit rules of a system. Not only do they not change the system, but they affirm the system by repeating its assumptions, rules, and patterns. When therapists enter into therapy with patients such as these, we often enter into a "game without end," a vicious cycle wherein our therapeutic solutions become the problem. This is often the case when therapists enter into therapy with clients who fit the criterion of borderline personality disorder (BPD), a problem pattern in which chronic self-harming behaviors are most commonly seen.

In this chapter, our final one on empirically supported treatments (ESTs), we focus on dialectical behavior therapy (DBT) for BPD. DBT has become one of the emerging ESTs for patients and therapists caught in the distressing pattern of symptoms referred to as *borderline personality disorder*. By now, it may come as no surprise that we believe the most potent therapeutic element in this approach, similar to the other ESTs we have reviewed, is that it is built on a firm foundation of second-order change. In this chapter, we show how the dialectical basis of DBT is the same as the systemic perspectives on change presented in the first several chapters of this book. The dialectical philosophy or worldview is represented in the actions of first- and second-order change. We also note how the dialectical perspective is infused into the working alliance and therapeutic relationship in such a way as to integrate relationship and intervention into a true second-order relationship between therapists and clients. First, however, we define what is meant by BPD and offer some of the history of the term and the defining behaviors. Finally, we present an overview of the DBT approach, including research support; rationale; and procedures, particularly those involving second-order change. We describe the kind of second-order change involved, not only for the client but for the therapist as well.

DEFINING THE PROBLEM

Too little and too much spoils everything.

—Danish proverb

The idea of BPD has a relatively long history yet a relatively recent translation into a formalized diagnostic category. The roots of the term *borderline* are firmly planted in psychodynamic theory. John Gunderson (2000) traced this early history from the early clinical observations of Adolph Stern in the 1930s; to Robert Knight in the 1950s; to Otto Kernberg and Roy Grinker's contributions in ego psychology and object relations in the 1960s; and then to Gunderson's own work (2000) on formalizing the diagnosis into a diagnostic category in the *Diagnostic and Statistical Manual of Mental Disorders* (e.g., 4th ed. [DSM–IV]; American Psychiatric Association, 1994) in the late 1970s. The term *borderline* itself comes from an early diagnostic assumption of a continuum from normal to neurotic to psychotic behavior. The cluster of behaviors in question was seen as fitting on the borderline between neurotic and psychotic. Although evolving psychodynamic perspectives in object relations and self psychology have focused on the characteristic historic and present problems these clients tend to have in forming and maintaining relationships, other theorists have preferred a more theoretically neutral description of the symptoms of the problem as merely a cluster of related behaviors. Millon (1987) has been one of the most vocal dissenters from even using the term borderline. Stressing the divergent backgrounds and histories of clients fitting the diagnostic criteria but who don't fit the traditional dynamic view, Millon suggested that the term *cycloid personality* be used as a better reflection of the behavioral and mood instabilities that characterize the cycles in which these people become trapped. At its worst extreme, for many therapists caught in the frustrating cycles of working with clients fitting these criteria, the term borderline has become synonymous with a four-letter word used to label and blame clients for the characteristic challenges they present therapists. The term borderline itself, however, has persisted in use and is defined in the *DSM–IV* (American Psychiatric Association, 1994).

Formal Definitions

Borderline personality disorder has been defined by the *DSM–IV* and also by the commonly used research instrument the "Diagnostic Interview for Borderlines" (J. G. Gunderson & Kolb, 1978; Zanarini, Gunderson, Frankenburg, & Chauncey, 1989) as including the following characteristics:

1. Frantic efforts to avoid real or imagined abandonment.
2. A pattern of unstable and intense interpersonal relationships characterized by alternating between extremes of idealization and devaluation.
3. Identity disturbance: persistent and markedly disturbed, distorted, or unstable self-image or sense of self.
4. Impulsiveness in at least two areas that are potentially self-damaging (e.g., spending, sex, substance abuse, shoplifting, reckless driving, and binge eating—not to include suicide or self-mutilating behavior, which are covered in Criterion 5).
5. Recurrent suicidal threats, gestures, or behavior, or self-mutilating behavior.
6. Affective instability: marked reactivity of mood (e.g., intense episodic dysphoria, irritability, or anxiety) usually lasting a few hours and rarely more than a few days.
7. Chronic feelings of emptiness.
8. Inappropriate, intense anger or lack of control of anger (e.g., frequent displays of temper, constant anger, recurrent physical fights).
9. Transient, stress-related severe dissociative symptoms or paranoid ideation.

The *DSM–IV* requires that at least five of these nine criteria be met for the diagnosis.

Marsha Linehan (1993; Robins, Ivanoff, & Linehan, 2001) has organized these *DSM–IV* criteria is in five areas in which the individual is dysregulated:

1. *Emotional dysregulation*: the individual's biological predisposition to be highly emotionally sensitive and reactive to one's environment. BPD clients are proposed to have difficulty controlling emotions of all kinds (Criteria 6 and 8).
2. *Interpersonal dysregulation*: patterns of intense, unstable relationships, including those with therapists (Criteria 1 and 2).
3. *Self-dysregulation*: persistently unstable self-image and chronic feelings of emptiness (Criteria 3 and 7).
4. *Behavioral dysregulation*: impulsivity in at least two of the self-damaging areas of the *DSM–IV* criteria (Criteria 4 and 5).
5. *Cognitive dysregulation*: the transient, stress-related paranoid ideation or severe dissociative symptoms that are sometimes seen (Criterion 9).

Linehan (1993), the major developer of DBT, has not developed an independent definition of BPD, but she has organized a number of behavioral patterns associated with a set of individuals who fit these criteria, including the following:

- *Emotional vulnerability*: a pattern of pervasive difficulties in regulating negative emotions including high sensitivity to negative emotional stimuli, high emotional intensity, and slow return to emotional baseline, as well as awareness and experience of emotional vulnerability. This may include a tendency to blame the social environment for unrealistic expectations and demands.
- *Self-invalidation*: A tendency to invalidate or fail to recognize one's own emotional responses, thoughts, beliefs, and behaviors. Unrealistically high standards and expectations for self. May include intense shame, self-hate, and self-directed anger.
- *Unrelenting crises*: A pattern of frequent, stressful, negative environmental events, disruptions, and roadblocks—some caused by the individual's dysfunctional lifestyle; others by an inadequate social milieu; and many by fact or chance.
- *Inhibited grieving*: A tendency to inhibit or overcontrol negative emotional responses, especially those associated with grief and loss including sadness, anger, guilt, shame, anxiety, and panic.
- *Active passivity*: A tendency toward a passive interpersonal problem-solving style involving failure to engage actively in the

solving of one's own life problems, often together with active attempts to solicit problem solving from others in the environment, learned helplessness, and hopelessness.

- *Apparent competence*: A tendency for the individual to appear deceptively more competent than she actually is; usually due to failure of competencies to generalize across expected moods, situations, and time, and to failure to display adequate nonverbal cure of emotional distress. (Linehan, 1993, p. 10)

Prevalence

Gunderson (2000) reported that individuals fitting the criteria of BPD constitute about 2% to 3% of the general U.S. population: 25% of all inpatients, and about 15% of all outpatients. Linehan, Cochran, and Kehrer (2001) reported that at least 70% to 75% of all persons fitting the BPD criteria have a history of at least one parasuicidal act (defined as any intentional, acute, self-injurious behavior with or without suicidal intent including both suicide attempts and self-mutilative behaviors). Linehan (1993) also noted that most individuals meeting the BPD criteria, and indeed most people who engage in self-injurious behavior, are women. She cited reviews concluding that 74% of the people in this population are women (hence the use of *she* in this chapter) and that 75% of instances of nonfatal self-injurious behavior include people between the ages of 18 and 45 years. She also reported that up to 76% of women meeting BPD criteria have been victims of childhood sexual abuse along with neglect and physical abuse. Millon (1987), however, cautioned against locating the cause of the disorder in any single event or time period. Although much is made of the general finding that most people fitting BPD criteria have experiences of what are called *invalidating environments* in their childhoods, recent reviews have suggested that sexual abuse is not a major direct cause of or risk factor for BPD (Fossati, Madeddu, & Maffei, 1999). Despite the relatively small percentage of the general population fitting BPD criteria and the relatively small portion of the outpatient and inpatient populations fitting these criteria, people with BPD take up a disproportionate amount of time and resources of mental health services and exact an equally high toll on the emotional resources of these providers.

IMPACT OF DIALECTICAL BEHAVIOR THERAPY

The DBT approach to this BPD pattern has been found to be more effective than treatment as usual in at least three major clinical trials to date (Koons et al., 2001; Linehan, Armstrong, Suarez, Allmon, & Heard, 1991; see Koerner & Dimeff, 2000, and Koerner & Linehan, 2000, for other reviews). In more severely impaired populations, DBT has been shown to increase treatment retention, improve global functioning, and reduce parasuicidal behavior and substance abuse (Linehan et al., 1991, 1999; Linehan, Heard, & Armstrong, 1993; Linehan, Tutek, Heard, & Armstrong, 1994). Similar results have been found in matched and randomized control trials for less severely affected populations (Koons et al., 2001; Stanley, Ivanoff, Brodsky, Oppenheim, & Mann, 1998; Turner, 2000). Limited follow-up data indicate that outcomes were maintained in 1-year follow-ups (Linehan et al., 1993). Regarding cost-effectiveness, Heard (2000) found that 1-year treatment costs were no more expensive than treatment as usual, with average costs more predictable and predictably lower for DBT. Koerner and Linehan (2002) further reported on a study that followed 14 clients 12 months after completing a DBT program in a mental health center in New Hampshire. They found a 77% decrease in hospital days, a 76% decrease in partial hospital days, a 56% decrease in crisis bed use, and an 80% decrease in emergency services used by the group. There have been no studies to date, however, that dismantle the several components of DBT to learn which of the components are essential or most important to the treatment's effectiveness. Given the impressive recent results of the DBT approach to the challenging problems of BPD, we will spend the major focus of our discussion understanding the key elements of this approach. A look at how the DBT approach describes BPD, and how BPD develops, will lead us to a better understanding of how this approach has designed its interventions.

Problem Development

The DBT approach is based in a biosocial theory similar to that of Millon (1987). In her original treatment manual, Linehan (1993) explained this.

> The major premise is that BPD is primarily a dysfunction of the emotion regulation system; it results from biological irregularities combined with certain dysfunctional environments, as well as from their interaction and transaction over time. The characteristics associated with BPD . . . are sequelae of, and thus secondary to, this fundamental emotional dysregulation . . . Invalidating environments during childhood contribute to the development of emotion dysregulation; they also fail to teach the child how to label and regulate arousal, how to tolerate emotional distress, and when to trust her own emotional responses as reflections of valid interpretations of events. (p. 42)

Linehan (1993) described the interaction of emotional dysregulation and invalidating environments as a transactional vicious cycle. She noted that a slightly emotionally vulnerable child in a slightly invalidating environment can evolve over time into one in which the child and the family are both highly sensitive to, vulnerable to, an invalidating of each other. A *validating environment* is described as one that affirms the child and her emotions as understandable within the context of her experience. A more emotionally reactive child calls for caregivers who can be more patient, understanding, and flexible and more willing to adapt their own needs to those of the child. Linehan described several types of families in which invalidation may be a by-product of the family structure. In a *chaotic family*, in which there is considerable parental absence, substance abuse, and emotional conflict, a child may get little attention, be overstimulated by the conflict, and be punished or disaffirmed for their responses. In *perfect families*, there is pressure for all members to conform to perfect ideals, little tolerance for negative affect, and the child gets the message that her emotional response is bad or a character flaw that needs correcting. In what is called *typical families*, the so-called Western ideal of individual autonomy, self-control, and self-directedness can translate into children getting told that their out-of-control emotional displays are out of norm and simply need to be gotten under control. No matter what the mode or reasons for the invalidation, high, biologically based emotional reactivity and invalidating environments are the key ingredients proposed to contribute to the development of BPD in adults. Inflexibility and invalidation of the child's emotions can initiate a vicious cycle, as we noted in chapter 8. Invalidation not only shuts down the child but inevitably leads to power struggles. In invalidating family environments

> emotional experiences and interpretations of events are often not taken as valid responses to events; are punished, trivialized, dismissed, or disregarded; and/or are attributed to socially unacceptable characteristics such as overreactivity, inability to see things realistically, lack of motivation, motivation to harm or manipulate, lack of discipline, or failure to adopt a positive attitude. (Linehan et al., 2001)

As a result, it is suggested that the child never gains an ability to label, tolerate, manage, and appropriately express her emotions; she learns to feel bad about her reactions and never gains a coherent sense of herself. The invalidating family's style eventually shapes an expressive style in the child that is later seen in the adult. This style vacillates between suppression of emotion at one pole to extreme emotional displays or the other. A person who develops BPD patterns eventually is described as operating along three dimensions defined by their opposite poles. One pole is the product of biology, created through problems in emotional dysregulation, and the other pole is the product of social reinforcement in the invalidating environment. The first dimension is defined by the poles of blaming the self for emotional pain, and the other represents blaming the universe for being treated unfairly (emotional vulnerability vs. self-invalidation). The second dimension is defined by active passivity (helplessly approaching problems while demanding that others solve them) at one pole, versus apparent competence exceeding one's abilities at the other. The third dimension is defined by the person experiencing life as a series of unrelenting crises on one pole versus her inability to experience emotions related to significant trauma and loss on the other. Clients are said to vacillate between these poles, characterizing their ongoing dilemmas. People fitting the criteria for BPD are said to have a deficit in balance, or a failure to synthesize the dialectically opposed poles of their struggles with life. One of the main goals of therapy is consequently to help these clients integrate these polar opposite dimensions or to form a *synthesis*. This form of "thesis," "antithesis," and "synthesis" is the essence of the dialectical perspective that is at the heart of the effectiveness of the DBT approach to BPD.

DIALECTICS

A great truth is a truth whose opposite is also a truth.
—Thomas Mann

As we noted earlier, the dialectical worldview, which is at the heart of the DBT approach, is the same as the perspective that gives rise to the fibers of the golden thread, namely, first- and second-order change. The dialectical view is a systemic perspective that views all elements of human interaction as parts of a dynamic, ever-changing whole. Apparently polar opposite elements are viewed as poles of related dimensions and are therefore integrated at a higher order level of logic or organization. Furthermore, change and not stability is the essence of this view of human interaction. Life problems come from vicious cycles as we get stuck at one level and are unable to move to the next to synthesize the poles of the dilemma. One way of viewing this is as movement from one pole to the opposite and, finally, to the integration of the two; or from thesis to antithesis to synthesis. Integration or synthesis is always moving to, accepting, and experiencing the world at a higher level of organization, or a higher logical level. Truth in this view is not fixed and externally discovered and verifiable. Truth is relative to the system in which it evolves, and it is an emergent product of interaction within a social domain. This is similar to the social constructionist perspective. Although there are Eastern and Western philosophical traditions that embrace the dialectical perspective, this view is most often related to Eastern philosophies. The dialectical perspective is essentially the same as such non-Western perspectives as Zen Buddhism and Taoism. Because this perspective is so different from most Western assumptions, it is often experienced by therapists in most Western cultures as illogical, counterintuitive, or paradoxical. This non-Western perspective affirms a balance and affirmation of all actions and ideas. This is represented in the classic yin–yang symbol, which has dark on one side, light on the other, and a dot of each shade in the middle of its polar opposite. The opposing elements combine into a circular whole; the synthesis of opposites define the essence of the whole at another level. These are but a few of the major bases of the dialectical perspective.

Recall that the idea of second-order change involves the assumption that all human interaction is part of a dynamic, ever-changing whole, consistent with the dialectic point of view. The way we negotiate interactions and change within a systemic whole is the focus for understanding and changing people within these systems. This is a perspective that focuses more on the process of change and less on the content and formal structure of the issues or systems at hand. Reality, truth, premises, and related assumptions on the way things are evolve and emerge from cocreated social interaction among group members. In this view, the only thing constant is change. Ideas from group theory and the theory of logical types are used to describe the types of change.

Recall that first-order change is that which occurs yet does not change the system. Because changes are in accordance with the accepted premises, rules, and assumptions guiding the system, these changes are logical or make sense to those within the system. First-order change operates according to the rules of group theory. Second-order change is a change that changes the system itself. This happens by moving to a higher order of organization in understanding and interacting within one's world, to a synthesis or integration of the poles of the first-order level. Because second-order change alters the assumptions and related rules of interaction within systems, such change is often experienced as counterintuitive or paradoxical when viewed from within the assumptions of the system undergoing second-order change. Second-order change operates according to the theory of logical types. First-order change typically involves the acceptance of a set of assumptions on the nature of correct and incorrect, right and wrong parameters for action within a given system. Problems are often resolved by applying negation or the opposite of what needs correcting. Frequently, this action works; often, it creates escalating cycles; yet it always it maintains the system. Second-order change resolves the polemic and escalating vicious cycles of first-order solution patterns by redefining the nature of the system, integrating the poles in a new synthesis, and thus eliminating the solution patterns that are the essence of the problems at the first-order level. Said another way, second-order change alters the solutions of the first-order level and changes the assumptions on which they were based. The dialectical perspective and the process view of systems from which first- and second-order change emerge are one and the same. We contend that it is the use of this dialectical perspective that is the core of the DBT approach's effectiveness.

Dialectics and Borderline Personality Disorder

In her original treatment manual for DBT, Linehan (1993) described how she came to use the dialectical view to describe and guide her work.[1] It

---

[1]Paul Watzlawick and his colleagues had already independently developed the systemic concepts of this work through first- and second-order change in their classic book *Change: Principles of Problem*

flowed naturally from what she seemed to be doing that worked with these clients. Discussing what people who observed her work told her, she said,

> These techniques were things such as matter-of-fact exaggerations of the implications of events, similar to Whitaker's (1975, pp. 12–13); encouraging the acceptance rather than change of feelings and situations, in the tradition of Zen Buddhism (e.g., Watts, 1961); and double-bind statements such as those of the Bateson project directed at pathological behavior (Watzlawick, 1978). These techniques are more closely aligned with paradoxical therapy approaches than with standard cognitive and behavioral therapy. (p. 29)

The fascinating thing that has emerged from Linehan's use of a dialectical perspective is that it has matched the problem processes of people who fit the criteria of BPD so well. From a dialectical view, BPD clients are caught vacillating between dialectically opposite poles on a range of core issues relating from who they are, to how competent they are, and how they express and tolerate the distress of their lives. Without integrating these poles, they become trapped in escalating vicious cycles in relationship to themselves and especially in relationship with others.

Vicious Cycles

The typical BPD client, being highly emotionally reactive and feeling emotionally flooded and overwhelmed by very real life issues, looks for solutions. She feels bad about herself and her situation because she feels personally empty, unworthy, and ineffective. Feeling incapable of resolving her challenges, and looking to others as idealized helpers, she regularly feels let down and abandoned when those helpers can't resolve her dilemmas or can't be there for her. Feeling intensely angry and disappointed with others drives them away in a self-fulfilling prophecy of abandonment. Feeling abandoned, and seeing her part in it, she becomes even more distressed and despondent and so down on herself that she now considers harming herself or committing suicide. Sometimes self-harm provides emotional relief, thus reinforcing its use for relief in the future. Also, when others become alarmed at the self-harming or suicidal gestures and offer support, affirmation, and problem-solving solutions, this reinforces these actions as ways of gaining the validating help and connection with others she so feels she needs. The cycle then continues to the next life dilemma only now with renewed confirmation of each phase and increased intensity of all of the elements. Like the "perfect storm," this is the perfect vicious cycle, which usually escalates to become one of the most intense, exhausting, and dangerous of those experienced by clients, their friends and family members, and their therapists.

Formation and Problem Resolution (Watzlawick, Weakland, & Fisch, 1974). Afraid that naïve therapists would misapply paradoxical interventions, Linehan turned to the parallel ideas of the dialectical view to describe and direct her work. The views, however, are one in the same.

Role of Others in the Cycle

These vicious cycles don't occur in vacuums. They occur in relationship with others, as they have evolved from childhood in relationship with family members. Recall that the hypothesis and rationale for the DBT approach are that the patterns of BPD evolve from the early interaction of a biologically dysregulated child interacting with an invalidating environment. According to almost all views of BPD, these clients bring this same dilemma into their current adult life and relationships. It is hard for the client to tolerate and control her strong emotional reactions. This is distressing to others who are in relationships with her. After several iterations of crises, these others may eventually burn out, become invalidating and resentful of her, and eventually abandon her. This reaffirms her basic lack of self-worth, creates validly intense pain, and escalates her wish to harm herself. This is when all others involved are drawn into the same self-fulfilling pattern. The most important point for therapists is to realize that we are equally susceptible to this cycle and its outcomes.

Parasuicide and the Threat-Rigidity Hypothesis

There is an infrequently referenced perspective on responding to perceived threat and uncertainty in larger systems, such as businesses, called the *threat-rigidity hypothesis* (Staw, Sandelands, & Dutton, 1981). Although this perspective is not used in DBT, it does well in explaining both the actions of clients and helpful others around them at points of crisis. It describes how people get pulled in to self-defeating patterns during crises out of the best of intentions, and yet it shows how those very solutions make the crisis worse. This is what is quite evident in the patterns surrounding suicidal and parasuicidal crises in BPD clients and those in relationships with them. What the threat-rigidity hypothesis suggests is that at times of perceived crisis and uncertainty, a cycle is initiated. The cycle evolves through initial distress and hypervigilance to a mechanized shift to more conservative efforts to manage risks and centralize decision making, excluding other relevant options and adopting more rigid conservative solutions that have been used in the past. These solutions perpetuate and exacerbate the crises they are designed to resolve. Changing this threat-rigidity cycle represents a second-order change, or a reversal of all of these patterns, including introducing new information and options that may be creative and even appear paradoxical and risky from the original perspectives of the individuals caught in the system under threat. Although this has been well demonstrated in larger systems, such as corporations, it is equally applicable to individuals caught in the parasuicidal crises of persons struggling with BPD.

It is only logical for friends, family, and therapists to respond to self-harming threats or actions with attempts to stop them. If someone wants to hurt herself, then you must tell her that she must keep herself safe. If she intends to die, then you must convince her to live, and so on. The problem with these reasonable and logical responses is that they may not only be invalidating of the pain being experienced, but they also set up another dialectical dilemma. Self-harm is contrasted with its opposite of safety; death wishes are matched with affirming life. All involved are drawn into trying to resolve the threat by negating it, applying the opposite. This parallels the polar dilemmas of the BPD client. As we have explained in our discussions of group theory and first-order change in earlier chapters, such solutions only perpetuate the system, may well escalate the intensity of its dilemmas, and ensure that a subsequent cycle will occur. Suicide attempts and parasuicidal actions become a solution-generated problem for all involved. These clients' threats of death and self-harm are so great that they cannot be ignored. Yet responding to these threats with rigidly logical attempts to stop them becomes invalidating for the client and perpetuates the essence of the emotional dysregulation and invalidation that form the core of the BPD dilemma. As noted earlier, emergency responses of others may also represent one of the few times when the person caught in the borderline pattern feel affirmed, genuinely helped, and connected with, while reaffirming that they, themselves are somehow incapable of solving their own dilemmas and that they are basically flawed because of that. The results of the resolution have the seeds of the next cycle within them. Both the BPD client and her friends and therapists become more concerned and committed to their rigidly held views of the situation and their solutions to resolve it.

Second-Order Change for Therapists

The DBT approach represents a second-order change targeted not only at clients but also, even more important, therapists. Therapists are compassionate. We are here to help clients with their problems. When we make therapeutic contracts with clients to resolve their problems, we expect they will work actively with us to achieve their goals. Most therapy is built on the mechanics of change, and often this change is of the first-order type. However, when we contract with a client who is engaged with the BPD patterns, the implicit rules change. Therapists can never be their clients' saviors, and yet it appears that this is what their clients expect. When these clients feel let down or betrayed in this contract and become suicidal or self-harming, the therapist is drawn in to rescue the client. The eventual burnout, frustration, anger, and alienation that both clients and therapists feel after several cycles of these crises actually replicates the problem the BPD client is there to resolve. They remain emotionally dysregulated in a now-invalidating relationship with a therapist whose job is to change all that. Once caught in this first-order pattern with our clients, we are trapped in a "twilight zone" dilemma whereby the more we try to change the problem, the more we affirm it and make it worse. This is a true solution-generated problem for therapists. The key target of DBT is to institute a second-order change in the therapeutic relationship. The goal of this second-order change is to release both clients and therapists from the deadly trap of their therapeutic relationship. To do this, therapists must learn a new integration of their usually polar concepts of facilitating change of painful problematic behavior on the one hand, and validating the existence and reasons for this behavior on the other. They must come to the new idea that validating stuckness and pain often frees clients to change and heal. They may often best help these clients to change by not pushing them to change. The apparent paradox that emerges from these and other similar shifts for therapists is a sure sign of the second-order change that is occurring for therapists. The new dialectical premises and assumptions about these clients and about the rules of therapy represent moving to a new logical level of organization according to the theory of logical types. Once adopted, these formerly counterintuitive positions and interventions eventually make perfect sense from the premises and assumptions of the new synthesizing and integrating point of view.

Therapy for the Therapists

No matter how compelling and potentially effective this new dialectical perspective and its related interventions are, they remain different from the way most of us think and act in our lives and with many other clients. Thus, it is necessary for therapists using this new rationale for treatment to meet regularly with other therapists and consultants to reaffirm the view and retain its focus in treatment. Furthermore, the very nature of the recurrent crises, and the often-angry blaming of therapists and others by these patients, requires that therapists have regular support for themselves to keep from burning out and becoming angry at and blaming of these clients. These therapist group meetings further reinforce the new perspective for all members of the treatment team and keep everyone on the same page with these clients, whose actions will easily split treatment team members and put them at odds with each other. Only when all therapists can retain the ability to validate these clients and keep a good balance between acceptance and change, reciprocity and irreverence, in their relationships with these clients will the approach achieve its full potential.

It's All About the Relationship

In our first several chapters, we discussed the controversies among therapists who argue whether techniques or relationships represent the active ingredients of effective psychotherapy. Some have come to the conclusion that it is both, but this doesn't take the resolution far enough. We have argued that techniques *are* relationships and that relationships *are* techniques. This is another second-order change for therapists. This represents a synthesis of the dialectical poles of the argument. As we discussed in earlier chapters on the relationship, as we see it the active ingredient in DBT is the *second-order relationship* offered to the BPD client by the therapist. Particularly for BPD clients who are used to being invalidated for who they are, what they are capable of, how they express their emotions, and what they can expect in relationships, this new kind of relationship certainly represents a second-order change from what they have come to expect in their ongoing relationships. No matter what they do, they are both affirmed and expected to change and evolve their life into one that is worth living. This affects first how they relate to their therapist and eventually how they relate to themselves and others.

The style of this new therapeutic relationship blends a number of elements, themselves representative of a balance between two poles, and the client and therapist often shift rapidly between those poles in moment-to-moment interactions in session. Linehan et al. (2001) wrote that

> A dialectical therapeutic position is one of constant attention to combining acceptance with change, flexibility with stability, nurturing with challenging, and a focus on capabilities with a focus on limitations and deficits. The goals are to bring out the opposites, both in therapy and the client's life, and to provide conditions for synthesis. The presumption is that change may be facilitated by emphasizing acceptance and acceptance by emphasizing change. (p. 479)

One of these dimensions is a balance between what is called *reciprocal communication* on one pole and a more *irreverent communication* style on the other. Reciprocal communication is what therapists have become most familiar with. It is designed both to convey acceptance and validation while reducing perceived power differentials between clients and therapists. It embodies all of those qualities of warmth, genuineness, transparency, engagement, and genuine interest in and affirmation of the client that are the hallmark of what has been commonly seen as establishing and affirming a therapeutic bond between clients and therapists. Irreverent communication balances this style with relational interventions that address the dialectical or second-order issues with the client. It is characterized as an often direct; sometimes confrontational; and still rather matter-of-fact, humorous, off-beat, or off-the-wall style. Its goal is most often to move the client from a rigid polar stance to one that must admit more uncertainty and new perspectives or options and therefore promotes the potential for change. It may include irony or exaggeration of a client's positions but never sarcasm, mocking, or mean-spirited derision. All communication is framed within a therapeutic relationship that is broadly affirming and offers validating respect for the client, her strengths, her potentials, and her goals to create a better life.

Validation

With clients who are caught in the borderline dilemmas of having a history of emotional dysregulation in invalidating environments, validation is one of the most prominent qualities that must permeate the therapeutic relationship. Not only does this seem to be an almost self-evident element of most positive relationships, but it is also a crucial intervention with BPD clients. They have rarely had this before. Linehan (1993) broke these down into levels of validation including emotional, cognitive, behavioral, and cheerleading forms of validation. The essence of these are to communicate to clients that they are listened to; the therapist is interested in them for who they are; that they are understood through accurate reflections of their feelings and experiences; that the therapist can almost read their mind in showing how natural their experience is to another; that their behavior is understandable in terms of both its historical and current causes; that their experience is understandable given the context in which it has occurred; and that they can be accepted for the person whom they are, knowing that they aspire to become more. All of these related elements of validation are critical elements of the therapeutic relationship for a BPD client who has mainly experienced invalidation throughout her life. This is a basic reversal or second-order relationship for these clients.

Acceptance and Change

Finally, an overlapping quality of the therapeutic relationship echoed in the discussion thus far is for the therapist to maintain a balance in their emphasis on both change and acceptance interventions. Linehan (1993) has suggested that the basic dialectic in all therapeutic relationships, much less in those for BPD, is that there is a balance between accepting what is and changing what is. As noted earlier, *change* interventions represent much of the traditional behavioral repertoire of interventions. They include such things as problem solving, skills training, contingency management, cognitive modification, exposure, and other related strategies that focus on directly creating change. *Acceptance* interventions prominently include validation, as discussed earlier, as well as practicing and having the client learn and practice a form of mindful awareness and present acceptance of what currently is without the need to act to change it. This also involves both the client and therapist in learning to accept and tolerate emotional distress and move forward, among other variations.

INTERVENTION

We must accept finite disappointment, but we must never lose infinite hope.

—Martin Luther King Jr.

Linehan (1993) laid out eight assumptions that underlie her approach to treatment: (a) patients are doing the best they can; (b) patients want to improve; (c) patients need to do better, try harder, and be more motivated to change; (d) patients may not have caused all of their own problems, but they have to solve them anyway; (e) the lives of suicidal, borderline individuals are unbearable as they are currently being lived; (f) patients must learn new behaviors in all relevant contexts; (g) patients cannot fail in therapy (it is the job of the therapy to help them succeed); and (h) therapists treating borderline patients need support. These assumptions set the background against which the treatment is applied.

Major Goals

Although DBT has numerous related goals, the overall goal is increasing dialectical behavior patterns. In the terms of this book, this means facilitating second-order change in the way these clients engage with their lives. This includes helping clients to reduce extreme and rigid patterns in both thought and behavior through learning to balance these elements within new frames and within a balanced lifestyle. Primary behavioral targets include decreasing suicidal behaviors Suicidal behaviors are seen as understandable and yet relatively ineffective problem-solving attempts. The goals are to reduce suicide crisis behaviors, parasuicidal acts, suicidal ideation, communications, expectations and beliefs, and suicide-related affect. A related behavioral goal is decreasing therapy-interfering behaviors. These include not attending sessions, not collaborating, not complying, interfering with other patients, doing things to burn out the therapist through pushing the therapist's personal limits or the organization's limits, or doing things that tend to decrease the therapist's milieu or another group member's motivation. Another behavioral goal is to decrease behaviors that interfere with quality of life. These include decreasing such things as substance abuse, high-risk sexual behavior, extreme financial difficulties, dysfunctional interpersonal behaviors, employment- and school-related dysfunctional behaviors, housing-related problems, repeated use of the hospital or prescription drugs, and so on. Another targeted set of goals is decreasing behaviors related to posttraumatic stress. These include accepting the fact of the trauma or abuse; reducing stigmatization, self-invalidation, self-blame; reducing denial and intrusive stress responses; and increasing self-respect. The other side of these targeted goals includes increasing positive behavioral skills. These include learning mindfulness skills, distress tolerance, emotional regulation skills, interpersonal effectiveness skills, and self-management skills. Finally, a set of related secondary behavioral targets are pursued. These include increasing emotion modulation and decreasing emotional reactivity; increasing self-validation and decreasing self-invalidation; increasing realistic decision making and judgments and decreasing crisis-generating behaviors; increasing emotional experiencing and decreasing inhibited grieving; increasing active problem solving and decreasing active–passivity behaviors; and, finally, increasing accurate communication of emotions and competencies and decreasing mood dependency of behavior.

The major DBT categories of intervention can be divided between the more traditional change strategies and the dialectically oriented acceptance strategies. All of these strategies are organized into four phases of treatment, with a critical pretreatment phase that sets the expectations and therapeutic contract for the rest of therapy. Therapy itself is multimodal; including individual treatment, group treatment and skills training, telephone consultation, consultation teams, and case management consultations. Given the range and detail of all of these modes, it is not possible or even desirable to go thoroughly through all of these elements. Instead, we arrange our discussion according to the categories of Jerome Frank's (Frank & Frank, 1991) contextual model, which we have used throughout this book. As we have said, this contextual model presents the main categories of all organized and effective treatments, and it provides the structure within which second-order change in clients' problem occurs. Second, we emphasize acceptance strategies more than change strategies. Acceptance strategies are most closely associated with second-order change (although many change strategies have implicit second-order shifts inherent in them). Given that change strategies tend to be more familiar to therapists, these will be noted yet discussed in less detail. Thus, we organize the following discussion according to Frank's categories of the relationship, the rationale or "myth," and the procedures used in treatment.

The Relationship

As we noted earlier, DBT is all about the relationship, and this relationship is dialectical at its core. For persons who are used to being abandoned and invalidated within the context of their strong emotional reactions, being validated, accepted, and confirmed in a relationship that at the same time firmly demands change is a powerful new experience. This dialectical relationship is a second-order one in the true sense of the way we discussed it in chapter 5. It breaks the cycle of first-order escalations with others by offering very different reactions from the therapist to actions that would usually either draw anger, blame, invalidation, and rejection from others. The therapist offers a combination of validation for the clients' pain and their actions, combined with problem solving to find, develop, and practice new and more effective solutions.

The Rationale or "Myth"

The two related rationales or therapeutic "myths" offered in DBT are (a) the dialectical worldview and explanation for the clients' behavior and

(b) the emotional dysregulation–social invalidation premise used to explain their problem. It is critical to successful therapy that the client accepts these rationales and that the therapist maintains the structure of these two rationales or therapeutic frames throughout treatment. The dialectic rationale is put forward as a worldview for the client and therapist, as an explanation for the client's problem cycles, and it is used as a method of treatment to guide the therapist's interventions. The emotional dysregulation–social invalidation frame is used to explain the client's problem, to absolve her from blame for it, to understand the repeated cycle of crises, and to structure the need for new learning and better problem-solving skills. Once the client and therapist accept these rationales and start working within them, the related procedures of therapy can move forward.

The critical pretreatment stage of orientation and commitment is crucial to delivering these rationales, setting clear therapeutic contracts, and establishing the roles of the client and therapist in this new second-order therapeutic relationship. Along with the dialectical rationale for treatment and the emotional dysregulation–social invalidation explanation, this stage has two goals. The first is for the client and therapist to make a mutual informed decision to enter treatment to make changes in the client's life. The second is to modify any dysfunctional beliefs about or expectations of therapy the client may have that may interfere with the therapy process and goals or lead to premature termination. First of all, this is not a brief form of therapy. Clients are asked to commit to at least 1 year of treatment, making an agreement to keep themselves alive at all costs during that time. The contracting itself has the core elements of dialectical paradox within it. The therapist both validates the client for her pain and for wanting to harm herself while simultaneously asking her if she wants to stay alive to see whether she can learn some new ways to make her life more worth living. Through this process, the therapist typically positions with the client by wondering why the client would want to change her current patterns. They note how this will be hard work and will often feel frustrating. The client will need to agree to commit to change, to complying with and attending multiple treatment sessions and modes, and to not harming herself during this time. This is quite a contract and should not be entered into lightly. This elicits the client's commitment to work toward treatment goals. DBT is presented as a supportive, collaborative therapy designed to create a life worth living for the client. It is presented as a treatment that analyzes problem behaviors, replaces them with more effective skills, and changes ineffective beliefs and rigid thinking patterns. Finally, it is described as a skill-oriented therapy with special emphasis on behavioral skill training. It will always include tensions between skill enhancement and self-acceptance, problem solving versus problem acceptance, and affect regulation and affect tolerance. Once this rationale and the related goals and responsibilities of the therapeutic contract are accepted, the procedures of therapy can go forward through its four stages, multiple modes, and balance of new skills training and acceptance and validation of the client for who she is.

Therapeutic Procedures

As noted earlier, the therapeutic procedures of DBT are divided between acceptance and change categories, spread across four stages of treatment and several therapeutic modes. Stage 1 focuses on attaining basic capacities, including first reducing suicidal and self-harming behaviors, then therapy-interfering behaviors, and quality-of-life-interfering behaviors, and then moving to increase behavioral skills. Stage 2 focuses on reducing posttraumatic stress reactions through exposure to trauma-related cues within the therapeutic setting. As noted earlier, this exposure itself is a second-order shift in that it offers a new rationale for the client to reverse her prior patterns of mastering trauma by avoiding it. Stage 3 focuses on resolving problems in living and increasing respect for the self. Here the therapist begins to pull back as the client is helped to trust and validate herself. Stage 4 focuses on helping the client in attaining the capacity for sustained joy, expanding awareness, spiritual fulfillment, and the ability to experience the flow of her life without alarm or judgment.

Change Strategies

Problem-solving strategies are the main change strategies in DBT. They all imply a collaborative agreement on the problem target and a commitment to actively working to learn new skills and practice them. This is often quite a challenge for any client, much less for one who is not used to active collaboration in relationships. This is when more of the acceptance interventions enter. For now, however, several related change interventions should be noted.

Behavioral Analysis

Behavioral analysis is simply a tracking process to understand the factors that lead to and maintain the problem behavior. To this end, clients are asked to actively keep DBT diary cards (see Figure 6.1, Linehan, 1993, p. 185) to track their misery levels, alcohol and medication use, and suicidal ideation and self-harm behaviors, along with other triggers and reactions in their daily life. Problem behaviors are tracked in fine detail by means of chain analysis of events, antecedents, thoughts and behaviors, and contexts. These analyses represent a second-order pattern shift in that they ask clients to engage in and track numerous problematic patterns and observe and record them for therapeutic ends. This sort of observing task, as noted in a number of earlier chapters, gains valuable information about the contingencies reinforcing problem patterns while subtly disengaging clients from these patterns and putting them in charge of those patterns. All suicide attempts and self-harm behaviors are immediately subjected to such analyses. The idea is to see what common patterns surround these incidents and to find alternative problem-solving options to try in future situations.

Problem-Solving Procedures

Once the problem pattern has been identified, the therapist and client brainstorm on possible new solution options and decide on what is needed to put them into practice. This often includes some combination of common behavior therapy procedures, such as skills training, contingency management, cognitive modification, and exposure. Behavioral skills are taught in the areas of distress tolerance, emotion regulation, interpersonal effectiveness, self-management, and the capacity to respond with awareness without being judgmental (mindfulness skills). These skills are typically taught in weekly skills training groups while clients are monitored and the skills are applied to specific problem situating with the individual therapist.

Mindfulness

Mindfulness helps patients bear pain skillfully. Mindfulness skills are seen as central or core skills in DBT. They are described as the behavioral translation of meditation and include observing, describing, spontaneous participating, being nonjudgmental, focusing awareness, and focusing on effectiveness. Mindfulness skills are the essence of a second-order change for clients who normally are triggered into more extreme emotional responses. This is an acceptance skill learned by the client. It is similar to the mindfulness acceptance taught to depressed clients to keep them from relapsing, or the skills of acceptance learned by couples who come to accept their partner's behavior without needing to change it, or of the parents of the disruptive child who learn not to respond to a certain class of disruptive behaviors in their child. Once clients learn this mindfulness skill, they become able to move toward formerly distressing events, thoughts, or situations while remaining at a peaceful center and without the need to try to respond to or solve the situation. This skill reverses another cycle of mastering emotional stimuli by avoiding them, and it blocks new vicious cycles from starting.

Distress Tolerance

Distress tolerance is the next step in mindfulness skills. Clients are asked to experience their thoughts, emotions, and behaviors without attempting to change or control them. Emotional distress is reduced through repeated exposure in a nonjudgmental atmosphere. *Emotion regulation* includes experiencing and identifying emotions in a present and nonjudgmental way. Obstacles to changing these emotions are identified, and ways to express the opposite emotion and increase more positive emotions are worked out. Each exposure and skill-building technique essentially builds on reversals of first-order solution patterns while teaching new mastery skills.

Stage 2 of therapy further extends this exposure training by focusing mainly on reducing posttraumatic stress. Through repeated exposure in session, and remembering and accepting the facts of earlier trauma, stigmatization and self-blame are reduced and emotional reactions and intrusive thoughts and images are decreased. All of this is based on mastery by exposure rather than avoidance; it is an exact reversal of the first-order solution-generated patterns of mastery by avoidance.

Interpersonal skill training then takes these skills into interpersonal relationships. Clients work out what objectives they have in typically conflictual situations. They then assign priorities among these objectives and balance them with the importance of maintaining valued relationships and their own self-respect. Interpersonal conflict situations are practiced in group and then generalized to the clients' lives. Rather than avoiding conflict and then finally exploding, clients are trained to go toward controlled conflict situations and practice their newly learned skills. They are taught to accept themselves and the results of these interchanges as simply new information on how to get better at gaining what they desire while maintaining desired relationships. In Stages 3 and 4, clients are then taught to reinforce these skills.

Acceptance Strategies

Although there are numerous second-order shifts in change strategies, the essence of second-order change in DBT is in its acceptance strategies. We have already discussed the prominence of validation in DBT for BPD clients, who have rarely been validated. Validating the reasons for self-harm, or the sense of relief a client gains from burning herself with cigarettes, for example, offers rare confirmation. This is exactly the opposite of what most helpful others have offered. It is often seen as paradoxical from the naïve perspective of therapists and other people who wanting to help these clients more directly. Recall that second-order change is often experienced as paradoxical or counterintuitive from the logic of the first-order level. Many of the acceptance strategies used in DBT explicitly address this paradoxical experience. Because we have already discussed validation at some length, we now turn to a range of other acceptance or dialectical strategies to further explain this position. In essence, each stance is related to the other, in that they all reflect the dialectical second-order shift that is the ultimate aim of the therapy.

Entering the Paradox

Dialectical behavior therapy views psychotherapy with borderline patients as a basic paradox. The psychotherapeutic relationship is seen as a dynamic balance between accepting and affirming the client for who she is and what she does to deal with her life. At the same time, the relationship demands that the client change what she is doing, and how she is doing it, to become more satisfied with and fulfilled in the life she is leading. As therapists and clients enter this special therapeutic relationship, they enter the paradox of it. The therapist continually stresses that things can be both true and not true and that answers can be both yes and no. Clients trapped in the first-order dilemmas of the BPD cycles get caught in rigid ideas of viewing themselves, others, or situations as either all good or all bad, catastrophic or blissful, fully committed or abandoning, and so on. Life is either worth living, or death is the only answer. The major second-order shift for these clients must be to move to a higher level of understanding and experiencing themselves and their lives in which all of these seemingly contradictory elements become accepted and affirmed as the ongoing flow of life. Readers familiar with Eastern views will recognize this as very Buddhist. Linehan (1993) repeatedly emphasizes that the dialectic springs from Zen and other related Eastern philosophies. To enter the paradox of the DBT therapeutic relationship is to help the client as a Zen master would help his or her student. The objective is to move to another level of experience, wherein the world of opposites is integrated and no longer in tension and conflict. (It should also be noted that this new integration will also contrast with another opposite in a never-ending hierarchy of dialectics.) If readers are becoming confused at this point, this may itself be the experience of the confusing contrast of levels of assumptions that is the paradoxical essence of the dialectic and second-order change. Both therapists and clients must be coached to maintain this often-counterintuitive framework. Entering the paradox is entering this.

Clients are affirmed in their wish to harm themselves and simultaneously helped to affirm life and live in new ways. The therapist acknowledges the client's wish that the therapist become her savior while confirming that only the client has the power to save him- or herself. In keeping with this position, a therapist may say "If I didn't like you so much, I would try to save you right now." This reflects on the cycle wherein repeated attempts to save clients disempowers them; confirms their weakness; and leads to another cycle of the client feeling helpless, unable to deal with the next crisis, and needing the therapist and others to help her. This and other seeming paradoxes are offered in the therapeutic relationship, which uses these very contradictions to help drive change to a new second-order level. Clients are urged for example, to get control of their excessive attempts to gain control. Linehan (1993) suggested the following:

> Struggling with, confronting, and breaking through these paradoxes forces the patient to let go of rigid patterns of thought, emotion, and behavior so that more spontaneous and flexible patterns may emerge. Likewise, genuine entering of the paradox, within both the therapeutic relation-

ship and the consultation group, forces the therapist to let go of rigid theoretical positions and inflexible therapy rules, regulations, and patterns of action. (p. 209)

This dialectical worldview and its process and related positions are the core of what helps therapists and clients negotiate a second-order change. Such change integrates the first-order assumptions and contradictions into a second-order synthesis. Such second-order integration alters the premises and assumptions of the first-order dilemmas, just as we have noted that it does with the range of other problems we have reviewed, from anxiety, to depression, to couple difficulties, and so on. It changes the rules of the system (and its solution-generated problems) and thus changes the system itself. This is true for the therapist as well. Therapists come to break free from their rigid ideas, theories, and practices and become open to the process of working with the client as a positive and evolving other. Through the dialectical stance, therapists resist the draw of the relationship these clients typically co-create with others in their lives. As therapists evolve to an acceptance and understanding of the clients in their context, they can then truly affirm the clients for whom they are while offering them the option to become more.

Acceptance Variations

There are a number of closely related positions and ways on framing interventions that are inherent in this basic DBT stance, including the use of metaphor, devil's advocacy, extending, using "wise mind," making lemonade out of lemons, allowing natural change, and practicing dialectical assessment. The most important thing to remember is that these are not techniques that stand alone but actions that flow from the basic dialectical position and that are inherent in the relationship.

Use of Metaphor

Metaphor is used in DBT the same way as it is used in the teaching stories, metaphors, and analogies of Zen and most other religious perspectives. Through metaphor, stories, and analogies, people are helped to understand some new relationship, idea, or issue by using something they do understand to introduce something to be learned. For example, the idea of savoring the current moment may be shown in the story of a man hanging onto a cliff by a twig above a hungry tiger. He picks a tasty berry from the twig and, savoring it, decides that life is sweet. Metaphors and analogies help clients to open themselves to potential alternative assumptions about themselves and their relationships in ways that are less susceptible to logical or emotional argument and instead offer models of something new, more, and different. Metaphors and analogies find their way around the client's current firmly held assumptions and introduce alternatives. As can be imagined, metaphor is used extensively throughout the DBT approach.

Devil's Advocacy and Extending

Devil's advocacy and the related position of extending are both used to help the client with the extreme implications of their firmly held ideas and emotions. In devil's advocacy, the therapist usually argues gently for a position of no change or caution, or a similar position held by the client, thus freeing the client to examine and argue for its alternative and potentially come to some middle path. This is most always applied in pretreatment sessions, when the therapist takes the position that the client may not want to enter therapy for a range of very valid reasons. Similarly, extending achieves the same ends by exaggerating the implication of strongly felt emotions and their consequences to their logical extreme. The client is faced with evaluating these extremes and thus enters dialogue with their therapist about there these emotions may lie again along a more middle path. For example, when a client threatens to commit suicide from the pain of not being able to see her therapist at a given time, the therapist may quite literally discuss how they might want to arrange for hospitalization in that case. The client and therapist then become freed to affirm the pain and still negotiate a suitable next meeting.

Activating Wise Mind

The term *wise mind* is certainly related to the practice of mindful meditation, which is a skill taught in DBT. Wise mind is compared with the complementary states of reasonable mind and emotion mind. *Reasonable mind* refers to the mode of reason and logic, or the premises and assumptions that guide the first-order interactions of the client's world. Similarly, *emotion mind* refers to the related emotions that spring from the ideas and interpretations of the first-order interactions driving the client's life. Wise mind is the integration of the two. Wise mind adds intuitive knowing to logical analysis and emotional experience. In George Lucas's epic Star Wars sequence of movies, there is a set of core ideas around how the opposing sides of the drama relate to the central force. Those who follow the dark side get drawn into systems of rigid reason and emotion that move them toward judgments of right and wrong and to seizing power for their own way. The Jedi, however, follow the middle path and resist giving way to the temptations of the world of opposites and absolutes. In the most recent and final episode of this series, the young man, Anakhin Skywalker, who will become the evil Darth Vader, confronts his former master, Obi Wan Kenobi, saying "You are either with me, or you are my enemy." Obi Wan's reply comes from the position of wise mind when he says "A Jedi doesn't deal in absolutes." When clients are able to practice this position of wise mind, they become able to act from their calm center without being unduly influenced by strong pulls of logic or emotion. Wise mind is another term for moving to a higher level in the theory of logical types, or akin to the position of experience in second-order change.

Making Lemonade Out of Lemons, Allowing Natural Change,
and Practicing Dialectical Assessment

These three related therapeutic positions come out of the dialectical view. "Making lemonade from lemons" simply refers to reframing all client and therapist experiences, no matter how intense, as opportunities for learning and pathways to eventual success. This deconstructs the common BPD client's experience of viewing all life events as successes or failures, good or bad. It throws clients off center by stopping the vicious cycle of catastrophizing and seeing their experiences as failures. Instead, it allows them and their therapist to take each apparent crisis as a learning experience to be tracked, learned from, and problem-solved to devise a better option for the future. Allowing natural change and dialectical assessment become part of the same position. Change is assumed to be a constant flow that evolves. There is no absolute right and wrong, only different patterns along an ultimately desired path. As the client and therapist accept this view, they simply support positive movement, address surprises, and evolve more effective future ways of negotiating the flow toward closer approximations to what they wish. Dialectical assessment simply affirms a constant analysis of the context and flow of the client's life and the interaction of the therapeutic relationship to keep constant focus on the structure of the dialectic and a flexibility to help guide the process of change. This is the essence of movement to the second-order shift of successful therapy with clients fitting the diagnosis of BPD.

Putting It All Together

As noted earlier, the complete treatment package of DBT includes several integrated modes of therapy. These include individual and group treatment, which we have already discussed. They also include telephone consultation and case management consultation. Telephone consultation is viewed as a crucial part of treatment. Its three functions include (a) real-time coaching in helping clients apply and generalize skills; (b) supporting planned emergency and crisis intervention; and (c) a forum for resolving conflicts and misunderstandings that arise between sessions. Clients are encouraged to call, and calls are prescribed and scheduled if clients appear to be reluctant. This reverses a common pattern. In this case it is therapists who are urging clients to call rather than the clients who are intruding with unwanted or unscheduled crisis calls. Clients are strongly encouraged to call before suicidal crises or self-harm. Proactive coping is shaped by forbidding supportive contact for 24 hours after a client has already harmed herself (other than contact to manage safety; Robins et al., 2001). Case management strategies include consultation to the patient, environmental intervention, and consultation to the therapist. These strategies broaden the influence of the treatment by including others who are active in the client's world to adopt a similar stance and thus reinforce skill generalization while extinguishing old cycles. The primary therapist role is to consult with the patient by empowering her to manage her own social and professional networks and not to consult with the network on how to manage the patient. The therapist always coaches the client in applying her new skills within her own social environment. It is only when the client does not possess the required skill that the therapist directly advocates by modeling the skill needed, and then only in the presence of the client and in order to avert negative consequences. Patients are consulted with on how to manage other professionals and other members of their social network. Other professionals are not told how to treat the client, although they are told of the nature and rationale of treatment. Environmental intervention, such as patient advocacy and providing information to others independent of the client, is offered only under emergency conditions. These include direct life risk, risk of having housing or sustenance removed, when the patient is a minor, or when she is unable to act on her own and the risk of negative outcome is high. Remember that a goal of treatment is client empowerment. Finally, consultation to therapists is provided to keep them with the dialectical therapeutic structure and rationale and to prevent burnout. As can be seen, this is a total wraparound set of treatment modes that combine to drive home the ultimate dialectical intervention of second-order change.

FOLLOWING THE THREAD

Chronically suicidal and self-harming client problems are described as vicious cycles between these clients and themselves and between them and significant others. Extremely dangerous actions become reinforcing for these clients and draw others to the rescue in an affirming way. Vicious cycles of emotional reactivity in historically invalidating relationships are repeated with significant others as well as with therapists. The second-order interventions revolve around therapists affirming their clients' distress and wish to self-harm while simultaneously working to build new skills to master such distress personally and interpersonally. Therapists provide second-order relationships for these clients through this position. Second-order reversals have clients go toward distress to practice new skills. From this point of view, both therapists and clients undergo a second-order change through the balanced synthesis of dialectically opposing poles. The DBT approach is an appropriate one to finish our section on ESTs, because its dialectical underpinning is the same one that gives rise to the golden thread of first- and second-order change. The golden thread runs richly throughout the fabric of this uniquely effective approach to these uniquely distressed and distressing clients.

12

FOLLOWING THE GOLDEN THREAD OF SECOND-ORDER CHANGE IN EFFECTIVE PSYCHOTHERAPY

The art of progress is to preserve order amid change and to preserve change amid order.

—Alfred North Whitehead

Throughout this book we have argued that the concept of second-order change, as described by the Mental Research Institute (Watzlawick, Weakland, & Fish, 1974), is the underlying dynamic that activates the change process in psychotherapy. Moreover, second-order change answers questions that have been raised about how and why change occurs (Kazdin, 2002; Miller & Rollnick, 2002). It also lends further understanding to issues surrounding how and why change in psychotherapy often occurs before formal interventions are introduced and how diverse intervention techniques produce equally effective results.

The concept of second-order change is both simple and complex. Simply put, it is about difference. Any difference in what is done about a problem or how it is viewed produces a shift. However, complication comes with the term *difference*. Difference, by definition, implies sameness, because there must be sameness to have deviation. Here, the concept of first-order change explains the vagaries of sameness and how difficult it is to produce a view or action that is different from an established behavioral pattern. Together, first- and second-order change comprises the golden thread that runs through the labyrinth of effective psychotherapies.

In this chapter, we briefly review the major ideas related to second-order change. We then outline implications for practical theorists, professors and students, researchers, administrators, and policymakers.

COMMON GROUND

I invent nothing. I rediscover.

—August Rodin

Effective psychotherapy does not directly target symptoms such as depression, anxiety, marital discord, and the like. Instead, it is aimed at the process that maintains and exacerbates symptoms—clients' solutions. Clients' problem-generating solutions become a problematic pattern. All that is required for such a pattern to be established is that failed solutions be repeatedly applied despite unwanted outcomes. In effect, it is this failed solution pattern (or first-order folly) that is the focus of attention in psychotherapy. This pattern may be described directly, or understood more implicitly as we have shown in many of the empirically supported treatments (ESTs).

From the perspective of second-order change, problematic solution patterns emanate from three basic problem-solving errors: (a) unnecessary actions are taken to solve a problem; (b) actions are not taken that are necessary; or (c) efforts to solve the problem occur at the wrong level. These three basic errors translate into the six corollaries noted in chapter 3 (this volume). These corollaries are important because they establish the direction problem solvers must take to create a second-order shift:

1. If the first-order solution is *to go away from the problem*, then the second-order solution will have something to do with *going toward it.*
2. If the first-order solution is *to overpursue the problem*, then the second-order solution will have something to do with *stopping and reversing the pursuit.*
3. If the first-order solution is *to not attend to the problem*, then the second-order solution will involve *acknowledging the problem* and *taking necessary problem-solving action.*
4. If the first-order solution involves *making the problem overly complex*, then the second-order solution will involve *simplifying the problem* and *narrowing problem-solving efforts* down to the problem at hand and clarifying the problem's parameters.
5. If the first-order solution is *to overintervene* with normal ups and downs of daily living, then second-order solutions will involve *tolerating and accepting* the amount of unpleasantness that is a natural part of the human condition.

6. If the first-order solution *reads to little into the difficulty*, or *simplifies the problem so much as to trivialize it*, then the second-order solution will *honor the complexity of the problem*.

These three basic errors that initiate vicious cycles and their six related corollaries of second-order change lead to specific therapy interventions. Referred to differently by different approaches, these general second-order strategies, discussed in chapters 3 and 5 (this volume), include blocking and acceptance; reversals; restraining change; normalizing; framing, reframing, and deframing; positioning; prescribing symptoms; predicting or prescribing difficulties or relapses; and adopting a goal-oriented future position.

DIALECTICS

A great truth is a truth whose opposite is also a truth.

—Thomas Mann

Another way we have looked at vicious cycles and their resolution is through a dialectical perspective that underlies much of the recent emphasis in effective treatments on the idea of integrating change and acceptance strategies. Looking more closely at the etiology of human behavioral problems, we can generalize that symptomatic behavior is rooted in a cycle of opposites. Extreme behavior, or behavior that is viewed as the opposite of normal, is addressed with an oppositional approach. Persons who are anxious try to flee from anxiety, depressed persons attempt to retreat from depressing feelings and life experiences, parents attempt to oppose their child's unruly behavior, and significant others oppose the alcoholic's drinking. Each failed solution pattern has something in common; each involves efforts at coercing change. In effect, symptomatic behavior is maintained by efforts to make it go away. As we have shown, coerced change can be self-generated, imposed on others, or both. However, the effect is to restrict freedom, which results in rebellion against self or others and further symptom generation.

Second-order change can be understood as a sequence or pattern that counters symptom-generating cycles. It does so in the case of coercion by blocking or reversing attempts to restrict the symptom. In the second-order pattern the first step in the sequence is to validate or justify the symptom. This is done through rationales that explain how and why the symptom is occurring. The next step is to validate the desire to change and to collaborate on goals. This is done within a context wherein change is not yet expected. So, at this point, much of the restriction may have already been reversed. The client is in a position in which he is justified for having a problem and justified for not changing it. He knows what he wants, and at the same time pressure for changing has been removed, because he is not expected to change until the change method has been introduced, and this has not yet occurred. The evidence shows that in many cases this initiates the change cycle and that once change has begun nothing more is needed. When needed, the next step is to introduce a change method. Our review of ESTs demonstrates that here again we see a commonality. Change methods are designed to block or reverse attempts at coercing change. Methods range from bold reversals to more subtle blocking efforts. Symptom prescriptions are bold reversals and in essence involve therapeutic permission to behave symptomatically. This occurs when therapists ask clients to simulate the sensations of panic attacks, when depressed clients are asked to test out their depressing hypotheses by engaging in the depression-producing situations, when couples are asked to stage a fight when they are not angry to learn about how they fight, and when emotionally dysregulated clients are asked to engage in distressing relationships to track how things escalate and try out alternative skills. Stimulus avoidance techniques in chemical dependency treatment involve blocking at a subtle level. Clients are asked to perform tasks involving thinking or doing that are mutually exclusive from the symptomatic behavior. Again, these efforts are directed at helping the client stop fighting change and to take more of a "let it happen" approach. The second-order change sequence in the treatments reviewed can be summarized as follows: Validate the symptom; validate the desire for change; and then restrain, block, or reverse current efforts to bring about change.

It should also be added that the change sequence we are describing is relative. It assumes that solution attempts involve coercion. However, because we are dealing with opposites, the contrary can also occur. Here, a vicious cycle may ensue when there are not sufficient efforts to bring about change when efforts are needed. Although not the general rule, this does occur. As expected, the reversal of this pattern involves applying more pressure to change. This is an important point, because it illustrates the need for clinical flexibility. All effective psychotherapy reverses, blocks, or redirects first-order vicious cycles depending on how that cycle is generated and how it continues. Second-order change is flexibly applied to the unique patterns of first-order cycles.

THE CONTEXTUAL MODEL

We have argued that the battle between advocates of technique and proponents of relationships and common factors is a classic polarized dialectical battle. It has all the earmarks of typical vicious cycles that perpetuate problems, only at a higher level of abstraction. As an integrating synthesis, we have proposed that therapists adopt the classic unifying contextual model proposed decades ago by Frank and Frank (1991). As we argued in chapters 4 and 5, the major components of this model are not only common to all ESTs but also offer a vehicle for integrating the therapeutic alliance with rationales and techniques to facilitate second-order change. These components include a *relationship with a helping person*; a *healing setting*; *rationales, conceptual schemes, and "myths"*; and, finally, *procedures and rituals* designed to achieve the goals of change.

Wampold (2001), in his review of studies and meta-analyses, reached the same conclusions regarding the important conditions found across effective treatments for all problems. These conditions not only are supported by the research evidence reviewed but also match those projected as being important by Frank and Frank's (1991) contextual model. To support clients in making second-order changes, a set of key elements need to be offered in the relationship between clients and therapists. In brief, they include the following seven components from the working alliance and the contextual model: (a) empathically validating clients' distress, including their emotions and the context for them; (b) providing a rationale to explain the symptoms that makes sense to both the client and the therapist; (c) agreement between clients and therapists on the related goals and procedures of treatment, and enthusiastic agreement to collaborate and invest in the enterprise of it; (d) flexibly maintaining this agreed-on structure and focus of the treatment contract throughout the treatment; (e) supporting new learning and actively engaging in new skills and actions both within and outside therapy; (f) consistently appraising progress and flexibly adjusting to build success; and (g) reinforcing successes and predicting and inoculating against future challenges to build resilience and reduce relapse. These are the elements common to each of the effective treatments we have reviewed, with the exception of one overriding factor common to them all: All of these elements must be directed at altering the vicious cycles of the core solution-generated patterns that have come to characterize the patient's problem.

FOLLOWING THE THREAD

The chains of habit are too weak to be felt until they are too strong to be broken.

—Samuel Johnson

One change leaves the way open for the introduction of others.
—Niccolo Machiavelli

We have used the metaphor of the golden thread of second-order change to accurately describe a number of well-established ESTs for a wide range of clinical problems. Understanding how these approaches work opens a number of possibilities for clinicians. These include but are not limited to: enhancing the clinician's understanding about how to selectively integrate psychotherapy frameworks, meeting clients' individualized needs, and enhancing the clinician's knowledge of first-order patterns that represent exceptions to the rule on which a therapeutic framework is based on. The following is a thumbnail sketch of the approaches we have reviewed for the purposes of this book.

Anxiety is typically seen as the result of trying to master anxiety by avoiding it. The first-order vicious cycle is the result of hypervigilance and sensitivity to anxiety cues, which only provoke more anxiety and prevent mastery. Second-order interventions offer rationales explaining the cycle and the difference between fear and anxiety. They then prescribe reversals in the pattern by moving clients toward their anxiety so that they can master it.

Depression is commonly seen as a vicious cycle of attempts to cope with overwhelming stress through self-disconfirmation, oversimplification of complex situations, and withdrawal. The first-order vicious cycle results in self-doubt, blame, and withdrawal from life situations that only get worse. Negative cognitions become self-fulfilling. Second-order interventions offer various rationales to affirm clients' depression as appropriate to context and to their habitual solutions. They then reverse the pattern through exercises in which clients check out their assumptions and address their challenges.

Parent–child relationship problems are widely viewed as the result of vicious cycles wherein parents try to force compliance to their demands and children and adolescents resist. Second-order interventions reverse the change sequence for parents by offering rationales for why the escalating battles happen and then having parents deescalate their demands by connecting and validating their children first before gradually shaping collaboration.

Couple difficulties are typically described as vicious cycles wherein partners try to force change on each other. These conflicts become polarized and erode positive feelings within the couple, making it harder to tolerate common couple conflicts. The more they try to fix the relationship, the worse it gets for the fixing. Second-order interventions first offer rationales to affirm the universal and more unique reasons for conflict. Reversals include asking partners to go toward conflicts, develop dialogue around them and accept those irresolvable differences, and evolve positive experiences and futures with each other.

Chemical dependency and alcohol problems have also been broadly described as the result of mastery through avoidance. The person does not properly attend to addictive behavior or take other necessary actions for change. One vicious cycle is between the person and the chemical, whereby the more the person denies addiction or dependence, the more he or she is drawn into addiction. The other cycle is triggered as significant others try to coerce the addict out of his or her addictive behaviors. A second-order intervention of Alcoholics Anonymous and similar 12-step programs is to have the addict win over the addiction by admitting defeat. Significant others are encouraged to reverse their positions, stand aside, and allow the addict to seek his or her own resolution. The other major second-order interventions are reversals for therapists. Therapists reverse their attempts to have the addict acknowledge and change the addiction; instead, they validate the addicted person's position on change and collaborate with the person on what he or she might decide to change, if anything.

Chronically suicidal and self-harming client problems are described as vicious cycles of clients struggling with their own emotions and views of themselves and between them and significant others. Extremely dangerous actions become reinforcing for these clients and draw others to the rescue in an affirming way. Vicious cycles of emotional reactivity in historically invalidating relationships are repeated with significant others as well as with therapists. The second-order interventions revolve around therapists affirming their clients' distress and wishes to self-harm while simultaneously working to build new skills to master such distress personally and interpersonally. By taking this position, therapists provide second-order relationships for these clients. Second-order reversals have clients go toward distress to practice new skills.

Describing how psychotherapy works from this level of abstraction has an additional advantage. Once it can be established that problems have common patterns and solutions, it becomes clear that a wide variety of methods can achieve the same result. For example, once it is understood that anxiety is maintained by avoidance, and that solutions involve engaging the symptom, we can more easily understand how many different approaches might accomplish this task. We do not need to prove that one method is better than another. However, other questions arise that are of more importance. With this in mind, we offer recommendations for researchers, theorists, professors and graduate students, administrators, and policymakers. In this, our final section, we are as direct as possible by offering our recommendations in the form of bulleted lists. These will be listed in three domains: (a) integration; (b) practice; and (c) policy.

RECOMMENDATIONS: SYNTHESIS

Integration

- Change is the common ground from which all effective psychotherapy grows.
- Effective treatments unanimously describe client problems as first-order vicious cycles of client solutions.
- Second-order change is the key element in all treatments that work.
- The contextual model provides a unified vehicle for integrating techniques and relationships across effective therapies.
- Current research debates between professionals who advocate techniques versus those who advocate relationships and common factors are polemic vicious cycles that offer no more than a game without end. Second-order change offers a synthesizing format for future research.

Practice

- Look for the first-order patterns of solution-generated cycles in all problems.
- Know the general vicious cycle patterns of each various problem.
- Know the typical second-order change patterns across various effective treatments.
- Attend to the unique, specific values and language of your clients.
- Integrate your clients' uniqueness with your own views.
- Blend what you believe in with what the client can invest in.
- Study the therapeutic alliance and put it into practice.
- Deliberately adapt the contextual model to your work and adapt it to your second-order goals and methods.
- Learn general second-order strategies.
- Become "outcomes-informed." Develop clearly measurable goals integrating your objectives with your clients' goals and values and in your clients' terms. Direct your goals to achieving second-order change as you determine that it is called for.

Policy

- Don't mandate rigid EST protocols. Research suggests that rigid protocol adherence is less effective than flexible matching with clients' needs. Request evidence of how second-order change is to be achieved and then require measurable outcomes.
- Look into general guidelines on what typical vicious cycle patterns are common to each general problem type.
- Ask therapists to be able to identify these common cycles.
- Ask therapists to be able to articulate how they plan to address these patterns.
- Ask therapists to have clear and measurable goals for their clients.
- Expect therapists to translate these goals in the client's terms and values, stating the problem as the client states it and according to the client's wishes.
- Ask therapists how they are adapting the contextual model to guide their practice.
- Ask how they are adapting it to produce second-order change for different clients and different types of problems.
- Ask for evidence of change. Look for the common thread or common ground across approaches to support flexible applications of "best practices." Understand second-order change and inform your policy choices with it in mind.

FOLLOWING THE THREAD TOWARD INTEGRATION

The main thing is to be original . . . to play in a way of your own.
—Coleman Hawkins

Regardless of whether we are looking at integration, policy, or practice, the golden thread of second-order change helps guide us through the labyrinth of seemingly different approaches and leads us to the goal of effective, integrated practice. These are exciting times for the practice of psychotherapy. We are beginning to integrate and blend the wisdom of expert therapists with the support of clinical research. Through our discussion of first and second-order change, we have demonstrated that techniques and relationship factors are equally important; they do not occupy opposite poles. Promising approaches to effective psychotherapy for common client problems are exciting, yet they don't occupy separate boxes of independent practices. They have a commonality; they produce difference. As Miller and Rollnick (2002) stated about motivational interviewing, "It is more than a set of techniques for doing counseling. It is a way of being with people, which is likely to be different from how others have treated them in the past" (p. 41). This simple statement reflects the common ground in which effective treatments are rooted. That common ground, the common thread, is second-order change. Knowledge is power. Knowing the fundamental truth of second-order change should empower even more effective practice. We thus invite you to follow the path of the golden thread of second-order change as it leads us all toward more integrated, effective psychotherapy.

REFERENCES

Abidin, R. R. (1986). *The Parenting Stress Index*. Charlottesville, VA: Pediatric Psychology Press.

Adams, J. (2001). *Conceptual blockbusting: A guide to better ideas*. Cambridge, MA: Perseus.

Alcoholics Anonymous. (1976). *Alcoholics Anonymous (The blue book)*. New York: Alcoholics Anonymous World Services.

Alexander, F. F., & Sexton, T. L. (2002). Integrative/eclectic. In F. W. Kaslow & J. L. Lebow (Eds.), *Comprehensive handbook of psychotherapy* (Vol. 4, pp. 111–132). Hoboken, NJ: Wiley.

American heritage dictionary of the English language (4th ed.). (2000). Boston: Houghton Mifflin.

American Psychiatric Association. (1994). *Diagnostic and statistical manual of mental disorders* (4th ed.). Washington, DC: Author.

Asay, T. P., & Lambert, M. J. (1999). The empirical case for the common factors in therapy: Quantitative findings. In M. A. Hubble, B. L. Duncan, & S. D. Miller (Eds.), *The heart and soul of change: What works in therapy* (pp. 33–56). Washington, DC: American Psychological Association.

Bachelor, A., & Horvath, A. (1999). The therapeutic relationship. In M. A. Hubble, B. L. Duncan, & S. D. Miller (Eds.), *The heart and soul of change: What works in therapy* (pp. 133–178). Washington DC: American Psychological Association.

Bandura, A. (1986). *Social foundations of thought and action: A social cognitive theory*. Englewood Cliffs, NJ: Prentice Hall.

Bandura, A. (1988). Self-efficacy conception of anxiety. *Anxiety Research, 1*, 77–98.

Bandura, A. (1997). *Self-efficacy: The exercise of control*. New York: Freeman.

Barkley, R. A. (1997). *Defiant children: A clinician's manual for assessment and parent training* (2nd ed.). New York: Guilford Press.

Barlow, D. H. (1988). *Anxiety and its disorders: The nature and treatment of anxiety and panic*. New York: Guilford Press.

Barlow, D. H. (2001). *Clinical handbook of psychological disorders: A step-by-step treatment manual*. New York: Oxford University Press.

Barlow, D. H. (2002). *Anxiety and its disorders: The nature and treatment of anxiety and panic* (2nd ed.). New York: Guilford Press.

Barlow, D. H., & Craske, M. G. (2000). *Mastery of your anxiety and panic (MAP–3): Client workbook for anxiety and panic* (3rd ed.). San Antonio, TX: Greywind/Psychological Corporation.

Barrett-Lennard, G. T. (1981). The empathy cycle: Refinement of a nuclear concept. *Journal of Counseling Psychology, 28*, 91–100.

Bateson, G. (1971). The cybernetics of "self": A theory of alcoholism. *Psychiatry, 34*, 1–18.

Bateson, G. (1979). *Mind and nature: A necessary unity*. New York: Basic Books.

Baucom, D. H., Shoham, V., Mueser, K. T., Daiuto, A. D., & Stickle, T. R. (1998). Empirically supported couple and family interventions for marital distress and adult mental health problems. *Journal of Consulting and Clinical Psychology, 65*, 53–88.

Beck, A. T., Epstein, N., Brown, G., & Steer, R. A. (1988). An inventory for measuring clinical anxiety: Psychometric properties. *Journal of Consulting and Clinical Psychology, 56*, 893–897.

Beck, A. T., Rush, A. J., Shaw, B. F., & Emery, G. (1979). *Cognitive therapy of depression*. New York: Guilford Press.

Beck, A. T., & Steer, R. A. (1987). *Manual for the revised Beck Depression Inventory*. San Antonio, TX: Psychological Corporation.

Beck, A. T., Weissman, A., Lester, D., & Trexler, L. (1974). The measurement of pessimism: The Hopelessness Scale. *Journal of Consulting and Clinical Psychology, 42*, 861–865.

Beutler, L. E., Crago, M., & Arizmendi, T. G. (1986). Research on therapist variables in psychotherapy. In S. L. Garfield & A. E. Bergin (Eds.), *Handbook of psychotherapy and behavior change* (3rd ed., pp. 257–310). New York: Wiley.

Beutler, L. E., Johnson, D. T., Neville, C. W., Jr., & Workman, S. N. (1972). "Accurate empathy" and the AB dichotomy. *Journal of Consulting and Clinical Psychology, 38*, 372–375.

Beutler, L. E., Johnson, D. T., Neville, C. W., Jr., & Workman, S. N. (1973). Some sources of variables in accurate empathy ratings. *Journal of Consulting and Clinical Psychology, 40*, 167–169.

Beutler, L. E., Molerio, C. M., & Talebi, H. (2002). Resistance. In J. C. Norcross (Ed.), *Psychotherapy relationships that work: Therapist contributions and responsiveness to patients* (pp. 129–144). New York: Oxford University Press.

Blatt, S. J., Sanislow, C. A., Zuroff, D. C., & Pilkonis, P. A. (1996). Characteristics of effective therapists: Further analyses of data from the National Institute of Mental Health Treatment of Depression Collaborative Research Program. *Journal of Consulting and Clinical Psychology, 64*, 1276–1284.

Bohart, A. C., Elliot, R., Greenberg, L. S., & Watson, J. C. (2002). Empathy. In J. C. Norcross (Ed.), *Psychotherapy relationships that work: Therapist contributions and responsiveness to patients* (pp. 89–108). New York: Oxford University Press.

Bordin, E. S. (1975, September). *The working alliance: Basis for a general theory of psychotherapy*. Paper presented at the annual meeting of the Society for Psychotherapy Research, Washington, DC.

Bordin, E. S. (1989, June). *Building therapeutic alliances: The base for integration*. Paper presented at the annual meeting of the Society for Psychotherapy Research, Berkeley, CA.

Bordin, E. S. (1994). Theory and research on the therapeutic working alliance: New directions. In A. O. Horvath & L. S. Greenberg (Eds.), *The working alliance: Theory, research, and practice* (pp. 195–230). New York: Wiley.

Borkovec, T. D. (1994). The nature, functions, and origins of worry. In G. C. L. Davey & F. Tallis (Eds.), *Worrying: Perspectives on theory, assessment, and treatment* (pp. 5–33). New York: Wiley.

Borkovec, T. D., & Sharpless, B. (2004). Generalized anxiety disorder: Bringing cognitive–behavioral therapy into the valued present. In S. C. Hayes, V. M. Follette, & M. M. Linehan (Eds.), *Mindfulness and acceptance: Expanding the cognitive–behavioral tradition* (pp. 209–243). New York: Guilford Press.

Bowlby, J. (1969). *Attachment*. New York: Basic Books.

Bowlby, J. (1977). The making and breaking of affectional bonds: II. Some principles of psychotherapy. The fiftieth Maudsley Lecture. *British Journal of Psychiatry, 130*, 421–431.

Brehm, S. S., & Brehm, J. W. (1981). *Psychological reactance: A theory of freedom and control*. New York: Academic Press.

Brown, G. W. (1996). Onset and course of depressive disorders: Summary of a research programme. In C. Mundt, M. J. Goldstein, K. Hahlweg, & P. Fiesler (Eds.), *Interpersonal factors in the origin and course of affective disorders* (pp. 151–167). London: Gaskell/Royal College of Psychiatrists.

Brown, J. M. (1998). Self-regulation and the addictive behaviors. In W. R. Miller, & N. Heather (Eds.), *Treating addictive behaviors* (2nd ed., pp. 61–73). New York: Plenum Press.

Brown, T. A., O'Leary, T. A., & Barlow, D. H. (2001). Generalized anxiety disorder. In D. H. Barlow (Ed.), *Clinical handbook of psychological disorders: A step-by-step treatment manual* (pp. 154–208). New York: Guilford Press.

Buckley, W. (1987). *Sociology and modern systems theory*. Englewood Cliffs, NJ: Prentice Hall.

Burns, D. D., & Nolen-Hoeksema, S. (1992). Therapeutic empathy and recovery from depression in cognitive–behavioral therapy: A structural equation model. *Journal of Consulting and Clinical Psychology, 60*, 441–449.

Cannon, W. B. (1927). *Bodily changes in pain, hunger, fear and rage*. New York: Appleton-Century-Crofts.

Castonguay, L. G., Goldfried, M. R., Wiser, S., Raue, P. J., & Hayes, A. M. (1996). Predicting the effect of cognitive therapy for depression: A study of unique and common factors. *Journal of Consulting and Clinical Psychology, 64*, 497–504.

Chamberlain, P., & Patterson, G. R. (1995). Discipline and child compliance in parenting. In M. H. Bornstein (Ed.), *Handbook of parenting: Applied and practical parenting* (Vol. 4, pp. 204–225). Mahwah, NJ: Erlbaum.

Chambless, D. L., Caputo, G. C., Bright, P., & Gallagher, R. (1984). Assessment of fear in agoraphobics: The Body Sensations Questionnaire and the Agoraphobic Cognitions Questionnaire. *Journal of Consulting and Clinical Psychology, 52*, 1090–1097.

Chambless, D. L., Caputo, G. C., Jasin, S. E., Gracely, E. J., & Williams, C. (1985). The Mobility Inventory for Agoraphobia. *Behavior Research and Therapy, 23*, 35–44.

Christensen, A., & Heavey, C. L. (1993). Gender differences in marital conflict: The demand/withdraw interaction pattern. In S. Oskamp & M. Costanzo (Eds.), *Gender issues in contemporary society* (pp. 113–141). Newbury Park, CA: Sage.

Christensen, A., & Jacobson, N. S. (2000). *Reconcilable differences*. New York: Guilford Press.

Claiborn, C. D., & Dowd, E. T. (1985). Attributional interpretations in counseling: Content versus discrepancy. *Journal of Counseling Psychology, 32,* 188–196.

Coyne, J. (1976). Depression and the response of others. *Journal of Abnormal Psychology, 85,* 186–193.

Craighead, W. E., Hart, A. B., Craighead, L. W., & Ilardi, S. S. (2002). Psychosocial treatments for major depressive disorder. In P. E. Nathan & J. M. Gorman (Eds.), *A guide to treatments that work* (2nd ed., pp. 245–261). New York: Oxford University Press.

Craske, M. G., & Barlow, D. H. (2001). Panic disorder and agoraphobia. In D. H. Barlow (Ed.), *Clinical handbook of psychological disorders: A step-by-step treatment manual* (pp. 1–59). New York: Guilford Press.

Craske, M. G., Barlow, D. H., & Meadows, E. A. (2000). *Mastery of your anxiety and panic (MAP–3): Therapist guide for anxiety, panics, and agoraphobia* (3rd ed.). San Antonio, TX: Graywind/Psychological Corporation.

Crits-Cristoph, P., & Mintz, J. (1991). Implications of therapist effects for the design and analysis of comparative studies of psychotherapies. *Journal of Consulting and Clinical Psychology, 59,* 20–26.

DiClemente, C. C. (2003). *Addiction and change: How addictions develop and addicted persons recover.* New York: Guilford Press.

DiClemente, C. C., Carbonari, J. P., & Velasquez, M. M. (1992). Alcoholism treatment mismatching from a process of change perspective. In R. R. Watson (Ed.), *Treatment of drug and alcohol abuse* (pp. 115–142). Totowa, NJ: Humana.

Donovan, D. M., & Rosengren, D. B. (1999). Motivation for behavior change and treatment among substance abusers. In J. A. Tucker, D. M. Donovan, & G. A. Marlatt (Eds.), *Changing addictive behavior: Bridging clinical and public health strategies* (pp. 127–159). New York: Guilford Press.

Duncan, B. L., Solovey, A. D., & Rusk, G. D. (1992). *Changing the rules: A client-directed approach to therapy.* New York: Guilford Press.

Elkin, I., Shea, T., Watkins, J. T., Imber, S. D., Sotsky, S. M., Collins, J. F., et al. (1989). National Institute of Mental Health Treatment of Depression Collaborative Research Program: General effectiveness of treatments. *Archives of General Psychiatry, 46,* 971–982.

Erikson, E. H. (1963). *Childhood and society* (2nd ed.). New York: Norton.

Fennell, M. J., & Teasdale, J. D. (1987). Cognitive therapy for depression: Individual differences and the process of change. *Cognitive Therapy and Research, 11,* 253–271.

Ferster, C. B. (1973). A functional analysis of depression. *American Psychologist, 28,* 857–870.

Feske, U., & de Beurs, E. (1997). The Panic Appraisal Inventory: Psychometric properties. *Behavior Research and Therapy, 35*, 875–882.

Festinger, L. (1954). A theory of social comparison processes. *Human Relations, 7*, 117–140.

Fisch, R., Weakland, J., & Segal, L. (1982). *The tactics of change: Doing therapy briefly.* San Francisco: Jossey-Bass.

Flores, P. J., & Georgi, J. M. (2005). *Treatment improvement protocol 41. Substance abuse treatment: Group therapy* (DHHS Publication No. SAM 05-3991). Rockville, MD: U.S. Department of Health and Human Services, Public Health Service, Substance Abuse and Mental Health Services Administration, Center for Substance Abuse Treatment.

Fossati, A., Madeddu, F., & Maffei, C. (1999). Borderline personality and childhood sexual abuse: A meta-analytic study. *Journal of Personality Disorders, 13*, 268–280.

Frank, J. D. (1961). *Persuasion and healing: A comparative study of psychotherapy.* Baltimore: Johns Hopkins University Press.

Frank, J. D. (1971). Therapeutic factors in psychotherapy. *American Journal of Psychotherapy, 25*, 350–361.

Frank, J. D. (1973). *Persuasion and healing: A comparative study of psychotherapy* (2nd ed.). Baltimore: Johns Hopkins University Press.

Frank, J. D., & Frank, J. B. (1991). *Persuasion and healing: A comparative study of psychotherapy* (3rd ed.). Baltimore: Johns Hopkins University Press.

Fraser, J. S. (1984). Paradox and orthodox: Folie à deux? *Journal of Marital and Family Therapy, 10*, 361–372.

Freud, S. (1940). The dynamics of transference. In J. Strachey (Ed.), *The standard edition of the complete psychological works of Sigmund Freud* (Vol. 12, pp. 99–108). London: Hogarth. (Original work published 1912)

Frick, P. J., Lahey, B. B., Loeber, R., Stouthamer-Loeber, M., Christ, M. A., & Hanson, K. (1992). Family risk factors to oppositional defiant disorder and conduct disorder: Parental psychopathology and maternal parenting. *Journal of Consulting and Clinical Psychology, 60*, 49–55.

Gelso, C. J., & Carter, J. A. (1985). The relationship in counseling and psychotherapy: Components, consequences, and theoretical antecedents. *The Counseling Psychologist, 13*, 155–243.

Gelso, C. J., & Carter, J. A. (1994). Components of the psychotherapy relationship: The interaction and unfolding treatment. *Journal of Counseling Psychology, 41*, 296–306.

Gloaguen, V., Cottrauz, J., Cucherat, M., & Blackburn, I. (1998). A meta-analysis of the effects of cognitive therapy in depressed patients. *Journal of Affective Disorders, 35*, 991–999.

Goldstein, A. P. (1962). *Therapist–patient expectancies in psychotherapy.* Elmsford, NY: Pergamon Press.

Goleman, D. (1985). *Vital lies, simple truths: The psychology of self-deception.* New York: Simon & Schuster.

Gonzalez, R. C., Biever, J. L., & Gardner, G. T. (1994). The multicultural perspective in therapy: A social constructivist approach. *Psychotherapy: Theory, Research, and Practice, 31,* 515–524.

Gotner, E. T., Gollan, J. K., Dobson, K. S., & Jacobson, N. S. (1998). Cognitive–behavioral treatment for depression: Relapse prevention. *Journal of Consulting and Clinical Psychology, 66,* 377–394.

Gottman, J. M. (1993). The roles of conflict engagement, escalation, and avoidance in marital interaction: A longitudinal view of five types of couples. *Journal of Consulting and Clinical Psychology, 61,* 6–15.

Gottman, J. M. (1999). *The marriage clinic: A scientifically-based marital therapy.* New York: Norton.

Gottman, J. M. (2000). *Clinical manual for marital therapy.* Seattle, WA: Gottman Institute.

Gottman, J. M., & Silver, N. (1999). *The seven principles for making marriage work.* New York: Three Rivers.

Greene, R. (2001). *The explosive child.* New York: HarperCollins.

Greene, R. W., Ablon, J. S., & Goring, J. C. (2003). A transactional model of oppositional behavior: Underpinnings of the collaborative problem solving approach. *Journal of Psychosomatic Research, 55,* 67–75.

Greene, R. W., Ablon, J. S., Goring, J. C., Fazio, V., & Morse, L. R. (2004). Treatment of oppositional defiant disorder in children and adolescents. In P. M. Barrett & T. H. Ollendick (Eds.), *Handbook of interventions that work with children and adolescents: Prevention and treatment* (pp. 369–393). West Sussex, England: Wiley.

Greene, R. W., Ablon, J. S., Goring, J. C., Raezer-Blakely, L., Markey, J., Monuteaux, M. C., et al. (2004). Effectiveness of collaborative problem solving in affectively dysregulated children with oppositional–defiant disorder: Initial findings. *Journal of Consulting and Clinical Psychology, 72,* 1157–1164.

Grilo, C. M., Money, R., Barlow, D. H., Goddard, A. W., Gorman, J. M., Hofmann, S. G., et al. (1998). Pretreatment patient factors predicting attrition from multicenter randomized controlled treatment study for panic disorder. *Comprehensive Psychiatry, 39,* 323–332.

Gunderson, J. G. (2000). *Borderline personality disorder: A clinical guide.* Washington, DC: American Psychiatric Publishing.

Gunderson, J. G., & Kolb, J. W. (1978). Discriminating features of borderline patients. *American Journal of Psychiatry, 135,* 792–796.

Ham, M. A. (1987). Client behavior and counselor empathic performance. In G. A. Gladstein & J. Brennan (Eds.), *Empathy and counseling: Explanations in theory and research* (pp. 31–50). New York: Springer-Verlag.

Hampton, B. B. (1988). The efficacy of paradoxical interventions: A qualitative review of the research evidence. (Doctoral dissertation, University of Texas, Austin, 1988). *Dissertation Abstracts International, 49,* 2378–2379.

Harris Interactive. (2004). *Therapy in America 2004*. Retrieved May 17, 2006, from http://www.psychologytoday.com/pto/topline_report_042904.pdf

Hayes, S. C., Follette, V. M., & Linehan, M. M. (2004). *Mindfulness and acceptance: Expanding the cognitive–behavioral tradition*. New York: Guilford Press.

Hayes, S. C., Strosahl, K. D., & Wilson, K. G. (1999). *Acceptance and commitment therapy: An experiential approach to behavior change*. New York: Guilford Press.

Heard, H. L. (2000). *Cost-effectiveness of DBT in the treatment of BPD*. Unpublished doctoral dissertation, University of Washington, Seattle.

Heisenberg, W. (1958). *Physics and philosophy: The revolution in modern science*. New York: Harper & Row.

Henggeler, S. W., Schoenwald, S. K., Rowland, M. D., & Cunningham, P. B. (2002). *Serious emotional disturbance in children and adolescents*. New York: Guilford Press.

Henry, W. P., Schacht, T. E., & Strupp, H. H. (1986). Structural analysis of social behavior: Application to a study of interpersonal process in differential psychotherapeutic outcome. *Journal of Consulting and Clinical Psychology, 54*, 27–31.

Henry, W. P., Schacht, T. E., Strupp, H. H., Butler, S. F., & Binder, J. (1993). Effects of training in time-limited psychotherapy: Mediators of therapists' responses to training. *Journal of Consulting and Clinical Psychology, 61*, 441–447.

Henry, W. P., Strupp, H. H., Butler, S. F., Schacht, T. E., & Binder, J. (1993). Effects of training in time-limited psychotherapy: Changes in therapist behavior. *Journal of Consulting and Clinical Psychology, 61*, 434–440.

Herrigel, E. (1989). *Zen in the art of archery*. New York: Vintage Books.

Hill, K. A. (1987). Meta-analysis of paradoxical interventions. *Psychotherapy, 24*, 266–270.

Hinshaw, S. P., & Anderson, C. A. (1996). Conduct and oppositional defiant disorders. In E. J. Mash & R. A. Barkley (Eds.), *Child psychopathology* (pp. 113–152). New York: Guilford Press.

Hofmann, S. G., & Barlow, D. H. (2002). Social phobia (social anxiety disorder). In D. H. Barlow (Ed.), *Anxiety and its disorders* (2nd ed., pp. 533–565). New York: Guilford Press.

Horvath, A. O., & Bedi, R. P. (2002). The alliance. In J. C. Norcross (Ed.), *Psychotherapy relationships that work: Therapist contributions and responsiveness to patients* (pp. 37–69). New York: Oxford University Press.

Horvath, A. O., & Goheen, M. D. (1990). Factors mediating the success of defiance- and compliance-based interventions. *Journal of Consulting and Clinical Psychology, 37*, 363–371.

Horvath, A. O., & Greenberg, L. S. (1986). Development of the Working Alliance Inventory. In L. S. Greenberg & W. M. Pinsof (Eds.), *The psychotherapeutic process: A research handbook* (pp. 529–556). New York: Guilford Press.

Horvath, A. O., & Symonds, B. D. (1991). Relation between working alliance and outcome in psychotherapy: A meta-analysis. *Journal of Counseling Psychology, 38*, 139–149.

Howard, K. I., Lueger, R. J., Maling, M. S., & Martinovich, Z. (1993). A phase model of psychotherapy outcome: Casual mediation of change. *Journal of Consulting and Clinical Psychology, 61*, 678–685.

Hubble, M. A., Duncan, B. L., & Miller, S. D. (1999). *The heart and soul of change: What works in therapy.* Washington, DC: American Psychological Association.

Hyman, H. H., & Singer, E. (1968). *Readings in reference group theory and research.* New York: Free Press.

Ilardi, S. S., & Craighead, W. E. (1994). The role of nonspecific factors in cognitive–behavior therapy for depression. *Clinical Psychology: Science and Practice, 1*, 138–156.

Imber, S. D., Pikonis, P. A., Sotsky, S. M., Elkin, I., Watkins, J. T., Collins, J. F., et al. (1990). Mode-specific effects among three treatments for depression. *Journal of Consulting and Clinical Psychology, 58*, 352–359.

Jacobson, N. S. (1984). A component analysis of behavioral marital therapy: The relative effectiveness of behavior exchange and problem solving training. *Journal of Consulting and Clinical Psychology, 52*, 295–305.

Jacobson, N. S., & Addis, M. E. (1993). Research on couples and couple therapy: What do we know? Where are we going? *Journal of Consulting and Clinical Psychology, 61*, 85–93.

Jacobson, N. S., & Christensen, A. (1996). *Integrative couple therapy: Promoting acceptance and change.* New York: Norton.

Jacobson, N. S., Dobson, K. S., Fruzetti, A. E., Schmaling, K. B., & Salusky, S. (1991). Marital therapy as a treatment for depression. *Journal of Consulting and Clinical Psychology, 59*, 547–557.

Jacobson, N. S., Dobson, K. S., Truax, P. A., Addis, M. E., Koerner, K., Gollan, J. K., et al. (1996). A component analysis of cognitive–behavioral treatment for depression. *Journal of Consulting and Clinical Psychology, 64*, 295–304.

Jacobson, N. S., & Follette, W. C. (1985). Clinical significance of improvement resulting from two behavioral marital therapy components. *Behavior Therapy, 16*, 249–262.

Jacobson, N. S., Follette, W. C., & Pagel, M. (1986). Predicting who will benefit from behavioral marital therapy. *Journal of Consulting and Clinical Psychology, 54*, 518–522.

Jacobson, N. S., & Margolin, G. (1979). *Marital therapy: Strategies based on social learning and behavior exchange principles.* New York: Brunner/Mazel.

Jacobson, N. S., Schmaling, K. B., & Holtzworth-Munroe, A. (1987). Component analysis of behavioral marital therapy: Two-year follow-up and prediction of relapse. *Journal of Marital and Family Therapy, 13*, 187–195.

Jacobson, N. S., & Truax, P. (1991). Clinical significance: A statistical approach to defining meaningful change in psychotherapy research. *Journal of Consulting and Clinical Psychology, 39*, 12–19.

Johnson, V. E. (1973). *I'll quit tomorrow.* New York: Harper & Row.

Jones, R. A. (1977). *Self-fulfilling prophecies: Social, psychological, and physiological effects of expectancies*. Hillsdale, NJ: Erlbaum.

Kabat-Zinn, J. (1990). *Full catastrophe living: Using the wisdom of your body and mind to face stress, pain, and illness*. New York: Delta.

Kabat-Zinn, J. (1994). *Wherever you go, there you are: Mindfulness meditation in everyday life*. New York: Hyperion.

Kabat-Zinn, J., Massion, A. O., Kristeller, J., Peterson, L. G., Fletcher, K. E., Pbert, L., et al. (1992). Effectiveness of a meditation-based stress reduction program in the treatment of anxiety disorders. *American Journal of Psychiatry, 149,* 936–943.

Kanfer, F. H. (1986). Implications of a self-regulation model of therapy for treatment of addictive behaviors. In W. R. Miller & N. Heather (Eds.), *Treating addictive behaviors* (pp. 29–47). New York: Plenum Press.

Kazdin, A. E. (2002). Psychosocial treatments for conduct disorder in children and adolescents. In P. Nathan & J. M. Gorman (Eds.), *A guide to treatments that work* (2nd ed., pp. 57–86). New York: Oxford University Press.

Keijers, G. P. J., Schaap, D. P. D. R., Googduin, C. A. L., & Lammers, M. W. (1995). Patient–therapist interaction in the behavioral treatment of panic disorder with agoraphobia. *Behavior Modification, 19,* 491–517.

Keller, M. B., McCullough, J. P., Klein, D. N., Arnow, B., Dunner, D. L., Greenberg, A. J., et al. (2000). A comparison of nefazodone, the cognitive behavioral-analysis system of psychotherapy, and their combination for the treatment of chronic depression. *New England Journal of Medicine, 342,* 1462–1470.

Kelley, H. H., Berscheid, E., Christensen, A., Harvey, J. H., Huston, T. L., Levinger, G., et al. (1983). *Close relationships*. New York: Freeman.

Kelly, G. A. (1955). *The psychology of personal constructs*. New York: Norton.

Kessler, R. C., McGonagel, K. A., Zhao, S., Nelson, C. B., Hughes, M., Eshleman, S., et al. (1994). Lifetime and 12-month prevalence of *DSM–III–R* psychiatric disorders in the United States: Results from the National Comorbidity Survey. *Archives of General Psychiatry, 51,* 8–19.

Klein, K. D., & Ross, D. C. (1993). Reanalysis of the National Institute of Mental Health Treatment of Depression Collaborative Research Program: General effectiveness report. *Neuropsychopharmacology, 8,* 241–251.

Klerman, G. L., Weissman, M. M., Rounsaville, B. J., & Chevron, E. S. (1984). *Interpersonal psychotherapy of depression*. New York: Basic Books.

Klinger, E. (1975). Consequences of commitment to and disengagement from incentives. *Psychological Review, 82,* 223–231.

Koerner, K., & Dimeff, L. A. (2000). Further data on dialectical behavior therapy. *Clinical Psychology: Science and Practice, 7,* 104–112.

Koerner, K., & Linehan, M. M. (2000). Research on dialectical behavior therapy for borderline personality disorder: Dialectical behavior therapy. *Psychiatric Clinics of North America, 23,* 151–167.

Koerner, K., & Linehan, M. M. (2002). Dialectical behavior therapy for borderline personality disorder. In S. G. Hofmann & M. C. Tompson (Eds.), *Treating chronic and severe mental disorders: A handbook of empirically supported interventions* (pp. 317–342). New York: Guilford Press.

Koons, C. R., Robins, C. J., Tweek, J. L., Lynch, T. R., Gonzalez, A. M. Morse, J. Q., et al. (2001). Efficacy of dialectical behavior therapy in women veterans with borderline personality disorder. *Behavior Therapy, 32,* 371–390.

Kropnick, J. L., Simmens, S., Moyer, J., Elkin, I., Watkins, J. T., & Pikonis, P. A. (1996). The role of the therapeutic alliance in psychotherapy and pharmaco-therapy outcome: Findings in the National Institute of Mental Health Treatment of Depression Collaborative Research Program. *Journal of Consulting and Clinical Psychology, 64,* 532–539.

Lambert, M. J. (1992). Implications of outcome research for psychotherapy integration. In J. C. Norcross & M. R. Goldfried (Eds.), *Handbook of psychotherapy integration* (pp. 94–129). New York: Basic Books.

Leake, G. J., & King, A. S. (1977). Effect of counselor expectations on alcoholic recovery. *Alcohol Health and Research World, 11*(3), 16–22.

Levy, R., O'Hanlon, B., & Goode, T. N. (2001). *Try and make me! Simple strategies that turn off the tantrums and create cooperation.* New York: Rodale Press.

Lewinsohn, P. M., & Gotlib, I. H. (1995). Behavioral theory and treatment of depression. In E. E. Becker & W. R. Leber (Eds.), *Handbook of depression* (pp. 352–375). New York: Guilford Press.

Liepman, M. R. (1993). Using family influence to motivate alcoholics to enter treatment: The Johnson Institute intervention approach. In T. J. O'Farrell (Ed.), *Treating alcohol problems: Marital and family interventions* (pp. 54–77). New York: Guilford Press.

Linehan, M. M. (1993). *Cognitive–behavioral treatment of borderline personality disorder.* New York: Guilford Press.

Linehan, M. M., Armstrong, H. E., Suarez, A., Allmon, D., & Heard, H. L. (1991). Cognitive–behavioral treatment of chronically parasuicidal borderline patients. *Archives of General Psychiatry, 48,* 1060–1064.

Linehan, M. M., Cochran, B. N., & Kehrer, C. A. (2001). Dialectical behavior therapy for borderline personality disorder. In D. H. Barlow (Ed.), *Clinical handbook of psychological disorders* (2nd ed., pp. 470–522). New York: Guilford Press.

Linehan, M. M., Heard, H. L., & Armstrong, H. E. (1993). Naturalistic follow-up of a behavioral treatment for chronically parasuicidal borderline patients. *Archives of General Psychiatry, 50,* 971–974.

Linehan, M. M., Tutek, D. A., Heard, H. L., & Armstrong, H. E. (1994). Interpersonal outcome of cognitive behavioral treatment for chronically suicidal borderline patients. *American Journal of Psychiatry, 151,* 1771–1776.

Loeber, R. (1990). Development and risk factors of juvenile antisocial behavior and delinquency. *Clinical Psychology Review, 10,* 1–41.

Loeber, R., Wung, P., Keenan, K., Giroux, B., Stouthamer-Loeber, M., Van Kammen, W. B., et al. (1993). Development of pathways in disruptive child behavior. *Developmental Psychopathology, 5,* 101–131.

Luborsky, L., Singer, B., & Luborsky, L. (1975). Comparative studies of psycho-therapies: Is it true that "Everyone has won and all must have prizes"? *Archives of General Psychiatry, 32,* 995–1008.

Markowitz, J. C. (1998). *Interpersonal psychotherapy for dysthymic disorder.* Washington, DC: American Psychiatric Press.

Marks, I. M., & Mathews, A. M. (1979). Brief standard self-rating for phobic patients. *Behavior Research and Therapy, 17,* 263–267.

Martin, D. J., Garske, J. P., & Davis, K. M. (2000). Relation of the therapeutic alliance with outcome and other variables: A meta-analytic review. *Journal of Consulting and Clinical Psychology, 68,* 438–450.

Masters, W. H., & Johnson, V. E. (1966). *Human sexual response.* Boston: Little, Brown.

Masters, W. H., & Johnson, V. E. (1970). *Human sexual inadequacy.* New York: Little, Brown.

McCrady, B. S., Noel, N. E., Abrams, D. B., Stout, R. L., Nelson, H. G., & Hay, W. M. (1986). Comparative effectiveness of three types of spouse involvement in outpatient behavioral alcoholism treatment. *Journal of Studies on Alcohol, 47,* 459–467.

McCullough, J. P. (2000). *Treatment of chronic depression: Cognitive behavioral analysis system of psychotherapy.* New York: Guilford Press.

Meichenbaum, D. (1984). The nature of the unconscious process: A cognitive behavioral perspective. In K. S. Bowers & D. Meichenbaum (Eds.), *The unconscious reconsidered* (pp. 273–298). New York: Wiley.

Miller, W. R. (1985). *Living as if: How positive faith can change your life.* Philadelphia: Westminster Press.

Miller, W. R. (Consensus Panel Chair). (2003). *Treatment improvement protocol series 35. Enhancing motivation for change in substance abuse treatment* (DHHS Publication No. SMA 03-3811). Rockville, MD: U.S. Department of Health and Human Services, Public Health Service, Substance Abuse and Mental Health Services Administration, Center for Substance Abuse Treatment.

Miller, W. R., Benefield, R. G., & Tonigan, J. S. (1993). Enhancing motivation for change in problem drinking: A controlled comparison of two therapist styles. *Journal of Consulting and Clinical Psychology, 61,* 455–461.

Miller, W. R., & Brown, J. M. (1991). Self-regulation as a conceptual basis for the prevention and treatment of addictive behaviors. In N. Heather, W. R. Miller, & J. Greeley (Eds.), *Self-control and the addictive behaviors* (pp. 3–79). Sydney, Australia: Maxwell Macmillan Publishing.

Miller, W. R., & Rollnick, S. (2002). *Motivational interviewing: Preparing people for change.* New York: Guilford Press.

Millon, T. (1987). On the genesis and prevalence of the borderline personality disorder: A social learning thesis. *Journal of Personality Disorders, 1,* 354–372.

Mohr, J. J., & Woodhouse, S. S. (2000, June). *Clients' visions of helpful and harmful psychotherapy: An approach to measuring individual differences in therapy priorities.*

Paper presented at the 31st annual meeting of the Society for Psychotherapy Research, Chicago.

Mowrer, O. H. (1950). *Learning theory and personality dynamics*. New York: Ronald Press.

Nathan, P. E., & Gorman, J. M. (2002a). *A guide to treatments that work* (2nd ed.). New York: Oxford University Press.

Nathan, P. E., & Gorman, J. M. (2002b). Efficacy, effectiveness, and clinical utility of psychotherapy research. In P. E. Nathan & J. M. Gorman (Eds.), *A guide to treatments that work* (pp. 643–654). New York: Oxford University Press.

National Institute of Mental Health. (1999). *The numbers count* (NIH Publication No. NIH-99-4584). Retrieved October 25, 2004, from http://www.NIMH.NIH.gov/publicat/numbers.CFM

Noonan, W. C., & Moyers, T. B. (1997). Motivational interviewing. *Journal of Substance Abuse, 2*, 8–16.

Norcross, J. C. (2002). *Psychotherapy relationships that work: Therapist contributions and responsiveness to patients*. New York: Oxford University Press.

Norcross, J. C., & Goldfried, M. R. (2005). *Handbook of psychotherapy integration* (2nd ed.). New York: Basic Books.

O'Farrell, T. J., Choquette, K. A., & Cutter, H. S. G. (1998). Couples relapse prevention sessions after behavioral marital therapy for alcoholics and their wives: Outcomes during three years after starting treatment. *Journal of Studies on Alcohol, 59*, 357–370.

O'Hara, M. M. (1984). Person-centered gestalt: Towards a holistic synthesis. In R. F. Levant & J. M. Shlien (Eds.), *Client-centered therapy and the person-centered approach: New directions in theory, research, and practice* (pp. 203–221). New York: Praeger.

O'Leary, K. D., & Beach, S. R. H. (1990). Marital therapy: A viable treatment for depression and marital discord. *American Journal of Psychiatry, 147*, 183–186.

Olweus, D. (1980). Familial and temperament determinants of aggressive behavior in adolescent boys: A causal analysis. *Developmental Psychology, 16*, 644–660.

Orford, J. (1985). *Excessive appetites: A psychological view of addictions*. New York: Wiley.

Orlinsky, D. E., Grawe, K., & Parks, B. (1994). Process and outcome in psychotherapy—Noch einmal. In A. E. Bergin & S. L. Garfied (Eds.), *Handbook of psychotherapy and behavior change* (4th ed., pp. 270–378). New York: Wiley.

Orsillo, S. M., Romer, L., Lerner, J. B., & Tull, M. T. (2004). Acceptance, mindfulness, and cognitive–behavioral therapy: Comparisons, contrasts, and application to anxiety. In S. C. Hayes, V. M. Follette, & M. M. Linehan (Eds.), *Mindfulness and acceptance: Expanding the cognitive–behavioral tradition* (pp. 66–95). New York: Guilford Press.

Parker, M. W., Winstead, D. K., & Willi, F. J. P. (1979). Patient autonomy in alcohol rehabilitation: I. Literature review. *International Journal of Addictions, 14*, 1015–1022.

Parloff, M. B., Waskow, I. E., & Wolfe, B. E. (1978). Research on therapeutic variables in relation to process and outcome. In S. L. Garfield & A. E. Bergin (Eds.), *Handbook of psychotherapy and behavior change: An empirical analysis* (2nd ed., pp. 233–282). New York: Wiley.

Parsons, T. (1951). Illness and the role of the physician: A sociological perspective. *American Journal of Orthopsychiatry, 21*, 452–460.

Patterson, G. R. (1982). *Coercive family process*. Eugene, OR: Castalia.

Patterson, G. R., Dishion, T. J., & Chamberlain, P. (1993). Outcomes and methodological issues related to treatment of antisocial children. In T. R. Giles (Ed.), *Effective psychotherapy: A handbook of comparative research* (pp. 43–88). New York: Plenum Press.

Patterson, G. R., Reid, J. B., & Dishion, T. J. (1992). *Antisocial boys*. Eugene, OR: Castalia.

Peake, T. H., & Archer, R. P. (1984). *Clinical training in psychotherapy*. New York: Haworth.

Peake, T. H., & Ball, J. D. (1987). Brief psychotherapy: Planned therapeutic change for changing times. *Psychotherapy in Private Practice, 5*, 53–63.

Phillips, K. (1996). *The broken mirror: Understanding and treating body dysmorphic disorder*. New York: Oxford University Press.

Phillips, S. D., Burns, B. J., Edgar, E. R., Mueser, K. T., Linkins, K. W., Rosenheck, R. A., et al. (2001). Moving assertive community treatment into standard practice. *Psychiatric Services, 52*, 771–779.

Piaget, J. (1950). *Psychology of intelligence* (M. Piercy & D. E. Berlyne, Trans.). New York: Harcourt Brace. (Original work published 1947)

Piaget, J. (1960). *The moral judgment of the child* (M. Gabin, Trans.). Glencoe, IL: Free Press. (Original work published 1932)

Presidential Task Force, American Psychological Association. (2005, February 25). *Draft policy statement on evidence-based practice in psychology*. Washington, DC: American Psychological Association.

Prochaska, J. O. (1979). *Systems of psychotherapy: A transtheoretical analysis*. Homewood, IL: Dorsey Press.

Prochaska, J. O., & DiClemente, C. C. (1982). Transtheoretical therapy: Toward a more integrative model of change. *Psychotherapy: Theory, Research, and Practice, 19*, 276–288.

Prochaska, J. O., & DiClemente, C. C. (1983). Stages and processes of self-change of smoking: Toward an integrative model of change. *Journal of Consulting and Clinical Psychology, 51*, 390–395.

Prochaska, J. O., & DiClemente, C. C. (1986). Toward a comprehensive model of change. In W. R. Miller & N. Heather (Eds.), *Treating addictive behaviors: Processes of change* (pp. 3–27). New York: Plenum Press.

Prochaska, J. O., & DiClemente, C. C. (1992). Stages of change in the modification of problem behavior. In M. Hersen, R. Eisler, & P. M. Miller (Eds.), *Progress in behavior modification* (Vol. 28, pp. 184–214). Sycamore, IL: Sycamore.

Prochaska, J. O., DiClemente, C. C., & Norcross, J. C. (1992). In search of how people change: Application to the addictive behaviors. *American Psychologist, 47*, 1102–1114.

Prochaska, J. O., Norcross, J. C., & DiClemente, C. C. (1994). *Changing for good.* New York: Morrow.

Project MATCH Research Group. (1997). Matching alcoholism treatments to client heterogeneity: Project MATCH post-treatment drinking outcome. *Journal of Studies on Alcohol, 58*, 7–29.

Rapee, R. M., Craske, M. G., & Barlow, D. H. (1995). Assessment instrument for panic disorder that includes fear of sensation producing activities: The Albany Panic and Phobia Questionnaire. *Anxiety, 1*, 114–122.

Rapee, R. M., Craske, M. G., Broen, T. A., & Barlow, D. H. (1996). Measurement of perceived control over anxiety-related events. *Behavior Therapy, 27*, 279–293.

Rehm, L. P. (1977). A self-control model of depression. *Behavior Therapy, 8*, 787–804.

Rehm, L. P. (1990). Cognitive and behavioral theories. In B. B. Wolman & G. Stricker (Eds.), *Depressive disorders: Facts, theories, and treatment methods* (pp. 64–91). New York: Wiley.

Reiss, S., Peterson, R. A., Gursky, D. M., & McNally, R. J. (1986). Anxiety sensitivity, anxiety frequency, and the prediction of fearfulness. *Behavior Research and Therapy, 24*, 470–472.

Robins, C. J., Ivanoff, A., & Linehan, M. M. (2001). Dialectical behavior therapy. In W. J. Livesley (Ed.), *Handbook of personality disorders: Theory, research, and treatment* (pp. 437–460). New York: Guilford Press.

Robinson, L. A., Berman, J. S., & Neimeyer, R. A. (1990). Psychotherapy for the treatment of depression: A comprehensive review of controlled outcome research. *Psychological Bulletin, 108*, 30–49.

Rogers, C. R. (1957). The necessary and sufficient conditions of therapeutic personality change. *Journal of Consulting Psychology, 21*, 95–103.

Rogers, C. R. (1980). *A way of being.* Boston: Houghton Mifflin.

Rogers, E. M. (2003). *Diffusion of innovations* (5th ed.). New York: Free Press.

Rohrbaugh, M. J., & Shoham, V. (2002). Couple treatment for alcohol abuse: A systemic family-consultation model. In S. G. Hoffmann & M. C. Tompson (Eds.), *Treating chronic and severe mental disorders: A handbook of empirically supported interventions* (pp. 227–295). New York: Guilford Press.

Schmidt, N. B., Trakowski, J. H., & Staab, J. P. (1997). Extinction of panicogenic effects of a 35% CO_2 challenge in patients with panic disorder. *Journal of Abnormal Psychology, 106*, 630–638.

Segal, Z. V., Williams, J. M. G., & Teasdale, J. D. (2002). *Mindfulness-based cognitive therapy for depression: A new approach to preventing relapse.* New York: Guilford Press.

Shapiro, A. K. (1971). Placebo effects in medicine, psychotherapy, and psychoanalysis. In A. E. Bergin & S. L. Garfield (Eds.), *Handbook of psychotherapy and behavior change: An empirical analysis* (pp. 439–473). New York: Wiley.

Shaw, B. F., Elkin, I., Yamaguchi, J., Olmsted, M., Valis, T. M., Dobson, K. S., et al. (1999). Therapist competence ratings in relation to clinical outcome in cognitive therapy of depression. *Journal of Consulting and Clinical Psychology, 67*, 837–846.

Shoham-Solomon, V., & Rosenthal, R. (1987). Paradoxical interventions: A meta-analysis. *Journal of Consulting and Clinical Psychology, 55*, 22–28.

Skinner, B. F. (1953). *Science and human behavior.* New York: Free Press.

Snyder, C. R. (1996). To hope, to lose, and hope again. *Journal of Personal and Interpersonal Loss, 1*, 1–16.

Snyder, C. R. (1998). A case for hope in pain, loss, and suffering. In J. H. Harvey, J. Owarzu, & E. Miller (Eds.), *Perspectives on loss: A sourcebook* (pp. 63–79). Washington, DC: Taylor & Francis.

Snyder, C. R., McDermott, D., Cook, W., & Rapoff, M. (1996). *Hope for the journey: Helping children through the good times and the bad.* San Francisco: HarperCollins.

Snyder, C. R., Michael, S. T., & Cheavens, J. S. (1999). Hope as a psychotherapeutic foundation of common factors, placebos, and expectancies. In M. A. Hubble, B. L. Duncan, & S. D. Miller (Eds.), *The heart and soul of change: What works in therapy* (pp. 179–200). Washington, DC: American Psychological Association.

Snyder, J., & Patterson, G. R. (1995). Individual differences in social aggression: A test of the reinforcement model of socialization in the natural environment. *Behavior Therapy, 26*, 371–391.

Solovey, A. D., & Duncan, B. L. (1992). Ethics and strategic therapy: A proposed ethical direction. *Journal of Marital and Family Therapy, 18*, 53–61.

Stanley, B., Ivanoff, A., Brodsky, B., Oppenheim, S., & Mann, J. (1998, November). *Comparison of DBT and "treatment as usual" in suicidal and self-mutilating behavior.* Paper presented at the 32nd annual meeting of the Association for the Advancement of Behavior Therapy, Washington, DC.

Staw, B. M., Sandelands, L. E., & Dutton, J. E. (1981). Threat-rigidity effects in organization behavior: A multilevel analysis. *Administrative Science Quarterly, 26*, 501–524.

Stuart, R. B. (1969). Operant-interpersonal treatment for marital discord. *Journal of Consulting and Clinical Psychology, 33*, 675–682.

Stuart, R. B. (1980). *Helping couples change: A social learning approach to marital therapy.* New York: Guilford Press.

Sue, S., & Lam, A. G. (2002). Cultural and demographic diversity. In J. C. Norcross (Ed.), *Psychotherapy relationships that work: Therapist contributions and responsiveness to patients* (pp. 401–421). New York: Oxford University Press.

Sullivan, H. S. (1953). *The interpersonal theory of psychiatry.* New York: Norton.

Szapocznik, J., Rio, A. T., Hervis, O. E., Mitrani, V. B., Kurtines, W. M., & Faraci, A. M. (1991). Assessing change in family functioning as a result of treatment: The Structural Family System Rating Scale (SFSR). *Journal of Marital and Family Therapy, 17*, 295–310.

Szapocnik, J., Robbins, M. S., Mitrani, V. B., Santisteban, D. O., & Williams, R. A. (2002). Brief strategic family therapy. In F. W. Kaslow & J. L. Lebow (Eds.), *Comprehensive handbook of psychotherapy* (pp. 83–110). New York: Wiley.

Task Force on Promotion and Dissemination of Psychological Procedures. (1995). Training in and dissemination of empirically-validated psychological treatment: Report and recommendations. *The Clinical Psychologist, 48,* 2–23.

Truax, C. B., & Carkhuff, R. R. (1967). *Toward effective counseling and psychotherapy.* Chicago: Aldine.

Tryon, G. S., & Winograd, G. (2002). Goal consensus and collaboration. In J. C. Norcross (Ed.), *Psychotherapy relationships that work: Therapist contributions and responsiveness to patients* (pp. 109–125). New York: Oxford University Press.

Tschann, J. M., Kaiser, P., Chesney, M. A., Alkon, A., & Boyce, W. T. (1996). Resilience and vulnerability among preschool children: Family functioning, temperament, and behavior problems. *Journal of the American Academy of Child and Adolescent Psychiatry, 51,* 732–738.

Turecki, S. (1989). *The difficult child.* New York: Bantam.

Turk, C. L., Heimberg, R. G., & Hope, D. A. (2001). Generalized anxiety disorder. In D. H. Barlow (Ed.), *Clinical handbook of psychological disorders: A step-by-step treatment manual* (pp. 114–153). New York: Guilford Press.

Turner, R. M. (2000). Naturalistic evaluation of dialectical behavior therapy-oriented treatment for borderline personality disorder. *Cognitive and Behavioral Practice, 7,* 413–419.

Veroff, J., Kulka, R. W., & Douvan, W. (1981). *Mental health in America: Patterns of help-seeking from 1957–1976.* New York: Basic Books.

von Bertalanffy, L. (1962). General system theory—A critical review. *General Systems: Yearbook of the Society for General Systems Research, 7,* 1–20.

Wampold, B. E. (2001). *The great psychotherapy debate: Models, methods, and findings.* Mahwah, NJ: Erlbaum.

Wampold, B. E., Minami, T., Baskin, T. W., & Tierney, S. C. (2002). A meta-(re)analysis of the effects of cognitive therapy versus other therapies for depression. *Journal of Affective Disorders, 61,* 104–108.

Watson, J. C. (2002). Revisioning empathy. In D. Cain, & J. Seeman (Eds.), *Humanistic psychotherapies: Handbook of research and practice* (pp. 445–472). Washington, DC: American Psychological Association.

Watzlwawick, P., Beavan, J., & Jackson, D. D. (1967). *The pragmatics of human communication.* New York: Norton.

Watzlawick, P., Weakland, J., & Fisch, R. (1974). *Change: Principles of problem formation and problem resolution.* New York: Norton.

Weiner, N. (1961). *Cybernetics* (2nd ed.). New York: Wiley.

Weiss, R. L., Hops, H., & Patterson, G. R. (1973). A framework for conceptualizing marital conflict, technology for altering it, some data for evaluating it. In L. A. Hamerlynck, L. C. Handy, & E. J. Mash (Eds.), *Behavior change: Methodology, concepts, and practices* (pp. 309–342). Champaign, IL: Research Press.

White, K. S., & Barlow, D. H. (2002). Panic disorder and agoraphobia. In D. H. Barlow (Ed.), *Anxiety and its disorders* (pp. 328–379). New York: Guilford Press.

Wickramasekera, I. (1985). A conditioned response model of placebo effect: Predictors form the model. In L. White, B. Tursky, & G. Schwartz (Eds.), *Placebos: Theory, research, and mechanisms* (pp. 255–287). New York: Guilford Press.

Wilkins, W. (1979). Expectancies in therapy research: Discriminating among heterogeneous nonspecifics. *Journal of Consulting and Clinical Psychology, 47,* 837–845.

Wilkins, W. (1985). Placebo controls and concepts in chemotherapy and psychotherapy research. In L. White, B. Tursky, & G. Schwartz (Eds.), *Placebos: Theory, research, and mechanisms* (pp. 83–109). New York: Guilford Press.

Williams, K. E., & Chambliss, D. L. (1990). The relationship between therapist characteristics and outcome of in vivo exposure treatment for agoraphobia. *Behavior Therapy, 21,* 111–116.

Yerkes, R. M., & Dodson, J. D. (1908). The relation of strength of stimulus to rapidity of habit-formation. *Journal of Comparative Neurology and Physiology, 18,* 459–482.

Young, J. E., Weinberger, A. D., & Beck, A. T. (2001). Cognitive therapy for depression. In D. H. Barlow (Ed.), *Clinical handbook of psychological disorders* (3rd ed., pp. 264–308). New York: Guilford Press.

Zanarini, M. C., Gunderson, J. G., Frankenburg, F. R., & Chauncey, D. L. (1989). The revised Diagnostic Interview for Borderlines: Discriminating BPD from other Axis II disorders. *Journal of Personality Disorders, 3,* 10–18.

AUTHOR INDEX

SUBJECT INDEX

Christenson, Andy, 61–62, 195, 196–199, 200
Class, in logical theory, 43–44
Classification errors, 34–38, 52–53, 95, 226, 272
Client factors
    assumptive world and, 75–76, 80, 100
    measures of empathy and, 70
    need for empathy and, 71
    priorites for change and, 231–232
    selection of strategies and, 109
    understanding and, 121
Client profile, 125
Clinical depression, 144–145
Clinical Manual for Marital Therapy (Gottman), 195
Clinical significance, 194
Closeness, 196
Codependency. *See* demand–withdraw interaction
Coercion, 273, 274
    couple problems and, 198–199
    parent–child problems and, 171–173, 174–175, 182
    substance abuse and, 226–227, 236
Cognitive–behavioral group therapy (CBGT), 131–133
Cognitive–behavioral therapy (CBT). *See also* Cognitive–behavioral group therapy; Panic control treatment (PCT); Rationale, investment in
    anxiety disorders and, 120–122, 131–134
    assessment scales in, 149
    cognitive change component in, 158–159
    for depression, 137, 140–142, 145–146, 147–151
    empathy and, 71
    notion of vicious cycle in, 28–29
Cognitive dissonance, 76
Cognitive errors, 140, 141–142
Cognitive restructuring, 131–132, 160
Cognitive therapy
    generalized anxiety disorder and, 133
    parent–child problems and, 177
Cognitive triad in depression, 140–141, 148
Collaborative empiricism, 148
Collaborative involvement, 69–70
Collaborative problem solving (CPS), 177, 178, 187. *See also* Greene, Ross
    basket framework of, 182–183, 186–187

treatment procedures in, 179, 181–187
Columbo method, 238–239
Combined behavioral couple treatment, 193–195
Commitment, 194
    borderline clients and, 262–263
    couple problems and, 208
Common elements. *See* Contextual model; Golden thread; Second-order change model
Common-factors group. *See also* Contextual model
    debate between best-practices group and, 8, 10–13
    outcome variance studies and, 10–11, 66
Communication. *See also* Empathy; Validation
    influence and, 74
    second-order relationship and, 258, 259
Communication and problem-solving training (CPT) approach, 193–195
Conceptual Blockbusting: A Guide to Better Ideas (Adams), 46–47
Conceptual scheme. *See* Rational
Conduct disorder (CD), 167. *See also* Disruptive behavior disorders
Confirmatory bias, 77, 79, 81
Conflict theory, 226–227
Conformity, pressure toward, 8, 12
Confrontational approach, 228–229, 230, 238, 242
Consensual validation, 78–80, 81, 92, 98, 102, 229. *See also* Validation
Contemplation, as stage of change, 233–234
Contempt, 200, 202
Context bound, as term, 88
Contextual events, and disruptive behavior, 171
Contextual model, 11, 13, 54, 65, 74–85. *See also* Common-factors group; Interpersonal psychotherapy (IPT); Rationale ("myth"); Therapeutic procedures; Therapeutic relationship
    anxiety disorders and, 120
    assumptive world and, 75–77
    borderline clients and, 261–265
    common elements in, 75, 88
    demoralization and, 77–80
    depression and, 143–144, 145, 146–147, 160–161, 162–163
    interventions and, 92–94

Dichotomous thinking, 142
Difference, and second-order change, 271–272
Discipline, 170–171
Discrepancy model, 89–90, 105, 231, 233
    motivational interviewing and, 239–240
Disruptive behavior disorders, 165. *See also* Parent–child relationship problems; Parent Training (PT)
    child characteristics and, 168–170
    definitions of, 166–171
    need for theory and, 165–166
    parental errors and, 174–175
    risk factors for, 167–168, 170–171
    second-order change and, 175–177
    vicious cycle in, 171–174
Distraction, 119, 128
Distress. *See also* Frustration tolerance skills
    degree of, 208
    tolerance of, 264–265
Divisive issues in couple problems, 208–209
Divorce
    approaches to marital therapy and, 193
    predictors for, 201–205
    U.S. rates for, 191
Dodo bird verdict, 72, 110
Domestic violence, 79–80, 208
Don't change position, 103–104
Double approach–avoidance conflict, 226–227
Dow-Jones ratios, 201. *See also* Behavior exchange (BE) approach
Drug problems. *See* Substance abuse
DSM–IV. *See Diagnostic and Statistical Manual of Mental Disorders, Fourth Edition*
Dysthymic disorder, 138–139

Eastern philosophy, 21, 30, 252, 266
Ego dystonic acts, 27
Einstein, Albert, 23
Emotional arousal, 94
Emotional disengagement, 194, 203
Emotional dysregulation, 248, 250–251, 255, 256–257
Emotional regulation, 264–265
Emotional vulnerability, 248
Emotion mind, 268
Empathy. *See also* Validation
    anxiety disorders and, 121–122
    couple problems and, 219
    definition of, 70, 88

    depression and, 161
    motivational interviewing and, 239
    parent–child problems and, 169, 187
    therapeutic relationship and, 67, 69, 70–71, 82, 98
Empirically supported treatments (ESTs). *See also* Best-practices group
    for anxiety disorders, 119–135
    arguments for, 11–12, 121
    for borderline personality disorder, 246, 253–257
    client selection and, 40–41
    for couple problems, 195–205
    for depression, 146–157
    outcome variance and, 10–11, 66–67
    for parent–child relationship problems, 177–189
    recognition of first- and second-order change in, 61–62
engagement, 69, 82, 179
Erickson, Milton, 34
ESTs. *See* Empirically supported treatments (ESTs)
Executive function, and disruptive behavior, 169
Exposure techniques, 119, 127, 128–129, 131, 264–265
Extending, 268
Externalizing. *See* Disruptive behavior disorders

False dichotomies, 72–73
Family crises, and disruptive behavior, 171, 181
Family-oriented therapies. *See also* Parent–child relationship
    shift to, 177, 180
    substance abuse and, 227
Faulty information processing, 140, 141–142
Fear, 114–115
Finger trap, 45–46
First-order change, 15, 26, 40, 271–272. *See also* Solution-generated problems; Vicious cycle
    anxiety disorders and, 118–119, 135, 136
    contextual reinforcement of, 96
    couple problems and, 197–200, 207
    depression and, 162, 163
    dialectical perspective and, 31
    finger trap and, 45–46
    group theory and, 42–43

role of formulation in, 214–215

Integrative Couple Therapy (Jacobson & Christenson), 195, 196, 199

Intent vs. actions, 180–181

Intermittent reinforcement, 181

Interoceptive avoidance, 119

Interoceptive exposure, 128–129

Interpersonal deficits, 144, 153, 154

Interpersonal psychotherapy (IPT), 137, 142–146, 151–154, 158

Interpersonal skill training, 265

Interpretation, discrepancy vs. content model of, 89–90

Intervention. *See also* Therapeutic procedures
  balance between change and acceptance in, 259
  common change strategies in, 56–61, 97–106
  contextual model and, 92–94, 99
  definition of, 71, 73
  integrated view of, 94–108
  procedural level strategies and, 56–61, 106, 109
  as relational act, 87, 107–108
  two-step process in, 92, 99

Interviewing
  assessment of panic disorder and, 122
  enhancement of motivation and, 237–240

Invalidating environment, 249, 250–251, 255, 256–257

In vivo exposure, 129

IPT. *See* Interpersonal psychotherapy (IPT)

Irreverent communication, 258

Jacobson, Neil, 61–62, 192–193, 195–200

Klerman's interpersonal model. *See* Interpersonal psychotherapy (IPT)

Labyrinth of Crete, 3, 16–17

Learning experiences, 94

Learning theory. *See* Parent Training (PT); Token economy

Levels in problem solving
  theory of logical types and, 43–45
  wrong-level solutions and, 36–37, 40–41, 44–45

Linehan, Marsha, 248–249, 253–254. *See also* Dialectical behavior therapy (DBT)

Logical systems, 42

Logical types, theory of, 42, 43–45, 269

Magnification and minimization, 142

Maintenance stage, 23–236, 240

Major depressive disorder, 138

Marital therapy. *See* Couples therapy

Marital Therapy: Strategies Based on Social Learning and Behavior Exchange Principles (Jacobson & Margolin), 193

Marriage Clinic (Gottman), 192, 195, 200–205

MBSR. *See* Mindfulness-based stress-reduction approach (MBSR)

Meaning, and reversals, 97

Medical model, 65–66, 225. *See also* Best-practices group; Empirically supported treatments (ESTs)

Medication
  vs. clinical management with depression, 139–140
  problem framing and, 59–60
  psychotropic, 12–13

Meltdown, 174, 183, 186

Mental Research Institute (MRI), 32–34, 174, 196, 239
  evolution of problem cycles and, 34–37

Metaphor, in DBT approach, 267–268

Mindfulness and Acceptance: Expanding the Cognitive–Behavioral Tradition (Hayes et al.), 134

Mindfulness approach
  borderline clients and, 264–265
  definition of, 134
  with depression, 62, 155, 156–157
  with generalized anxiety disorder, 134–135
  pain and, 22

Mindfulness-based stress-reduction approach (MBSR), 62, 156–157

Moral deficit model, 225

Motivational factors
  disruptive behavior and, 169–170
  enhancement of motivation and, 237–240
  overcomplication and, 53
  pro-change positioning and, 101–102
  psychotherapy setting and, 91
  substance abuse and, 231–232

Motivational interviewing, 237–240, 243

Mountain climbing example, 20

MRI. *See* Mental Research Institute (MRI)

MST. *See* Multisystemic therapy (MST)

reversing the change sequence and, 174–177, 184–187

risk factors for disruptive behavior and, 167–168, 170–171

role of consequences and, 187–189

second-order change model and, 175–189, 276

validation in, 180–182, 187

vicious cycles and, 171–174

Parents

coaching of, 184–187

goal revision and, 182–184

lack of monitoring and, 173

reactive vs. proactive parenting and, 182

risk factors for disruptive behavior and, 167–168, 170–171

validation of, 178–179, 180–181

Parent Training (PT), 171, 177. *See also* Barkley, Russell A.

assessment in, 178

effectiveness of, 187

role of consequences in, 187–189

treatment inclusion criteria and, 166–167

treatment procedures in, 179, 180–188

vicious cycles and, 171–173

Passivity, 248–249

Pattern shifts

framing and, 58–60

nature of, 43–44, 45–48

questions for pattern understanding and, 51–52

Perpetual problems, 204–205

Personalization, 142

Personal relationships, and borderline patients, 255–256, 265

Persuasion and Healing (Frank), 74–75

Phillips, Katherine, 29

Physiological reactivity, 202–203

Polarization, 198, 199–200, 209, 214

Policymakers

conduct of psychotherapy and, 7, 8, 12

cost of treatment and, 250

second-order change perspective and, 9–10

Positioning, 60, 101–106, 109, 268

Positive feedback loop, 30–31, 37–38

Positive regard, 67, 201

Practical theorists, 9

Precontemplation stage, 232–233, 237, 239

Predicting, 61, 106, 109

Premises. *See* Assumptions

Preparation stage, 234–235

Prescribing. *See* Symptom prescription

Problem formation. *See also* Contextual model

common errors in, 34–38, 52–53, 95, 272, 273

contributions of MRI and, 32–34

framing strategies and, 58–60, 105

in panic disorder, 127

second-order corollaries of errors in, 53–54, 272–273

stages of, 22–26

typology of, 33, 34, 72

vicious cycle in therapeutic models and, 26–32

Problem persistence, 33–34

Problem resolution. *See also* Second-order change model

application to clinical problems and, 51–56

clinical strategies and, 56–61

essence of, in interventions, 39–40

first-order change as sufficient and, 40–41

golden thread in, 62–63

human dilemmas and, 48–51

puzzles in, 45–48

second-order change as needed for, 41–42

theoretical roots and, 42–45

Problem solving. *See also* Collaborative problem solving (CPS); Problem formation; Problem resolution; Second-order change model

CPT approach and, 193–195

DBT strategies and, 263, 264

generalized anxiety disorder and, 134

group theory and, 43

mind-set and, 47–48

win–win approach to, 186–187

Problem-solving skills therapy, 177

Procedural level strategies, 56–61, 106, 109. *See also* Therapeutic procedures

Process-level systems, 30–31

Process-of-change model, vii

Pro-change position, 101–102

Project MATCH, 237

Prosocial behavior, punishment of, 173

Psychoanalysis, vicious cycle in, 27–28

Psychotherapeutic profession. *See also* Outcome variance

application of second-order change to, 51–56

challenges to, 12–13
change strategies in, 56–61, 97–106
common-factors vs. best-practices models in, 8, 10–13
effectiveness studies and, 140
false dichotomies in, 72–73
integration of models in, 13–15, 94–108
shifts in views on substance abuse and, 229–232, 242–243
vicious cycles in, 26–32
Psychotherapy Relationships That Work: Therapist Contributions and Responsiveness to Patients (Norcross), 11
Psychotropic medication, 12–13
Punishment. *See also* Natural consequences
of prosocial behavior, 173
use of, 176, 187–189

Rationale, investment in, 93–94
anxiety disorders and, 120–122, 132, 133
borderline clients and, 261–263
cognitive–behavioral therapy and, 120–122, 132, 133
Rationale ("myth")
client context and, 93–94
cognitive behavioral therapy and, 148, 159–160
connection between procedure and, 93, 99
dialectical behavior therapy and, 261–263
marital therapy and, 192–195
parent–child relationship approaches and, 176, 179, 180, 181, 185
substance abuse and, 225
treatment of anxiety disorders and, 120–122
Reactive problem, 198, 204
Readiness to change, 231
Reasonable mind, 268
Reciprocal communication, 258
Reconcilable Differences (Christensen & Jacobson), 195, 196–199, 200
Reframing, 59, 105, 109, 269
Reinforcement system. *See* Token economy
Relapse
couples therapy and, 193, 194, 221
prevention strategies and, 61
substance abuse and, 236, 243
treatment of depression and, 61, 151, 156

Relaxation training, 134
Remoralization, 160–161
Repair attempts, 203–205
Repetition compulsion, 27–28
Researchers, 9. *See also* Outcome variance
Restraining
parent–child relationship and, 184–187
as therapeutic strategy, 57–58, 104, 109
Reversals, 56–57. *See also* Second-order change model
context and, 94
domains for, 97
finger trap and, 46
second-order relationship and, 87, 97–98
treatment of anxiety and, 119, 129, 132, 133–134, 135–136
Righting reflex, 238
Ritual. *See* Rational
Rogers, Carl, 73–74
Role disputes, 144, 153, 154
Role transitions. *See* Transitions
Rolling with resistance, 240

Sadness, 144
Safety behaviors, 119
Schemas, 29, 140, 141, 150, 151, 152
Second-order change model, 4, 9
addiction rationales and, 225
anxiety disorders and, 54–56, 120, 276
application to psychotherapy and, 51–56
borderline clients and, 277
clinical strategies in, 56–61, 97–106, 273
common first-order errors and, 34–38, 52–53, 95, 272
concept of second-order change and, 271–272
contextual model and, 76, 80–81, 94–108, 274–275
corollaries of problem-solving errors in, 53–54, 272–273
couple interventions and, 210–221, 276
definitions, 15, 41–42
demoralization and, 78–80
depression and, 149, 154, 156–157, 163, 276
dialectical perspective and, 31, 95–96, 253, 273–274
illustrations involving, 45–51
location of change in, 95

mindfulness approaches and, 135, 156–157

panic disorder interventions and, 122, 124, 127–128, 129

parent–child interventions and, 175–189, 276

recognition of, in ESTs, 61–62

shifts by therapists and, 106–107, 242–244, 256–257

substance abuse and, 241–244, 277

support system configuration and, 96

theoretical roots of, 42–45

Second-order relationship

anxiety disorders and, 120

borderline personality disorder and, 257–259

complex process of, 87

intervention as relationship and, 107–108

unified framework and, 108–110

Selective abstraction, 142

Self-awareness, 169

Self-care, 221

Self-change, 101

Self-efficacy, 231, 240

Self-fulfilling prophecies, 29. *See also* Solution-generated problems; Vicious cycle

anxiety reactions and, 55

depression and, 140–142

substance abuse and, 230

Self-harming, 245–246, 254. *See also* Borderline personality disorder (BPD)

Self-invalidation, 248

Self-mastery, 94

Self-monitoring, 123–124

Self-regulation theory, 231

Set theory. *See* Group theory

Seven Principles for Making Marriage Work (Gottman & Silver), 195, 216–218

Sexual abuse, 249

Sexual problems, 25, 30

Shakespeare, William, 137

Sick role, 152–153

Silkworth, Dr., 241

Social anxiety disorder

case of John and, 132–133

cognitive–behavioral group therapy (CBGT) and, 131–132

definition of, 116–117

description of, 130–131

Social avoidance, 29, 80, 97

Social withdrawal, 91

Soft restraint, 57–58

Solution-generated problems, 23–26, 272–273. *See also* First-order change

anxiety disorders and, 55, 116, 117–119, 131

couple problems and, 197–200, 204–205

depression and, 140–142, 145–146

for therapists, 256–257

wrong-level solutions and, 36–37, 43–44

Sound marital house theory, 206, 214, 215–216

Stability and change, 19–22, 40, 252

Stages of change model, 101, 223, 232–236

interventions based on, 236–237, 243–244

Standardized inventories

with couple problems, 206, 207

with depression, 149

with panic disorder, 122–123

Stonewalling, 202–203

Substance abuse, 223–244. *See also* Stages of change model

anxiety disorders and, 117, 132

conceptual shift in views of, 229–232

confrontational approaches to, 228–229

definitions and, 223, 224–225

driving under the influence case and, 233, 234

golden thread in approaches to, 244, 277

historical view of, 228–229

motivational interviewing and, 237–240

rationales and, 225

second-order change and, 229–232, 241–244

stages of change model and, 232–237, 276

vicious cycle in models for, 225–228

Substance dependence (addiction), 223, 224. *See also* Substance abuse

Suicidal clients, 245–246. *See also* Borderline personality disorder (BPD)

Sullivan, Harry Stack, 142

Support system. *See also* Family-oriented therapies

bipolar clients and, 255–256

demoralization and, 79–80

second-order change model and, 97, 98, 99, 242
Symptom prescription
in specific interventions, 124–125, 183, 186
as strategy, 60, 105, 109
Synthesis, 252
Systemic family consultation model, 227
Systems theory, 29–31

Technique, as term, 71, 108. *See also* Therapeutic procedures
Telephone consultation, 269
Temperament. *See also* Fit, goodness of
definition of, 168
in development of disruptive behaviors, 168–169
no-fault framing and, 182
treatment of parent–child problems and, 180–181
"Terrible simplifications," 44
Theme, and couple problems, 214
Therapeutic alliance, 67, 81. *See also* Common-factors group; Therapeutic relationship
anxiety disorders and, 120
collaboration and, 69–70
definition of, 68–69
depression and, 147–148, 159–162
emotional arousal and, 94
empathy and, 67, 69, 70–71
engagement and, 69, 82
goal consensus and, 69–70
influence and, 73–74
one-down position and, 238–239
righting reflex and, 238
solution level and, 41
symptom prescription and, 60
Therapeutic model, allegiance to, 161–162
Therapeutic procedures. *See also* Intervention
of dialectical behavior therapy, 263–265
in marital therapies, 215–221
procedural level strategies and, 56–61, 106, 109
resistance and, 230
second-order change strategies and, 56–61, 106
therapy with anxiety disorders and, 126–130
Therapeutic relationship. *See also* Common-factors group; Second-order relationship; Therapeutic alliance

borderline personality disorder and, 256–259, 261
CBT approach to depression and, 147–148
client rating of, and outcomes, 121
contextual model and, 74–85, 88–92
definition of, 67–68
elements of, 67
healing setting and, 90–92
hope and, 82–85
as intervention, 81–82, 83–85, 107
interventions with depression and, 146–147
interventions with parent–child problems and, 179
research on, 65–74
second-order changes for therapists and, 106–107, 242–244, 256–257
in substance abuse counseling, 230
Therapeutic relationship skills, 108–109
Therapist group meetings, and dialectical perspective, 257
Theseus (mythological warrior), 3, 8, 16–17
Threat-rigidity hypothesis, 255–256
Time management, 134
Token economy, 183, 184–185, 188
Toxic cures. *See* Toxic triad (accusaton, blame, coercion)
"Toxic negativity cycle," 179, 188
Toxic triad (accusaton, blame, coercion), 198–199, 202
Traditionality, 194
Transitions, and depression, 144, 153, 154
Transtheoretical, as term, 75
Triggers
couple problems and, 197, 205
depression episodes, 141
disruptive behavior and, 171
problem formation and, 25–26
12-step approaches, 223, 240–241, 244
Tyrol, Margareta Maultasch, Duchess of, 49–50

Uncertainty principle, 9
Underreaction, 35, 53, 54, 110, 272
Unified framework, 108–110
Unrelenting crises, 248, 255–256
Unsuccessful coping, 197–198
"User-friendly" environment, 181, 182, 184. *See also* Healing setting

Validation. *See also* Acceptance strategies; Consensual validation; Empathy; Normalizing

borderline clients and, 259
of incorrect assumptions, 99
invalidating environment and, 249, 250–251, 259
between parent and child, 175, 176, 179, 181–182, 184–187
of parents, 178–179, 180–181
in second-order change model, 98–101, 109
steps in therapeutic process of, 98
"validate, then work for change" approach and, 175–177, 187
Vapor lock metaphor, 174
Vicious cycle
in anxiety disorders, 117–119, 135–136
in borderline clients, 254–255
common errors leading to, 34–38, 95
contextual model and, 75–77, 80–81
in couple problems, 195–205, 206, 207
in depression, 142–145
parent–child problems and, 171–174, 178
problem formation and, 23–25

schism in psychotherapy as, 13–14
in substance abuse, 225–228
in therapeutic models, 26–32
Vietnam War demonstrations, 48–49
Virtuous cycle, 30–31
Vulnerability, and couple problems, 196–197

Weakland, John, 51. *See also Change: Principles of Problem Formation and Problem Resolution* (Watzlawick, Weakland, & Fisch)
Western philosophy, 30, 252
Willingness to change, 231
Win–win approach, 186
Wise mind, activation of, 268–269
Worry behavior prevention, 134
Worry exposure, 133–134
Wrong-level solutions, 36–37, 40–41, 53, 272

Yin–yang symbol, 252

Zen Buddhism, 21, 31, 252, 266

ABOUT THE AUTHORS

J. Scott Fraser, PhD, is professor and former director of clinical training and former director of internship training at the School of Professional Psychology of Wright State University in Dayton, Ohio. He also served for 14 years as director of the Crisis/Brief Therapy Center at the Good Samaritan Hospital and Health Center in Dayton. In addition to his doctoral teaching, he directs a community-based brief therapy center, where he trains doctoral students and interns in clinical psychology along with mental health center staff. He also supervises psychology trainees in a primary health care center and an internal medicine residency program. He has authored a number of articles and book chapters over his 30-year career. He is board certified in family therapy by the American Board of Examiners in Professional Psychology. Scott has been the recipient of several distinguished teaching awards and "best-in-conference" workshop and panel presentations at national meetings. He consults to a wide range of centers and organizations and has presented nationally and internationally on effective approaches to brief therapy, family therapy, crisis intervention, and integrated best practices.

Andrew D. Solovey, ACSW, LISW, is associate director of clinical services at Scioto Paint Valley Mental Health Center in Chillicothe, Ohio. As such, he is responsible for the provision and evaluation of a broad range of mental health and substance abuse programs across the Scioto Paint Valley Mental Health Center's five-county area. He has also developed a highly respected center-based clinical training program that has been in existence since 1985. In addition to his work at Scioto Paint Valley Mental Health Center, Andy is clinical assistant professor of psychiatry at The Ohio State University School of Medicine in the Department of Psychiatry. He is also in private practice at Solutions Counseling in Dublin, Ohio.

Andy has a diverse background and has worked with many client populations during his 30-year career. He has provided psychotherapy to adults, children, and adolescents with severe mental and emotional disorders. He has worked in the substance abuse field and has provided psychotherapy in a medical rehabilitation setting. He has had extensive training in family therapy. He taught "Brief Strategic Therapy" as a faculty member at the Dayton Institute for Family Therapy, where he achieved the status of senior faculty. Andy coauthored a book, *Changing the Rules: A Client-Directed Approach to Therapy*, in 1992 and has coauthored many journal articles. More recently, he coauthored a chapter in *Quickies: The Handbook of Brief Sex Therapy* with J. Scott Fraser (2004). Andy is very interested in the phenomenon of change and the importance of client determination in the change process. He has conducted many workshops on this subject throughout Ohio and the United States.